D0758906

FABLES OF THE SELF

FABLES OF THE SELF

Studies in Lyric Poetry

ROSANNA WARREN

W. W. NORTON & COMPANY   NEW YORK LONDON

ILLUSTRATION CREDITS

Figure 1: *Première fenêtre simultanée*, by Robert Delaunay:
reprinted from F. Gilles de la Tourette, *Robert Delaunay*
(Paris: Charles Massin, 1950).

Figure 2: *La colombe poignardée et le jet d'aeu*, by Guillaume Apollinaire:
reprinted from Guillaume Apollinaire, *Calligrammes*
(Paris: Gallimard, 1925).

Figure 3: *Il pleut*, by Guillaume Apollinaire: reprinted from
Guillaume Apollinaire, *Calligrammes* (Paris: Gallimard, 1925).

For information about permission to reproduce selections from this book,
write to Permissions, W. W. Norton & Company, Inc., 500 Fifth Avenue,
New York, NY 10110

For information about special discounts for bulk purchases, please contact
W. W. Norton Special Sales at specialsales@wwnorton.com or 800-233-4830

Manufacturing by Courier Westford
Book design by Brooke Koven
Production manager: Julia Druskin

Library of Congress Cataloging-in-Publication Data
Warren, Rosanna
    Fables of the self : studies in lyric poetry / Rosanna Warren. — 1st ed.
    p. cm.
  Includes bibliographical references and index.
  ISBN 978-0-393-06613-5 (hardcover)
1. Lyric poetry—History and criticism. 2. Self in literature. I. Title.
  PN1356.W29 2008
  809.1'4—dc22   2008021348

W. W. Norton & Company, Inc.
500 Fifth Avenue, New York, N.Y. 10110
www.wwnorton.com

W. W. Norton & Company Ltd.
Castle House, 75/76 Wells Street, London W1T 3QT

1 2 3 4 5 6 7 8 9 0

For Katherine and Chiara

Contents

SECTION II: FRANCE: "I" AS ANOTHER

SECTION III: POETRY AND CONSCIENCE: "I" AT WORK

List of Illustrations

Preface

Wが　hat is the self imagined, tested, symbolized, and performed in literature? What does it look like, sound like, feel like? What risks can it take? How does it relate to the singular, workaday social self, and to the documentary ego heavy with its pedantry of doings and injuries? I take these questions to be all the more urgent in the climate of aggressive literalism and therapeutic self-proclamation in the United States in the early twenty-first century. Furthermore, the imagined self behaves and means differently from one era and one literary culture to another.

The studies in literary criticism presented here compose an occult autobiography, and an investigation into the nature of literary selfhood. The book opens with a description of my experience, at ages twelve and thirteen, of living with my family in the South of France, and it closes with excerpts from a notebook recording my absorption of the death of my father. Between the personal opening and the coda are assembled critical analyses and translations I have written over a quarter of a century. They emerged from my work as a writer of poems, and are side effects of that work. This long-evolving book, however personal, tries paradoxically to define a notion of selfhood not founded on, or confined to, the psychological ego. And yet one needs some notion of selfhood, or else one abolishes the realities of love, guilt, acts of conscience, and dying. These are problems that this book explores through the medium of literary analysis, in the conviction that poetry—a presentational, dramatic art—brings us close to the quick and mystery of being and also to its ethical consequences.[1]

My readings are literary and subjective rather than academic, though scholarship and criticism have helped to shape them. Their deeper logic derives from matters of place and time, as suggested by the childhood memoir and the notebook of mourning. For being must start from place and work out its propositions in time. The Mediterranean coast of France, where we lived in the region known as the "Midi" (noon), had been heavily colonized by the Romans, and my memoir recalls my learning French and Latin in that landscape layered with French, Provençal, and Roman pasts. My later reading of the Latin poets, especially Catullus, Horace, and Virgil, was steeped in a feeling of immediacy drawn partly from my young year in the neighborhood of Orange, Arles, and Nîmes, and from still younger years in Italy.

The first section of this book examines a few classical poets and some of their modern heirs: Sappho, Alcaeus, Theocritus, and Virgil, in relation (variously) to Baudelaire, Swinburne, Auden, Hollander, Strand, H.D., Bidart, and Glück.

Over the years I have built up an argument for a kind of living classicism, a sense of the Greco-Roman tradition as a force at work in the recombinant DNA of certain modern imaginations. Some of that DNA is formal: I try to show that key structures of ancient verse—the Sapphic and Alcaic stanzas, the heroic hexameter, the elegiac couplet—carry with them allusive and suggestive power that modern poets can draw on actively, not passively. I propose as well that such metrical shapes still afford opportunities for powerful discovery and self-testing. Some of the inheritance is thematic: Sappho's eroticism, Alcaeus's poetry of exile, Virgil's sorrowful assessments of imperial power. The modern poets whose work I ponder have taken their cues from the classics in differing and idiosyncratic ways, and part of my task has been to consider those differences.

To feel the ancient poems as present, dangerous, and at work in us is to accept the light of a living classicism. It requires one to live bifocally: to have an ironic awareness of history and of the separateness from the past, at the same time that the imagination collapses time and sees the past as radiantly present. In such a state did Petrarch write to Cicero as to a contemporary; of a similar state, more mystically conceived, Blake declared in "Proverbs of Hell," from *The Marriage of Heaven and Hell*: "Eternity is in love with the productions of Time."

In the second section of the book, I regard France not as a Roman colony, but as a modern nation, the laboratory of modern art and poetry. From my year in the Lycée de Jeunes Filles in Grasse when I was twelve, through frequent returns to France in adolescence and later life, I adopted France as the country of my soul, and French poetry and painting as the arts that gave me the keys of form and spirit. Of course, one doesn't easily divorce France from the Roman heritage: how could one, why should one, with Ronsard, du Bellay, and Racine in mind, not to mention the chiseled Latinate architecture of Baudelaire's verse? But I am speaking here of the France of modernity, France of revolutionary aesthetics, France ever leaping to some artistic barricade and proclaiming a new order. Only a powerful classicism can engender so powerful, so lucid, a modernism. I see no contradiction in a book that celebrates classicism in the first section, and modernism in the second: that is the natural order of things, the systole-diastole motion of art's temporal and formal development. The second section, in considering Nerval, Mallarmé and Max Jacob, Rimbaud, and Apollinaire, explores those revolutions in form—the invention of the prose poem, *vers libre, calligrammes*, concrete poetics, and Cubist and post-Cubist painting—that opened up new kinds of self-knowledge and new knowledge of the world.

Two shadow masters preside over this book. One is Mallarmé. I find that in almost every essay, for years, I have invoked Mallarmé's phrase *la disparition élocutoire du poète* (the elocutory disappearance of the poet) from his definitive essay "Crise de vers." Eliot made a life work of translating it into his own personal terms.[2] How does the poet "disappear"? One answer is, he doesn't—as recent scholarship on Eliot has rightly pointed out. But in a deeper sense, a certain social and psychological version of the poet (or artist) does disappear in the fully realized work of art. One can argue about the force of "elocutory" in Mallarmé's formulation: I take it to be the inscribed personal presence of the writer that the Symbolist magus wished to eliminate, and did, from his own work. His is an extreme version of such askesis. He alchemized his own experience of despair and literal suicidal temptation in Tournon in 1866 and 1867 into a figurative suicide, the extinction thereafter in his poems of the personal sign. He converted loss into substance, and his favorite word, *rien* (nothing), into a positive metaphysical denomination. For most writers, the sublimation of the personal takes less radical form. Henry James allegorized this withdrawal in his story "The Private Life," in which the narrator and his friend, the actress Blanche Adrey, at a typically Jamesian house party, discover that while the public figure of the esteemed author Clare Vawdrey is outside chatting conventionally with Blanche, the "real" Vawdrey—the writer self—is hidden in his room, writing. Proust, that great spelunker in the caves of selfhood, described a similar division in *Contre Sainte-Beuve*: ". . . that a book is the product of another *me* than the one we show in our habits, in social life, in our vices. If we want to understand this other self, we can reach it in the depths of ourselves, trying to re-create it within us. . . ."[3] Proust's radical interiority differs from Mallarmé's erasure of self, but in a strange way the two extreme positions meet in a rejection of social, and to some extent psychological, selfhood.

I encountered Mallarmé's phrase in my youth around the same time I was living in the imaginative space carved out by T. S. Eliot. Having concluded, in my sixteen-year-old reading of Pascal, that the "self" as ego was a source of torment, I had already devoted myself to art as to a discipline for subliming away the appetitive self. Little did I know, in my teenaged absolutism, what strains and resistances such a vocation would internally encounter, what sacrifices it would exact, and how intricately an experienced self, grounded in life, capable of love and suffering, would need to be involved in the creation of art. The "I" at work in this preface, for instance, can be taken as a fairly straightforward, documentary "elocutory" presence in a piece of writing whose purpose is primarily informational and argumentative. That is, hardly literary. Such an "I" differs from the more fictive speaker in the memoir "Midi," and cannot even be thought of in the same metaphysical space with the first-person singular pronoun in a poem.

We might describe literature as the symbolic space in which we make formal, imaginative verbal experiments in consciousness and conscience (both contained in the rich French word *conscience*). In works whose "I" has a realistic referent, autobiography collaborates with fable to fashion a distinct sort of fictive presence—which does not mean an "untrue" presence. The self is a locus, a meeting place of multiple presences organized, in the individual person, by will, experience, and character, while the authorial self in the work of literature is organized by rhetorical structures and patterned language. With such a notion of selfhood, it is important to distinguish the involuntary, psychotic fluidity of personality we see in Nerval's illness (though not in his art), from the achieved asceticism and willed anonymity in Mallarmé, as from the conscious self-erasure of Rimbaud's "Je est un autre" (I is another). I draw a further inference, perhaps more North American than French: that the self thus ascetically prepared, by the practice of literature and other forms of meditation, is still capable of moral knowledge and moral agency, and that the work of art can (though does not necessarily) lead toward that knowledge.

The sketch of erased, dispersed, or withdrawn selfhood I have presented may be aligned with a major inclination of twentieth-century thought, much of it French, much of it derived from Mallarmé, about the displacement of subjectivity and "the death of the author." I distinguish my own search from the mischievous overstatements of Roland Barthes in his essay "The Death of the Author." Barthes, too, takes off from Mallarmé: "In France, Mallarmé was doubtless the first to see and to foresee in its full extent the necessity to substitute language itself for the person who until then had been supposed to be its owner."[4] But Barthes's replacement of the author with the "scriptor," and of "expression" with "inscription," leaves one in a moral void, a disagreeable situation made more disagreeable by the arrogance of the scriptor-critic: "Having buried the Author, the modern scriptor can thus no longer believe, as according to the pathetic view of his predecessors, that this hand is too slow for his thought or passion and that consequently, making a law of necessity, he must emphasize this delay and indefinitely 'polish' his form. For him, on the contrary, the hand, cut off from any voice, borne by a pure gesture of inscription (and not of expression), traces a field without origin—or which, at least, has no other origin than language itself, language which ceaselessly calls into question all origins."[5] The physically violent metaphor of cutting off the hand and the cultic claim of purity combine in a dangerous and sentimental absolutism.

My thinking has been shaped more by poetry, fiction, painting, literary criticism, and religious tradition than by philosophy and linguistics. But in seeking to place my quest in a context of ideas, I would call on Emmanuel Levinas and Paul Ricoeur, who are not naïve about the contingent nature of the self, but who recognize the need to found ethical life on some form of selfhood. Ricoeur, especially in *The Symbolism of Evil* and *Oneself as Another*, finds his way into philosophical questions through philology, the study of words, and his method can work congruently with literary criticism while expanding poetry's conceptual reach. And I find myself in sympathy with a radical reader of Mallarmé, Maurice Blanchot, who has pursued a rigorous inquiry into the sacrifice of selfhood all his writing life, and who cares about its ethical consequences.[6] Throughout *L'Espace littéraire*, Blanchot is less blithe than Barthes and weighs more fully the psychic and metaphysical cost of the renunciation of the first-person singular. His thinking is deeply shaped by Mallarmé's *Igitur* and *Un Coup de dés jamais n'abolira le hasard*; Blanchot's whole book can be seen as an explication of Mallarmé's letter to Henri Cazalis of November 14, 1869: "I am now perfectly dead. . . . It's to let you know that I am now impersonal, and no longer the Stéphane whom you knew."[7]

Even while acknowledging, and—for myself—declining, Mallarmé's extremism, I keep faith with his essential perception: that in the making of an art of value, the social and psychological self labors and disappears, leaving the impersonal power of the work. Along with the social ego, Mallarmé teaches, any documentary literalism is also transformed into symbolic shape by the work of art. Literary art is not journalism, though it comes into being through encounters with the unworded "real." It is the shapeliness of the art, the form, that transforms the material, as James Merrill wittily described in his poem "The Thousand and Second Night": ". . . 'Ah. How and when / Did he 'affirm'? Why constantly. And how else / But in the form. Form's what affirms. That's well / Said, if I do—.'"[8] Or, as Louise Glück concisely puts it: "The material is subjective, but the methods are not."[9]

I have learned to read, partly from literature itself (our best teacher), and partly from literary criticism. My approaches in these studies are eclectic and pragmatic, varying according to the pressures of the subjects. In differing ratios, I have needed philological analyses of style adapted from Leo Spitzer; attention to formal structures of prosody; studies of allusion, semantics, and imagery; literary and cultural history; and biography. I can't conceive of a responsible criticism that was not, in some sense, "practical," nor can I imagine a useful reading that did not pay "close" attention to words. The New Criticism hardly had a monopoly on close reading. No school or method of criticism has a monopoly on reading, on what Mallarmé called "la lecture comme une pratique désespérée" (reading as a desperate practice).[10] So neurologically and cognitively mysterious, so subtly demanding is the practice of reading—this progressive making sense of written patterned language—that we need all the help we can get. That is, we need multiple forms of attentive criticism, and we need to see how the various approaches interact with one another.

The central section of this book, "France," includes translations as well as critical examinations: stories and sonnets by Gérard de Nerval, poems by Max Jacob. In keeping with the model of literary impersonality I have been sketching, translations take their place alongside "original" work as a demonstration of, an intensification of, the interactions of consciousness that constitute all reading and writing. Language is both shared and personally inflected; translation occupies a vibratory median position between scribal reading and copying, at one pole, and original composition at the other. It reminds us that in reading and writing we are, in complex ways, not alone. As writers, we are composite, as well as composed.

My other shadow master is Thomas Hardy, though he may be more obscurely present in these pages than Mallarmé. In the memoir "Midi," I recount how, as a young woman experimenting with expatriate life in Italy, I came upon a volume of Hardy's poems and was flooded with the conviction that, after all, the English language was where I had my true home. Hardy's experimental adoption of classical meters, combined with his powerful sense of his own Dorset and Standard English vernacular in speech, song, and story, presented a model of a synthetic and grounded art of poetry, one whose precepts I have tried to honor. The other geographical place I mention in this book, the Vermont landscape touched on in the final journal entry, coordinates for me with the linguistic homecoming in my reading of Hardy. New England—that land of second-growth woods, rocky farms, lost homesteads, crowded suburban development, and successive European dreams foisted on an older woodland—lies under all the classicizing and European imagination in these essays. At times I feel like a late colonial subject, living in the North America felt as a New World, with memories of an older civilization active within me: and is that not still a workable description of the hybrid cultures of the United States?

The nearest I come to acknowledging "Americanness" in this book is in the chapter on Melville, which is also a homage to my father. The book describes an imaginative and emotional arc from an often-foreign childhood to an adulthood that can hold in mind the death of the father and acceptance of the father's country and language, the fatherland, the Northern and Southern United States in their conflict and sorrow. Perhaps it is in meeting one's native sorrow that one ultimately wrests one's own being into shape, however far afield one has gone to find out what "shape" can mean. I have called the third section of the book "Poetry and Conscience." Not that the works discussed earlier disregarded conscience, for no work of art can afford to do so. But the chapters in the last section focus more particularly on poetry as an art in quest of difficult knowledge, and I ask what forms poetry gives us for that search. The study of Geoffrey Hill's poetry develops out of the earlier piece on Mallarmé, and brings to the surface metaphysical and ethical concerns latent in the French poet's

Symbolist aesthetics: Hill's poetry provides a model of the dispersal of the ego to make way for moral and spiritual consciousness. The study of Melville tries to show how poems about battles are themselves battles, within the field of language and poetic structure. The chapter on H.D. argues that the weakness in her poems stems, in corollary ways, from vatic self-delusion and an inflated rhetoric: an insufficiency of language mirroring an insufficiently tested knowledge.

I should say a word more about the idea of home. I grew up in a literary family; by what I think of as an accident of biology, my parents were well-known writers. As a young person in love with stories and poems from an early age, I came to struggle with the self-consciousness induced by a growing sense of literature as the parental preserve. For years, I tried to be a painter, and kept my writing private. When, around the age of twenty, I began to show my writing and to acknowledge it as an integral and necessary part of my life, I took pains to distinguish my work from anything created by my parents, and I tried to erase, in public, any connection to them. The last thing in the world I could have written was a memoir or any account appearing to draw on, or exploit, that familial line. It is only after my parents' deaths, and in the light of my stubborn, by now middle-aged persistence in my own writing, that I feel balanced enough to refer to my parents as writers without fearing that I am withdrawing funds from an account that is not mine. So my parents are lightly present in this book, and I hope it will be felt that they are there so I can properly acknowledge genuine debts.

On the cover of this book is a reproduction of a painting by Poussin, *The Ashes of Phocion*. I had daydreamed of calling this collection by that title, but realized it would describe the book only in a most roundabout way. But here is what I had in mind. Phocion, the fourth-century B.C.E. Athenian general, is described by Plutarch as a man of doughty virtue who helped guide and defend Athens in the city's late, humiliating years of subservience to the Macedonians. He was finally betrayed by a populist uprising and put to death on specious charges. Nor was he allowed burial within Athens: his body had to be conveyed discreetly out of the city and burned in a spot beyond Eleusis. His wife had an empty tomb constructed there, and brought his ashes and bones back at night to Athens, where she buried them in the floor by her own hearth. Before long, Plutarch tells us, the Athenians repented of their madness, gave Phocion an honorable burial within the city, and put his accusers to death.

Why Poussin, why Phocion? I am struck by Poussin's hierarchy of effects in his storytelling. He places the human story, the widow's grieving over the ashes, as an almost minuscule event within the larger rhythms of the landscape: the interlocking olive green, ochre, and smoky gray planes of field and woods, sky and hill, with the city itself subordinate to its natural setting and to the billowing of foliage and cloud above it. Yet the tiny figures of the widow and her servant in the foreground do command our attention. Poussin managed to convey a complex wisdom about our human story, so important to the participants, and yet chastened by the much larger perspective of life's plenitude. Poussin's classicism also proposes a dual sense of time: in his imagination, in his rhythms of color planes and lines, the ancient world is given to us as present, saturated, alive, and palpitating in Grecian light. It is such an experience of the past I hope to have suggested here. The story of Phocion is a tale of the transformation of selfhood into ash and symbol, into patterned force. It is also, finally, a tale of homecoming. In a nonfunereal sense, that idea as well contributes to the understory I hope this book tells.

—Rosanna Warren
Marfa, Texas

Acknowledgments

I gratefully acknowledge the following journals and books in which some of these chapters first appeared.

"Midi" is reprinted from *The Most Wonderful Books: Writers on Discovering the Pleasures of Reading*, edited by Michael Dorris and Emilie Buchwald (Milkweed Editions, 1997). "Alcaics in Exile" was given first as a lecture for the Association of Literary Scholars and Critics; it subsequently appeared in *Philosophy and Literature*, April 1996, and was reprinted in *Unrelenting Readers: The New Poet-Critics*, edited by Paul M. Hedeen and D. G. Myers (Storyline Press, 2004). "The End of *The Aeneid*" was given as a lecture at a conference at the University of Georgia, and was printed in *Poets and Critics Read Vergil*, edited by Sarah Spence (Yale University Press, 2001). "In Classic Guise" was given as a talk, under a different title, at the Modern Language Association convention in 1999; Part I appeared in *Literary Imagination*, Spring 2001; Part II was originally published as "Night Thoughts and *Figurehead*" in *Raritan*, Fall 2000. The first half of Chapter 7, "Contradictory Classicists," first appeared in *Threepenny Review*, Summer 2002. "The 'Last Madness' of Gérard de Nerval" and the accompanying translations of Nerval's prose appeared in the *Georgia Review* in Spring 1983. The translations of Nerval's sonnets were published in *Comparative Criticism* (Cambridge University Press, 1984). I first gave "Rimbaud: Insulting Beauty" as a talk at the Symposium on Changing

Ideas of Art at the Accademia dei Lincei, Rome, with the American Academy of Arts and Sciences in May 2004. "Orpheus the Painter: Apollinaire and Robert Delaunay" appeared in *Criticism*, Fall 1988, and was reprinted in *Conversant Essays: Contemporary Poets on Poetry*, edited by James McCorkle (Wayne State University Press, 1989). "Dark Knowledge: Melville's Poems of the Civil War" was given as a lecture for the ID 500 University Professors Seminar at Boston University, and appeared in *Raritan*, Summer 1999. "Words and Blood" appeared in *The Poets' Dante*, edited by Peter Hawkins and Rachel Jacoff (Farrar, Straus and Giroux, 2001). "Hardy's Undoings" was given as a talk at the Modern Language Association convention in 1997, and reprinted in the *Berlin Journal*, Spring 2006. "Meeting H.D." was given as a talk first at the ID 500 University Professors Seminar at Boston University, and then at the University of Missouri, Columbia. "Adventures of the 'I': The Poetry of Pronouns in Geoffrey Hill" also took shape first as a talk for the ID 500 Seminar; it was published in the *Cincinnati Review*, Winter 2005. "Coda" appeared in *The Poet's Notebook*, edited by Stephen Kuusisto, Deborah Tall, and David Weiss (W. W. Norton, 1995).

Many people have helped to shape this work. Stephen Scully was my unofficial tutor in classics, and generous life companion, for many years. William Arrowsmith is the great teacher who stands behind much of my learning. Over the years, Donald Carne-Ross, John Hollander, and Christopher Ricks have given me invaluable criticism on some of these pieces. Anne and Avigdor Arikha, Michael Putnam, and Gary Smith read several of the chapters with generous vigilance, and Deborah Tall helped me to press the preface through a sequence of metamorphoses. Jonathan Aaron, Linda Gregerson, and Ken Gross—long-suffering friends—gave me critical readings of the whole manuscript, and Frances Whistler commented acutely on the preface and on "Midi." While I was in Berlin, Katherine Scully helped me with research in the United States, Aude Pivin with research in Paris. I could not have finished this book without the blessing of a quiet month in Marfa, Texas, at the Lannan Foundation, and the more extended blessing of five months at the American Academy in Berlin. In Berlin, the beautifully efficient staff of the Academy contributed in practical ways, especially Yolande Korb, the librarian, and Benny Dreischner, the computer guru. At Boston University, Darius Barron and then Aubrey Hooser formatted this complex manuscript into one workable document, and without them the book would not exist. Aubrey Hooser also undertook the herculean task of asking many publishers for permissions. Sophie

Klein proofread the classical material, and Louisa Mandarino the book as a whole. Louisa also concluded the task of hunting down permissions. Finally, I owe an incalculable debt to my editor at Norton, Jill Bialosky, for her long patience, her faith in the book, and her gentle and perspicacious urgings which helped me envision its final shape. And Paul Whitlatch at Norton has graciously helped to guide the book into port.

To all of these people, I am more grateful than I can soberly express.

Section I

ANTIQUITY AT PRESENT

CHAPTER I

Midi

We lived, the winter I was twelve years old, in a two-hundred-year-old, decrepit, manorial farmhouse in a village of the Alpes-Maritimes, in southern France. The province is well named. The Alps there do pour down to the sea so steeply that all roads must zigzag, and the habitations barely maintain a toehold on their narrow terraces. The whole, large region, though, is called "le Midi," and as a child I thought that an even better name: it means "noon," and though the winter proved chill and gray enough, this was still the land of palms, cypresses, and flagrant meridional sunlight.

Our house, called a *mas* in local parlance, had stone walls about a meter thick, and was built into a cliff three stories high. One entered the massive front door to the *salon* and downstairs bedroom from the front of the house, which faced the plunge down the valley with its terraced vineyards, gardens, and tile-roofed villas; but one could just as well enter the back way, through the olive groves, by clambering up steps cut in the cliff face, coming in at the kitchen on the third floor through the broad old oak door at the back—and upper—story of the house. The *mas*, called "La Moutonne," was set in three hectares of ruined garden: half-tumbling terraces for olive trees, ivy cascading down stone walls, twisted fig and quince trees, tall sword-bladed cacti, nettles, tufted ochre-colored grass.

My ten-year-old brother and I roamed this wilderness with our white goat, Lily, who bounded ahead of us up walls and grizzled olive trees, then paused, and regarded with agate-yellow, unblinking eyes our struggles to follow her. The eucalyptus trees soared over the house and driveway, with their dark, massy foliage, and their mottled bark which peeled off in parchment strips. Above "our" property, the olive groves straggled up the slope, past the road, into the high, thistly pasture lands for goats and sheep. At our gate, half a kilometer down the rutted driveway, the village of Magagnosc perched on a spur over the valley, a cluster of gray stone and apricot stucco culminating in the church of the same terra-cotta color as the very earth of the Midi. On clear days, we saw the Mediterranean below us, a streak of lapis lazuli, or turquoise, or sometimes a blade of pewter held at the throat of the horizon. It was here, in the ruined garden, that I began to memorize poetry. It was here that I learned my school French for the daily exercises at the Lycée de Jeunes Filles. It was here that I began to learn Latin conjugations and declensions, to catch up with my *lycée* class, which had entered on its third year in those mysteries.

"Amo, amas, amat," "hic, haec, hoc," "ille, illa, illud," still evoke for me the scents of lavender, thyme, eucalyptus, cypress, dried goat turds: the sweet and acrid odors of the Midi. The Latin forms gave inward shape to this new world. "He, she, it," "this one, this one, this one"—and most of all, though I knew it only obscurely at the time—"I love, you love, he/she/it loves," ordered that world for me. And how eagerly did I collect, savor, and compare its forms, whether drawing in India ink and watercolor the spiky leaf shapes of the garden or copying and recopying Latin in my *lycée cahier*, with its neat pages ruled, not in horizontal lines like American paper, but in tiny boxes in whose confines I struggled, with cartridge ink pen and blue-stained fingers, to shape the fat, squat script required of French schoolgirls.

If there was *amor* at work in my hours of copying and memorizing, it sprang not only from the involuntary association of the discovery of Latin with the discovery of the wild garden and the latent, ruined, Mediterranean *Latinitas* that surrounded us. It must have come, as well, from my teacher. The good angel of pedagogy delivered me, that year, into the care of Madame Péron for both my Latin and my French classes. In the harsh regime of the *lycée*, with its daily humiliations and beratings and rankings, its *pions* (spies), concrete walls, and the smell of boiled lard in the refectory, she stood out in a radiance of generous wit. My other teachers, that year, all seemed angular. When I remember them, I see women with collapsed cheeks and lips pursed in permanent disapproval, and I hear the crack of rulers across desktops. But Madame Péron had a serene and stately largesse of figure which suited perfectly her fine Greek head, held always high, with her black hair coiled up behind.

My mother, when she had gotten to know Madame Péron, asserted that it was the half-Greek lineage that accounted for her remarkable humanity within the *lycée* system. Of that, I could not judge. But on the first day of school, as I stood awkwardly before the class in my regulation blue *tablier* (not so much an "apron" as a long-sleeved, buttoned smock), trying to muster my unsteady summer French to respond to Madame Péron's interrogation, I felt her amused sympathy, like sunlight across frost. "Alors," she concluded, with a hint of smile and a tilt of her chin, "vous allez vous débrouiller?" (meaning, roughly, in that wonderful French verb, that I would "manage"). "Oui, Madame," I replied, pulling myself together, "je vais me débrouiller." "Bien," she said, and sent me back to my desk.

And so it was my fortune, on Thursday afternoons, when the other schoolchildren had been released from classes, to climb the steep, unevenly paved street from the Lycée de Jeunes Filles in Grasse to Avenue Fouques, an even steeper and narrower street leading to the Pérons' house. In spring, the walled gardens of Grasse send forth hazy bursts of yellow mimosa blossom and tumbling, starry veils of jasmine. In autumn and winter, the first months of my tutorials, those gardens revealed, over their stone and stucco ramparts, only dark green foliage, occasionally the deeper green of cypress. But whatever the season, the ascent of Avenue Fouques was a progress past mysteries, with the glimpses of inner courtyards through iron grille gates, the ruddy roof tiles, the tawny walls (some studded with broken glass along the rim), the green shutters, all suggesting interiors ripe with domestic narrative. But it was in Madame Péron's apartment— at the top of the street, up two flights of stairs—that the real mysteries began to unfold.

There, in the small rooms made somehow enormous by the balconied window giving over the swoop of valley down to the sea, and by the entire interior wall space being given over, Pitti Palace–fashion, to the watercolor scenes—Breton seascapes, Provençal landscapes—painted by her husband Yves, she led me, step by step, into the chambers of Latin grammar. Looking back, I remember not so much toiling at home, back at La Moutonne with its drafty rooms in the early winter dusks, as those sessions over the smudged *cahiers* in Madame Péron's eyrie. Night would fall and still I would be staggering through the imperfect tense—perhaps even in the subjunctive!—side by side with Madame Péron at her oaken dining room table as she coaxed me forward into still-stranger regions. The subjunctive mood, for instance: I think it must have been that winter that I found there were verbal forms reserved for purely hypothetical states of being or action. Finally, Madame Péron's daughter Sylvie would come in—my age, but, I thought, infinitely sophisticated—and Monsieur Péron would arrive with his shy, sweet grin, and my lesson would be over. Three or four years later, back in New England, when another teacher had opened for me the poems of Catullus, Horace, and Virgil, and in solitary, early morning hours I labored to make sense of First Asclepiadean meters and ablative absolutes, I could shut my eyes and call back the sensation of climbing the corrugations of Avenue Fouques toward Madame Péron, and her window opening over the Mediterranean.

It didn't take a lot of imagination, in that landscape, to feel the Romans as a parent civilization only recently departed. We were, after all, on the Côte d'Azur, just above Nice and Cannes; a slide eastward down the coast would land us in Monaco, and another two steps would take us over the border into Italy. But one didn't need to cross a border to feel the Romans. In late spring, we left Lily for a long weekend with the local shepherd, and our parents took us off exploring the Roman sites of Provence. As my brother and I scampered in the ruins of Roman theaters in Nîmes, Orange, and Arles, or teetered across the great aqueduct, le Pont du Gard, we felt—or I imagine now that we felt—those stones as an extension of the stone terraces in our garden at La Moutonne.

Latin, of course, went hand in hand (or hand to mouth?) with French: Madame Péron taught both. French pedagogy in those days was based on memorization. We were expected, if called on, to be able to recite the lesson in any subject, every day, which was a little like playing Russian roulette, since it was impossible to be prepared in algebra, geometry, history, geography, Latin, French, and English, all of which we were learning. I remember standing in front of the class to recite, to the approval of the math teacher, the lesson involving fractions: "A fraction is a number composed of two numbers separated by a horizontal line." And I dutifully recited for the history and geography teacher what I knew from observation to be untrue: that "Vermont has an economy based on metallurgy and the cultivation of grain." For Madame Péron, however, I memorized with love. Every lesson in French grammar—and with what beautiful precision did those chapters tease us with the behavior of dependent clauses and the agreements of tense and mood!—was linked to a literary passage.

So it was that, as my classmates and I learned to hitch dependent clauses within main clauses, we filled our minds with the verse rhythms of La Fontaine and Leconte de Lisle, the prose rhythms of Chateaubriand and Alphonse Daudet. For me, La Fontaine's rat is still annoyingly proclaiming his parity with the elephant; Daudet's flocks of sheep and goats are still trampling through dust clouds to return to the farmyard from their summer grazing in the Alps, the peacocks screaming from the walls, with chickens, guinea hens, ducks, and turkeys careering around the yard in the welcoming din; and in Leconte de Lisle's ponderous and mesmerizing Alexandrines I can still taste the "supreme and baleful *volupté*" I reveled in, at age twelve, as I chanted his "Midi" and imagined my heart dipped seven times in divine oblivion:

> Viens! Le Soleil te parle en paroles sublimes;
> Dans sa flamme implacable absorbe-toi sans fin;
> Et retourne à pas lents vers les citées infimes,
> Le cœur trempé sept fois dans le Néant divin.

> (Come! The Sun speaks to you in sublime words; / Absorb yourself forever in its implacable flame; / And return with slow steps toward the minuscule cities, / Your heart dipped seven times in divine oblivion.)

I had grown up in a house of stories told and read aloud, of poems recited as naturally as breathing. Our parents were both writers. Reading had been for me, early on, an experience of *volupté*, a perfect absorption such as Leconte de Lisle's "Midi" described. But those were poems and stories in English. And English was my parents' language. They wrote in it; they wrote whole books in it; all their friends—as far as I could make out—wrote books in it. English was a terrain already occupied. The year of the garden in Magagnosc, I found languages I thought "my own." The first poems I memorized for myself were in French and Latin; the first verse forms I intuited, and imitated, for myself were in French and Latin. So I date my life as a reader, in one sense, to my twelfth year, when I began not only to take *dictée* from Madame Péron's clear, expressive reading aloud, but to memorize; when I entered language consciously; when I had the illusion of living in languages neither maternal nor paternal, but ancestral in a much vaguer sense, and therefore possessable.

To read is to take possession. But it is also to give oneself completely, if temporarily, to the keeping of another mind, and to enter another world. If the spell holds, it is a sensuous world, alive with texture, odor, and rhythm. It is voluptuous. At the age of twelve, one experiences imaginative absorption unreservedly, even as one glimpses the farther reaches of another *volupté* promised as yet obscurely by adult life in its unfolding. To read fully as an adult must be—I believe—to relive something of that childhood incipience tempered with the adult's chastened backward vision.

For me, the trail from the decrepit and promising garden led to years of sounding myself out in languages other than English. The road back to English was the road of growing up, the true falling away of childhood. That is another and a private story. But two scenes especially mark it for me. One occurred when I was eighteen, living for the first time on my own, attending art school in Rome, and visiting my family in the house they had rented for a year in Grenoble. Awkwardly no longer *jeune fille*, not yet young woman, out of sorts and out of place, I stayed up late at night while my parents and brother slept. By the weak lightbulb in the small, stone-flagged kitchen, I started reading poems I had picked up from my father's table: Roethke's *The Lost Son and Other Poems*. Here were not Latinate stanzas, but a perilous groping, the small, dark lives of plant cuttings, bulbs, and slugs feeling their way out across the page:

> One nub of growth
> Nudges a sand-crumb loose,
> Pokes through a musty sheath
> Its pale tendrilous horn.
>
> (from "Cuttings")

And:

> When sprouts break out,
> Slippery as fish,
> I quail, lean to beginnings, sheath-wet.
>
> (from "Cuttings, later")[1]

I knew this poetry was dangerous, because it leaned too intimately into my own, late-adolescent sprouting; I also knew it had lodged itself in my psyche for life.

The second scene took place some years later, when I had graduated from college and had spent a year living in Paris, vaguely painting and translating, surreptitiously writing poems. From France I had migrated to Crete for four months where I lived in an empty flat for forty dollars a month and pursued my exercises in oblivion. By October I was in Venice. Elder friends let me stay in their apartment during their absence, and I found myself invited, one grim weekend in late November, to a Palladian country house in the Veneto. I remember the house rising, in its rect-angular majesty, from the flat, muddy fields, the whole scene swathed in mists and gusts of rain. Inside, the house was damply, dimly, magnificent, with high ceilings and little furniture. It rained all weekend. In the hours when my host was absorbed in his study and my hostess had disappeared on duties of her own, I wandered like a ghost from room to room. On a shelf in one of the sitting rooms, I found, among an international mis-cellany of books, a small edition of selected poems of Thomas Hardy. It seemed, in that room, in that landscape, perfectly incongruous. It opened to "Neutral Tones":

> We stood by a pond that winter day,
> And the sun was white, as though chidden of God,
> And a few leaves lay on the starving sod;
>   —They had fallen from an ash, and were gray.[2]

It was a poem my father loved, a poem his teacher had loved. Years of suppressed apprehensions broke upon me. I shuddered at the sturdy, homely particularities of this verse and its held-back breath, not French, not Italian, not Greek, not Latin. By the time the roadkill smile had died on the woman's lips in Hardy's poem—"The smile on your mouth was the deadest thing / Alive enough to have strength to die"—and the color had drained from its four stanzas, leaving "a pond edged with grayish leaves," I found myself weeping. I knew, with a definite and half-heartsick knowledge, that this hard language was mine, and that I should have to live in it.

So I went home. "Home," that is, to North America. But more than that, "home" to English, which has always been a hospitable, hodgepodge tongue, and which has room in it, I have found, for parents and children, for the scent of eucalyptus, Leconte de Lisle's sun trance, and Latin verbs, as well as for Hardy's earthbound, mortal, cryptically Latinate poems.

CHAPTER 2

Sappho: Translation as Elegy

For Ruth Jaeger

> *Our dreams pursue our dead . . .*
> —Swinburne, "Ave atque Vale"

ILLE MI PAR . . .

He's like a god, that man; he seems
(if this can be) to shine beyond
the gods, who nestling near you sees
    you and hears you

laughing low in your throat. It tears me
apart. For when I glimpse you,
Lesbia, look—I'm helpless:
    tongue a frozen

lump, and palest fire
pouring through all my limbs; my ears
deafened in ringing; each eye
    shuttered in night. . . .

You're wasting your time, Catullus,
laying waste to your life. You love it.
Whole kingdoms and blissful cities
    have wasted away, like you.

I seem to have given a misleading title, for the poem I present is not by Sappho, but by Catullus. And I revise further by pointing out that it is not "by" Catullus either, but "by" me. There may seem to be downright foolishness and no little immodesty in putting forward my own translation of Catullus's famous translation of Sappho's famous poem "Phainetai moi."

My translation of Catullus's "Ille mi par . . ." occurs, with another Catullus poem in the Sapphic meter, in a volume of my own poems. But these possessive phrases become obtrusive, as indeed they ought in matters of authorship. The purpose in focusing on another translation of a translation is not to claim that the world *needs* yet another version of this perennially retranslated poem, nor is it to demonstrate that I have outpaced all my predecessors and found a perfect English equivalent for Catullus. Rather, I should like to offer it, impersonally, as a small instance of lyric lineage, a model for poetry's perpetual reengendering of itself. It is to argue that poetry is, finally, a family matter, involving the strains of birth, love, power, death, and inheritance; and that, given such strains (in every sense), one is never "by oneself," however isolated the act of writing may appear. The so-called original poems in my book are, in their own way, translations of several lyric traditions into personal experience and idiom, and are possible only thanks to strenuous acts of reading, one form of which we know, conventionally, as translation. I am concerned here with the way in which the individual poet inherits poetry, or, in Eliot's formulation, is catalyzed by it; and I take translation as a specific and especially focused instance of the reception and transformation of literary tradition.

I was drawn to Catullus 51 ("Ille mi par . . .") not only because it has haunted me since adolescence, not only because I am more at home in Latin than in Greek, but because I was touched by the pathos of its being a translation and not "the real thing." In Catullus's forging of a new poetry from his still rather primitive native traditions and Greek models, I recognized the situation of any poet in the strain of self-creation through confrontation with the foreign and the past, the choosing of a parentage. And that situation may be seen as an analogy for the self-creation of a whole literature which develops by exposure to the "other," as English literature, also fairly barbaric in its early stages, has done in burst after burst, and as American literature, given its colonial inception, could not avoid doing.

The word "inheritance" implies death, grief, contest, and riches. In presenting the literary genre of elegy as a model for translation, I shall be relying on Peter Sacks's *The English Elegy*.[1] This book traces the work of mourning from its anthropological origins on into complex literary codification. In elegy, with its association with the ritual death and rebirth of a fertility god, I see a figure for the work of translation, which involves the death, dismemberment, and (one hopes!) rebirth of a text, with relative consolation for the mourners, or readers.

Sacks's work is essential in restoring our sense of the primitive vigor, I could almost say sacred power, at the source of our inherited rituals of mourning, of elegiac writing, and, I will argue, of all writing. In recalling the rites of sacrifice and cannibalism associated with early cults of Dionysus, and the survival of such rites symbolically in ancient Greek and later funerary practice, Sacks reveals the terror and *virtù* latent in such an apparently artificial form as English pastoral elegy. He shows how individual loss may be integrated within larger rhythmic structures dramatized by the poem, and he provides a vision of literature as a communion perpetually renewed in the light of death. In considering Sappho and some of her progeny, I am trying to recover that visceral sense of the rite of poetry: that sense in which, as Auden said of Yeats, "the words of a dead man / Are modified in the guts of the living," and in which Pound, also translating a translation, envisioned Odysseus summoning the dead in Canto I of the *Cantos*: ". . . A sheep to Tiresias only, black and a bell-sheep. / Dark blood flowed in the fosse, / Souls out of Erebus. . . ."[2]

The term "elegy" requires more than a little elucidation. The word is a rather mysterious one, with veiled origins and auspicious dual associations with death and with love. The original Greek elegiac couplets were not necessarily associated with funerals, but were used for a wide variety of exhortation and reflection.[3] But Hellenistic grammarians derived *elegos*, in an imaginative etymology, from *e e legein* (to cry "woe, woe").[4] In Euripides it is used as a song of mourning associated with the *aulos*, a flute whose tone was considered woeful as opposed to the *barbitos*, the lyre associated with lyric. In *Heroides* 15, Ovid has Sappho say, in elegiac couplets, "Flendus amor meus est—elegiae flebile carmen; / non facit ad lacrimas barbitos ulla meas"[5] (11.7–8: My love is lamentable—a weeping song of elegy; no lyre suits my tears). "Elegy," in that passage, is doubly anachronistic: in Ovid's time the term was used for witty amatory complaint, and in Sappho's seventh century B.C.E. the elegiac meter had no necessarily doleful connotation. However, there is a strong possibility that the *elegos* was at an earlier period specifically associated with ritual grief.[6] Sacks describes the evolution of elegy through Latin love poetry into the English pastoral elegy, which reclaims some of the primitive features such as structures of repetition, myth of a vegetation god, bursts of anger and cursing, procession of mourners, detachment from the deceased, and consolation through symbolic substitution.[7] For my purposes, which are to define a private ritual figure for translation, the perhaps fictive origin of elegy as the art associated with funerals, and thus with the death and resurrection of vegetation gods and the rechanneling of eros into song, serves beautifully. We are considering the death and resurrection of texts in a myth of literary metamorphosis whose deities are those grieving poet-lovers whose nymphs turn into the tools—or emblems—of the trade: Pan's Syrinx into the panpipes, Apollo's Daphne into the laurel. Its other forces are those vegetation figures Dionysus, Adonis, Hyacinth, who survive sacrifice to reemerge as myths of eternal song.[8] It becomes apparent then that two senses of elegy, love and loss, can only rarely be disentangled.

We shall find our way back to Sappho through "Lycidas." The death of Edward King provided Milton with an occasion to dramatize grief—in this case a rather ceremonial grief—and, more pointedly, to explore the inherited genre of pastoral elegy and his own ambition and fear of death. His apparent heartlessness, or at least jauntiness, in the twitch of the mantle blue and the turn from pastoral to epic has often been noted. A poet's elegy for another poet is somehow a translation of that poet or at least of a tradition, and involves some kind of transfer of powers, perhaps aggressively asserted by the survivor. In any case, the underlying question is not that of personal survival, but of the survival of poetry. If all real poetry is, as I believe, writing in the light of death, elegy is the genre which performs most consciously in that light.

In "Lycidas" Milton's grief, anger, and fear crystallize appropriately around the figure of Orpheus, in classical mythology the mystic singer whose death by dismemberment could be read either as the failure of art or as its resurrection and purification.[9] Orpheus's *sparagmos* and drowning in the Hebrus not only suit the fate of Edward King, but fit within Milton's cosmic pattern of drownings and ascensions of stars and the sun. Such a pattern is hinted at early in the poem when the shepherds sing undisturbed by the passage of time ("Oft till the star that rose, at Ev'ning, bright /

Toward Heav'n's descent had slop'd his westering wheel"); the pattern is fulfilled at the end, in Christian design: "So sinks the day-star in the Ocean bed, / And yet anon repairs his drooping head." The final couplet astonishingly detaches the surviving poet, the uncouth swain, from the natural cycle to which the dead poet has been assimilated; yet the solar association haunts the conclusion in the ambiguous pronoun "he": "And now the Sun had stretch'd out all the hills, / And now was dropt into the Wester n bay; / At last he rose, and twitch'd his Mantle blew: / To morrow to fresh Woods, and Pastures new."[10]

In a crucial turn "Lycidas" associates Orpheus with Sappho:

> What could the Muse her self that Orpheus bore,
> The Muse her self, for her inchanting son
> Whom Universal nature did lament,
> When by the rout that made the hideous roar,
> His goary visage down the stream was sent,
> Down the swift Hebrus to the Lesbian Shore?
>
> (lines 59–63)

The classical Orpheus envisaged in his humiliation emphasizes the death of Lycidas, in this phase, as horror. This Orpheus serves as antitype to, and will give way before, "the dear might of him that walked the waves"; cut off from Christian revelation, he is an inadequate figure for resurrection. Even at this nadir, however, when the "hideous roar" of the Thracian women seems to overwhelm the "inchanting" powers of music, Milton hints at the resurrection of those powers by imagining the current of the Hebrus flowing south over a hundred miles along the coast of Asia Minor to wash Orpheus's head to the shores of Sappho's island. That "supreme head of song," as Swinburne called her, and the possibilities of poetry she represents, are immediately challenged in "Lycidas" by the speaker's questions and the visions of the blind Fury. In Milton's poem Sappho remains a faint allusion. It is significant, however, that she should be glimpsed here in the context of the drowned poet who will be raised, like the "day-star," into the morning sky, and into a familiar mythology of resurrected divinities. Sappho, too, is said to have drowned, disappointed in love, by leaping from the Leucadian Rock; as Gregory Nagy has shown,[11] she rises, in her legend if not in "Lycidas," into a similar myth of solar resurrection as Sappho/Aphrodite pursuing Phaon/Phaethon.

But why Sappho? I have been considering her as a legend, not as a

poet. Indeed, it is partly as legend that she presides over the family matters I want to trace, in translation, through Catullus, Baudelaire, and
Swinburne. Nagy's argument linking her to Aphrodite/Ishtar/Eos and
a solar myth of recurrent death and rebirth—an argument so intricate
as to deserve Sappho's own epithet for Aphrodite, *doloplokos*, weaver of
wiles—derives to some degree from Sappho's invocations to the goddess,
but for the most part from a fragment of Menander's *Leukadia* preserved by
Strabo, from Ovid's *Heroides* 15, and from a bristling array of mythological sources. Through Menander and Ovid and earlier comic traditions,
Sappho entered the Western imagination as a priestess of song and of
illicit love who died by flinging herself off the white cliff at Cape Leukas
for the love of the handsome ferryman Phaon. Satirically viewed in various plays of the Middle Comedy, the story is one of the insufficiency of
poetry, and perhaps also of the just comeuppance meted out to a woman
who has spurned too long the love of men. Even the burlesque plays and
Ovid's arch diagnosis, however, veil a glorious Sappho linked to ancient
cults at Cape Leukas. Through "Longinus," that is, through the treatise
"De sublimitate" to which we owe the preservation of "Phainetai moi,"
Sappho has imposed herself as the exemplary sublime poet, with a halo of
primacy for the lyric akin to that of Homer for epic. She was known in
the *Palatine Anthology* as the Tenth Muse, and comes down to us as a kind
of mother goddess of poetry, of whom Swinburne said, "Judging even
from the mutilated fragments fallen within our reach from the broken
altar of her sacrifice of song, I for one have always agreed with all Grecian
tradition in thinking Sappho to be beyond all question and comparison
the very greatest poet that ever lived."[12]

But again, why Sappho? Why such a legend? Why should she seem
to have engendered the Western lyric not once, but over and over again,
as we see in the twentieth century's rapture over the Oxyrhynchan fragments and their shaping touch on Aldington, Pound, H.D., Guy Davenport . . . ? We must turn to these fragments, to the poems. If the legendary
Sappho rising from the sea as the evening star gives us an emblem of the
translation and survival of song, the actual survival of her texts in quoted
snippets and in the papyri of grave wrappings is all the more eloquent. In
the idea of elegy, with its dual allusions to love and death, we can sense
something of the power of these mutilated poems stripped from mum-
mies but still casting erotic spells.[13]

The enchantment resides, however, not in an idea, but in her "visible
song," as Swinburne so rightly understood; supremely, in the Sapphic

stanza, which burned its shape into Catullus's brain five centuries after Sappho's death, and which has shaped our desire ever since. If we consider Sappho as a myth, it must be as a myth not of love, but of form.

> Phainetai moi keinos isos theoisin
> emmen oner ottis enantios toi
> izanei kai plasion adu phonei-
> sas upakouei
>
> kai gelaisas imeroen, to m'ei man
> kardian en stethesin eptoaisen;
> os gar es s'ido, broke', os me phona
> s'oud'en et eikei
>
> alla kam men glossa eage, lepton
> d'autika kroi pur upadedromeiken,
> oppatessi d'oud' en oreimm', epirrom-
> beisi d'akouai,
>
> kad de m'idros kakkheetai, tromos de
> paisan agrei, klorotera de poias
> emmi, tethnakein d'oligo pideueis
> phainom' em' auta. . . .

It is a haunting shape. In Sappho's hands it plays release against restraint with unrivaled cunning: the poem runs from stanza to stanza like water pouring from basin to basin down a trout stream, twisting and flashing, unfurled and checked. As Charles Segal has observed, its very motion is the erotic persuasion, *peitho*, of which Sappho so often writes. Within each hendecasyllabic line the opening trochaic feet give way to the impulse which throbs forward in the choriamb, to be teasingly checked by the concluding bacchiac: $- \cup - \times \mid - \cup \cup - \mid \cup - -$. The halt teases because more often than not the sentence's propulsion launches us into the next line, sometimes through enjambment within a word: *phonei-/sas* (lines 3–4), *epirrom-/beisi* (lines 11–12). After three such hendecasyllables the adonic seems to dam up the current with its wedgelike, truncated shape and final pair of long syllables; but Sappho admits no such resolution, and spills her poem over barrier after barrier. Within this flow, the eddies of assonance and consonance complete the work of hypnotic enchantment.

In its expansions and contractions this is a stanza fatally gauged to register the pulse of desire.

Can a living stream be translated? One of Sappho's finest interpreters, Swinburne, has testified:

> To translate the two odes and the remaining fragments of Sappho is the one impossible task; and as witness of this I will call up one of the greatest among poets. Catullus "translated"—or as his countrymen would now say "traduced"—the Ode to Anactoria—"Eis Eromenan": a more beautiful translation there never was and will be; but compared with the Greek, it is colourless and bloodless, puffed out by additions and enfeebled by alterations. . . . Where Catullus failed, I could not hope to succeed.[14]

Swinburne is here mourning the death of the original. To pursue the elegiac analogy, he has brought himself to that stage of grief which recognizes irreplaceable loss. But just as the work of mourning proceeds by rehearsal of the trauma and ritual self-mutilation to detachment from the deceased and acceptance of a symbolic substitute, so the work of translation repeats the destruction of the original, dismembers and ingests it as in the Thracian sacrifice of Orpheus or the rites of Dionysus, and finally offers its transubstantiated version as consolation for, and recognition of, loss. In the passage just quoted, Swinburne was defending his free translation of Sappho in his poem "Anactoria":

> "That is not Sappho," a friend once said to me. I could only reply, "It is as near as I can come; and no man can come close to her. . . . I have striven to cast my spirit into the mould of hers, to express and represent not the poem but the poet. . . . Here and there, I need not say, I have rendered into English the very words of Sappho. I have tried also to work into words of my own some expression of their effect: to bear witness how, more than any other's, her verses strike and sting the memory in lonely places, or at sea, among all loftier sights and sands—how they seem akin to fire and air, being themselves "all air and fire"; other element there is none in them."[15]

We shall presently consider the fruits of such devotion; before that, we need to turn to her first translator, Catullus.

SAPPHO AND CATULLUS

51

Ille mi par esse deo videtur,
ille, si fas est, superare divos,
qui sedens adversus identidem te
    spectat et audit

dulce ridentem, misero quod omnis
eripit sensus mihi: nam simul te,
Lesbia, adspexi, nihil est super mi. . . .

lingua sed torpet, tenuis sub artus
flamma demanat, sonitu suopte
tintinant aures, gemina teguntur
    lumina nocte.

otium, Catulle, tibi molestum est:
otio exsultas nimiumque gestis:
otium et reges prius et beatas
    perdidit urbes.

Though Catullus seems to have written only two poems in the Sapphic meter, the extent of his debt to the poet of Lesbos may be judged from the name he gave to the woman he loved: Lesbia. The two Catullan Sapphic poems record stages in that affair. The translation of "Phainetai moi" can be seen either as celebrating an early, happy phase, substituting erotic rapture for Sappho's distress,[16] or, as has been plausibly argued, as commenting ironically on the destructiveness of his love for Lesbia through allusion to supposed marriage elements in Sappho's poem.[17] "Furi et Aureli," Catullus's other Sapphic poem (Catullus 11), is a savage and lyrical farewell to the unworthy lover. However Lesbia is seen by Catullus in these poems, it is through a Sapphic lens which emphasizes, by contrast, Lesbia's Roman corruption.

This is not the occasion to pore, syllable by syllable, over the transposition from Greek to Latin; a few details will have to suggest the enterprise. Most tellingly, however, we can observe right from the start that Catullus has "lost it" (to use current parlance) with the very first word. *Phainetai,* from *phaino* (to appear), shares a root with *phaos* (light), and with the verb *phao* (to give light, to shine). The "appearance" Sappho indicates is no mere seeming or being seen, but something more on the order of our "epiphany," an English cognate of *phaino*. It is used of the apparitions of deities. The man of Sappho's poem, *keinos*, that one, whoever he is who sits next to the beloved girl, blazes in the first stanza with a radiance reflected from Aphrodite, through the girl. It is an epiphany of Love, working upon the man and, beyond him, upon Sappho (or let us call her "the speaker") observing. We are confronted here not simply with a relative poverty in Latin and English verbs of seeming, but with an entirely different conception of the manifestation of the divine.

Another detail: Sappho's *imeroen* (line 5). A long-drawn-out, caressing neuter adjective used adverbially ("and listens to you laughing *enticingly*"), it contains the word *eros*, and is charged with desire, with the dread and sacred power of love, to a degree that annihilates most dippy English substitutes and far outstrips Catullus's merely sensory *dulce* (sweetly). As if *imeroen* had not sufficient voltage, Sappho renews the charge in a phonetic echo, completing the line "kai gelaisas imeroen, to m'ei man," whose sensuous alliteration and assonance can be savored even by the Greekless reader. A few final points: Catullus inserts a legalistic clause into line 2: "si fas est, superare divos" (if it is permitted, [he seems] to surpass the gods). It testifies to a peculiarly Roman attitude toward men and gods, but it also slows up the poem, and a good deal is lost in line 6 in the replacement of Sappho's heart shuddering in her breast by the abstract *sensus* (general powers of apprehension).

What has Catullus salvaged? First and foremost, the stanza form, through which he knowingly pours his own poem. It was Catullus's muscular twining of sentences through lines and stanzas that mesmerized me years ago when I did not know the Greek. He has taken over, likewise, something of Sappho's vowel and consonant play, though his seems more programmatic and symmetrical: "flamma demanat, sonitu suopte" (line 9). Where Sappho was entirely flexible, Catullus moves toward practices which will be codified in Horatian Sapphics, often making the fourth syllable of the hendecasyllable long, and ending a word after the fifth syllable. He does not have Sappho's radiance, but he grasps the simplicity with which she lists the medical symptoms of love, symptoms taken over from Homeric descriptions of shock and fear, the drama of war imported to the love chamber, epic into lyric. Where Sappho emphasized intimacy in stanza 1, Catullus insists on the recurrent nature of the scene with the rare adverb *identidem* (again and again), which appears in his other Sapphic poem, "Furi et Aureli," in an obscene context. He misses the ring structure in her poem that linked the apparition (*phainetai*) of the rival man in line 1 through the sundering of her own body to a reunification of self in the strongly enjambed verb "to be" (*emmi*, line 15) and felt apparition of self "I seem" (*phainomai*, line 16). Where her poem went at this juncture is a wild surmise. Catullus seems to have omitted her remarkable fourth stanza, and his poem may or may not have ended with the famous *otium* stanza. If the *otium* lines did close his poem, as I sense they did, they set Catullus's passion in the typically Roman context of politics and empire at odds with private erotic life, and glance out again in the direction of epic.

That epic glance is given more scope in the "Furi et Aureli" poem. There Catullus addresses his two enemies as his "companions" and charges them, in a torrent of bombast mimicking imperial rhetoric, with a simple message of farewell to his "girl." After the calculated understatement "non bona dicta" (not good words) explodes a stanza of obscene abuse which gives way to one of the most delicate of all Latin lyrics, the stanza recalling Sappho's cut flower[18]:

> But she'd better not look, like last time, for my
> love reviving. It's her fault it's fallen,
> a flower at the rim of the meadow, touched
>   by the plow passing.[19]

Not surprisingly, the anatomy of love, and perhaps jealousy, in "Phainetai moi" has never lost its grip on the Western imagination. But the history of Sappho in English is by and large a sorry one. It is the story of the awkward adaptation of classical quantitative prosody to the English accentual-syllabic system.[20] The faint presence of stress in Latin meter only complicates the problem further. John Hall, translating "Phainetai moi" in 1652, sensibly opts for a loose stress equivalent to Sappho's quantities, and gives tetrameters with a dimeter for the adonic. The poor man can muster almost no other poetic resources beyond his common sense, however: his instinct for the rhyming couplet wars with the shape of the stanza, his meter thuds, his vocabulary is trite; to top it all off he has misunderstood (willfully perhaps) the gender relations in the poem, rendering stanza 2:

> How did his pleasing glances dart
> Sweet languors to my ravish'd heart

At the first sight though so prevailed
   That my voyce fail'd.[21]

E. M. Cox's 1925 version exemplifies the mess that results when a quantitative system is clamped arbitrarily onto English. One line will suffice. The conflict between natural word stress and fictive quantity results in verse which, if pronounced according to its own system, sounds downright idiotic: "Peér of thé góds | thé happiést | man Í seém."[22] J. A. Symonds in 1887 was more successful in aligning English stress with the requirements of length; his version is hardly felicitous syntactically ("Nothing see mine eyes, and a noise of roaring/Waves in my ear sounds"), but his first line at least shows how an accommodation might plausibly be reached: "Peér of góds hé | seémeth to mé, | the blíssfúl. . . ."[23] For an approach which ignores the Sapphic stanza but tries to approximate its simplicity and concision, we can turn to Mary Barnard's 1958 version:

He is more than a hero

He is a god in my eyes—
the man who is allowed
to sit beside you—he . . .[24]

Hers has the virtue of cleanliness, but it lacks the rhythm of expansion and contraction which sustains life in Sappho's form.

The twentieth century has been rich in appropriations of Sappho's poem. In "Three Letters to Anaktoria" from *Imitations* (1958), Robert Lowell supplies in hyperbole, exaggerated assonance and alliteration, extraneous similes, and sheer gusto what he lacks in subtlety: the man sits next to the girl "like a cardplayer"; "refining fire," filched from Dante's Arnaut Daniel, perhaps by way of Eliot, purifies the speaker's flesh in a discordantly Christian way; and Sappho's pale grass becomes blindingly verdant: "I am greener than the greenest green grass."[25] Basil Bunting, working freely from Catullus in 1965, turns the poem back to Sappho by imitating her ring structure: "O, it is godlike to sit selfpossessed / when her chin rises and she turns to smile," he begins, and concludes the last stanza: " . . . I dissolve / when her chin rises and she turns to smile. / O, it is godlike!"[26]

I would like to close, not by nagging at the innumerable translations of "Phainetai moi" in English, but by penciling briefly a larger sketch of translation as an elegiac genealogy. I spoke of poetry as a family matter; a record of translations is a family tree. I want now to trace, through a series of elegies, a perpetuated acknowledgment of Sappho as lyric mother, and therefore of her progeny as siblings. At issue is the enduring life of poetry. The poems to bear in mind are Catullus's elegy for his real brother ("Multas per gentes," poem 101), Baudelaire's Sapphic poems, Swinburne's "Sapphics," and his elegy for Baudelaire, "Ave atque Vale." Through these elegies, we can sense Sappho, the lyric impulse, rising again and again like Hesperus from the waters of language, and perpetually lost; and we will sense translation in action as the blood pulse of our continuing, shared literary life, keeping time with the larger cycles of nature. I freely confess it: this is a myth. A working myth for a poet and translator.

BAUDELAIRE AND SWINBURNE

Baudelaire studied Greek as well as Latin in the *lycée*, and was surely familiar with Sappho's "Phainetai moi." But the Sappho reincarnated in Baudelaire is not a metrical essence, as she was in part for Swinburne. Rather, Baudelaire is haunted by the myth of Sapphic sexuality. In a number of poems, two of which were excluded from *Les Fleurs du mal* by the censor in 1857, he celebrates an eros which has nothing to do with the Greek Sappho's frank and splendid pleasure. Baudelaire's lesbian love is consecrated, not as joy, but as deviance. Set in the ghoulish context of Christian damnation on the one hand, and of "natural," socially useful, reproductive mating on the other, his lesbians are artists and outcasts in their pure search for beauty and sensation. "O vierges, ô démons, ô monstres, ô martyres, / De la réalité grands esprits contempteurs, / Chercheuses d'infini . . ." ("O virgins, O demons, O monsters, O martyrs, / great spirits contemptuous of reality, / seekers of infinity . . ." from "Femmes damnées").[27] Theirs is the true spirituality in, and against, a materialistic world, and, not surprisingly, they are associated with Baudelaire's cherished images of infinity: the abyss and the gulf, and their corollary, death: "—Descendez, descendez, lamentables victimes, / Descendez le chemin de l'enfer éternel! / Plongez au plus profond du gouffre, où tous les crimes . . ." ("Descend, descend, sad victims, / Descend the path of eternal hell! / Dive to the depths of the gulf, where all crimes . . ." from "Femmes damnées: Delphine et Hippolyte").[28] This *gouffre* has its analogies in Baudelaire's sense of Sappho's poetry: the nearest he comes to describing her verse is his evocation, in "Lesbos," of the lesbian embraces where the imaginary cascade behaves rather like a Sapphic stanza:

> Lesbos, where the kisses, like cascades
> teeming and turbulent yet secret, deep,
> plunge undaunted into unplumbed gulfs
> and gather there, gurgling and sobbing till
> they overflow in ever-new cascades![29]

At issue for Baudelaire is not the survival of Sappho's poetry. His Sapphic poems suggest something of the hell created in French nineteenth-century society for homosexual lovers, but his true absorption is with his own deflected eroticism as a figure for art. For him, art is and must be profoundly antinatural; it joins in holy alliance with a sterile eros and with death, with infinity and the soul, in opposition to the squalid claims of nature and literal fact.

Though he claims to be Sappho's sentinel keeping vigil on the Leucadian cliff, Baudelaire takes us far afield from Sappho's hyacinths and the "dew on the riverside gleaming."[30] With Swinburne, the inheritance is much more complex because it is expressed "genetically"—that is, in meter and stanza form. Sappho's strain is crossed, however, with the strong influences of Baudelaire and, at his worst, the Marquis de Sade. Before considering the fraternal relationship between Swinburne and Baudelaire, I want to address the matter of Sappho's more direct incarnation in Swinburne's poetry.

First, the meter. Swinburne's Greek was excellent and, more than excellent, it was passionate, so that he writes the Sapphic stanza naturally, translating long and short syllable to stress with an ease scarcely ever matched in English. I will now make a risky claim: that Sappho lives in English, not in any word-by-word reproduction of her texts, but in Swinburne's poems "Sapphics" and "Hendecasyllabics." I would claim in addition that Sappho's rigor and subtlety saved Swinburne from his own worst propensities toward prosodic exaggeration, and that his finest poems, to which we do not sufficiently confess our gratitude,[31] are those disciplined by Greek. In "Sapphics" Swinburne has allowed himself to be possessed by Sappho's "visible song," and his poem, in places, surges and pauses as delicately as hers down its streambed, its vowels and consonants as cunning in play:

. . . and I too,
Full of the vision,

Sáw thĕ whíte ímplácăble Áphrŏdíté,
Saw the hair unbound and the feet unsandalled
Shine as fire of sunset on western waters;
    Saw the reluctant

Feet, the straining plumes of the doves that drew her . . .[32]
                       (lines 7–13)

I scan one line to show with what grace the stress corresponds to the Greek's requirements for length. In "Anactoria" the rhyming pentameter couplets make for a cruder versification. Here, however, actual translation of Sappho rises out of hyperbolic Sadean rhetoric, and so filially imbued is Swinburne with her spirit that those fragments from the "Hymn to Aphrodite" seem intrinsic to his own poem:

Saw Love, as burning flame from crown to feet,
Imperishable, upon her storied seat;
Clear eyelids lifted toward the north and south,
A mind of many colours, and a mouth
Of many tunes and kisses; and she bowed,
With all her subtle face laughing aloud,
Bowed down upon me, saying "Who doth thee wrong,
Sappho?"

                       (lines 67–74)[33]

Swinburne is straining to render the first lines of the ode, "poikilothron athanat' Aphrodite / pai Dios doloploke"; literally, "Richly (dappled, intricate, with various colors) enthroned immortal Aphrodite, child of Zeus, weaver of wiles." Swinburne has at least made incantatory what in Barnard seems blunt and curt, though clean ("Dapple-throned Aphrodite / eternal daughter of God, / Snare-knitter!"), and in Davenport rococo ("God's stunning daughter deathless Aphródita / A whittled perplexity your bright abstruse chair . . .").[34]

    Swinburne has taken from "Phainetai moi" the conceit of love as a pathology, "Yea, all thy beauty sickens me with love" (line 56); he has grossly exaggerated it with Sadean extrapolation that shies not from cannibalism: "Ah that my mouth for Muses' milk were fed/On the sweet blood thy sweet small wounds had bled!" (lines 107–8). For a modern reader such a passage can only be comic; nor is there much to be said in defense of the workaday verse. I pause for a moment, however, on the theme of cannibalism. For all its hysteria, the passage points back to primitive rites of communion associated with funerals, and may recall my elegiac emblem of translation for which Sacks provided the model. The erotic communion Swinburne solicits, an invitation to, rather than a defense against, death, is itself a figure for the poet's real communion with the spirit of Sappho, and, as such, is an elegiac act. At the end of "Anactoria" the poetic eros does fend off death, for it allows Sappho, resurrected through Swinburne, to assert the immortality of song:

> I Sappho shall be one with all these things,
> With all high things forever; and my face
> Seen once, my songs heard in a strange place,
> Cleave to men's lives. . . .
>
> (lines 276–79)[35]

Communion with a ghost from antiquity is one thing; acceptance of the death of an immediate poetic forebear is quite another and more shocking matter. The loss is felt more urgently, as is the threat to one's own life and voice. The news of the (supposed) death of Baudelaire was, for Swinburne, such a shock, and one that elicited from him one of the majestic pastoral elegies in English, "Ave atque Vale."[36] The title conjures up Catullus's farewell in elegiac couplets to his brother, and proclaims a fraternity between Sappho's lyric offspring: Catullus, Baudelaire, and Swinburne.

Sappho, the mother, is immediately invoked in stanza 2:

> Thine ears knew all the wandering watery sighs
> Where the sea sobs round Lesbian promontories,
> The barren kiss of piteous wave to wave
> That knows not where is that Leucadian grave
> Which hides too deep the supreme head of song.

Peter Sacks has charted this poem with exemplary intelligence and learning. For my purposes, it will suffice to emphasize the way in which an elegy involves translation. In rejecting the traditional garland "rose or rue or laurel," in favor of "Half-faded, fiery blossoms, pale with heat," Swinburne is translating "Lycidas" into *Les Fleurs du mal*. The poem proceeds to "translate" Baudelaire's own "translation" of Sappho: "Fierce loves and lovely leaf-buds poisonous . . ." (line 25). Facing the death and, worse still, the silence of his brother poet, Swinburne is led to question whether poetry itself survives: "Thou art far too far for wings of words to follow / Far too far off for thought or any prayer" (lines 89–90); note the lack of caesuras streamlining the distance. In this crisis, the poem attempts to assert poetic communion as the symbolic consolation proffered in traditional elegy: " . . . and not death estranges / My spirit from communion with thy song" (lines 103–4); the whole lyric tradition appears as one long, shared lament: "Or through mine ears a mourning musical / Of many mourners rolled" (lines 109–10). But this death and the impotence of Apollo and Aphrodite, poetry and love, seem to blight consolation: ". . . not all our songs, O friend, / Will make death clear or make life durable" (lines 171–72). After much synaesthesia, the elegy seems to end in silence; the dead poet is not to rise as day-star or genius of any shore, and the figure of Sappho has blended into that of a more tragic mother: "And chill the solemn earth, a fatal mother, / With sadder than the Niobean womb . . ." (lines 191–92).

The dead poet seems beyond the reach of poetry. This crisis corresponds to the moment in Moschus's lament for Bion in which "Bion is dead, and with him dead is music, and gone with him likewise the Dorian poesy."[37] The work of mourning, that is, would be completely blocked were it not for the *translation* of Catullus that opens the final stanza, and in its very nature as translation belies the silence of death which it asserts. As long as Catullus speaks through Swinburne, he is neither dead nor silent, and neither, in some sense, is Baudelaire: "For thee, O now a silent soul, my brother, / Take at my hands this garland, and farewell" (lines 188–89). Besides being one of the noblest versions of the Catullus we are likely to get, Swinburne's closing echo ensures that Hesperus will once again rise from Okeanos, that Sappho lives on, transmuted, in her children, and that poetry will continue to voice us to ourselves.

CHAPTER 3

Alcaics in Exile: W. H. Auden's "In Memory of Sigmund Freud"

On September 23, 1939, Sigmund Freud died in exile in London, a refugee from Nazi Austria. Within a month, Auden, who had been living in the United States since January of that year, wrote a friend in England that he was working on an elegy for Freud.[1] The poem appeared in the *Kenyon Review* early in 1940. A stately public ode, the poem mourns not only the death of a publicly significant individual, but the collapse of a world. Hitler had overrun Austria, Czechoslovakia, Poland; assaults on Jews had intensified; England and France had just declared war on Germany. There would be, indeed, many who would have to be mourned:

> When there are so many we shall have to mourn,
> when grief has been made so public, and exposed
>   to the critique of a whole epoch
>   the frailty of our conscience and anguish,
>
> of whom shall we speak? . . .

Someone encountering this poem for the first time, on the page or in the ear, might be pardoned for puzzling over its form. It sounds prosy. It seems to have some recognizable English cadences, pentameters ("When there are so many we shall have to mourn"), tetrameters ("so many plausible young futures"), and even trimeters ("the frailty of our conscience and anguish"). But the pattern seems unruly, with some lines stretching out beyond five traditional beats, and ignoring any iambic order: "turned elsewhere with their disappointment as he." Groping for a more satisfactory principle of organization, a reader with some knowledge of versification may be moved to count syllables. Such a reader will discover that the poem is indeed organized syllabically in lines of eleven, eleven, nine, and ten syllables. "Aha," says the reader, alert to Auden's intimacy with classical civilization: "A Horatian ode. Not inappropriate for a formal elegy." Reflecting further and leafing through the pages of Horace, that reader will find, or remember, that two-thirds of Horace's odes are in these quatrains, the Alcaic stanza. Auden, it appears, has composed his elegy in some version of the meter of Alcaeus, the seventh-century B.C.E. Greek poet whose stanza became second nature to Horace. And we cannot enter the world of Auden's poem without asking, Why Alcaics? And how do they work here?

"In Memory of Sigmund Freud" is sometimes said to be Auden's first syllabic poem.[2] Others demur, proposing both earlier and later examples.[3] Whatever the spats about dating Auden's early syllabic practice, scholars conventionally agree that his turn toward syllabic composition reflects his evolving interest in a discursive poetry; in the poet as a private intelligence with a public voice; and in the work, respectively, of Horace and Marianne Moore. Having identified the poem as syllabic, many critics move on to heftier topics like psychoanalysis versus Marxism, Auden more than most poets having laid himself open to an overridingly thematic criticism of Big Ideas. But if, having acknowledged the influence of Horace and Moore in Auden's refusal of English iambic lyricism here, we stay with the question of meter, we are led back to the older progenitor, Alcaeus, a great poet of exile, whose stanza Auden adopts and adapts. I shall ask how it affects our reading to observe that the stanza itself has a genealogy, and brings its expressive burden to bear on Auden's poem.

"In Memory of Sigmund Freud" relies on a counterpoint of two metrical systems, the largely iambic accentual-syllabic system, traditional in English since Wyatt, and a flattened version of Greek quantitative meter, which was a musical notation of syllable length. For Auden, whose great prosodic facility was almost a handicap, the problem was "not how to write iambics but how not to write in them from automatic habit."⁴ Throughout his poetic life, he reached for cadences to interrupt the "natural" iambics, sometimes recalling the Old English alliterative beat, and often turning to ballads and popular tunes for rhythmical variation. By the late thirties, he was not only disillusioned with the Spanish Civil War and his role as quasi-Socialist bard, but was seeking new compositional principles as well. Free verse was not an alternative: his ear required an evident prosodic order, a perceptible "law like love." On the other hand, Auden had been stirred by his encounter with Moore's syllabics in 1935. As he confessed later, he had at first been unable to "make head or tail of her poems. . . . A syllabic verse like Miss Moore's, in which accents and feet are ignored and only the syllables count, is very difficult for an English ear to grasp."⁵ He persevered, however, sensing the integrity of her rule. The syllabic verse Auden eventually made his own hardly resembled Moore's, but she helped deliver him from habitual cadences and perhaps helped him imagine the shape of a modern Horatian ode in rhythms trained more on speech than on song.

It is no mystery why Auden should have been drawn to a Horatian stance. The Roman poet stood squarely in the center of his era and mastered it with the authority of his verse, as Auden appeared to have done in 1939. But Horace leads us back to Alcaeus, who haunts Horace's odes as a symbolic figure. In the declaration of his own poetic immortality (III.30: "Exegi monumentum aere perennius," I have built a monument more lasting than bronze), Horace links his power to his having first brought Aeolian song into Latin verse, and specifically invokes contentious, exiled Alcaeus in many of his odes. More deeply than in mere reference, however, Horace honors Alcaeus in incorporating his stanza. He insisted on the caesura after the fifth syllable in the first two lines, and lengthened that syllable in the first three lines, giving weight and stability where Alcaeus had often allowed a rapid forward trill of short syllables. By accentuating weight and pause, Horace points up the principal beauty of the Alcaic, its shifts in rhythm in midcourse, its calculated imbalance as the iambic and choriambic first two lines yield to iambs in the third and resolve in racy dactyls in the fourth. As exemplum of poetry's task, to act out the dynamic equilibrium between order and disorder, the Alcaic has no rival. Listening to it in Horace's Cleopatra ode, I.37, will tune our ears for Alcaeus's Greek and Auden's English. Here, celebrating in disorder the imposition of order, is the pounding dance step of the Romans after Actium:

Nunc est bibendum, nunc pede libero
pulsanda tellus, nunc Saliaribus
    ornare pulvinar deorum
        tempus erat dapibus, sodales.

(Now is the time to drink, now with freed foot / to beat the
earth, now, companions / we must decorate the couches of the
gods / for the feasts of Mars.)

And what of Alcaeus, to whom Horace owed his lyre? He was born
in Mytilene on Lesbos around 630 B.C.E.; he was an aristocrat; he lived
during the collapse of the traditional political order in Mytilene; with
his brothers he fought the tyrant Pittakos, was defeated, and spent years
in exile. His poetry has the directness of statement, clarity of image, and
eerily swift transitions that should be the envy of any modern. His social
role as a poet allies him more closely with Auden than with any other
modern poet. For Alcaeus's lyrics are so intrinsically social, the very distinction between private and public loses its relevance in regard to them.
His songs were performed in and for the *hetaireia*, the aristocratic kinship
club of his clan. Song consecrated the fellowship, which was based on the
sacramental bonds of common drinking and fighting. But hunted into
exile, Alcaeus the social poet becomes a solitary man among wolf-thickets,
lukaimiais, as he says in poem 130.[6] In the two poems of Alcaeus I offer
here, the actual community has been replaced by divine order, the ideal
spiritual community visible on earth in its temples where the exile prays
for revenge and consolation, and where, in the astonishing last stanza of
poem 130, in an Aeolic meter related to the Alcaic, the girls of Lesbos go
to and fro trailing their robes, being judged for beauty, and all around
there rings the wondrous sound of the loud, holy cry of women. In the
prose translation by David Campbell in the Loeb edition, the surviving
fragments of the poem read as follows:

. . . I, poor wretch, live with the lot of a rustic, longing to hear
the assembly being summoned, Agesilaidas, and the council: the
property in possession of which my father and my father's father
have grown old among these mutually destructive citizens, from it
I have been driven, an exile at the back of beyond, and like Ono-
macles I settled here alone in the wolf-thickets (?) (leaving the?)
war . . . for to get rid of strife against . . . is not . . . to the precinct

of the blessed gods . . . treading on the black earth; . . . meetings
themselves I dwell, keeping my feet out of trouble, where Lesbian
women with trailing robes go to and fro being judged for beauty,
and around rings the marvellous sound of the sacred yearly shout
of women; . . . from many [troubles] when will the Olympian
gods [free me]? . . .[7](16 ff.)

If we recall how Auden, all his life, sought some version of the *hetaireia*,
an ideal brotherhood; how he tried one form after another of such a
community—public school, Socialism, the fraternity of art, the Anglican
Church; how deeply embedded in his poetry and prose was the dream of
that brotherhood, of "the poet and the city," we shall begin to sense the
poignant relevance of Alcaeus, the poet of exile, to Auden in 1939, mourning another masterful exile. But we might then ask, as some of Auden's
English readers did, whether his continued residence in the United States
after the outbreak of war was not more a vacation than an exile proper in
the sense in which Alcaeus and Freud both suffered it; we might even be
tempted to see the formality of his ode as a refuge from, or a displaced
shape for, tormenting questions about his own status as an exile.

   Let us hear, now, Alcaeus's own music, the song from his broken world,
in a meter which seems to lose its footing, mid-stride, but recovers its
balance, and heals in the order of the ear what on earth and in politics
remains in ruins. The Alcaic is scanned:

    _ _ ∪ _ _ /_ ∪ ∪ _ ∪ _ (twice)
    _ _ ∪ _ _ _ ∪ _ _
    _ ∪ ∪ _ ∪ ∪ _ ∪ _ _

I give the first three stanzas of poem 129 in Greek transliterated from
Campbell's text, and in Campbell's translation:

       . . .]. .ra. . . . a tode Lesbioi
       . . .]. . . . eudeilon temenos mega
       xunon ka[te]ssan, en de bomois
       athanaton makaron etheikan,

       kaponumassan antiaon Dia
       se d' Aioleian [k]udaliman theon
       panton genethlan, ton de terton
       tonde kemeilion onum[a]ssan

zonnusson omeistan. a[gi]t' eunoon
thumon skethontes ammetera[s] aras
akousat', ek de ton[d]e moxthon
argaleas te phugas r[uesthe.

(. . . The Lesbians established this great conspicuous precinct to be
held in common, and put in it altars of the blessed immortals, and
they entitled Zeus God of Suppliants and you, the Aeolian, Glorious Goddess, Mother of all, and this third they named Kemelios,
Dionysus, eater of raw flesh. Come, with gracious spirit hear our
prayer, and rescue us from these hardships and from grievous
exile. . . .)[8]

Turning to Auden's poem, we hear nothing of the subtle kinship
between choriamb (_ ∪ ∪ _) and dactyl (_ ∪ ∪) so essential to
Alcaeus's music. Auden's poem is oratory, not song: "When there are so
many we shall have to mourn . . ." In fact, his elegy is an exercise in the
sacrifice of song. We note that Auden has not followed the practice of
most English poets adapting quantitative meter, aligning English stress
with Greek long syllables as Tennyson does in his Alcaics to Milton: "Óh
míghty-móuth'd ínvéntor of hármoníes . . ." This was not for lack of
know-how on Auden's part: he had spent years in school translating Greek
and Latin into English and vice versa. But he thought "the attempt of
Spenser, Harvey and others to be good little humanists and write English
verse in classical meters" futile[9] (though he granted that "English poetry
owes much to their forlorn attempt");[10] nor, clearly, did he want to make
his Freud elegy a piece of pyrotechnic classicizing by reproducing stress
analogues to Greek meter.

The Alcaic stanza as Auden deploys it here allows him to sidestep an
iambic tune, and to mark the progression of a prosaic rhetoric, moving
logically through stanzas as through stages of argument: When—For—
No wonder—Of course—Like weather—But—But. It also allows him
an invigorating asymmetry, further to defy the consoling recurrences of
English lyric. Yet the ghost of Alcaeus still haunts it, and one way to read
this poem of disenchantment and reenchantment, of fracture and union,
is to measure the ways in which it both invites in and resists the lyric
ghost of its ancestor.

"In Memory of Sigmund Freud" is not, in fact, Auden's first poem in
syllabics or even in adapted English Alcaics. From the mid-thirties on,

Auden had been fooling around with the ode form, gesturing with stanza shape toward the Sapphic and the Alcaic, eschewing rhyme but retaining an iambic accentual-syllabic meter, in poems such as "Casino," "Journey to Iceland," "Oxford," and "Orpheus." These poems are not organized by syllable count. But in April 1939 Auden wrote a disciplined, numerical Alcaic poem called "Crisis."

A sinister poem, "Crisis" seems as stilted in its habitation of the Alcaic stanza as in its generalized drama of plural pronouns, "they" versus "we": "Where do they come from? Those whom we so much dread . . ." The poem suffers, I think, in never breaking through its symbolic generalities. What energy it does muster derives from its semi-submerged imagery of rape and (perhaps) of homosexual dread as an allegory for the onset of fascism (in which "rector" elicits "rectum" in a semi-pun one cannot exclude):

> For the barren must wish to bear though the Spring
> punish; and the crooked that dreads to be straight
>   cannot alter its prayer but summons
>   out of the dark a horrible rector.[11]

By contrast, "In Memory of Sigmund Freud," composed five months later, has an urgently particular subject which is both individual and public (Auden's own intense experience of Freud's work giving him, no doubt, a sense of private loss at this death).[12] The first-person plural pronoun here is far more charged and personal than in "Crisis": "we" are all those who mourn the passing of a great healer, we who mourn the dominion of Hate over family life and nations, we who have suffered privately our own demons. Similarly, the Alcaic stanza is far more daringly managed, its prosaic potentiality liberated, syntactic units no longer packaged by line as they were for the most part in "Crisis," but allowed to flex over lines and stanzas where the argument needs to make a pointed move. Here, poetry is startled to life: a formal vernacular disposed in argument strains against the local constrictions of unrhymed quatrains with unequal line lengths. In that rejection of lyric narcosis, Auden has found a shape for a loss which should afford no easy consolation.

This very public poem builds off the interplay of singular and plural, the "he" and the "we." In theme, let us note briefly how the literal exile of line 24 ("an important Jew who died in exile") expands to embrace figuratively the objects of the unconscious in lines 82–85: "while, as they lie in the grass of our neglect, / so many long-forgotten objects / revealed by his undiscouraged shining // are returned to us and made precious again." By the end of the poem, the image of exile extends to the fauna of the night, the psychic formations which, in being recognized, contribute to healing: ". . . With large sad eyes / its delectable creatures look up and beg / us dumbly to ask them to follow: / they are exiles who long for the future // that lies in our power. . . ." It expands further, we might suggest, to include the not-quite-exiled poet-speaker who never writes himself into this poem in the first-person singular. Further, in our pursuit of theme, we should notice how Time structures the poem, not only in the classroom allegories of Past, Present, and Future, but in the disposition of temporal adverbs and conjunctions and the play of tenses: "*still* at eighty he wished . . ."; "For about him *till* the very end were *still* / those he had studied, the fauna of the night, / and shades that *still* waited to enter / the bright circle of his recognition / turned elsewhere . . ."; "They are *still* alive . . ." In line 68, the adverb "now" takes hold of the poem, and the tenses shift from past to present as the absent one is called into his afterlife: "to us he is no more a person / *now* but a whole climate of opinion. . . ." The retrospective "still" gives way to the prospective "till" in line 75 as Freud is seen affecting not only the present, but the future:

> he quietly surrounds all our habits of growth
> and extends, till the tired in even
> the remotest miserable duchy
>
> have felt the change in their bones and are cheered,
> till the child, unlucky in his little State,
> some hearth where freedom is excluded,
> a hive whose honey is fear and worry,
>
> feels calmer now and somehow assured of escape. . . .

A fuller reading of the poem would explore how images swell into theme in the structural antitheses of private and public life; childhood and adulthood; small and large; night and day; imagination and reason; disorder and order. I will merely remark that, as Freud's triumph is seen here in his power to "unite / the unequal moieties fractured / by our own well-meaning sense of justice," restoring night to day, maternal feeling to son, and so forth, the poem's triumph is to unite its antitheses in a single encompassing movement. This it achieves through the Alcaic stanza.

Auden's obsession, as a poet, was to tell the truth. Hence his draconian self-revisions. As he said in *The Dyer's Hand*, "Poetry is not magic. In so far as poetry, or any of the other arts, can be said to have an ulterior purpose, it is, by telling the truth, to disenchant and disintoxicate."[13] Freud was, for Auden, one of the great, liberating truth-tellers, and one way the Alcaic honors him here is by disenchanting the lyric, by interrupting English iambic flow and forcing dissonant enjambments. A look at a few of those enjambments will show some of the pressure points of the poem, where the stanza shape is intrinsic to the motion of thought. At line 36, the break between stanzas reenacts the moment of clarification in therapy: ". . . he merely told / the unhappy Present to recite the Past / like a poetry lesson till sooner / or later it faltered at the line where // long ago the accusations had begun." The collapse of oppressive structures is reflected at line 47: "No wonder the ancient cultures of conceit / in his technique of unsettlement foresaw / the fall of princes, the collapse of / their lucrative patterns of frustration." In line 54, "down," clamping the line fore and aft, carries us appropriately down to Dante's Hell: "down among the lost people like Dante, down / to the stinking fosse. . . ." To adduce one last example, we can note how the exposed preposition "to" in line 95 suspends and intensifies the restoration of maternal energy to the son: ". . . would give back to / the son the mother's richness of feeling."

I should not want to suggest that Auden leaves no trace of accentual-syllabic meter in his poem. It is powerfully audible through the resistant syllable count and periodic syntax. In the last stanza, you hear, distinctly, two pentameters followed by two tetrameters, and John Hollander has beautifully observed how the suppressed dactyls, the trace of the original Greek lyric, rise again in the end-stopped concluding lines of quatrains, as in "puzzled and jealous about our dying" (line 16). But the life of the poem inheres in its play of prose against its lyric model. In "In Memory of Sigmund Freud," Auden made himself at home in the Alcaic stanza, and happily, since he used it in numerous later poems, most immediately in the "Prologue" and "Epilogue" to the long "New Year Letter" written early in 1940.

By September 1939, Auden had outgrown the fantasy of belonging to a literal community. He had accepted exile as the essential, not the accidental, human condition: "Aloneness is man's real condition," he wrote in "New Year Letter" (line 1542).[14] To his friends Professor and Mrs. E. R. Dodds back at Oxford, Auden wrote a series of letters between September 1939 and March 1940 in which he strained to justify his stay in the United States during England's struggle in the war with Germany. "At least I know what I am trying to do, which most American writers don't [*sic*], which is to live deliberately without roots," he wrote in January.[15] In March, he sent the Doddses an invented questionnaire in which he argues with himself about his actions; he confesses to being "embarrassed at being so happy when many of my greatest friends are having an unpleasant time,"[16] but he determines that as his responsibility is to the language, nothing a writer could do in England "justifies smashing his private life. . . . I am neither a politician nor a novelist, rapportage is not my business."[17] From Edward Mendelson's account in *Early Auden* it is clear that the decision to leave England preceded the outbreak of war by well over a year, and was motivated by inward, poetic urgencies, not by expediency. The same forces that brought Rilke as a guardian spirit into Auden's sonnet sequence "In Time of War" (1938) were leading him away from a poetry of partisan politics toward a stance at once more private and more cosmopolitan.[18] His trajectory, that is, runs counter to that of Alcaeus: the ancient poet longs to return home, while his modern cousin flees it. But they meet in the Alcaic stanza.

However one judges Auden's position—and some English readers still hold him, and the Freud elegy, accountable for a shirking of duty—his adoption of the Alcaic stanza coincides with his stepping clear not only of the nation of his birth, but of the very idea of community as a defining force. He found in Alcaeus's stanza what he would call in another context a "civitas of sound."[19] If we think of the word "stanza" etymologically, as a room, we may think of Auden coming to celebrate an ageless cult at the *temenos*, or sacred precinct, marked out by Alcaeus. In that *temenos*, in the presence of divinities invoked by Alcaeus and Auden alike, we say farewell to Freud:

> One rational voice is dumb. Over his grave
> the household of Impulse mourns one dearly loved:
>   sad is Eros, builder of cities,
>   and weeping anarchic Aphrodite.

CHAPTER 4

The End of The Aeneid

In the last lines of *The Aeneid*, a vast chord is swelling. Almost every word has some complex harmonic relation to the preceding twelve books. I want to look at one word in particular, *immolat*, as it appears in line 949: "Pallas te hoc vulnere, Pallas / immolat et poenam scelerato ex sanguine sumit" (Pallas sacrifices you with this wound, and Pallas / demands payment with your criminal blood). In turn, *immolat*—the verb "to sacrifice"—draws into its magnetic field a sequence of earlier scenes and variations, and exerts its own pressure on the triumphant and civilizing goals of the Roman race as announced in the prophecies of Jupiter in Book I and of Anchises in Book VI.

I think most readers agree that the conclusion of *The Aeneid* is shocking. The shock derives partly from narrative pace. In effects imitated, and transformed, from *Iliad* XXII, the long-delayed duel of the two heroes plays itself out in agonizing detail: Turnus's sword shattering in his hand, a circular chase of figurative hound and stag, weapons lost and restored to each combatant, and a time-out on Mount Olympus where Jupiter and Juno come to terms and determine Turnus's fate. By the time the scene shifts back to the battlefield, the winged fiend has driven Juturna from her brother Turnus's side, and the Rutulian hero faces his death alone. And now the poem grinds massively into slow motion. The nightmare of immobility, transferred from Achilles' pursuit of Hector around the walls of Troy, here freezes Turnus as he tries to hurl the boulder, which is not any old stone, but by a sad irony a boundary stone set to prevent quarrels over property. He cannot complete the throw, and, most eerily, this huge and powerful man does not "know himself": "sed neque currentem se nec cognoscit euntem / tollentemve manu saxumve immane moventem . . ." (XII.903–4: But he did not recognize himself running nor going / nor lifting with his hand nor moving the huge stone). The drag of spondees in these lines, the hallucinatory piling up of ineffectual participles, and the gluing alliteration of n's and m's all suggest that Turnus's paralysis has impeded the verse itself. That undertow of delay gathers force in the simile of the dream which follows the boulder sequence, in Turnus's strange inward and outward vision as he stands in a trance facing Aeneas's spear-cast, and in the repetition of the verb "to hesitate," *cunctari*. Aeneas seems to throw in slow motion; the spear takes eight lines to leave his hand and pierce Turnus's thigh. Even Death hesitates in this scene, and that hesitation, as Aeneas stands (*cunctantem*) over the wounded Turnus and "represses" his own sword arm, seems to hold in balance all the mighty values of justice, clemency, and *pietas* the poem has celebrated. When the scales tip in favor of *ira*, rage, the poem goes into fast-forward: three lines for Aeneas's infuriated speech, three lines for him to plunge his sword into Turnus's chest and for that abused spirit to flee to the Underworld. End of poem.

The shock of shifting velocities in this scene, the lurch from almost frozen motion to savage swiftness, recapitulates the suddenness and shock of an actual death. Nor is there an aftermath. Here is Turnus, whom we have known and followed since Book VII; whose courage, fears, desires, and delusions we have intimately observed; who was just now breathing and speaking: gone. More shockingly, his "going," the last line of the poem, borrows the precise line of verse from the warrior-maiden Camilla's death in Book XI: "vitaque cum gemitu fugit indignata sub umbras" (and life fled with a groan of indignity into the shades). But Camilla, in her dying, has about fifteen lines in which to slip away from life, whereas Turnus is quenched instantaneously. To compound the abruptness, memories of *The Iliad* crowd in. The originating scene, the duel of Hector and Achilles, occurred in Book XXII, leaving two more books for the consequences of Hector's death to eddy and take their course in shapes of grief, rage, reconciliation, and foreshadowed doom. Virgil allows no such space for imaginative absorption of Turnus's death.

A noble if deluded creature is killed in a fit of fury; the act that founds the city in blood also closes the poem. If the word *indignata*, used for Camilla's death, described the protest (her own and possibly the poet's) at young and brilliant life cut off—a life that would have no place in the Roman order—*indignata* in Turnus's case carries a far more somber cast of outrage at the *way* he dies: at the failure of supplication, the failure of enlightened mercy.

A shock of pacing, that is, bears a deeper, moral shock. It is one of the weird brilliances of Virgil, not unnoticed by his devotees, to have used the same verb for *founding* the city of Rome in the opening lines (I.5: "dum conderet urbem") and for Aeneas *planting* (or *founding*) his sword in Turnus's chest at the poem's conclusion: "hoc dicens ferrum adverso sub pectore condit / fervidus" (XII.950–51: saying this, he planted his sword in the opposing chest / in fury). Virgil will not let us gloss over the cost of this founding: its price was blood, and, it appears, blood spilled in rage, not justice. Rage, *ira*, presides over the opening and closing of the poem just as the verb *condere* does: Juno's rage sets things in motion—"saevae memorem Junonis ob iram" (I.4: because of the relentless rage of cruel Juno)—but Aeneas's rage, the rage of the *pius* hero who was to found a city dedicated to the arts of peace, with Furor chained in the temple, brings it all to a savage halt. If the reader feels taken aback at Turnus's death, it is partly at the contradiction between the scene itself and the values of moderation and justice associated with Aeneas and the city he is to father. *Ira* and *furor* have been the insatiate forces of evil throughout the poem; they have been linked with the female violence of Juno, Allecto, and Amata, and with the monstrous Cacus, and both Jupiter and Anchises have laid out for their earnest hero a blueprint for a city that was to repress such rage. But *ira* also helped Hercules to defeat the monster Cacus in Book VIII, and from Book X onward, fluctuations of *ira* seem to fuel Aeneas's heroism on the battlefield. It is as if a Latin poem of *dolor*, of *lacrimae rerum*, had been invaded by Iliadic *menis*, wrath.

The noun *ira*, the participle *indignata*, the verbs *cunctari* (to hesitate) and *condere* (to found) help organize any reading of Turnus's death. But the word I want particularly to interrogate, as I have said, is *immolare*, to sacrifice. It is not a word used often in the poem, and a feel for its weight and valence may help us, in turn, chart the forces which join in Turnus's death. In what sense is Turnus a sacrifice? Does his death ritually sanctify the imperial destiny the poem projects? How does his immolation extend and complicate the pattern of the many previous sacrifices the poem has presented? Looking at the death of Turnus, we see a multiple exposure of immolations, some animal, some human, all of which color Aeneas's final act in the poem. Finally, I would suggest, the offering up of Turnus draws its power not only from association with the poem's many recorded acts of sacrifice, but, even more eloquently, from one unrecorded one: the death of Remus at the hands of his brother Romulus. That murder haunted the mythic founding of Rome, but is never explicitly mentioned in *The Aeneid*, though Romulus and Remus enter the prophecies of the poem as figures of law and imperial power. In more than one way, Rome is founded on ritual bloodshed; and how we interpret that fact will depend partly on how we read the silence at the heart of the poem, the unacknowledged but central murder of Remus.

To say "ritual bloodshed," of course, is already to beg the question. The death of Remus is not technically a sacrifice, and we would have to admit that Aeneas is using the word *immolat* in a metaphorical sense when he vents his fury on Turnus: "Pallas te hoc vulnere, Pallas / immolat et poenam scelerato ex sanguine sumit" (Pallas sacrifices you with this wound, and Pallas / demands payment in your criminal blood). Strictly speaking, Turnus has not been offered ritually to the gods, but has been killed in single combat. Aeneas's figurative use of *immolat* needs to be heard in the context of a taxonomy of deaths, ranging from the bulls, sheep, and boars offered ceremonially at altars; through the eight young men Aeneas destines for Pallas's pyre; through Priam murdered at his altar in Troy; Dido on her pyre; Palinurus and Misenus; who seem to pay the price of Aeneas's entry to the Underworld and arrival in Italy with their lives; Silvia's stag; the loss of Anchises; and on up to the great scenes of warrior deaths in battle, particularly the young, like Nisus and Euryalus, Lausus, and Camilla, culminating in Turnus himself. As the idea of sacrifice widens in range, one could see whole panoramas as sacrificial offerings: Troy in flames in Book II, and the weary burning of the Italian and Trojan war dead in Book XI. To return for a moment to *immolat* as Aeneas uses it, we need to note that as a figure of speech it has ambiguous rhetorical and moral consequences. In an immediate sense, it seems to absolve Aeneas of wrongdoing in his slaying of Turnus: that death is claimed as a price justly paid for the death of Pallas. In a larger sense, it justifies the invasion of Latium. At the same time, however, that holy word uttered by a man enraged (lines 946–47: "furiis accensus et ira / terribilis"—kindled in fury / and terrible in rage) casts doubt on both the smaller and the larger justifications, and sets up a vibration of doubt that reverberates back through the entire poem. When, in fact, does a sacrifice become a murder?

The place to start would seem to be with the animals, those patient creatures whose blood flows so freely throughout the poem that it almost seems a substitute for ink. The bullocks, sheep, and boars die, their throats slit at altars, at fairly regular intervals; and their deaths serve not only to punctuate august events (prophecy, celebration, funeral rites, truce-making), but to confirm a system of contact and reciprocity between humans and gods, and a sense of regularity and justice in the workings of fate, as well as of sanctity in the shedding of blood. The vocabulary describing sacrifice varies considerably from scene to scene, and each rite is quite individual and unformulaic in presentation, but the essential form remains the same, and a single phrase returns now and again to describe it: the beasts are slaughtered *de more*, according to custom. These scenes combine variation and continuity, the variations displaying a rich choice of words for killing (*mactare*, to slay; *caedere*, to cut, kill; *ferire*, to strike dead; *sacrare*, to dedicate to a god), and emphasizing transactions of particular intensity between humans and gods. Offerings presented in such a spotlight include the sacrifice to Hecate in Book VI, with details of the bullock's forelock bristles cast on the flames, and his blood caught in cups; and the sacrifice to ratify the treaty between the Latins and the Trojans in Book XII. The latter rite has a drama quite its own mingling darkness and light, interior secrets and exterior revelation, the quick and the dead, as it takes place at sunrise and requires that the viscera be ripped from the living sheep to be loaded on platters at the altar flame.

A gulf divides these sacred, sanctioned, customary killings from Neoptolemus's stabbing of Priam in his son's blood at the altar at Troy in Book II. But between these extremes of the sacred and the impious, most of the deaths of *The Aeneid* take place; and in that doubtful space even the purity and justice of the gods may suffer some stain. They, after all, sponsor much of the killing. And this is the acting space of this poem of *pietas*: the highly charged, obscure arena in which piety is not always so clearly discernible from impiety. The poem unrolls, for the most part, in a moral twilight only stabbingly illuminated by the glare of sacrificial flames, pyres, torches, and—more rarely—the radiance cast by a goddess.

Turnus falls heavily, immensely. He tumbles down in an enjambment from the main verb and participle as if the line itself had suffered the jolt of Aeneas's spear: ". . . incidit ictus / ingens ad terram duplicato poplite Turnus" (XII.926–27: Turnus fell, struck / huge to the earth, his knee bent). When he falls, what does it mean that he has just a hundred odd lines above been compared to a stag? In Fitzgerald's translation:

> . . . As when a stag-hound
> Corners a stag, blocked by a stream, or by
> Alarm at a barrier of crimson feathers
> Strung by beaters, then the dog assails him
> With darting, barking runs; the stag in fear
> Of nets and the high river-bank attempts
> To flee and flee again a thousand ways,
> But, packed with power, the Umbrian hound hangs on,
> Muzzle agape: now, now he has him, now,
> As though he had him, snaps eluded jaws
> And bites on empty air. . . .[1]

Most immediately, such imagery seems to contribute to the legitimacy of the word *immolat* as used by Aeneas, animals being the designated victims of sacrifice, and appropriately offered to the gods. But a stag is the prey of hunters, not customarily dispatched on an altar. In Turnus's death, then, hunting imagery complicates the claim of sacrifice. Furthermore, Turnus-as-stag inevitably recalls the death of Silvia's tame stag, carelessly, even brutally slain by Ascanius in Book VII in the act of aggression that starts the war between the Latins and Trojans. That earlier scene establishes a code we can't help applying to the death of Turnus. Virgil calls our attention to it all the more by altering the analogous Homeric simile. Hector pursued by Achilles in Book XXII was seen as a fawn beset by a hound: "As through the forest, o'er the vale and lawn, / The well-breath'd beagle drives the flying fawn, / In vain he tries the covert of the brakes, / Or deep beneath the trembling thicket shakes; / Sure of the vapour in the tainted dews, / The certain hound his various maze pursues. / Thus step by step, where'er the Trojan wheel'd, / There swift Achilles compass'd round the field."[2] To cast Turnus as a stag insists on the Latin leader's stature and nobility, not on his weakness, and insists as well on neural pathways of imagery peculiar to *The Aeneid*.

Silvia's stag is hardly the first to be killed in the poem. When the battered Trojan ships draw up on the Carthaginian coast in Book I, Aeneas's first act as a responsible leader is to kill seven deer to feast his crew. He accomplishes this robustly and matter-of-factly, and the narration hints neither at sacrificial ritual nor at pathos in the fate of those deer. But

Silvia's stag was half tame, and we suffer his death from his point of view. In Fitzgerald's version:

> Now as he wandered far from home, the hounds
> Of Iulus on the hunt, furiously barking,
> Started the stag. He had been floating down
> A river, keeping cool by the green bank.
> Ascanius himself, now on the chase
> And passionate for the honor of the kill,
> Let fly a shaft from his bent bow: Allecto's
> Guidance did not fail his hand or let him
> Shoot amiss, and the arrow whizzing loud
> Whipped on to pierce the belly and the flank.
> Mortally hurt, the swift deer made for home
> In the farm buildings. Groaning, he found his stall,
> And coated with dark blood he filled the house
> With piteous cries, as though imploring mercy.[3]

The deer, half tame, half wild, had personified the innocent harmony between humans and nature that prevailed in the pre-Roman world of Latium. He is wounded not only in the belly, but, literally, in the groin, or genitals (*ilia*), so that this pastoral world loses its future, its power of propagation. And he is killed through the direct agency of the Fury Allecto, who inflames Ascanius and his hounds in vocabulary contaminated by association with the poem's other infuriated characters, Juno, Dido, the Trojan women who set fire to the ships in Book V, Amata. Allecto rouses *rabiem*—frenzy—in the dogs, so that they would "burn" to chase the deer, "ut cervum ardentes agerent"; the killing of the deer ignites the country people to war, "belloque animos accendit agrestis" (VII.481); Ascanius himself is kindled by love for outstanding praise ("eximiae laudis succensus amore," VII.496); and not for the first time in the poem has *amor* gone up in smoke, fired by some baser passion. At this juncture one might think not only of Dido, but of Brutus in Book VI, putting his own sons to death, conquered by love of the fatherland and immense greed for fame ("vincet amor patriae laudumque immense cupido," VI.823).

To see Turnus as a stag, then, is to contradict the sense of *immolat* on which Aeneas insists: the justification of Turnus's death as the due price for the death of Pallas, and an offering to the destiny of Rome. From the perspective established by the imagery of Book VII, Turnus's death is a needless, infuriated act of aggression, a perverted immolation. Both forces of the word are at work in the last scene, and that huge dissonance endows the scene, and the entire poem, with uncanny, reverberating power. Furthermore, the image of Turnus as a stag culminates an extended metamorphic sequence. Turnus was seen as a lion as he prepared to fight Pallas in Book X, and at the opening of Book XII; fighting with Aeneas, he is several times portrayed as a wild bull (and in the simile preceding the stag simile in Book XII, the combatants are both seen as bulls, quite recasting the Iliadic model which gives Achilles overwhelming superiority). Turnus has also been envisioned as Mars, as wind, as fire, and as a mountain crag. Only in his last confrontation does he slip into focus as a stag: no longer a predatory force, no longer enraged, but restored to his original state of natural nobility and peacefulness from which Allecto's torch had hurled him.

If we track the word *immolat* in the poem, it only compounds the perplexities folded into the last scene. With all the variety of words for ritual killing, Virgil never uses *immolare*, which would seem to be the obvious choice, to describe animal sacrifice in *The Aeneid*. He reserves it, blood-chillingly, for human sacrifice, and in contexts that hardly shore up the claims for justice and sanctity in the poem's final act. Dido on her pyre had been acting as a human sacrifice. But in Book X Aeneas literally engages in that grim rite, capturing eight young Latins—four sons of Ulmo, four of Ufens—to be killed at Pallas's funeral: ". . . Sulmone creatos / quattuor hic juvenes, totidem quos educat Ufens / viventis rapit, inferias quos immolet umbris / captivoque rogi perfundat sanguine flammas" (X.517–20: Four young sons of Sulmo, / as many whom Ufens raised, / he took alive, whom he would immolate to the shades of the Underworld, / and with whose blood he would sprinkle the flames of the pyre). Virgil proceeds briskly from those lines to recount Aeneas's further prowess in battle. But the model passage in *The Iliad* calls out in protest. Achilles in Book XXIII throws on the pyre of Patroclus not only countless sheep and cattle, but four high-necked horses (for which he grieves), two dogs, and twelve noble sons of great-hearted Trojans, slashing them with the sword: "dodeka de Troon megathumon uieas esthlous / khalko deioon . . ." (XXIII.175). And, the narrator declares, in doing so Achilles contrived an evil thing in his mind, "kaka de phresi medeto erga."

The narrator's judgment of human sacrifice as *kaka* is conspicuously absent from—but, I think, obscurely operative in—*The Aeneid*. The events immediately following the capture of the eight sacrificial victims would suggest as much. First, Aeneas refuses the supplication of Magus, who is at his mercy: in Fitzgerald, ". . . And with this he took / The man's helm in his left hand, bent the neck / Backward, still begging, and drove home the sword / Up to the hilt."[4] Then, in the second appearance of *immolare*, Aeneas hunts down and slaughters a priest of Phoebus and Diana: in Fitzgerald, ". . . Next, not far off, he met / Haemonides, a sacred minister / Of Phoebus and Diana of the Crossroads, / Wearing the holy headband, all in white / And shining priestly robes. Over the field / Aeneas drove him till the man went down, / Then stood, his mighty shadow covering him, / And took his life in sacrifice."[5] ". . . lapsumque superstans / immolat ingentique umbra tegit . . ." (X.540–41). Here, not only the paradox of a priest in holy regalia being the victim of sacrifice, but the collision of light and dark carries the moral argument: the glittering robes of the priest flutter against Aeneas's shadow, which extends hugely over him, and, in a sense, snuffs him out.

By the time the sacred verb *immolare* makes its third and last appearance in the poem, in Aeneas's final speech to Turnus, it carries a burden of implicit desecration. As Aeneas's sword hesitates over Turnus, the vision of Rome hangs in the balance. Jupiter has foretold, in Book I, that in Rome the gates of War will be shut, and unholy Fury (*impius Furor*) chained in the temple. Anchises, in Book VI, has confirmed that vision in his famous definition of the Roman arts: "tu regere imperio populos, Romane, memento / (hae tibi erunt artes), pacique imponere morem / parcere subjectis et debellare superbos" (VI.850–52: Remember, Roman, to rule the peoples with power, / (those will be your arts), and impose the rule of law, / and spare the conquered and beat down the proud). Aeneas himself has often acted as the agent of such a destiny, displaying self-control and *pietas*. During the funeral games for Anchises in Book V, Aeneas provided the very pattern of enlightened rule, restraining fury (*iras*) when it threatened to break up the community, and in the boxing match between Dares and Entellus, substituting an animal for a human victim in what can be seen as an archetypal sacrifice: in Fitzgerald, "Fatherly Aeneas would not sit by / While this fury went further—so berserk / Entellus was in the rancor of his soul. / He stopped the fight, and saved bone-weary Darës. . . ."[6] When the victor Entellus receives the prize bullock, Fitzgerald continues, "He set himself to face the bull that stood there, / Prize of the battle, then drew back his right / And from his full height lashed his hard glove out / Between the horns. The impact smashed the skull / And fragmented the brains. Down went the ox / Aquiver to sprawl dying on the ground. / The man stood over it and in deep tones / Proclaimed: 'Here is a better life in place of Darës, / Eryx; here I lay down my gauntlets and my art.'"[7] Entellus's rage has almost broken the boundaries of law, and the games—the model of aggression organized and contained—have almost collapsed into fury. But Aeneas imposes order, and the bull's life ransoms Dares.

It is all the more tragic, with this example in view, and with the prophecies of justice and order echoing through the poem, that Aeneas should give way to *ira* at the end. But if we look back at the prophecies, we find just that dark potentiality already inscribed there in the story of Romulus and Remus. And here, too, we find an example of the height of Virgil's art, an art which in its most stringent form consists in *not* saying; an art of the unspoken, perhaps of the unspeakable (*infandum*). Versions vary as to the story of Romulus and Remus, and they vary importantly (for our purposes) in justifying or not justifying the fratricide. Plutarch himself in his *Life of Romulus* cites contradictory sources and versions of the tale; genealogies of the twins vary, as do accounts of their bringing up, and in some versions it is not Romulus but his companion Celer who slays Remus. The violent death of the twin brother, however, remains at the heart of the tale. In many accounts, Remus is said to have provoked the murder by leaping over the ditch his brother had plowed to mark his city wall on the Palatine Hill. As we see in Plutarch, uncertainty hangs about the ancient tale, and about the potential curse of a city's being founded on a killing. In a poem roughly contemporaneous with the composition of *The Aeneid*, Propertius refers to the walls of Rome as "established by the slaying of Remus," suggesting a ritual aspect to the slaying: "ordiar et caeso moenia firma Remo" (also I will establish the strong walls by the slaying of Remus, Ode III.9, 50). Virgil handles the problem by shoving it into a black hole and simply eliding the murder in both prophecies. But like a black hole in space, the unspoken murder exerts a magnetic pull on the entire poem.

Jupiter, in Book I, famously promises nothing less than the world to his distraught daughter Venus: "Romulus excipiet gentem et Mavortia condet / moenia Romanosque suo de nomine dicet. / His ego nec metas rerum nec tempora pono: / imperium sine fine dedi" (I.276–79). In Fitzgerald, ". . . young Romulus / Will take the leadership, build walls of Mars, / And call by his own name his people Romans. / For these I set no limits, world or time, / But make the gift of empire without end."[8] Brother Remus, over whose dead body, so to speak, this glorious future comes to fruition, appears some seventeen lines later, as—paradoxically—a lawgiver, along with the deities Fides, Hestia, and Quirinus, guarantors of social order in the same sentence that shuts the gates of War and enchains Furor. This conjunction of figures is more peculiar and complex than we can explore here, but we need to note, at least, that Quirinus, that ancient Roman god, is sometimes used as another name for Romulus, and he seems in this list to represent Romulus alongside his "brother Remus" ("Remo cum fratre Quirinus"). In a terrific sleight of hand, this dream of future peace has reconciled the brothers and healed fratricide and civil war by promoting both Romulus and Remus to the status of gods. This line gives us a spectacularly bifocal view: through one lens, the dream of peace and restoration, and through the other (more veiled), unassimilable horrors of mythic murder and historic civil war. Anchises, in Book VI, doesn't even mention Remus. Rome is now embodied in the figure of Romulus, who as son of Mars turns the fratricidal force of civil war outward, in the legitimate aggression of imperial conquest. In Fitzgerald, "Look now, my son: under his auspices / Illustrious Rome will bound her power with the earth, / Her spirit with Olympus."[9]

But Remus's death is not so easily exorcised. If his story remains unspoken, it is not unknown. Other hidden murders rise up to haunt the poem: Sychaeus, Dido's husband, cut down by her brother in *furor* at the altar, appears as a ghost and inspires her escape; and in Book II Aeneas recounts to Dido how he tore violently at the bleeding tree in Thrace (in a ghastly prefiguration of his wrenching the Golden Bough) until the voice of Polydorus cried out from the earth to tell how he had been murdered.

Turnus dies, in a sense, *because of* a mythological scene of massacre: the story of Aegyptus's forty-nine sons slain by their brides on their wedding night is inscribed in gold on Pallas's fatal sword belt. A whole chorus of indignities, not just the deaths of Camilla and of Silvia's stag, resound in the word *indignata* in the last line of the poem: "vitaque cum gemitu fugit indignata sub umbras." And the choral effect includes the dissonances in the various senses of *immolat*. Like Remus, Turnus is both innocent and guilty. His death, like that of Remus, allows for the founding of Rome. What are we to make of such sorrow? Of a poem that tallies up so grievously, so relentlessly, the cost of the order it celebrates? In one mood, the modern poet W. H. Auden holds the whole dolorous matter at arm's length. In "A Walk After Dark" (1948), he quips,

> Yet however much we may like
> The stoic manner in which
> The classical authors wrote,
> Only the young and the rich
> Have the nerve or the figure to strike
> The lacrimae rerum note. . . .[10]

A decade later, Auden resists Virgil more directly in "Secondary Epic," which opens, "No, Virgil, no. . . ." In rejecting the prophetic structure of *The Aeneid*, Auden colludes with the Roman poet in ignoring Remus: "That Romulus will build a wall,/Augustus found an Age of Gold. . . ." But in his long last sentence which unwinds torturously toward its own prophetic revelation, Auden substitutes for the initial sacrifice of Remus a terminal blood offering, the last boy emperor of Rome, Romulus Augustulus, whose names, obviously, could not appear in Anchises' prophecy, but which in their ironic diminutiveness linger in the ear of the student of Roman history: "The names predestined for the Catholic boy / Whom Arian Odovacer will depose."[11]

Auden's sinister prophecy delivered with modernist hindsight hardly found a redemptive power in that death, except insofar as "*Alaric has avenged Turnus . . .*" The Augustan Empire in "Secondary Epic" prefigured Hitler's Germany. But in "Vespers," composed a few years earlier in 1954, imagining a meeting between himself-as-Arcadian and his Utopian, totalitarian antitype, Auden seems disposed to accept the price of memory, and mindfulness, that Virgil demanded:

> Was it (as it must look to any god of cross-roads) simply a fortuitous intersection of life-paths, loyal to different fibs?
>
> Or also a rendezvous between accomplices who, in spite of themselves, cannot resist meeting
>
> to remind the other (do both, at bottom, desire truth?) of that half of their secret which he would most like to forget?
>
> forcing us both, for a fraction of a second, to remember our victim (but for him I could forget the blood, but for me he could forget the innocence),

on whose immolation (call him Abel, Remus, whom you will,
it is one Sin Offering) arcadias, utopias, our dear old bag of a
democracy, are alike founded:

For without a cement of blood (it must be human, it must be
innocent) no secular wall will safely stand.[12]

Between the poles of Auden's readings of *The Aeneid*, between the cyni-
cism and dread of empire motivating "Secondary Epic" and the acceptance
of sacrifice as a political sacrament in "Vespers," we may locate the terms
of the debate continuing in our day about the price of peace. Virgil refuses
to ease our reading. In that refusal may lie at least part of the secret of the
enduring life of his poem.

CODA

It will be obvious that I am deeply indebted to Michael C. J. Putnam
in my reading of Virgil, especially to his *The Poetry of The Aeneid* (1965)
and *Virgil's Aeneid: Interpretation and Influence* (1995). The dark version of
The Aeneid he presented, now a generation ago, has shaped the American
discussion of the poem for many years.

When I presented this paper at the Symposium on Virgil at the University of Georgia in March 1995, I was unaware of T. P. Wiseman's
superb book, *Remus*, which appeared in 1995 from Cambridge University Press. Whereas the figure of Remus, for me, remained a literary and
mythological intuition, Wiseman has integrated a full array of Roman
source material with archaeological and historical evidence to produce
a richly suggestive and (to my mind) convincing explanation of Remus.
For him, Remus personifies distinct political and religious forces in distinct periods of Roman history. His argument is too complex to be sum-
marized easily, but to put it in the simplest terms, Wiseman associates
the mythological twins with the struggles of plebeian-patrician power-
sharing in the fourth century B.C.E., and in pointing to an unusual grave
beneath the altar of the Temple of Victory on the Palatine he associates
Remus with a specific if obscurely attested instance of human sacrifice
to ward off the threat from Samnites, Etruscans, and Gauls in 496 B.C.E.
Wiseman traces the vagaries of the later Romulus and Remus myth as

political iconography through vicissitudes in the reign of Augustus: in the earlier years Remus was celebrated in association with Augustus's colleague Agrippa, and was later suppressed after the death of Agrippa and the murder of Agrippa Postumus, the rival heir with Tiberius. Wiseman's book is a model of erudition dynamically organized in the service of argument; it would seem to command the field in any further investigation of Romulus and Remus.

Chapter 5

Negative Idylls: Mark Strand and Contemporary Pastoral

Pastoral poetry seems to be an eerily enduring genre, in spite of, or perhaps because of, its power to shift shapes over the centuries. One might not think of Mark Strand as having much to do with it. But in attending to the way in which Strand has evolved as a poet of field, and, more recently, of mountain and sea, we will be able to isolate some distinguishing features of his imagination. These features literally distinguish him, reveal him as distinct from more obviously agrarian and descriptive poets of our day—say, Maxine Kumin, Wendell Berry, Gary Snyder, and Hayden Carruth. Strand has a closer kinship with the ancient bucolic poetry of Theocritus and Virgil than do most of his American contemporaries, like the poets just mentioned whose work more accurately falls into the category of georgic, poems of earth, celebrating the labor demanded by earth. The pastoral slant also suggests a model of poetic selfhood that sets Strand far apart from the practice currently prevailing in another large set of poets, the use of autobiographical anecdote (usually traumatic) as the justification for utterance. To pursue the argument, we will need to dip back into Theocritus and Virgil, and then trace certain paths in the poetry of Mark Strand, particularly in *The Continuous Life* of 1990 and *Dark Harbor* of 1993.

From the first—that is, from the publication in 1964 in limited edition of *Sleeping with One Eye Open*—Strand has been intent on purifying his poetic practice. Throughout the first five collections and well into the sixth, he severely restricted his vocabulary; used a simple declarative syntax, the present tense, and line lengths rarely venturing beyond the trimeter; and sublimated anecdote, description, and lyric self-enunciation. In this austerity, inspired, one imagines, in part from Stevens' "The Snow Man" to honor "nothing that is not there and the nothing that is," Strand set himself quite at odds with one dominant strain of North American poetry: the personal confession crudely derived from Lowell and continuing in our day, much debased, in narratives of personal injury.

We may well ask what Mark Strand, the poet of absence, the mid-century surrealist, might have to do with the pastoral tradition. I will propose a few answers, and then return to specific poems to test these notions against, and along, their grain. Let me make clear at the outset, however, that I shall not attempt to construct Strand as a strict pastoralist or even as a student of Theocritus. But let us consider some categorical resemblances. In the first place, pastoral archetypally situates itself in an idealized and artificial landscape. Whether in the Greek Arcady often invoked by Virgil or Theocritus's Sicily, the scenery is standard (tamarisks, beeches, willows, galingale, olive trees, musical brooks), and it is understood that nature here has obliged by providing an elemental poetic space. We shall find an analogous space in Strand's moonlit fields. Unlike the georgic with its workaday worries and provisos (though not without its own mythology), pastoral—or, to call it by its Theocritean name, bucolic or herdsmen's poetry—celebrates and in fact depends on leisure, a fact Renato Poggioli emphasized in his masterful reconnaissance of the subject, *The Oaten Flute*. Pastoral re-creates the Golden Age, the *bella età del'oro* of Tasso's *Aminta*; and when the young Alexander Pope composed his "Discourse on Pastoral Poetry," he asserted that idealization must underlie any conception of the genre: "If we would copy Nature, it may be useful to take this Idea along with us, that pastoral is an image of what they call the Golden age," and, some twenty lines later, "We must therefore use some illusion to render a Pastoral delightful; and this consists in exposing the best side only of a shepherd's life, and in concealing its miseries."[1] Such concealment was precisely what rendered the genre obnoxious to Johnson, who called pastoral "easy, vulgar, and therefore disgusting," and who famously wrote of Milton's "Lycidas," "It is not to be considered as the effusion of real passion; for passion runs not after remote allusions and obscure opinions. Passion plucks no berries from the myrtle and ivy, nor calls upon Arethuse and Mincius, nor tells of rough 'satyrs' and 'fauns with cloven heel.' Where there is leisure for fiction there is little grief."[2] We shall find Strand making just the opposite, the antimimetic, case, and asserting that where there is fiction there can be, on the contrary, all the more grief.

Pastoral landscape streams with song; the very brooks and breezes move musically; and all the lolling herdsman has to do is pick up his panpipes and harmonize, as Theocritus murmurs in the opening lines of his first Idyll:

> adu ti to psithurisma kai a pitus, aipole, teina,
> a poti tais pagaisi, melisdetai, adu de kai tu
> surisdes. . . .
>
> (In Robert Wells' translation: "That pine tree by the spring
> and your touch on the pipe: / Both whisper a music to draw
> the listener in / With its sweetness, goatherd. . . .")[3]

In the first two lines and a fraction, the poet repeats *adu*, sweetly, twice; draws out his whisper in four syllables, *psithurisma*; and sets the key with two major musical verbs, *melisdetai* (warbles) and *surisdes* (whistle, pipe). The Arcadian landscape is also steeped in eros, with unrequited love, often homoerotic, providing the motive force for much of the singing. But like nature, love serves only as a pretext in these euphonious glades, as Marvell's couplets in "The Garden" remind us: "Apollo hunted Daphne so, / Only that She might Laurel grow. / And Pan did after Syrinx speed, / Not as a Nymph, but for a Reed."[4] In Strand, as well, we find this sublimation of nature and love into song.

The idealization of the landscape requires, as a corollary, a principle of exclusion, and this feature also characterizes Strand's poems. Pastoral *seems* to provide shelter from city, family, politics, illness, and the biological consequences of love. It is the *locus amoenus* whose very conventionality affords it blessed protection. But the power of pastoral paradoxically rests in its fragility, its evanescence. Its generic purity and artificiality direct our attention inevitably to all it has excluded. We are invited to study the ways in which pastoral poems willingly suffer contamination, and derive from it their most poignant strengths. We will need to focus on the exclusive impulse in Strand's diction and narrative structures. To set him in the larger landscape, however (and that setting is my main intent), we may glance at a few instances of pastoral's intrinsic contamination.

Instructed by Erwin Panofsky, we know that the phrase *Et in Arcadia ego* (Even in Arcady I—Death—dwell) originated in Guercino's painting in 1621 in which two shepherds contemplate an enormous skull on a tomb. But as Panofsky argues, and as is plain to see in any case, the Renaissance inscription draws on an ancient topos, the presence of sorrow and death in Arcady. The fancy, that is, cannot cheat so well, and didn't, even in Theocritus, the source of the dream. The delicate, playful realm of the *Idylls* shudders even within its borders at the anguish of frustrated desire, and occasionally acknowledges the pressure of a larger, political world beyond its frontier, as in the urban, Alexandrian Idyll II where Simaetha weaves a vengeful spell for her lover, or Idyll XIV where Aeschines, after a row with his girlfriend, considers joining Ptolemy's army. More hauntingly, Idyll I, to which we shall return, works inward to a core of grief, the death song of Daphnis, while Idyll VII in a sense defines the genre as it stages the meeting between the sophisticated urban and the archaic rural worlds in the exchange of songs between Simichidas and Lycidas. Paul Alpers, in *What Is Pastoral?*, prefers to characterize pastoral not through landscape, but through what he calls the "representative anecdote" of "herdsmen and their lives"; it is such meetings and exchanges that matter to him more than the woods and streams.[5] In Virgil's *Eclogues*, of course, the excluded realities—war, Roman politics, death—press even harder on the twilit Arcadian world. One feels epic stirring within and tapping at the shell of the bucolic; the very first lines of the first Eclogue call up the tears for things in Meliboeus's lament for his lands dispossessed by Roman soldiers: "Tityre, tu patulae recubans sub tegmine fagi / silvestrem tenui Musam meditaris avena: / nos patriae finis et dulcia linquimus arva. / nos patriam fugimus . . ." (in David Ferry's translation: "Tityrus, there you lie in the beech-tree shade, / Brooding over your music for the Muse, / While we must leave our native place, our homes, / The fields we love, and go elsewhere; meanwhile, / You teach the woods to echo 'Amaryllis' ").[6] Michael Putnam has subtly argued for a political reading of the *Eclogues* that engages the questions of justice and injustice the genre would seem to obscure: of Eclogue I he writes, "This is not an easy poem. There is a mood of crisis about it. . . ."[7] Eclogue IV famously envisages the birth of a new, political Golden Age, while Eclogue V transplants Daphnis from Theocritus and mourns at his tomb, and Eclogue IX worries at the threat of dispossession of the poet's own lands. In both Theocritus and Virgil, in different ways, Arcady stands as a gossamer design of compensation for loss; as such, it figures the essence of art, as lucent in its failures as in its structures of restitution. Poets often play on this dual nature of pastoral, its ideality and its fragility, by setting it within the larger context of epic or drama. The greenwood in *As You Like It*, Milton's Eden already in etymological declension before the Fall, instruct us, among other things, in the permeability of boundaries, and the ephemeral nature of refuge from time, politics, and death.

A few more generic points. Lament is not incidental, but integral, to ancient pastoral. Two wordplays in the first Idyll of Theocritus insist upon the connection. When the goatherd asks Thyrsis to sing the elegy for Daphnis, he concludes:

> Kouti tu kertomeo. potag', ogathe. tan gar aoidan
> ou ti pai eis Aidan ge ton eklelathonta phulaxeis.

> (. . . Do you think I mock you? / No holding back! You
> cannot take your song with you / In the end. Hades and
> forgetfulness are the same.)[8]

The Greek stresses the pun on *aoidan* (song) and *Aidan* (Hades). Similarly, as Charles Segal has observed in his indispensable book *Poetry and Myth in Ancient Pastoral*, Thyrsis concludes his song with the juxtaposition of *Moiran* (Fate) and *Moisais* (the Muses) in identical metrical positions, linking death and poetry. To stretch the point, let us observe that though Theocritus's *Idylls* and Virgil's *Eclogues* are all "about" song, they are composed not in lyric meters, but in heroic hexameters, so that something of the contamination, the importing of time, loss, politics, and death, occurs even in the texture of the prosody. The cult of texts, not songs, dominated Alexandria in the third century B.C.E., and it is perhaps not outlandish to think of Theocritus mourning, even as he celebrates, a lost world of song and myth. In that sense, the true object of mourning in the Idylls would not be the poet-cowherd Daphnis or lost loves like Hylas and Galatea, but song itself, the ancient oral tradition represented by the shaggy goatherd, Lycidas, smelling of rennet, who passes his crook to the urban poet Simichidas in a gesture of benediction.[9] When we consider Strand, a highly allusive, "literary," self-consciously belated poet—one could almost say a Hellenistic poet—we will find that he makes explicit the connection between writing and elegy, and devotes a mysterious little prose book called *The Monument* to that kinship. "Even the Monument is little," writes the dead anonymous author, who has become nothing but his text to his future translator. "How it wishes it were something it cannot be—its own perpetual birth instead of its death again and again, each sentence a memorial."[10]

The idea of elegy leads to one final generic point of congruence between ancient pastoral and Mark Strand. At the heart of pastoral lies an archaic myth of sacrifice. This sophisticated genre employed the mask of its bergeries not, or not merely, to enact the rural, nostalgic, weekend-getaway fantasies of a cosmopolitan culture, but to recover the mystery of death and regeneration, of sorrow and restitution, in the symbolic structures of song. Only a mystery this powerful, I think, could account for the perennial allure of pastoral, which has survived, among other things, the dead weight of so many dull poems over so many years. A shepherd's genre, yes, not only because shepherds proverbially and actually have time to roam the hills and need to amuse themselves and are sexually frustrated and lonely, but because the culture of flocks and fields is linked to rituals of sacrifice. Segal has explored in detail, as he says, "what form mythic representation may take in a post-mythic age," and has related the death of Daphnis to the death of Adonis.[11] In the opening lines of Idyll I, it is a question of which goat to sacrifice to Pan, which ewe to set aside for the Muses; but the death song of Daphnis, himself a sacrifice to Aphrodite, occupies the heart of the poem. In the realm of vegetal sacrifice, the benediction, the passing of the crook from Lycidas to Simichidas, occurs in Idyll VII under the auspices of the harvest festival, the sacrifice of first fruits to Demeter. The *Idylls* of Theocritus and the *Eclogues* of Virgil are haunted by the same sacrificial figures—Daphnis, Hylas, Orpheus. The poems are also characterized by a generic doubling of poetic energies; many are amoebean, split into alternating competing song units, and most involve some form of polyphony and dialogue. No shepherd wanders Strand's moonlit fields and sunset mountains; but his entire oeuvre has developed through intricate erasures and doublings of the poetic self, until it reached a temporary fulfillment in his embrace of the figures of Orpheus and Marsyas. Our route will take us, then, through some of the sacrificial structures in Theocritus and Virgil, before it leads into Strand's landscapes and the sacrifices enacted there.

Let us look briefly at Theocritus's first Idyll. Several voices interweave: those of the goatherd and Thyrsis, and within Thyrsis's song, the voices of Hermes, Priapus, Aphrodite, and Daphnis. The landscape, the realm of the dangerous god Pan, is lush with song and sex, all musical streams and the frank and bounteous fertility of goats. The poem sets frame within frame as it modulates scenes of grief and trouble within scenes of pleasure. Between Thyrsis and the goatherd, it is understood that song partakes of the joy of life, along with plump lambs and the charm of good cheese. Their view would seem to be confirmed by the inset ekphrasis, the cup the goatherd offers to Thyrsis as a reward for his song (prompting Pope to complain of the length of the description). The goatherd promises Thyrsis:

> . . . a deep, two-handled cup new made
> Washed in fresh wax, still fragrant from the knife.
> About the lip of the cup an ivy pattern
> Is carved, with golden points among the leaves:
> A fluent tendril flaunting its yellow bloom.
> Beneath is a woman's figure, delicately worked:
> She is robed and wears a circlet to keep her hair.
> On either side of her stand two bearded suitors
> Arguing their claim. But she takes no notice,
> Looks smilingly at one man, so it appears,
> Then at the other; while, hollow-eyed with love,
> They struggle against her kindly indifference.
> Beside these is carved an aged fisherman
> On a jutting rock. He strains at the very edge
> Of his strength to draw in a net with its heavy catch.
> You can see the effort bunching in each tense limb
> And in his neck, as he gives himself to the task.
> He has white hair, but his strength is supple and fresh.
> A little distance from the old man's sea-labour
> There is a vineyard hung with darkening clusters.
> A small boy perches on a dry stone wall to guard them.
> Two foxes shadow him. One sneaks along the rows
> For plunder; another has fixed her tricky eye
> On the quarter loaf the boy keeps for his breakfast
> And will not let him alone till she has snatched it.
> Blithely intent, he shapes a cage for a cricket
> From asphodel stalks and rushes. The bag with his food
> Is forgotten; so are the vines. The toy absorbs him.[12]

The cup with its curling ivy pattern seems almost natural. Yet it is art, vying with the shield of Achilles in the wholeness of vision it sets forth, not the epic, cosmic perspective of Homer, but—polemically, I think—the smaller pastoral world and the disruptions it must heal: frustrated desire, labor, hunger, thievery. *Pace* Alexander Pope, the description *had* to be this long to stand up against the shield.

Several points about the cup. (1) Like all classical ekphrasis, it is an aesthetic object described with such *verismo* that it seems "real," the protocinematic dream of unmediated representation, of stasis turning dynamic, directing our attention even to the bunching of muscles. In its play of illusion, it is an *ars poetica*, making us see the raw material of life—not only its action, but its suffering—and the stabilization of all that activity and loss into a beautiful object: cup, cricket cage, or poem. (2) An ekphrasis within an ekphrasis, made from the materials of the natural world, the boy's cricket cage exemplifies the essential achievement of pastoral, the redirection of desire from primary objects—food and sex—to aesthetic ones, the conversion of the natural into the artificial. At this juncture, I hear the ghost of that Arcadian, Sir Philip Sidney, protesting, "'But ah,' Desire still cries, 'Give me some food!'" Theocritus's poem will cry out also against the insufficiency of the bargain.

Bargaining, in fact, structures the entire idyll, and most idylls. Shepherds trade prizes (goats, cheeses, cups, and crooks) for songs, and the songs propose the consoling deal of art for love. The boy will lose his lunch for his artwork, as Polyphemus in Idyll XI finds relief in song from his passion for Galatea. The end of the cup passage suggests an even bigger deal: art is the temporary bargain we make with death, knowing full well that death's audit, though delayed, answered must be, and that its quietus is to render us. "Do you think I mock you?" asks the goatherd. "No holding back! You cannot take your song with you / In the end. Hades and forgetfulness are the same."[13]

The image of the cup and the images on the cup propose a charming but too easy resolution to the struggle between art and life's sorrow. Thyrsis immediately begins his song, and the possibilities latent in the pun on *aoidan* and *Aidan*, song and death, spring terribly to life in the story of Daphnis. Several features demand our attention. First, as Segal points out, it's not clear why Daphnis dies. He's like Kafka's Hunger Artist, simply refusing the terms of his world—terms offered, most conspicuously, by Priapus and Aphrodite, who come to upbraid him. All we know is that he has offended Love; Priapus claims that he has spurned some girl, but there is no way to judge the truth of that claim or to know, if he has spurned her, whether it was for some other impossible passion or to maintain his purity. Reading extratextually for clues about Daphnis doesn't necessarily help; a Daphnis appears in Idyll VIII, winning a song contest and marrying the nymph Nais, and the sacrificial Daphnis is mentioned in Idyll VII in the song of Lycidas: ". . . and Tityrus beside me to sing / How Daphnis the cowherd sickened for Xenea's love, / How the hillside shared his pain, and how the oaks / By Himera's banks cried his lament, as he wasted / Like a snowfall on the slopes of some high mountain. . . ."[14] But identities are fluid in the mythic realm, so all we can strictly say of Daphnis in Idyll I is that he is a poet-cowherd and that he dies offending love, though Aphrodite tries at the end to save him: ". . . Aphrodite struggled to raise him / But the thread allowed by the Fates had run to its end. / Daphnis drew near the water and the current took him, / Unhappy child of the Muses, the Nymphs' lost friend."[15]

It is important that Daphnis's death remain mysterious, because an ancient mystery is being evoked here. Dying, he insults Aphrodite, and replaces her with his own tutelary deity, Pan, whom he calls to Sicily and to whom he leaves his panpipes in a reversal of the usual exchange of gift for song: "Come, master, and take this pipe of mine, sweet-smelling, / Fastened with wax, the lip-piece delicately bound. / Love drags me into the darkness where no songs abound."[16] These pipes are poised against the goatherd's cup washed in fresh wax, a counterartifact to symbolize a far more troubling vision of art. In the story of Daphnis, true to the pastoral model, art replaces love, and Pan displaces Aphrodite, but in this case the artist relinquishes love, art, *and* life, and disappears into the water like Hylas, who drowns in the pool of the nymphs in Idyll XIII.

The idyll ends, though, not in sacrifice, but in the cheerful return to the outer frame, where Thyrsis claims his prizes and the goatherd tells him to eat honey for the sweetness of his song. So Daphnis's death is absorbed—and yet resists absorption—into the sensuality of pastoral with its milk, honey, and capricious sex. Poetic consciousness is split and antiphonal, between Daphnis, the voice more than half in love with easeful death, and Thyrsis, the voice of living song. Quite contradictory spells have been cast, and they do not cancel each other out. To ears trained on English, it is hard not to hear in that pairing the dual energies of Milton's Lycidas and the uncouth swain who so blithely twitches his mantle blue.

We can only glance at Virgil's transformations of Theocritus. Daphnis reappears, consecrated and deified, as the subject of song in the contest between Menalcas and Mopsus in Eclogue V; Eclogue V in a sense institutionalizes Theocritus's sacrificial cowherd, and emphasizes the mysterious association of pastoral and lament. The very condition of song-making, it appears, implies absence: "et tumulo facite, et superaddite carmen: / Daphnis ego in silvis, hinc usque ad sidera notus, / formosi pecoris custos, formosior ipse" (Then build a tomb and place on the tomb these verses: / "Daphnis was known to these woods and known to the stars; / Lovely the flock, and lovelier still the shepherd").[17] Daphnis as a generic name occurs elsewhere in the *Eclogues*, and Hylas, the boy drowned in the pool, appears in the myths sung by Silenus in Eclogue VI. But the figure who haunts the *Eclogues* is Orpheus. This daemon of song is depicted on the cups offered by Damoetas in Eclogue III; the prophetic singer of Eclogue IV claims to rival Orpheus, and in Eclogue VI Silenus is said to outdo Orpheus and Apollo. Orpheus doesn't take on full narrative form for Virgil, however, until the *Georgics*, where for the first time the story of his failure is told. The tale serves as a crescendo and conclusion to the *Georgics* just before the poet looks back to his *Eclogues* and, one surmises, forward to epic. The scene of Orpheus's death, the severed head floating down the Hebrus River still calling "Eurydice," is recounted within the context of Aristaeus and his bees, and the need to bring life out of death; Aristaeus, hearing the Orphic tale from Proteus, must sacrifice to the nymphs so a new swarm of bees may arise from the dead bullock. In Virgil's myth, which is far darker in its implications than anything in Theocritus, new life is brought not by the artist, but by the violent farmer, Aristaeus. Art has an afterlife only as an echoing song; it is severed from life by what we might call aesthetic distance, and while we might see in the death of Orpheus that remove from realism that distinguishes pastoral as a genre, it also suggests doubts about the powers of any art to heal or to console. It makes particular sense that Virgil should have told the failure of Orpheus in the *Georgics*, not the *Eclogues*, and that it should signal a transition out of pastoral to a sterner world of labor and loss.[18]

Turning to Strand's negative idylls, let me repeat that I'm not trying to prove that Strand is imitating Theocritus; for all I know, he has never read him. At any rate, he has received his Theocritus through Virgil, whose shade certainly moves through Strand's Orphic poems. The chief matter lies elsewhere: I want to argue that Strand is a poet of mythic patterns, who uses landscape as an allegory for poetic creation and who reenacts obsessively the sacrifice of the self as a condition for the making of the poem. In this reenactment, he fulfills even more than Eliot the dictum of that great modern pastoralist Mallarmé, who called for "the elocutory disappearance of the poet."[19]

What are the landscapes in Strand? As idealized in their way as the groves of Theocritus and Virgil, Strand's outdoor spaces—mostly fields in his earlier work, with seascapes and mountains in the recent books—have been so minimally furnished and so repetitively invoked that he can almost be credited with, or accused of, having single-handedly established a new convention. It's true that in the sixties and seventies in the United States many derivative poems floated about stocked with the standard "moonlight," "dark," "white," "tree," and "wind" of Strand's obsessional vision. But one can hardly hold the master responsible for his imitators. Strand himself observed a strict aesthetic in the disposition of his properties within his own poems, and has consistently outgrown his own conventions.

Let's look at a few of them. The field recurs often, because it is bare and elemental enough a word, and susceptible enough to metaphysical suggestion, to serve as ground for the eerie divestitures of self this poet needs to stage. Even more recurrently, his generic early landscapes are composed of wind, darkness, and moonlight, and sometimes simply of air—the potential for the sublime usually corrected by deadpan wit ("The future is not what it used to be," "The Way It Is").[20] One cannot ponder the wind, darkness, and air in these poems without at the same time observing the pronouns which seem precipitates of their ghostly surround. Who is the "you," for instance, in the title of "Taking a Walk with You," and what is the relation of "you" to the "we" of that poem? Is "you" a muse, a lover, Wallace Stevens, the reader? Unanswerable, and meant to be: the question remains as part of the force field of the poem, diffusing consciousness between writer, progenitors, and the reader, who form a mysterious plurality: "And yet, why should we care? / Already we are walking off / As if to say, / We are not here, / We've always been away."[21]

This is an early poem, from the first book, *Sleeping with One Eye Open*. Stevens broods over it, as over so much of Strand, the Stevens of "Notes Toward a Supreme Fiction": "From this the poem springs: that we live in a place / That is not our own, and much more, not ourselves."[22] The first word in Strand's "Taking a Walk with You," "lacking," sets the key, and calls forth the series of negative declarations that clear the space for awareness: "no less beautiful," "was never made to stand," "nor were," "we don't belong," "don't take into account." A poem of elementary refusal, then, a Daphnis poem of sorts, except that it courts not death but simply a state of being "away," the motion and motive of the walk being to walk not *in* a landscape, but out of it. The final, simple rhyme of "say" and "away" gives the poem's molecular formula as clearly as any notation in the periodic table: utterance rhymes with absence, and that union generates the entire poem, not to mention a poetics.

The *via negativa* is literally a "way" as well as a spiritual practice, and Strand's poems often involve motion. "One foot in front of the other. The hours pass. / One foot in front of the other. The years pass. / The colors of arrival fade" ("The Hill").[23] Or: "It is dark and I walk in. / It is darker and I walk in" (from "Seven Poems").[24] "Keeping Things Whole," one of the most famous of the early poems, progresses not by rhyme but by subtle repetitions: "In a field / I am the absence / of field. / This is / always the case. / Wherever I am / I am what is missing. . . ."[25] Ancient pastoral sacrificed a third-person singular figure, a Daphnis or a Hylas. Strand's protagonist here is "I," a character who subtracts himself from the landscape. This poem is as simple as a theorem, and inexhaustibly mysterious. What to make of a repeated self-assertion ("I am," "I am," "I am") that erases the self? What is the uneasy relationship between "I" and "my body"? What is this need for wholeness, for restoration, that excludes the self? Is "I" as insubstantial as the air it displaces, not merely "the absence of field," but, as the line break suggests, "the absence"? In its blend of philosophical abstraction and contemporary American idiom ("we all have reasons . . ."), the poem modulates and acts out the reduction it celebrates, moving from "a field" to "field"; minimally expanding and contracting line lengths; and leaving its own vacancy for the air to occupy after each stanza.

With his third book, *Darker*, in 1970, Strand surveyed his field, gauged his powers, and started with an *ars poetica* more concerned with the public and private power of poetry than with rules of craft. "The New Poetry Handbook" proceeds by numbered aphorisms. "6. If a man wears a crown on his head as he writes, / he shall be found out. / 7. If a man wears no crown on his head as he writes, / he shall deceive no one but himself."[26] Inching forward by paradoxes, the poem brings us to the familiar conclusion of renouncing Aphrodite for Pan, with the added Mallarmean touch of white paper: "21. If a man finishes a poem, / he shall bathe in the blank wake of his passion / and be kissed by white paper."[27] After this cautionary opening, the book turns the earlier erasures of self into rituals carried out in poem after poem with the drone and subtle variation of litany. These rites of purification, required perhaps to ward off the threat of false powers adumbrated in "The New Poetry Handbook," take place most often in the abstract field we recognize as Strand's own territory. In these poems, the doubled personae of classical pastoral have been internalized: inner self is divorced from its own being. Listen to the variations: "I empty myself of the names of others. I empty my pockets. / I empty my shoes and leave them beside the road" ("The Remains").[28] "I give up my eyes which are glass eggs. / I give up my tongue. / I give up my mouth which is the constant dream of my tongue. / I give up my throat which is the sleeve of my voice" ("Giving Myself Up").[29] "Slowly I dance out of the burning house of my head. / And who isn't borne again and again into heaven?" ("The Dance").[30] "I am becoming a horizon" ("Breath").[31] "Now I lie in the box / of my making while the weather / builds and the mourners shake their heads as if / to write or die, I did not have to do either" ("My Death").[32] "—Must I write *My Life* by somebody else? / *My Death* by somebody else? Are you listening? / Somebody else has arrived. Somebody else is writing" ("My Life by Somebody Else").[33]

In one of his rare pieces of expository prose, his essay "Views of the Mysterious Hill" (1991), Strand confirms much that one might have surmised about the mythological cast of his thought. In this piece, he surveys poems by Edwin Arlington Robinson, Dickinson, Stevens, and Hecht, and his own poem "The Hill" from *Darker*. "In the five poems that I shall look at," he states, "specific properties are at a minimum, but general properties suggest a remarkable similarity among hills"—a similarity he explains by proposing that they are all versions of Parnassus. Furthermore, he argues, remarking on the "resolute plainness" of the hills, "Parnassus for American poets must be cold and bare," "bare places for the myth of originality."[34]

We have Strand's word for it, if we needed it, that he conceives of landscape as symbolic poetic space, and its bareness as a distinctive feature of our American post-colonial myth of self-invention. We recognize in the poem "The Hill" the typical Strand landscape, complete with a tree rattling "black leaves," the "I" solitary, and a mild metrical pun about progress: "One foot in front of the other. The hours pass. / One foot in front of the other. The years pass. / The colors of arrival fade. / That is the way I do it."[35] But in the volume *Darker*, the laconic poems of vocation like "The Hill" make way for several expansive poems that do not so much mourn Daphnis, so to speak, as, like Virgil, use his tomb as an occasion for the celebration of song. "Breath," for instance, pursues one sentence through its five quatrains in one long exhalation. Though "I" here is "becoming a horizon," the poem insists "that if the body is a coffin it is also a closet of breath," and concludes, "that breath is the beginning again, that from it / all resistance falls away, as meaning falls / away from life, or darkness falls from light, / that breath is what I give them when I send my love."[36] This beginning again is hard-won in Strand's work, but keeps recurring as the reward for sacrifice. In fact, so many rituals of self-effacement seem to have released in him an impersonal lyric "I" fathered by Christopher Smart.

I am referring to "From a Litany." For our pastoral theme, we will want to observe what has happened to the field in the first line. The earlier bare field of so many of Strand's poems is now an "open field," and the hole he once dug—the grave he had fashioned over and over—now opens through a run-on sentence to blessing and a promise of poetic resurrection. In its acts of inclusiveness, the poem begins to build that poetic community which is the pastoral family—not Lycidas, Daphnis, or Thyrsis, but "the poets of Waverly Place and Eleventh Street, and the one whose bones turn to dark emeralds when he stands upright in the wind"[37] (Richard Howard, William Merwin, and James Wright). The word "nothing," another Stevensian inheritance from whose account Strand has drawn large sums, in this poem provides a reward beyond calculation. And after the catalogue of creation, the image of the shovel recalls the original field which was the ground and source of this rite, a rite that concludes with the claim of the nonbiological birth of the poet: "I praise myself for the way I have with a shovel and I praise / the shovel. / I praise the motive of praise by which I shall be reborn. / I praise the morning whose sun is upon me. / I praise the evening whose son I am."[38]

A more leisurely route would have included consideration of Strand's elegy for his father in *The Story of Our Lives*, in which for the first time in Strand's work "you" has a concrete, definite existence even as "you" quits existence, and in which the figurative extinction of the poetic self finds a terrible objective analogue. My argument would have gained fullness, as well, from examination of the doubled selves that agitate so many of the poems, narratives of self-murder or self-mutilation like "The Mailman," "The Accident," and "The Man in the Tree." Linda Gregerson has written the best account of these divided personae in her essay "Negative Capability."[39] For our purposes, we need to notice the way the split selves recapitulate the doubled poetic personae of idylls and eclogues. But the figure of Orpheus calls us onward.

The Continuous Life appeared in 1980, Strand's first collection of poems in ten years. Mortality in these poems is no longer merely a metaphor for *poiesis*; it is the fact that stares the older poet in the face. Landscape, too, exerts a new pressure. Strand had moved to Utah, and the sublime possibilities in the Western mountains leave their impress on the poems, even as sunset suggests the decline of a human life. Even the prosody responds to the new sense of scale; many of the poems here begin with "And" or "So," suggesting a larger sequence and a greater lungful of breath; the poems for the most part eschew stanza breaks and swell to pentameters and hexameters, even into prose poems; the imagery turns not just continental, but stellar and interplanetary at the approach of the larger dark. In different keys, Strand continues to explore the rite of self-extinction. In the Kafkaesque prose poem "Two Letters," Gregor Samsa personifies *la disparition élocutoire du poète*, and in the conscientiously impersonal poem "A.M.," the initials of the title connect Andrew Marvell of "To His Coy Mistress" with Archibald MacLeish of "You, Andrew Marvell"—with an added nod at the time of morning, A.M.—to probe the diurnal processes from which poetry springs. Even more fully, the poem "Se la vita è sventura . . . ," whose title alludes to Leopardi's poem "Canto notturno di un pastore errante in Asia" (Night Song of a Wandering Shepherd in Asia), hauls Leopardi's cosmic reach and melancholy into Strand's circumference, and adds a third character to the motif of poetic self doubled as assassin and victim. The third character now hovers over those two and participates in the rite as an observer, being born into himself out of the imaginary death. The poem unrolls in somnambulistic rhythms and long periodic sentences, with three stately repetitions of the opening question, "Where was it written?" That is the essential question, for the poet emerges from the amniotic sea of previous writing (including Leopardi's) and falls back into it if the rite is correctly performed. Through the puns on "writing" and "righting" and "line," this murder turns directly into poetry, "soundlessly, slowly, as if righting itself, into line." I quote from the conclusion:

> Where was it written—
> That, despite what I guessed was his will to survive, to enter
> Once more the unreachable sphere of light, he would con-
>   tinue
> To fall, and the neighbors, who had gathered by now,
> Would peer into his body's dark and watch him sinking
> Into his wound like a fly or a mote, becoming

An infinitesimal part of the night, where the drift
Of dreams and the ruins of stars, having the same fate,
Obeying the same rules, in their descent, are alike?
Where was it written that such a night would spread,
Darkly inscribing itself everywhere, or for that matter, where
Was it written that I would be born into myself again and
    again,
As I am even now, as everything is at this moment,
And feel the fall of flesh into time, and feel it turn,
Soundlessly, slowly, as if righting itself, into line?[40]

"Orpheus Alone," in *The Continuous Life*, celebrates a similar rite. It has a Virgilian portal: it is preceded by the short poem "Cento Virgilianus," which means "Virgilian patchwork." The cento indeed patches together the landscape of Carthage from Book IV of *The Aeneid* and the approach to the Underworld in Book VI, blending the stories of passion, loss, and mourning into one as it anticipates the tale of Orpheus: "We'd come to a place / Where everything weeps for how the world goes."[41]

"Orpheus Alone" starts with one of Strand's characteristic indefinite pronouns: "It was an adventure much could be made of: a walk. . . ."[42] "It," in Strand, usually invites us to savor mystery, to let an ostensible subject waver off and let the dreamwork begin. The first line also acknowledges the literariness of the subject, both prospectively and retrospectively: "It was an adventure much could be made of," indeed, and of which much has been made, by Virgil, by Milton, by Rilke, among others—though this poem needs innocently to set aside, even as it remembers, its ancestors.

In coming to this Orphic landscape of Strand's we reach in some sense the type toward which all his earlier landscapes were tending. Where but in the Underworld should the negative idyll be set, after all? The Underworld, however, occupies only the first phase of the poem; it will be replaced by nameless hills and skies, which will themselves give way to sheer light. Each landscape embodies a poetics, and the poem charts an evolution, perhaps the imaginary shape of Strand's own oeuvre. The first phase, introduced by deadpan demotic ("its marble yard / Whose emptiness gave him the creeps . . ."; "And, then, pulling out all the stops, describing her eyes . . ."), reproduces a poetry of erotic description, in which the enumeration of the absent lady's features almost conjures her presence. Far from rejecting the Petrarchan list ("My mistress' eyes are nothing like the sun . . ."), this poet dutifully totes up its elements,

". . . describing her eyes, / Her forehead where the golden light of evening spread, / The curve of her neck, the slope of her shoulders, everything / Down to her thighs and calves. . . ." But the uninspired tone and that vague, impatient "everything" hint that this descriptive procedure will soon be discarded. As it is, in the next half line: as soon as the issue is no longer the woman, but words, the diction, imagery, and rhythms all rouse and move upstream, reversing the flow of fate: "Down to her thighs and calves, letting the words come, / As if lifted from sleep, to drift upstream, / Against the water's will, where all the condemned / And pointless labor. . . ."

The first effort, which allows "the lost bride / To step through the image of herself and be seen in the light" (presumably, to step through Virgil and Rilke), avoids the crisis of Orpheus turning to Eurydice, the core of the story for Virgil and Rilke, and the source of the cry "Eurydice" which echoes in Georgic IV and down the Western tradition: ". . . Hebrus / volveret, Eurydicen vox ipsa et frigida lingua, / a miseram Eurydicen! Anima fugiente vocabat: / Eurydicen toto referebant flumine ripae" (lines 524–27: And as his head, cut off from his beautiful neck, / Was tumbling down the rushing course of Hebrus, / His voice and tongue, with his last breath, cried out, / "Eurydicé! O poor Eurydicé!" / And the banks of the downward river Hebrus echoed, / "O poor Eurydicé! Eurydicé!").[43]

Strand never names the lost bride. He simply assumes her loss (the title, "Orpheus Alone," tells that story), and Orpheus himself expels her from the second phase of poetry: ". . . and, finally, / Without a word, taking off to wander the hills / Outside of town, where he stayed until he had shaken / The image of love and put in its place the world / As he wished it would be. . . ."[44]

This second phase I would call the phase of pastoral consolation, the bargain of an ideal landscape of song exchanged for the loss of love. It's the bargain too easily struck in the first section of Theocritus's Idyll I. Strand allows his voice to gain more amplitude here, even echoing his own earlier lyricism, the miraculous fields of grain recalling the "miraculous hours of childhood" from his earlier poem "In Celebration." This phase rehearses the poetry of ideal essences. Like the first, it modulates from a high rhetoric to a dissonant minor chord: "And that was the second great poem, / Which no one recalls any more."[45]

The third and final phase enacts the sacrifice and clearly embodies Strand's credo. No longer a poetry of things, but of action, it rolls forward in one nineteen-line sentence, thrust into its own becoming by the repetition of "it came," "it came," "it came." The sexual climaxes implied in the verb are entirely rhetorical, as eros has been sublimed into language. The dominant figure of speech is no longer metaphor, but the more disembodied simile; and the similes describe evanescence, the moment of vanishing, the quintessential lyric momentariness:

> . . . The third and greatest
> Came into the world as the world, out of the unsayable,
> Invisible source of all longing to be; it came
> As things come that will perish, to be seen or heard
> A while, like the coating of frost or the movement
> Of wind, and then no more; it came in the middle of sleep
> Like a door to the infinite, and, circled by flame,
> Came again at the moment of waking, and, sometimes,
> Remote and small, it came as a vision with trees
> By a weaving stream, brushing the bank
> With their violet shade, with somebody's limbs
> Scattered among the matted, mildewed leaves nearby,
> With his severed head rolling under the waves,
> Breaking the shifting columns of light into a swirl
> Of slivers and flecks. . . .[46]

Things have become acts, the marble yard has become shifting columns of light, Orpheus has lost his name and become an anonymous "somebody"; the whole material world and the self have been reborn into language with the subject of the subjunctive clause of purpose seeking and seeking its postponed verb: ". . . it came in a language / Untouched by pity, in lines, lavish and dark, / Where death is reborn and sent into the world as a gift, / So the future, with no voice of its own, nor hope / Of ever becoming more than it will be, might mourn."[47]

One might have wondered where a poet could go in a subsequent volume. From the perspective of the next book, *Dark Harbor*, "Orpheus Alone" looks like a prelude. *Dark Harbor* is a single, book-length poem in tercets, though not in *terza rima*. It returns us to the pastoral theme in its sequence of symbolic landscapes and poetic sacrifices. Though the format might suggest epic, the lack of central narrative and the shifting tones and subjects still, for me, bespeak a collection of idylls or eclogues, though built into a larger argument. I shall concentrate on the overall sweep of the book, from its opening scene of entry to the Underworld to its culmination in a poetic Elysium reminiscent of the pastoral elysia in *The Aeneid* and *The Divine Comedy*. To connect the two scenes, I shall sketch out what I take to be Strand's argument about confessional poetry and his reenunciation of his faith in poetic impersonality through the figures of Orpheus and Marsyas.

The "Proem," set aside in italics and pagination from the body of the poem, launches us into allegorical landscape, a very American landscape at that: "'This is my Main Street,' he said as he started off / That morning, leaving the town to the others, / Entering the high-woods tipped in pink // By the rising sun but still dark where he walked. . . ." It concludes, "'This is the life,' he said, as he reached the first / Of many outer edges to the sea he sought, and he buttoned / His coat, and turned up his collar, and began to breathe."[48] At the edge of the sea of Whitman, Frost, and Stevens (not to mention Homer), the contemporary poet catches his breath and finds his voice. And having found it, where does he depict himself? In the transition between life and death, crossing the Styx so to speak, except in poem I of *Dark Harbor*, the landscape of small-town America has replaced the traditional decor of the entrance to Hades. Decorative elements like the "emerald trees" are held in check by the demotic: "Wings can be had / for a song. . . ." One notices how the familiar props (moonlight, black leaves) and the disappearance of "I" around the corner anticipate the larger argument, the topos of poetic trips to the Underworld with all the assumption of destiny such trips imply:

> In the night without end, in the soaking dark,
> I am wearing a white suit that shines
> Among the black leaves falling, among
>
> The insect-covered moons of the street lamps.
> I am walking among the emerald trees
> In the night without end. I am crossing
>
> The street and disappearing around the corner.
> I shine as I go through the park on my way
> To the station where the others are waiting.
>
> Soon we shall travel through the soundless dark,
> With fires guiding us over the bitter terrain
> Of the night without end. I am wearing

A suit that outdoes the moon, that is pure sheen
As I come to the station where the others
Are whispering, saying that the moon

Is no more a hindrance than anything else,
That, if anyone suffers, wings can be had
For a song or by trading arms, that the rules

On earth still hold for those about to depart,
That it is best to be ready, for the ash
Of the body is worthless and goes only so far.[49]

The argument about Orpheus in this book is bound up with an argument about genealogy. The pastoral model, from Theocritus through Virgil, the Astrophell of Sidney and Spenser, Milton's "Lycidas" and on, implies, in its continuance and in the recycling of the same names, a new structure of kinship to replace the biological family. The bonds in Arcady are the bonds of poetic fraternity. No other relationship—not erotic, not parental—endures in this landscape. I will conclude by pointing to the way in which Strand, acting out his own death in the poetic landscape, claims kin with a family of poets and rejects a poetics based on accidents of biology and autobiography.

Moving into the land of the dead in *Dark Harbor*, one finds oneself, as in Dante, very much in the land of the living. The scenes obsessively revisited are those that demanded attention in life. In poem III, the speaker evokes a myth of origin and a fall back into a particular identity ("Go in any direction and you will return to the main drag. / Something about the dull little shops, the useless items / That turn into necessities, a sense of direction, // Even the feel of becoming yourself on your return . . ."[50]); that return concludes, "From far away, life looked to be simpler back in the town / You started from . . . look, there in the kitchen are Mom and Dad, / He's reading the paper, she's killing a fly." Mom and Dad recur, in a tradition that has sources in *The Oresteia* and Plato's *Republic* (hardly repositories of family values), as the antimuses throughout this volume, and turn up in counterpoint to Orpheus and Marsyas. In IX, for instance, they reappear in a vain attempt to stabilize memory and the passage of time: ". . . Who can face the future, // Especially now, as a nobody with no past / To fall back on, nothing to prove one is / Like everyone else, with baby pictures // And pictures of Mom and Dad in their old-fashioned

/ Swimsuits on a beach somewhere in the Maritimes. / We are at work on the past to make the future // More bearable. . . ."[51]

Orpheus is primed to collide with Mom and Dad. He first appears in *Dark Harbor* in XXVIII as a failure, a lost dream of song: "There is a luminousness, a convergence of enchantments, / And the world is altered for the better as trees, / Rivers, mountains, animals, all find their true place, // But only while Orpheus sings. When the song is over, / The world resumes its old flaws. . . ." The poem ends by evoking "the well of our wishes / In which we are mirrored, but darkly as though // A shadowed glass held within its frozen calm an image / Of abundance, a bloom of humanness, a hymn in which / The shapes and sounds of Paradise are buried."[52] The hymn, a song of praise, supplication, and deep wishfulness, rises phonetically from the human condition, our "humanness," in the occult chime of "hymn" and "human." The poem immediately following, however, breaks the paradisal tone and rises to angry accusation of confessional poetry: it is diatribe, as angry as the passage about the "blind mouths" in Milton's "Lycidas." The elevation of self, the poetry of me, me, me and Mom and Dad, stands in direct opposition to the sacrificial poetry we have been considering, and one particularly senses Strand's anger at the desecration of "his" moonlight, the light of the imagination *par excellence*. This is a poetry he reviles as ". . . the savage // Knowledge of ourselves that refuses to correct itself / But lumbers instead into formless affirmation, / Saying selfhood is hating Dad or wanting Mom, // Is being kissed by a reader somewhere, is about me / And all my minutes circulating around me like flies— / Me at my foulest, the song of me, me in the haunted // Woods of my own condition, a solitaire but never alone. / These are bad times. Idiots have stolen the moonlight. / They cast their shadowy pomp wherever they wish."[53]

Orpheus hardly has the last word in this volume. He gives way to Marsyas, the faun flayed alive by Apollo for poetic presumption, a far more violent and earthbound figure for poetry. In XXXVI the poet cannot decide ". . . whether or not to stroll / Through the somber garden where the grass in the shade / Is silver and frozen and where the general green // Of the rest of the garden is dark. . . ."[54] The woman waiting in the garden has a Eurydice feel to her which implies that the "I" persona who enters the garden has been somewhat assimilated to an Orphic role. In the next poem, the woman sitting and waiting in an echoing hall is clearly confirmed as Eurydice: "Orpheus came to visit her, came several times. // Each time he left he wished her well, but he was a fool, / Preferring the moonlit chords of his melancholy, / The inward drift of notes to anything of hers. And yet, // What does it matter now? He's gone for good. The floating / Darkness of the cries seems more and more the prompting / Of a distant will, a fatal music rising everywhere."[55] Orpheus, now glimpsed in the slightly foolish solipsism to which lyric is prey, disappears from that last stanza, leaving only his music. The poet, by now an old expert at giving things up, has shrugged off even the mythological identification with the spirit of poetry, Orpheus. But the full-bodied, alliterative pentameters survive, in cadences of impersonal mastery.

Strand ends his volume, reasonably enough, with a poetic Elysium, in a quiet idiom which at first sounds like a postcard from an artists' colony: "I am sure you would find it misty here, / With lots of stone cottages badly needing repair. . . ." The poets gathered in this posthumous society tuck their heads under their wings at the approach of the newcomer: anonymity, not fame, blesses this poetic afterlife. And the spirit of song which ends this book so affirmingly can be attributed to no individual poet. The passage, and indeed the whole book, rise to a restrained dignity as they imagine the necessary angel: ". . . Then it stopped in mid-air. / It was an angel, one of the good ones, about to sing."[56]

Elysium represents one important version of pastoral. But I prefer to end with a darker pastoral, the sacrificial pastoral, which charges Strand's language with a stronger current: the Marsyas poem. For Marsyas is a pastoral figure, a creature of hill and grove and song. In this poem, the impersonal "one" of poetic consciousness turns into a provisional lyric "I" as he ponders the torture of Marsyas becoming "a body of work"; as he ponders, that is, the mystery by which brute life experience is transmuted into poetic figuration and patterned language. What "I" considers, though, is whether that suffering is legible beyond the confines of private experience. I love this poem for its physical resistances, its syntax probing forward past line ends and stanza breaks, its intrication of myth in flesh and oil paint, and the meshing of the "I" in the body of song. And let us note that transfiguring touch, the repetition in the last line of "the moment, the moment," by which mortal transience is—fleetingly—arrested and held in the timely illusion of verse.

XXXIX

When after a long silence one picks up the pen
And leans over the paper and says to himself:
Today I shall consider Marsyas

Whose body was flayed to excess,
Who made no crime that would square
With what he was made to suffer.

Today I shall consider the shredded remains of Marsyas—
What do they mean as they gather the sunlight
That falls in pieces through the trees,

As in Titian's late painting? Poor Marsyas,
A body, a body of work as it turns and falls
Into suffering, becoming the flesh of light,

Which is fed to onlookers centuries later.
Can this be the cost of encompassing pain?
After a long silence, would I, whose body

Is whole, sheltered, kept in the dark by a mind
That prefers it that way, know what I'd done
And what its worth was? Or is a body scraped

From the bone of experience, the chart of suffering
To be read in such ways that all flesh might be redeemed,
At least for the moment, the moment it passes into song.[57]

CHAPTER 6

In Classic Guise:
John Hollander's Shadow Selves

1.

John Hollander has been fooling, all his life as a poet, with types of shape. The explicitly pictorial calligrams collected in 1969 under the title *Types of Shape* formalized hauntings that had already given, and would continue to give, both form and fictive sense to all his poems, and substance to his literary scholarship. How, he has asked over and over, does pattern turn into signifying figure? How does scheme distill into trope? I want to consider a particular pair of patterns—the Alcaic and Sapphic stanzas—in the light of questions Hollander himself has taught us to ask about the signifying, tropic, and allusive power of shape.

These questions all turn on the question of turning. In Hollander's calligram of a cracked Etruscan cup, "A Possible Fake," the column asks: "Is it / mere mire / column of / common or / even rare / clay that / carries a / proud cup / so dry so / empty now"? The poem answers itself, and, distantly, Keats: "Lo what the / potter twists / on his flat / turning wheel / is his idea. . . ."[1] Mire, or the literal, on the turning wheel of trope becomes form: idea, cup, image, poem, body. Another figure for this metamorphosis we know as art could be the distillery. In the Cognac region, any farmer will show you the great, hand-hammered, bulbous brass still, uniquely shaped to distill its uniquely flavored brandy. Like the Cognac stills, the Alcaic and Sapphic stanzas have generic shape which is modified in each particular instance. As with Cognac, the ratio of modification to inherited genre, combined with the quality of raw material—sun, soil, grapes—determines the essence of the poem.

Hollander's classical stanza shapes come down to us from seventh-century B.C.E. Lesbos charged with allusive force. They bring this allusiveness, in Hollander's delicate phrase from *The Figure of Echo*, "into the range of [their] subject."[2] Declaring their genealogies, the stanzas establish lines of continuity from ancient Ionia through Rome to the United States, and other continuities within the scope of Hollander's own poetic life. They allow us to trace, for instance, lines of thought from the Alcaic poems of *Movie-Going and Other Poems* of 1962 through the Sapphics of *Spectral Emanations* in 1978 to the Sapphics of *Figurehead and Other Poems* in 1999. To consider these poems is also to meet head-on the challenge of the literariness of a *poeta* as *doctus* as Hollander. Do these poems taste of sun and soil and grape, or are they mere neoclassical exercises?

The Alcaics in *Movie-Going*, "Off Marblehead" and "On the Sand Bar," occur in the book's penultimate section called "Sea Pieces," accompanied by two poems in a related meter, Fourth Asclepiadean, but introduced and concluded by poems in free verse. This ranginess in formal choices reflects the spirit of the collection as a whole. Appearing in 1962, just three years after Lowell's *Life Studies*, *Movie-Going* vaulted over the sectarian divisions in American poetry of the period—the polarization between traditional and open forms—and boldly claimed as its own the entire continent of form, ancient and modern. Against his own ingenious command of convention—sonnet, pentameter eclogue, Marvellian rhymed tetrameter couplets, elegiac couplets, and so forth—Hollander plays a tense, vernacular prosiness. "Drive-ins are out, to start with. One must always be / Able to see . . ." begins the book with its populist title poem in anti-iambic hexameters.[3] Hardly nostalgic, Hollander's Alcaics provide a loom for this taut weave of prose and the conventionally poetic, speech and verse, contemporary and classical.

Convention, then, demands our attention. And not one convention, but a lineage of conventions: the Alcaic stanza draws into the arena of the poem's sense not only the originating figure of Alcaeus, the seventh-century compatriot and contemporary of Sappho, but also Horace, who shaped his own Roman authority in the odes by adapting the meters of Alcaeus and Sappho, and Auden, who in 1939 revived the English Alcaic. To what extent is this lineage active in Hollander's Alcaics?

A reader of Alcaeus will want to remember: (1) that he is a political and communal poet, often in exile, writing drinking and war songs to rally his aristocratic clan brotherhood, the *hetaireia*, to defiance of the tyrant; (2) that his poems are *songs*; and (3) that he is particularly known for the topos of the ship of state, which readers may or may not see allegorized in his very physical descriptions of ships and shipwrecks. For example, nothing demands that the poem numbered 208 in David Campbell's Loeb Library edition be read politically, though in the context of Alcaeus's whole surviving work, the inference might be drawn. In prose paraphrase, the fragment tells us:

> I fail to understand the direction of the winds: one wave rolls in from this side, another from that, and we in the middle are carried along in company with our black ship, much distressed in the great storm. The bilge-water covers the masthold; all the sail lets light through now, and there are great rents in it; the anchors are slackening; the rudders . . . my feet both stay (entangled) in the ropes: this alone (saves) me; the cargo . . . (is carried off) above. . . .[4]

Alcaeus's meter is more complex than most English meters, changing its pace three times in the course of each quatrain, from the choriambic first two lines, to the iambic third, to the dactylic fourth. Six hundred years later, Horace took over this flexible form for thirty-seven odes and a vast array of subjects, endowing the stanza with Roman solidity by standardizing as long the fifth syllable in the first two lines. Most importantly, he established Alcaeus, along with Sappho, as an almost allegorical figure for lyric poetry. In Horace, Alcaeus, often invoked by his lyre, represents no longer a vital, obstreperous political force, but "literature," the lyric itself as form and theme. Look at his appearance in Ode II.13, where Horace recounts his near brush with death from a falling tree. In James Michie's translation:

> . . . I half glimpsed the dire
> Judge of the dead, the blest in their divine
> Seclusion, Sappho on the Aeolian lyre

Mourning the cold girls of her native isle,
And you, Alcaeus, more full-throatedly
Singing with your gold quill of ships, exile
And war, hardship on land, hardship at sea.[5]

In Horace's Alcaics:

Sappho puellis de popularibus,
et te sonantem plenius aureo
    Alcaee, plectro dura navis,
        dura fugae mala, dura belli.

After Mary Sidney's Alcaic psalm in the 1590s, the Alcaic doesn't find much echo in English, aside from some odd quaverings by Tennyson, Bridges, and Clough, until it emerges as full-throated response in Auden's poems of 1939. Since Auden resounded, we may be sure, in Hollander's inner ear, we should hold one of his stanzas up as a tuning fork. In the elegy for Freud, as we have seen, song meter has become speech meter, the syllabic counting (lines of eleven, eleven, nine, and ten syllables) allowing Auden to elude his own innate tunefulness. An ancient song form has become an instrument of modern, discursive antilyric. In subtle ways, however, the figure of Alcaeus as exile works allusively in this evocation of Freud's exile, and the dactyls rise up to remind us of the all-but-vanished song in the last stanza of "In Memory of Sigmund Freud":

One rational voice is dumb. Over his grave
the household of Impulse mourns one dearly loved:
    sad is Eros, builder of cities,
        and weeping, anarchic Aphrodite.[6]

Here, now, is Hollander's "Off Marblehead":

A woeful silence, following in our wash,
fills the thick, fearful roominess, blanketing
    bird noise and ocean splash; thus, always
        soundlessly, rounding the point we go

gliding by dippy, quizzical cormorants.
One black maneuver moving them all at once,

they turn their beaks to windward then, and,
        snubbing the gulls on the rocks behind them,

point, black, a gang of needles against the gray
dial sky, as if some knowledge, some certainty
        could now be read therefrom. And if we
            feel that the meter may melt, those thin necks

droop, numbers vanish from the horizon when
we turn our heads to scribble the reading down
        on salty, curled, dried pages, it is
            merely our wearied belief, our strained and

ruining grasp of what we assume, that blurs
our eyes and blears the scene that surrounds us: tears
        of spray, the long luff's reflex flapping,
            crazy with pain, and the clenching sheet,

and, looming up, Great Misery (Named for whose?
When?) Island. Groaning, jangling in irons, crews
        of gulls still man a rolling buoy not
            marked on our charts. Overhead, the light

(impartial, general, urging of no new course)
spares no approving brightening for the sparse
        and sorry gains of one we hold to
            now, ever doubting our memory. But

no matter—whether running before the wind
away for home, or beating against the end
        of patience, towards its coastline, still the
            movement is foolishly close to one of

flight, the thick, oily clouds undissolving, crowds
of sea birds, senseless, shrill, unappeased, no boats
        about, and, out to sea, a sickening,
            desperate stretch of unending dark.[7]

If we face the question of Hollander's literariness, it is partly because the poet himself has raised it and fought it out so toughly. Throughout *Movie-Going*, and throughout Hollander's oeuvre, Fate suspends uncertaine victorie between the two equall armies of Literature and Life, each with its capital *L*. His poems are carefully staged battlefields where our souls are made to negotiate these forces, the artificial and the rawly prosaic. So it is in "Off Marblehead." In a book starting with a paean to the imagination and to America's movies, and concluding with another paean to art and tradition in "Upon Apthorp House," modeled on Marvell, "Off Marblehead" beats its wings against the faith in art affirmed so strongly elsewhere in the book. Not that the affirmation was ever more than provisional: whether imagining, like Horace, a monument in bronze, or the light that may shine bright in black ink, poems are always set against Chaos and Old Night, as Hollander well knows; he places his forms gallantly against the void, and "Movie-Going" and "Upon Apthorp House" both end in visions of engulfing night.

The night in "Off Marblehead," however, menaces with more sinister force, because the poem itself challenges more rudely the saving power of art. Against the "desperate stretch of unending dark," a sailboat makes its way. Nudging Alcaic form toward Alcaic theme, we may note, (1) that the nautical scene evokes Alcaeus; (2) that the plural first-person subject, "we," invokes, however distantly, the Alcaic notion of clan brotherhood; and (3) that Hollander has been more respectful than Auden of Alcaic metrical cola, not just counting syllables but letting us feel the swing of the choriamb $(-\cup\cup-)$ in the opening lines of each stanza: "fóllowing ín," "róominess blánk," "quízzical cór." The very title with its "marble head" may be a sidelong glancing pun at the idea of the classical displaced to modernity and the New World.

How then has Hollander's poem turned from its forebears? Partly in its contractions. Alcaeus's songs, on land or sea, railed, mourned, and celebrated events of the city; their themes were mythopolitical, and bound together a tribal and political group. Hollander's seascape, by contrast, is made of text. Alcaeus's full, vigorous, brilliantly thing-laden world of action and public consequence has shrunk to a literary seascape where "the meter may melt," "numbers vanish from the horizon," and "we" on the boat "turn our heads to scribble the reading down / on salty, curled, dried pages." The brotherhood implied in Hollander's "we" cares not about war, but about metrics and epistemology: ". . . it is / merely our wearied belief, our strained and / ruining grasp of what we assume. . . ." Alcaeus, having passed through the literary domestication of Horace's odes with their muted politics of patronage, seems to have dwindled still further in a passage through Mallarmé's "Brise marine" and its literary acedia—"La chair est triste, hélas! Et j'ai lu tous les livres"—to wash up here in the near-suffocating despair of "Off Marblehead."

Merely a complaint, then, of the jaded *littérateur*? Far from it. Within this unstable classical stanza, the modern poet proposes and refuses the consolation of the pseudoclassical, and faces his own nightmare temptation, that of living and pleasuring in a world of text alone. If the speaker wants to read the world as poetic text, the world resists. Utterance here is inscribed into "a woeful silence," and concludes in the dark. Midway, the attempt to impose prosodic order upon reality (by counting syllables, and gently rhyming the first two lines of most stanzas) founders in the recognition of the pathetic fallacy: ". . . it is / merely our wearied belief, our strained and / ruining grasp of what we assume, that blurs / our eyes and blears the scene. . . ." If this is the ship of poetry, it passes either Misery already named or facts "not / marked on our charts." Neither the literary future ("urging of no new course") nor the past ("ever doubting our memory") promises much, and the general movement in these quatrains occurs as flight within a world formless, "senseless," "unappeased," and dark. The one false note in the poem sounds in the phrase "crazy with pain," a hyperbole neither supported by the empirical conditions of the scene—after all, this is just an afternoon's sail off the North Shore of Boston—nor in tune with the skeptical, grim intelligence of the poem as a whole. What survives the dark is the stanza shape itself, flexible enough to allow the tussle between each restless sentence and the architecture of lines, the remembered cadences of song. Taking more than one cue from Auden, Hollander has used an ancient lyric form to break out of the dominant lyric convention of his own day, the versions of pentameter so characteristic of American poetry of the forties and fifties. The stanzas of "Off Marblehead," syllabic and anti-iambic, act out a newly self-conscious poetics of syntax.

"The classics can console. But not enough," wrote Derek Walcott in "Sea Grapes."[8] In "Off Marblehead," Hollander presses hard on his own sense of that "not enough," testing his medium and its consolations as only the finest works can afford to. With the rich Sapphic tradition, his instincts have been equally contrarian. Whereas the Alcaic doesn't arouse much recognition from modern American readers, the Sapphic stanza, far better known, resounds with the mythic personality of its supposed creator. In its three hendecasyllabics and final, five-syllable adonic, Sappho's stanza seems to exhale and inhale with rhythms almost heavingly erotic.

Hollander's "The Lady of the Castle" and "After an Old Text" in *Spectral Emanations* both play off the epiphanic eroticism of Sappho's lyrics to reveal a bitter, personal, and modern truth. To Sappho's Aphrodite, Romanized as "Venus Pudica" and presented as a three-dimensional sculpture, "The Lady of the Castle" opposes the obscene Sheela-na-gig, the crude medieval female figure carved on churches in England and France. This poem enforces reduction: sculpted goddess shrinks to primitive relief, full-blossomed mystery to a hideous explicitness in the vaginal slit. "Hieroglyphic / Of nature's own cuneiform," Hollander calls her, playing between more and less pictographic writing systems for this Linear C creature whose wedge-shaped meaning is all too clear.[9] Most reductively, the Sapphic music, which Swinburne caught with such choriambic grace, has petrified here into willfully prosaic syllabics:

> Hers is the closed door into the stone again.
> The soft traps having long since sprung, the marble
> Self-adoring dolls long crumbled, hers is the
>   Linear kingdom.

"After an Old Text," near neighbor to "The Lady of the Castle," revises, repossesses, and restages Sappho's famous "Phainetai moi" (He seems like a god to me . . .) in ways too complex to tease out here. Its power depends less on severe reduction (though it does lop off a stanza) than on a radical and punning sense of "revision." In the lines "This revision of you sucks out the sound of / Words from my mouth, my tongue collapses . . . ," the translator "revises" the Sapphic original, collapsing his own tongue, while the anguished lover has "revised" (reseen, reenvisioned) the beloved in the embrace of a rival man.[10]

I conclude with a Sapphic that works not by ironic, modernist counteracting of the classic, but by celebration and expansion. Hollander's *Figurehead* contains four poems in Sapphics. I shall be looking at "A Fragment Twice Repaired." It depends on one's sense, not only of the piecemeal nature of the poem numbered 43 by Edmonds, but of the brazen emendations he presented in his Loeb edition of 1922. I give Edmonds' "restorations" and his translation.

And then I answered: "Gentle dames, how you will evermore remember till you be old, our life together in the heyday of youth! For many things did we together both pure and beautiful. And now that you depart hence, love wrings my heart with very anguish."[11]

By contrast, David Campbell in the Loeb edition of 1982 gives the Greek text of the same poem (which he numbers 24a) with severely reduced conjecture, and his translation is similarly restrained:

"(a) . . . (you will?) remember . . . , for we too did these things in our . . . youth: many lovely . . . we . . . the city . . . us . . . sharp . . ."[12]

Now comes Hollander, full of devotion and hubris, to leap, not into the breach, but into Edmonds' closure of the breach. And might we not consider such tearing away of scar tissue, such reopening of gaps in the literary forms of the past, as a figure for all literary creation? Creation both rends and mends what has preceded it. Hollander's first two italicized stanzas relineate Edmonds' translation; the final stanzas invent a counter-voice for Sappho herself, filtered through the words of a later injured and redeemed lady, La Pia of Dante's famous chiasmus in *Purgatorio* V: "Siena mi fé, disfecemi Maremma" (Siena made me, Maremma unmade me).[13] In the light of Hollander's responsiveness to tradition, his understanding of originality as a wrestle with origins, we are invited to hear yet another injured female voice in this harmony, the anonymous, composite voice of the suffering woman of "The Fire Sermon" section of *The Waste Land*: "Highbury bore me, Richmond and Kew / Undid me. . . ."[14] Hollander's poem dramatizes and embodies Eliot's notion of tradition and the indi-vidual talent. The literary Sappho here has been made, unmade, and remade in the lines of those who adore her and seek to redeem her from the wrecked papyrus. She rises in Hollander's imagination as an emblem of the unity of time and eternity ("eras of eros"), of the blended passions of life and poetry, and of the communion of poets dead and alive in the embrace of song. For Hollander has allowed himself a lyric rendering; the lines pulse in their English accentual choriambs, and for a moment at least he proffers the vision of art not as critique, but as restoration. In its flight, song leaves text and the merely literary far behind, as Verlaine knew: "Et tout le reste est littérature."[15]

. . . *Then I replied to them, the delightful women,*
"How you will remember till you are old, our
Life together there in the splendid time of
      Youth, for we did so

Many pure and beautiful things together
Then, and now that you are all departing
Amorous passion gathers up my heart and
      Wrings it with anguish."

(Here the scrap of ragged papyrus gets to
Speak her piece, who, bearing textual witness
Down through all the violent aeons ever
      Sought restitution,

Sought to break the medium's silence, she who
Kept it while her fabric was rent and Chronos
Gathered up her heart and wrung it but not "with
      Anguish" or sorrow:)

"Sappho made me, Edmonds (J.M.) undid me
Now J.H., belated, restores the losses
Wrought on me by whatever at Oxyrhynchus
      Shredded me down to

Fifteen words, and a classicist's dusty guesses.
Hear me now who, virginal, carried down through
Many long and shifting but yet untiring
      Eras of eros—

Whether it were there in the splendid time of
Youth or all the afterwards I endured in—
Love's wild words, and those of jealousy standing
      Just at her shoulder,

Bore her character as my own and wore the
Impress of her singing hand in the darkness.
Cursed be those who patch me together but who
      Heed not the gleaming."[16]

II.

Movie-Going, from 1962, John Hollander's second book of poems, opened and closed with visions of the imagination resisting night. In each case, the title poem "Movie-Going" and the long, Marvellian "Upon Apthorp House," the form of imagination invoked is a public art: the movies, shining "Out from the local Bijou, truest gem, the most bright / Because the most believed in, staving off the night,"[17] and the eighteenth-century architecture of Apthorp House at Harvard depicted in Hollander's tightly rhymed tetrameter octets. Throughout *Movie-Going*, Hollander made the private lyric participate in "the state of the city"; with equal complexity of theme and variation he poised poetic form—sonnet, calligram, Alcaics, Alexandrines, quatrains, elegiac couplets, to name only a few—against formlessness, against the "sickening / desperate stretch of unending dark" ("Off Marblehead").[18] *Figurehead*, Hollander's seventeenth book of poems, triumphantly extends and complicates those youthful schemes.

Though *Figurehead* contains its share of public poems, such as "Fancying Things Up" with its Chaplinesque figure curled asleep "In the cold lap of stone Prosperity,"[19] or the prophetic castigations of "A Shadow of a Great Rock in a Weary Land" and "The Parade," its opening and concluding poems establish a far more intimate tone. Its nights, too, are different, and have been absorbed more gratefully than those in *Movie-Going*. In "Movie-Going" and "Upon Apthorp House," night threatens reason and imagination like Pope's Great Anarch in *The Dunciad*. *Figurehead* as a collection is haunted by images of night, but the first poem, "So Red," invokes the dark by implication only, as backdrop for the mortal blaze of leaves. Like the leaves, the sunset, and the dying fire of Shakespeare's Sonnet 73, Hollander's leaves glow (red, not yellow) against the dark. A complex poem running only two sentences through twelve haiku stanzas, "So Red" leads through a self-interrupting syntax of exploration to fulfill itself only in the last word and act, "acknowledgment." Along the way, the brilliant and dying leaves have acted out a "lastness / which itself can never last / longer than the few // moments—in this case / October days—it takes to make / itself intense in. . . ."[20] The exposed preposition ("to make / itself intense in") reveals a gesture characteristic of Hollander. Like his tendency to thrust words from noun to verb form ("lastness," "can never last") and, Hardy-fashion, to force an abstract noun from an adjective ("lastness"), the preposition points up the athleticism of a poetry that insists on acting out and acting up, a poetry that imposes clearly defined forms it then assaults from within. The "lastness," however, has still more work to do in "So Red":

> to put forth something
> of light that had either been
> waiting all along
>
> to reveal itself
> or more likely, escaping
> its dead body of
>
> leaf. . . .[21]

The first, high-strung sentence has taken nine stanzas to arrive at its crisis, which will inform the whole book to come: the liberation of the figurative from the literal, of light from the mere "dead body of / leaf." Unleashing a cadenza of figures ("It hits the road / with a visual halloo / as of a bright scarf // or a letting of / arterial blood . . ."), the poem winds up, like "Movie-Going" and "Upon Apthorp House," celebrating the imagination; it honors that power, however, not in public art, but in a private acknowledgment that accepts sacrifice and participates in nature's chiaroscuro.

"Beach Whispers," the last poem in *Figurehead*, also listens to the promptings of nature, and makes imaginative room for night, its mysteries, and death. This is not the night of the end of "Upon Apthorp House," where "noxious lights may bring about / A night, once more, of fear and doubt,"[22] *The Dunciad*'s universal darkness and certainty tempered with "noxious lights" and "doubt." The dune grasses whisper of mortality to hearers who "barely understand," but gently accept the message. If they, and we, do accept these nocturnal suggestions about orders far vaster than the human, it is partly because the poem itself has been schooled by Shakespeare's sonnets, though its twenty-five lines of irregularly rhyming tetrameters owe nothing to sonnet form. The grasses as "food for ruminant thought" lightly recall Sonnet 64, where "Ruin hath taught me thus to ruminate," a poem more explicitly invoked in *Figurehead*'s homage to Edward Hopper, "Sun in an Empty Room." "The fiefdom of the ocean, / The serfdom of the shore" intensify recollections of the same sonnet. But whereas Sonnet 64 ends in a spasm of antithesis and protest ("This thought is as a death, which cannot choose / But weep to have that which it fears to lose"), "Beach Whispers" stands in quiet receptivity, "Ears open and eyes shut," accepting that the sun, absentee landlord, reigns in "some otherwhere." Wit in "Beach Whispers"—with the puns on sound and being ("We are what we always whirr") and on the sun's solitude ("sole / Absentee landlord")—remains subordinate to the deeper simplicity of the one unrhymed line: "What they could be said to say."[23]

A suggestive and playful book, *Figurehead* explores a series of oppositions which turn out not to be contraries so much as complex marriages. Darkness and light achieve a delicate union in poem after poem; so do prose and verse, and so do the apparent opposites, the literal and the figurative. Readers familiar with Hollander's work are well acquainted with his obsession—not too strong a word—with the turnings, torques, tropes by which poetry turns the tables on the flatly factual. Puns, those quicksilver flashings of multiple sense, have always been central to his art; so have parables, iconic shaped poems, and the standard figures, metaphor and simile. In order to test such turnings, he has, all along, incorporated into his poems a stratum of brute fact. One might construct a model—but it could only be provisional—in which the apparently opposed terms of dark and light, prose and verse, literal and figurative, are lined up in parallel columns. In such a scheme, we would expect to find darkness, prose, and literalness associated. *Figurehead* often does suggest such a pattern, but only up to a point, when the poems' deeper and disruptive wisdom takes over.

The literal is the ground necessary for figuration, and like figuration, it is treacherous ground, as Hollander knows well. One of his strongest early poems made that clear. "Hobbes, 1651," from *Movie-Going*, following a lead from the philosopher who wrote with such excruciating awareness of the equivocal nature of language, presents a monologue in Hobbes' voice. Geoffrey Hill has insisted on the importance of equivocation in Hobbes, and his essay "The Tartar's Bow and the Bow of Ulysses," in *The Enemy's Country*, can provide a key as well for Hollander's poem. In terse elegiac couplets, "Hobbes, 1651" attempts statement of fact ("When I returned at last from Paris hoofbeats pounded"), but keeps breaking, as if irrepressibly, into personification: "the wind moaned."[24] Still, the poem manages to keep an air of grim factuality until the last word, the plainest of all and yet the most figurative, embodying the landscape itself as well as the Hobbesian concern for a language not to be undermined by double entendre: "If it was not safe / In England yet, or ever, that nowhere beneath the gray / Sky would be much safer seemed very plain."

Figurehead lays out this dangerous plain ground in poem after poem. In the first poem, "So Red," the literal is associated less with darkness than with death, "its dead body of / leaf." "Las Hilanderas," a virtuosic meditation on figure-making, establishes the literal as "the very here and now," and "a fabric of fact and pure, unthinking self."[25] In "Variations on a Table-Top," it appears as "the plain deal table in the kitchen" standing for nothing (and thereby for so much) but itself.[26] "Fancying Things Up" laments, "O that metal were not so literally / Massive. . . ."[27] In "Owl," "Medusa's visage gazed our bodies to / Literal stone unshaded. . . ."[28] "Figurehead" portrays the literal as "of darkness and of the peculiar vacancy of the busy"[29]; in "Emblem" it is "the merely visible"[30]; in "Sun in an Empty Room" it is "the clutter of incident"[31]; in "An Afterword," figuration appears as "the living twilight" as opposed to "Dark, the night that cancels all seeming; and so / literal, dying."[32] "Early Birds," in its more overtly narrative mode, presents the literal in monosyllabic plainness as incident not yet converted to plot: "That in fact was it," and "And that was all of that."[33]

As one would suspect, all of these literalnesses in *Figurehead*, like "plain" in "Hobbes, 1651," barely hold still, so eager are they to gambol in language's promiscuity, its slide into the figurative, its embrace of multiple partners of meaning. Consistently, Hollander associates the literal with darkness and death: the dead body of leaf, Medusa's petrifying gaze, and "literal, dying." By analogy, his more prosaic maneuvers—dangling prepositions, rough enjambments, slang, iambic meter akimbo in syllabic counts, dashes, conversational interruptions—suggest the raw material with which the formal imagination of verse must work. This play of prosiness against verse of course participates in the larger story of modernism, with *vers libre* and the prose poem, Frost's sentence sounds, Moore's syllabics, and Lowell's "words meat-hooked from the living steer"[34] representing just a few of the ways in which the unpoetic has been hauled in to jar poetry to life. Each generation in its turn redefines the poetic, indicating new fields of inclusion and exclusion. But Hollander's modes of braiding or colliding verse with prose have been entirely his own. From the first volume, *A Crackling of Thorns* (1958), he has experimented with tilting metrical lines into vernacular speech patterns; he has been ingenious in adapting verse to the manners of narrative fiction, most ambitiously in the book-length poem *Reflections on Espionage* (1974; 1999), in the hybrid Midrashic detective romance *Spectral Emanations* (1978), and in the prose poems of *In Time & Place* (1986). In *Figurehead*, his fine ear for American idiom, the demotic as well as the erudite, collaborates with verse-making of the highest sophistication to play out, in myriad forms, the book's central theme: the wresting of imaginative truth from fact, the visionary from the visible.

Not surprisingly for a poet who has long pondered the visual arts, Hollander uses a series of ekphrastic poems in *Figurehead* as laboratories in which to test different ratios of illusion, different levels of figuration. Two masterful poems about Arachne initiate this line of thought, "Las Hilanderas" and "Arachne's Story." "Las Hilanderas," out of Ovid by way of Velázquez, works in a vertiginous hierarchy of illusions, taking Velázquez's painted scene of the women spinning as "real," and the depicted tapestry in the back room as the realm of fiction. The poem maintains an illusion of the literal from Velázquez's pictorial illusion: the spinners, severely to be distinguished from the artists who wove the images, occupy "the very here and now / Where what is spun is skeined without contentiousness."[35] The pun upon "content" in "contentiousness" winks at the bifocal vision we must preserve if we wish to keep the spinners in their literal place. But these solid, warm young women, providers of raw material though they are, point "unwittingly" to the great fictions about the making of art, the tales about the two punished weavers, Arachne and Philomel. Those weavers, in turn (imagined, not seen in the painting), serve as figures for the two kinds of art Hollander is at pains to distinguish. Philomel, her tongue ripped out by her rapist Tereus, weaves "testimony," a documentary art of pain experienced and witnessed whose literalness is its point. Arachne, on the other hand, "filling with vivid / Wonder the texture of the very stuff of fiction / She herself was made of," weaves Ovidian myth. In her transformation into a spider, Hollander sees a parable of an art still higher than the fictive art he so repeatedly honors. The architecture depicted by Velázquez gives a clue to this hierarchy: as the eye moves from the foreground with the laboring spinners, to the tapestry above and beyond them, to the blank round window above all, we move from realistic representation, to imaginative fiction, to a structuralist art-for-art's-sake justified by form alone:

> Busy busy busy: they toil and also do
>   They spin and to what final cause is made
> Splendidly clear in the room behind—and, after all,
>   Above—them: the tapestry is what the thread
> Was for, the wonder of substantial image is what
>   The tapestry was for, and as for the wonder,

It serves itself—crowning the end of what has tied
   Know-how to craft and after that to high
Art. And, above all that, as in an afterthought,
   The unacknowledging eye of an oriel
Window's blank stare, yielding nothing. . . .[36]

The sense of the scriptural allusions in the first line (Matthew 6:28; Luke 12:27) takes hold only slowly as the scene builds up: in considering "the lilies of the field, how they grow; they toil not, neither do they spin . . ." we are asked to consider a nonutilitarian art, beautiful in itself and serving no purpose but wonder. Arachne becomes truly an artist in this poem when she leaves her represented fictions behind along with the selfhood that needed them. She becomes a pure Mallarmean artist, the poet of nothing, of the elocutory disappearance of the poet, "the spider / Spinning out of its own guts, not the 'expression' / Of pain and longing, of delight and hope, / But the more profoundly formed cord of whatever / Is woven into the matter of representation. . . ." But the poem that contains her is far from a Mallarmean poem, and it concerns, not "nothing," but many "somethings."

Hollander continues these meditations in "Arachne's Story," the sister poem that follows "Las Hilanderas." Instead of the web of elegiac couplets, he weaves (or spins) this poem in a canny free verse that floats its filaments off the central pentameter design: "The skill at weaving was itself a web. . . ."[37] Speaking out of Ovid, Arachne explores mysterious conjunctions of structure and image, literal and figurative, artistic selfhood and artistic selflessness. Central to this poem's labor are the puns, "texture itself becoming / Text rather than lying like painting / Lightly upon some canvas or some wall. . . ." In the prestidigitation of puns (texture/text; lying/lying; trope/trap; toil/*toile*), the ground of the literal, Hobbes' plainness, is revealed to be no ground at all. To the poetic eye, every datum is incipient metamorphosis, which is why Ovid presides over these poems. In the spider's art, the apparently literal sets out one more illusion, "not imaging things / That seem to be, but building traps that seem not to." The spider artist exemplifies an unconfessional ethos that might describe the poetic selfhood in Hollander's own poems: off-center, almost invisible, but powerfully present in design.

The spider spins "upward as I move down, hanging / Like life itself, after all, by a thread." "Hanging by a thread" suggests urgency. It is an urgency unrelated to the contemporary poetry which claims our attention in proportion to the extremities suffered by the authorial self, a self validated by supposed biographical authenticity. Amid such clamor, it is worth asking whether Hollander's impersonal dramas can be heard at all. Even more to the point, one can ask what kind of intensities his poems live by, so unlike the more popular violences. Among many answers one might propose—their storytelling, their antic wordplay—one would have to include his persistent lust for the truth of the eye. For years, a visual-philosophical hunger has driven his poems. Works of visual art have provoked him to question the nature of being in the nature of seeing, as in the brilliant "Effet de Neige" from *Harp Lake* (1988), a dialogue of voluble "Saying" with silent "Seeing." That poem of depths and surfaces, of robust prepositions breaking the picture plane, dramatized both "the obvious / Standing in the way of the truth," and, in conclusion, "the truth, blocking the path of the obvious."[38] *Figurehead*'s many ekphrastic poems keep worrying these questions with no diminution of energy or ingeniousness; and it is a tribute to them that their ingeniousness in no way detracts from their urgency.

The works by Hopper, Sheeler, Magritte, and others invoked in *Figurehead* are not the occasions for descriptive taxidermy, but pretexts for dramas, at once intimate and impersonal, of "the way we know and / Remember and represent . . ." ("Sun in an Empty Room").[39] The trick, the achievement here, is to stage the revelations so the reader is drawn in and taught to care. This Hollander manages through theater, as in the opening lines of "An Old Image": "Poor doggie! But that's where we all are, *nicht wahr?*"[40]; or of "Figurehead": "Wondering whether the position you had just taken"[41]; or of "Two Glosses on René Magritte": "You say you love my X my two Y's, my / Mysterious (as in French or British) Zed."[42] Even a more overtly descriptive poem like "Sun in an Empty Room" launches from visual data ("Early sunlight, even if at a late / Time . . .") into epistemological hypotheses and conundrums: "as if given substance thereby"; "as if in memory or in afterthought / Or in some mode of light's picturing of light as it / Composes a picture of the way we know and / Remember and represent. . . ."[43]

Do we care about "the way we know"? "Sun in an Empty Room" lures us into caring, partly through suspenseful syntax hovering across line ends; partly through the local arousals of paradox and wordplay; partly through the gathering seriousness of self-discovery which sets an austere demotic against wit: "And to ask ourselves what we are *doing* / In this space . . ."; "It was ourselves that we were after, / Filled with the minding of the light that dwells. . . ." That gerund, "minding," could work as an emblem of Hollander's art: an art in which intelligence acts as verb rather than as a noun ("minding" rather than "mind"), an art which shares the intellection, the watchfulness, and the faithful guarding all suggested by the verb "to mind." Hollander has "minded" Hopper before, in "Sunday A.M. Not in Manhattan" from *The Night Mirror* (1971), and "Edward Hopper's Seven A.M." from *Tesserae* (1993). The present poem, more reflective of mental process than of a particular painting, constitutes in many ways Hollander's "reminding" of the American painter.

Poems around and about paintings make up a goodly portion of *Figurehead*, and provide occasion for serious fooling with figuration. Another set of poems that appear to be games challenges the very idea of seriousness. These games, "Getting from Here to There," "Across the Board," and "Variations on a Table-Top," by emphasizing the arbitrary nature of their rules and pursuing whimsical non sequiturs in subject matter, assert the arbitrary and artificial character of literary form. In their teasing, they assault the literal from yet another vantage point, and with it, the naïve notion of art as validated by personal sincerity. But "Getting from Here to There," in its alphabetically shifting line endings (each last word engendering the next line's last word with only one letter changed), "Across the Board" with its repetitive triple rhymes, and the surrealist proliferation of tables in "Variations on a Table-Top," veer so close to ornate arbitrariness, even to nonsense, that they risk alienating a reader's emotional commitment. It is a risk well taken, however, and a measure of these poems' achievement, that out of the welter and frolic of word games, out of the non-sense of phonetic and alphabetic orderings, out of the recognition of language's conventionalities, each poem shapes a provisional sense. Such shapings, Hollander seems to suggest, are key to human meaning: forms poised against the void, their arbitrariness temporarily converted to significance. Words that have no kinship of sense are brought into brief, intense marriages: rune and ruse, dust and lust. These marriages are the substance of poetry.

Like the movie houses staving off the night in "Movie-Going," Hollander's game poems ask the reader to cherish sense-making itself as an activity. In the fraternity of poets he so often celebrates, he seems particularly responsive, in these poems, to James Merrill, the fellow spy who bears the code name "Image" in *Reflections on Espionage*. Merrill had memorably played "word golf" in his poem "Processional" from *The Inner Room* (1988), concluding: "Or in three lucky strokes of word golf

LEAD / Once again turns (LOAD, GOAD) to GOLD."[44] Following this game, which revels in the metamorphic forces of language, Hollander in "Getting from Here to There" pays oblique homage to Merrill; the end words of the last section lead through the sequence dust—lust—last—list—line—lone—tone—tune—rune—ruse—rust—dust, generating a little parable about art's insistence on harmony set against mortality, a tune and a rune drawn from dust. "Across the Board" nihilistically—or is it hedonistically?—entertains the Mallarmean proposition of formal meaninglessness: the passage "Here at the finish, nothing's left to win / Although, surely, something has taken place; / *As always, the bottom line is all for show*"[45] recalls "Nothing / Will have taken place / But the place" from Mallarmé's *Un Coup de dés*. But "Variations on a Table-Top," through its delirium of puns (the Bower of Tabel, *arrosto d'Ariosto, favola calda*), suggests that in confronting language's variabilities, and the instability of even canonical texts, the mind is delivered of illusions and gains a clear and stern regard. Undoing the famous emendation ("babble" for "table") in the scene of Falstaff's death in *Henry V*, Hollander both demonstrates the fragility of inherited orders and the quest to establish them: "He lay there at the end of things; what was it he still could see: / A table of green fields . . . ?"[46] This editorial diversion gives way to the "broad true plain," still the Hobbesian plain but less dangerous, for the moment snatched away from biblical and Miltonic allusion. The mountaintop may be Sinai, the sunset bay the landscape of the end of "Lycidas," but playing on the word "table," the poem concludes,

> . . . is at last
> To climb to the table land and see, not a fancy prospect
> As from a mountaintop, or across a bay at sunset, but
> Again the broad true plain, ungirded by any lofty hills.

The gamesmanship, in both its frivolity and its gravity, reaches a crescendo in "M and M's," a double elegy for James Merrill and "Muriel," the poet-speaker's mother. Trained on the Sapphic stanza, a form Merrill gracefully used and which has a long history in Hollander's work, "M and M's" bops around the field of memory like a pinball, lighting up one "Muriel" after another in a fit of high jinks and camp which leads, *via* a learned text on surnames and the spell-checker's *idiot savant* corrections, to "Merrill" and so to "Merlin," "Merit," "Merrily," all of which fit James Merrill to an M if not to a T. In the final fitting together, Hollander evokes the double losses, within six months of each other, of mother and poet companion, and finds in the stanza itself a shape sufficiently resilient to hold these divergent figures together in a "new constellation."

Figurehead, as a book, is steeped in darkness and the prescience of death. Beneath the games, over wit's shoulder, stands the shadow. "Wit with his wantonnesse / Tasteth deaths bitternesse," we might say of this collection, cribbing from Nashe; except that the modern poet does not terrify himself into prayer at the prospect. He sets his wrought stanzas against entropy, but increasingly these poems erode earlier oppositions and allow dark and light to embrace, death and life to illuminate each other. The Sapphic stanzas in *Figurehead*, not only in "M and M's" but also in "A Fragment Twice Repaired," "Digital," and "An Afterword," all meditate on the mystery of poetic form withstanding death, as Sappho's song-shape itself has survived wars, Alexandrian undertakers, Christian zealots, and two thousand six hundred years of battering and translation to reach our present.

Darkness in Hollander's poems maintains its association with menace and death. But for years, as well, he has been a master of shadows, observing how those children of the marriage of light and dark give us our primal images. He has also, in less antic moments, acknowledged the reconciliation of light with dark, spirit with matter, life with death. Such a poem is "August Carving" from *Blue Wine* (1979), a poem of quiet dignity and depth:

> The stone pair have been making love but that is as nothing:
> The he and she celebrate the embrace of light and stone.
> Light will fall from them, as from ourselves: they will pass
>   among
> Moments of astonishing shadow, then enter the dark,
> Coldly, invisibly, forms fractured from their radiance.[47]

"Owl," from *Figurehead*, deserves to be read in the company of "August Carving." A public poem—the Phi Beta Kappa poem for Harvard in 1996—"Owl" keeps faith with its ceremonial occasion but suggests as well the mind's most private moments of recognition. "August Carving" measured a kind of adult truce with transience; "Owl," a more explicitly philosophical poem, takes a reading of the intellect in action. As in "minding the light" from "Sun in an Empty Room," the truth discovered in "Owl," the prey of the owl, is less a noun than a participle in Hollander's dynamic conception: "Keep on Keep on knowing forth." In its allegory of intellection—Minerva's owl with its fixed vision, its nocturnal insight, as opposed to roving human daylight vision—"Owl" owes something to the tradition of Vaughan's "The Night." Both poems find enlightenment not in "thin / Spaces of ill-illumined day" (Vaughan's "and by this world's ill-guiding light"), but in insight delivered from mere visibility. Vaughan's insight is religious, Hollander's, here, philosophical, the search for "laws / Governing the unseen."[48] But his allegory, unfolded in rhyming quatrains, an even-numbered syllabic approximation of the more unstable Alcaic, works in poetry's realm and in poetry's sensuous terms. So the owl, in one of Hollander's most pointed puns, confers "the sounder darkness" upon the spruces, and "sounds the dark." "Sounding" must be given every valence: acoustical, spatial, and material. Wisdom in this poem is dramatic and interrogative as well as propositional: the owl sounds the dark with its famous question, so that "Wisdom arises on the wings / Of darkness and of doubt." It also arises on the wings of symmetrical alliteration. Furthermore, wisdom, in poetry's terms, must be dual in its powers, both the abstracting mind ("Great-winged, far-ranging consciousness") and the small fleshly victim, the object of intelligence, "the affrighted heartbeat on the ground." "Owl" acts out what it propounds, its concreteness and abstraction unified in pun and parable ("execution"), its allusive complexities coursing forward, recurrently, in song.

Figurehead does not stave off the night. Its forms in their resilience and variety, its language, its parables, accept the incursions of disorder, transience, darkness, death. In communion with shade, these poems generate light of mind and heart; in intimacy with death, they attain a vitality that is a deepest form of generosity. Playing, it turns out, is serious business. It may help us live. It may even help prepare us to die.

CHAPTER 7

Contradictory Classicists:
Frank Bidart and Louise Glück

Amerrican poetry in the early twenty-first century has an amiable heterogeneity, but a lack of vigor, focus, and scale. It is, of course, hard to see one's own time clearly; our vision tends to be that of the souls in Dante's Hell, able to see future and past, but not the present. Within these limitations, we can discern loose groupings of poets, the most visible of whom are, on the one hand, the Language Poets, with a self-announcing theory of abstraction and avant-garde pedigree, often of soft-Marxist derivation, and on the other a much less organized tribe of anecdotal poets. These latter stake their claim to our attention on the pledge of autobiographical authenticity, the presentation of experience—often the experience of private suffering—sanctified through public confession. For these poets, intensity of narrative subject matter tends to replace intensity of verbal construction, in diction, rhythm, or syntax. Frank Bidart and Louise Glück stand outside both of those arenas, and they seem to me among the liveliest of our contemporaries. Each rises authoritatively from the lyric tradition, projecting—and by that I mean, partly, distancing—private experience in poetic form. For each of them, the transfiguration of personal raw material occurs, not in traditional prosodic shapes, but in a shapeliness sought for in each new process of composition. And the personal material often finds its pattern in some analogue from Greek or Roman literature, or mythology. Glück's and Bidart's are both self-centered and self-uncentering poems, and it is in acting out that contradiction that they take shape.

In lyric classicism, poetic shape is precipitated as an act of mind and feeling, but also as a process of translation and adaptation of inherited forms: "We fill pre-existing forms and when we fill them we change them and are changed," Bidart has declared in his small *ars poetica*, "Borges and I," from *Desire*.[1] The translation may be more or less explicit, and I should like to consider in Bidart and Glück several fairly explicit modes of translation as composition, by way of thinking about their poems as exertions that lift psychic weight and move the burden of understanding from one state to another. It is in this sense that we may think of poems as "moving," and one of the things they move is an ego-bound conception of self.

Ezra Pound presides over the modern notion of translation as composition, though he was by no means alone in his practice; Eliot recombined much foreign DNA in his work, and Bidart's "Borges and I" could be considered a private riff on "Tradition and the Individual Talent." But Pound so thoroughly identified translation and composition, he was so thoroughly the ventriloquist and found his own voice so persistently in the voices of others, that he dramatizes the mode at an extreme, and so helps define both its dangers and its opportunities.

"O strange face there in the glass!" Pound addresses himself in one of his earliest poems, "On His Own Face in a Glass":

> O ribald company, O saintly host!
> O sorrow-swept my fool,
>
> What answer? . . .[2]

Pound's "The Seafarer" starts by demanding, in the free translation from the Anglo-Saxon, "May I for my own self song's truth reckon," requiring us to read the pronoun "I" as a multiple exposure of many fictive selves, and "my own self" similarly as a composite fiction that will make good the song's truth in the valor of the language presented.[3] Thinking of lyric selfhood as a ribald company or as the song's truth (not the singer's) may help us to understand the practices and visions of poets as seemingly distant from Pound as Bidart and Glück, and may help us to gauge some of the ways in which they undo the crudely packaged lumpen-self of the poetry of personal anecdote.

Merely to invoke Pound is to have to acknowledge and bracket his vile political manias. I do bracket them, for the moment anyway, as they do not in their pathology affect the point that Pound renewed and intensified, for his time, the recognition of poetry as a polyvocal art expressed through the medium of the individual. He makes clear certain ratios of inheritance and invention, of personal and impersonal matter, and of originality and origins. He does this not only thematically in his reinvention in English of the Provençal of Bertran de Born, the Italian of Guido Cavalcanti, the Chinese of Li Po, or the Latin of Propertius. More molecularly, he does it in the structure and texture of verse. "Who hath taught you so subtle a measure?" his Propertius asks.[4] Pound did not, all alone, "break the pentameter" of Victorian verse; much radical Victorian metrical experimentation, often from Greek models, by Patmore, Swinburne, Bridges, Hardy, Hopkins, and others had prepared the way. But Pound did, with his own practice, with his own fine listening to foreign metrics, as well as with his rowdy polemics, retune the ear of readers of English for the early twentieth century. And by attending to the vigor and directness of presentation in Sappho, Catullus, Cavalcanti, and Villon, he renewed modes of presentation in modern poems. His recombinant relation to poetry of the past is embedded in the pun with which he opens his Canto I: "And then went down to the ship, / Set keel to breakers, forth on the godly sea, and . . ."[5] And what is he continuing, conjoining, in this epic of conscience in search of civilization, in this staggered series of inheritances (Homer passed through Andreas Divus, Greek through Latin) but the heroism of the tradition, the hero being the word itself, the first word of *The Odyssey*: "Andra moi ennepe, Mousa . . ."(The man to me sing, Muse). *Andra* is accusative of *aner*, heroic man; the hero of this vision of poetry is the English conjunction "and." Tradition, we may say, *is* conjunction.

Frank Bidart is an occult Poundian. He has said in an interview that when he was young, Eliot was probably his favorite twentieth-century poet, but that Pound was the more liberating.[6] Bidart has published, so far, six books, the most recent being *Watching the Spring Festival* in 2008. From the appearance of his first collection, *Golden State*, in 1973, he has been known in some quarters for the scandal of his outré material: the monologue of the rapist, murderer, necrophiliac Herbert White, or the case study of the suicidal anorexic Ellen West, or the searingly autobiographical poems like "California Plush." He has also been known for his eccentric typography and lineation. I want to examine his classicism, and the figure that brings it into focus: contradiction.

At every level of Bidart's poems—syntactic, prosodic, propositional—contradiction provides the emotional fuel. Broadly, we can discern contradiction in the conflicting modes he inherited from his early companionship with Lowell: on the one hand, a vision of the poem as a document of lived experience; on the other hand, the poem as an impersonal form recognizable in a kinship system of forms. Bidart's poems crucify themselves between their confessionalism and their classicism; upon that crux, they find their shapes, and their signifying pain.

In theme, Bidart springs contradiction on us at every turn. In "Elegy" (1977): "I feel too much. I can't stand what I feel." "The Book of the Body" (1977) continues that leitmotif:

> Wanting to cease to feel—;
>
> since 1967,
> so much blood under the bridge,—
>
> the deaths of both my parents,
> (now that they have no
> body, only when I have no body
>
> can we meet—)
>
> my romance with Orgasm,
>
> exhilaration like Insight, but without
> content?—
>
> the NO which is YES, the YES which is NO—

In "Golden State" (1973), the speaker announces: "Your wishes were too simple: / or too complex." The long poem "Confessional" from *The Sacrifice* (1983) concludes, *"Man needs a metaphysics; / he cannot have one."*[7]

In each case, lineation and punctuation dramatize the impossibilities within which consciousness, and conscience, frame themselves. The figure is often asyndeton, the jamming of clause against clause with no conjunction: "I feel too much. I can't stand what I feel." *"Man needs a metaphysics; / he cannot have one."* Punctuation and lineation act as pivots—a period, a colon, or a semicolon will join these unjoinable statements. Chiasm, the abba structure, also focuses the equilibrium of contradiction: NO YES YES NO. If a conjunction does lend a hand ("Your wishes were too simple: / or too complex"), it is to underline the mutual incompatibility of the declarations. The dropped lines, white spaces, indentations further emphasize opposition. The page itself, for Bidart, is a magnetic field in which the reader learns to live in the shock of powerfully attractive and repellent forces.

Asyndeton and contradiction also shape the ordering of poems within the books. What appears contradictory, of course, resolves itself often as intimate collaboration, and that is the case with the juxtaposed personal and impersonal material. The table of contents of each of these carefully constructed books rewards study. For now, we can note, simply, that almost every one of his books opens and closes with an apparently impersonal poem—a persona clearly distanced from Bidart's educated, male, ruminative late twentieth-century lyric "I." *Golden State*, for instance, opens with "Herbert White," the rapist-murderer poem, and concludes with "Another Life," self-consciously framed in quotation marks to suggest that this dream of Kennedy and de Gaulle in Paris is recounted by someone "else," some imaginary person. Within each book, the logic of juxtaposition is subtle: *Golden State* does not plunge from the monologue of Herbert White with its crescendo of MYSELF in capital letters to the father poems of section II. That transition occurs through the small, Cavafyesque "Self-Portrait, 1969," in which the subject of self-scrutiny appears in the third person: "He's *still* young—; thirty, but looks younger— / or does he?"[8] Both of these selves—the mad rapist, the "he" of "Self-Portrait, 1969"—inform the "I" who becomes subject and object of attention in "California Plush":

> The need for the past
>
> is so much at the center of my life
> I write this poem to record my discovery of it,
> my reconciliation.[9]

The poems of spelunking in the cave of autobiography in *Golden State*— the obsessively rehearsed scenes of paternal abandonment and alcoholism, of maternal ruin, mania, and smothering—give way, after section II, to a free translation of the opening lines of *The Aeneid*. Only in context does one read this translation, aloof in its archaizing diction and word order, impersonal in its epic objectivity, as a commentary on and extension of the lava flow of (presumed) privacy in section II. "Muse, make me mindful of the causes, load upon me / knowledge of her sorrows, she whom men call the queen of the gods," prays the speaker, and we seem to hear the prayer of the son of the blasted parents of the preceding poems.[10] Bidart's wordplay here leads the weighty Virgilian verb *condere* (to found) to the English verb of finding ("found Italy, found Latium"), to city-founding, to foundering ("After foundering Troy"), and brings to the surface the elegy latent in Virgil's epic. By implication, he personalizes this elegy as lyric knowledge: "how heavy the burden, to found the Roman race," suggests how heavy the burden of Bidart's book, to know one human heart.

The juxtaposition of Virgil and the family poems opens up mirrors on both sides: if it invites us to read epic as lyric and translation as original composition, it equally invites us to project epic detachment back on the autobiographical poems, and to recognize the extent to which they, too, are a fiction. These reflections only gain in complexity when we move from the *Aeneid* passage to a harshly jocose scene of double rape in the voice of a lyric "I" that both does and does not belong to Catullus (from Carmen 56), and does and does not belong to the "I" of this book who announces, in "California Plush," "And so I made myself an Easterner," and "I look at my father," and "I want to change."[11]

What we see, in Bidart, is an art of figurative contiguity, not (for the most part) metaphor; and an art of dramatic voice, not song. These energies, and his central, contradictory logic, are hard at work in his three translations of Catullus's elegiac couplet, "Odi et amo." The elegiac couplet is an inherently self-divided form, and Catullus divides it still further:

> Odi et amo. Quare id faciam, fortasse requiris?
> Nescio, sed fieri sentio et excrucior.

> (I hate and love. Why do I do this, perhaps you ask?
> I don't know, but I feel it done and am tortured.)

In an elegiac couplet, a dactylic hexameter is followed by a pentameter composed of two amputated hexameters—two hemiepe, to be technical.

So we have one duality, the distich, divided into a subduality, the two hemiepe. Catullus keeps subdividing, and each subdivision points up a contradiction: "Odi et amo" (I hate and love) is balanced at the end by another verb-plus-verb unit: "sentio et excrucior" (I feel and am tortured). The central axis of the poem impales the active and passive forms of the verb *facio*, to do: *faciam* (I do, in the subjunctive), and *fieri* (to be done). In that crisis of active and passive doing lies the mystery of love as Catullus experiences it. The chiasm of alliteration reinforces the agonized equilibrium: *q f f q*—"quare . . . faciam . . . fortasse . . . requiris." Verbs of ignorance and conscious feeling contradict and balance each other, poised at the head of each hemiepis: *nescio* (I don't know), *sentio* (I feel). In the final, passive verb of torment, *excrucior*, we find the image of the cross, the crux, the Roman instrument of torture. Hate crosses love, active crosses passive, ignorance crosses awareness: in all of these mutually exclusive but joined states, Catullus finds his poetic life and Bidart borrows his.

He published his first version of "Odi et amo" in *The Sacrifice* in 1983, placing it just before the long, self-crucifying poem "Confessional."

> I hate *and* love. Ignorant fish, who even
> wants the fly while writhing.[12]

The italicized conjunction "and" emphasizes, and endows with a twinge of hysteria, Catullus's initial paradox. The address, in the Latin, to an interlocutor ("fortasse requiris"; perhaps you ask) has dropped out, replaced by the inward-turning metaphor of the fish, the figure of driven appetite; the couplet preserves something of Catullus's symmetrical contradictions in the alliteration of "wants" and "writhing." Fourteen years later, Bidart still can't leave it alone. The version in *Desire*, in 1997, reads:

> *I hate and—love.* The sleepless body hammering a nail nails
> itself, hanging crucified.[13]

The balance of power has shifted ambiguously between hate and love, now all italicized: hate occupies more of the sentence, but that dash sets off love with more prominence. This new version multiplies self-division, in the repetition of "nail"/"nails," in the enjambed reflexive verb "nails / itself," in the alliteration of "hammering" and "hanging," and in the double sense of body as object and subject. Most tellingly, Bidart highlights the physical image of torture latent in the verb *excrucior*, forcing us not just to read it generically as torment, but also to see the crux upon which love excruciates.

In a still later reworking of the couplet in 2006, Bidart removed the italics altogether:

> What I hate I love. Ask the crucified hand that holds
> the nail that now is driven into itself, why.[14]

In restoring Catullus's original question, "Quare id faciam?" (Why do I do this?), Bidart has moved from his first focus on the *fact* of contradiction (the italicized *and* in "I hate *and* love") through the longer exploration of self-torture in his second version ("The sleepless body hammering a nail nails / itself . . .") to *interrogation of motives*. We might almost say, he moves from the data of police work to psychoanalysis, except that good police work presumably involves induction about motives also. The contradiction of feelings is now presented as a given ("What I hate I love"), and the poem proceeds to ponder the why of the case. But Bidart has subtly shifted the focus of Catullus's question. In a worldly tone of social intercourse, Catullus creates an unnamed interlocutor and a situation of dialogue ("perhaps you ask") in which to present his fiercely interior state. Bidart's most recent version retains the presence of an interlocutor through the imperative mood of the verb ("Ask"), but the tone is harsh, not polite, and the poem now throws the weight of its attention on the question itself, isolated by a strong caesura at the end of the couplet: "why?" The projection of "I's" self-torture onto the image of the crucified and crucifying hand amplifies the self-division already present in Catullus's Latin: this new "I" as consciousness is somehow separated from its experience, the hand. Catullus's "Odi et amo" may turn out to be Bidart's "Well-Tempered Clavichord" in miniature, a theme and variation throwing into high relief the minutest poetic decisions.

Many of these forces are at work in the longer poem "In the Western Night," from the book of that title in 1990. Its irregular alternation of single lines and couplets acts as a figure for solitude and communion; its symmetrical repetitions and antitheses bear the familiar stamp of Bidart's imagination: harmonies/harmonies; I said/you said; my hands/your hands. Its epilogue, the last stanza detached from Horace's Ode IV.1, gives a laboratory example of Bidart's classicism in its crucified relation to his confessionalism.

IN THE WESTERN NIGHT

1. *The Irreparable*

First, I was there where unheard
harmonies create the harmonies

we hear—

then I was a dog, sniffing
your crotch.

I asked you why you
were here; your answer was your beauty.

I said I was in need. You said
that the dead

rule and confuse our steps—

that if I helped you cut your skin
deeply enough

that, at least, was IRREPARABLE . . .

This afternoon, the clouds
were moving so swiftly—

massed above the towers, rushing.

2. *In My Desk*

Two cigarette butts—
left by you

the first time you visited my apartment.
The next day

I found them, they were still there—

picking one up, I put my lips where
yours had been . . .

•

Our not-love is like a man running down
a mountain, who, if he dares to try to stop,

falls over—
my hands wanted to touch your hands

because we had hands.

•

I put the two cigarette butts
in an envelope, carefully

taping shut the edges.
At first, the thin paper of the envelope

didn't stop

the stale smell of tobacco . . .
Now the envelope is in my desk.

3. Two Men

The man who does not know himself, who
does not know his affections that his actions

speak but that he does not
acknowledge,

who will SAY ANYTHING

and lie when he does not know that he is
lying because what he needs to believe is true

must indeed
be true,

THIS MAN IS STONE . . . NOT BREAD.

STONE. NOT CAKE. NOT CHEESE. NOT BREAD . . .

The man who tries to feed his hunger
by gnawing stone

is a FOOL; his hunger is

fed in ways that he knows cannot satisfy it.

4. Epilogue: A Stanza from Horace

At night in dreams I hold you
    and now I pursue you
fleeing though the grass of the Campus Martius,
you, through the waters (you are cruel) fleeing.[15]

The apparently autobiographical material of humiliating love has already
been chastened into considerable objectivity by the first three sections:
in the echo of Keats in "unheard/harmonies," in the lines of sight moving from "I" and "you" to clouds rushing, in passion objectified in cigarette butts, in "I" and "you" being generalized into exemplary "man":
"The man who does not know himself," "The man who tries to feed his
hunger." The Horatian epilogue distances personal passion still further,
preserving it as a scene of perpetual motion-in-stasis and as a fragment of
ancient literature, an impersonal classic.

Horace's own poem, Ode IV.1, a marvel of shifting tones and intensities, arrives by surprise at its visionary last stanza. The speaker, comically
forswearing love early in the poem and requesting Venus to address herself
elsewhere, has broken through—unwillingly, it seems—to this chamber
of lively sorrow. Horace's light-footed Latin in the Second Asclepiadean
meter perfectly paces this fugitive scene, keeping in balance the acts of
holding and pursuing, *teneo* and *sequor*; associating fleeing boy and rushing
water in the alliteration of *volucrem* (flying) and *volubilis* (rolling); moving

swiftly through enjambment in the dream logic from flight across grass to
flight in swirling water. Into this movement of dissolution, the adjective
for the boy, *dure* (hard), stands fast:

> Nocturnis ego somniis
>   iam captum teneo, iam volucrem sequor
> te per gramina Martii
>   campi, te per aquas, dure, volubilis.

Bidart captures and makes his own this interplay of holding and losing:

> At night in dreams I hold you
>   and now I pursue you
> fleeing through the grass of the Campus Martius,
> you, through the waters (you are cruel) fleeing.

Symmetrical structures lock the feeling in place, in all of its contradicto-
riness: I hold you, I pursue you. Bidart repeats "you," Horace's poignant
te, and as poignantly enjambs "you/fleeing . . . /you . . . fleeing." The
participle "fleeing" begins and ends Bidart's last two lines in a static structure of enclosure; at the same time, it fluently modifies both "you" and
"waters," and flows away in Bidart's suave, assonantal pentameter. In such
writing, translation is composition, and one can feel that Bidart is most
himself when most apparently selfless.

Like Bidart, Louise Glück is primarily a poet of speech, not song.
Like Bidart, she has taken the lyric self as the theater for her conflicts.
Her poems seem to rise from an unstaunchable sense of private hurt.
Even more than Bidart, she risks Shelleyan pathos, not falling upon
the thorns of life and bleeding, but "I speak / because I am shattered,"
announces the Red Poppy in *The Wild Iris*.[16] All the more crucial,
then, is her power to distance the lyric "I" as subject and object of
attention. This she does, and has done in the course of ten books now,
in a variety of classicizing gestures, often as projections of Greek and
Roman myth. Lacking—having deliberately refused—the resources of
traditional prosody, the power of impersonal, formal song-shape, she
has chosen a poetry of exploratory syntax. She must invent anew, in
poem after poem, the free-verse form that will impose a discipline of
detachment upon urgently subjective material. The achieved balance of
tone, of passion and irony, of heat and cold, is key to the success of her

poems, a success often to be measured as a ratio of emotional risk to a parrying critical intelligence. The risk is large; so is the corresponding triumph of formal feeling.

Glück is aware of the dangers of formulaic mythologizing, of dipping into what Philip Larkin called the "myth kitty." In her essay "The Forbidden" she has remarked on "that most depressing of strategies, the obligatory elevation of the quotidian via mythic analogy."[17] She is also aware of the risk of stasis: the poem as a representation of congealed hurt. And she has meditated with scrupulous clarity on the subject of narcissism in the essays "American Narcissism" and "Against Sincerity,"[18] perhaps in a spirit of exorcism, since her own poems arise from fiercely inward experience. But the poetic selfhood Glück praises in "American Narcissism" is protected from self-infatuation by modesty, detachment, and humor, and is seen in vital interaction with an external and populated world beyond the self. It is also, on the evidence of her own poems, a self projected into impersonal realms and into chill and elemental dramas, scenes drawn sometimes from Greek and Roman mythology, sometimes from the Bible, and sometimes from the natural world. Whatever the terrain, it provides a structural matrix so that private experience is no longer experienced as private. As she formulated it in "Against Sincerity," "The artist's task, then, involves the transformation of the actual to the true."[19] From her earliest work in *Firstborn* in 1968 and *The House on Marshland* in 1975, Glück has established a severe mode whose restriction and dry wit press anecdote to a poetry of essences.

She has pursued this conversion of anecdote to essence with remarkable consistency over the years in spite of the transformations and expansions in her work from book to book. "Pomegranate," from the *The House on Marshland*, explores the tensions between mother and daughter in the story of Demeter and Persephone. The style is minimalist in theme and lineation:

> First he gave me
> his heart. It was
> red fruit containing
> many seeds, the skin
> leathery, unlikely.
> I preferred
> to starve, bearing
> out my training. . . .[20]

This early poem draws, with Glück's characteristic wit, on the American vernacular to relieve the portentousness of the classical subject: "Now *there* / is a woman who loves / with a vengeance . . ." says Hades of the enraged Demeter. In a move we will come to recognize in later poems, "Pomegranate" passes from carefully managed, almost comic dialogue (". . . My dear / you are your own / woman, finally . . .") to a conclusion of grim spiritual discovery and indictment, the fruit of knowledge earned. Hades says of Demeter's extravagant, narcissistic grief,

> . . . but examine
> this grief your mother
> parades over our heads
> remembering
> that she is one to whom
> these depths were not offered.

Glück has taken up and expanded the struggle between Persephone and Demeter as a leitmotif throughout her masterful new book *Averno*, thirty years after "Pomegranate." Among the dimensions she has added to her earlier contemplation of the tale is the introduction of an analytical voice we can take less as that of a narrator than as an outside, orchestrating, probing intelligence, a metanarrator. This voice interferes with the story, involving the reader in its creation. In "Persephone the Wanderer" we are told:

> I am not certain I will
> keep this word: is earth
> "home" to Persephone? . . .[21]

The voice turns imperative, leaving little leeway for interpretation:

> You are allowed to like
> no one, you know. The characters
> are not people.
> They are aspects of a dilemma or conflict.

But having imposed this degree of abstraction, the voice plunges us back into the conflict between mother and daughter in crude and startling terms ("as an argument between the mother and the lover— / the daughter is just meat"), and rises to a lyric crescendo that unites a general vision of natural life, to the individual voice crying out in pain, to a personal challenge to a "you" who is suddenly drawn into the poem's field of action and releases the poem from solipsism:

> Song of the earth,
> song of the mythic vision of eternal life—
>
> My soul
> shattered with the strain
> of trying to belong to earth—
>
> What will you do,
> when it is your turn in the field with the god?

Two poems from *Vita Nova* (1999) may serve as keys to Glück's classicism; instruments of self-knowledge, they turn static sorrow into dynamic awareness, and classical emblems (Dido, Aeneas, Orpheus) into argument. But before entering *Vita Nova*, it will help to glance back at a few earlier pieces. *The Wild Iris*, which won the Pulitzer Prize in 1992, vastly widened Glück's tonal range, and in expanding her dramatis personae, expanded her notion of lyric. Now the whole book became, in essence, a single poem and the lyric voice fractured and multiplied itself. The speakers fell into three categories. We hear human sufferers, Adam and Eve figures who address an absent God in poems with titles of prayer names, "Matins" or "Vespers": "What is my heart to you / that you must break it over and over?"[22] We also hear the voices of flowers and flowering trees, nonhuman consciousnesses that both reflect and criticize the human; and we hear an irritable creator deity who speaks as weather conditions ("Clear Morning," "Retreating Wind"): "I gathered you together; / I can erase you / as though you were a draft to be thrown away."[23] Here Glück depends on the Hebrew Bible, not Greek and Roman classics, for the great acoustic chamber giving resonance to her voice; and she depends on the multiplicity of voices to correct potential self-pity. In this powerful book, "Field Flowers" seems to me an especially fine achievement in the American demotic: its power arises from its querulous, insulting, completely recognizable speech rhythms. Yet behind the American "sentence sounds," George Herbert may be felt as well:

What are you saying? That you want
eternal life? Are your thoughts really
as compelling as all that? . . .[24]

Glück's is a deliberately self-limiting art. Its diction does not, on the whole, sound etymological depths. It has few complex rhetorical let alone prosodic structures. Its force is an effect of concentration, of self-restriction, of focused images, of pacing syntax—and therefore recognition—through lineation. At its most refined, it crystallizes an almost Zen-like fullness of feeling and perception into a medium of extreme simplicity, as in these lines from "October" in *Averno*, which could be taken as a miniature *ars poetica*: "I am / at work, though I am silent."[25] The canny line break keeps the mystery of being all to itself ("I am"), but associates it in the next line with the paradox of an expressive work through silence. In Glück's poems, Pound's dictum holds true: the natural object is always the adequate symbol. Such a natural object is the card-playing in "Widows," from *Ararat* (1990); nothing is explained, nothing feels forced, yet this modern suburban family could be the players of *The Oresteia*, so fated and desolate are their games of Spite and Malice, so simple and devastating is Glück's level tone: "the one who has nothing wins."[26] In the poems with classical sources, like the Odyssean poems of *Meadowlands* (1996), she does not translate and incorporate passages in the manner of Bidart; she absorbs and refashions narrative situations, usually with a view to exposing an ideal as an illusion. So, in the poem "Telemachus' Guilt," the son speaks with analytic coldness, the expression (we surmise) of injured love:

Patience of the sort my mother
practised on my father
(which in his self-
absorption he mistook
for tribute though it was in fact
a species of rage—didn't he
ever wonder why he was
so blocked in expressing
his native abandon?): it infected
my childhood. . . .[27]

One notices here the self-correcting intelligence of the line breaks, even down to the placement of the hyphen in "self- / absorption," so that each stage of awareness gives way to a new, more bitter and disillusioned view in the following line. The self-absorption of the father observed by the son is, in fact, broken apart and examined as the compound word is both joined and broken by the hyphen and enjambment, and the poem acts as the rhythmical instrument for that process of examination. The same process corrects the potential self-absorption of the poet-speaker-ventriloquist behind all the characters in *Meadowlands*. *Vita Nova* continues this method of critical refashioning in its kaleidoscopic views of *The Aeneid*, Dante's *Inferno*, and the Orpheus myth. The book has a considered architecture and implicit overall narrative; into the story of a modern woman's mourning a divorce and her return to life after a shattering, it splices poems in the consciousness of Dido, of Aeneas, of a critical outside observer, of Orpheus, of Eurydice. To elude the self-absorption of sorrow, it multiplies selves. I would like to consider a Dido poem, "The Queen of Carthage," and an Aeneas poem, "Roman Study," as an implicit duet and antidote to solipsism.

As always in Glück, tone is key. In "The Queen of Carthage," in relation to Books I and IV of *The Aeneid*, we note all sorts of strategic diminishment. Not only has epic shrunk to a single page; the free-verse lines contract and expand, but the main thrust is toward contraction; the tone of both narrator and queen is coldly dignified, nothing like Dido's arias in Virgil's poem. Glück's modern, wounded female psyche cannot afford such arias: she needs clarity, judgment, stoical acceptance. Glück's Dido seems already to have read *The Aeneid* before embarking on her affair; with terrible lucidity, she prays for love returned "even for a short time." Why write this poem? one might ask. Does it improve on or illuminate *The Aeneid*? Or Marlowe's *Dido, Queen of Carthage*, for that matter? Part of the answer, I think, is to see it in the context of the smashed life of the *Vita Nova* narrative. Where could any poem go, we might wonder, after the triple repetition of "brutal" in the first stanza, which seems to foreclose any other movement?

THE QUEEN OF CARTHAGE

Brutal to love,
more brutal to die.
And brutal beyond the reaches of justice
to die of love.

In the end, Dido
summoned her ladies in waiting
that they might see
the harsh destiny inscribed for her by the Fates.

She said, "Aeneas
came to me over the shimmering water;
I asked the Fates
to permit him to return my passion,
even for a short time. What difference
between that and a lifetime: in truth, in such moments,
they are the same, they are both eternity.

I was given a great gift
which I attempted to increase, to prolong.
Aeneas came to me over the water: the beginning
blinded me.

Now the Queen of Carthage
will accept suffering as she accepted favor:
to be noticed by the Fates
is some distinction after all.

Or should one say, to have honored hunger,
since the Fates go by that name also."[28]

The opening lines, I said, seem to preclude development. Yet precisely in this blockage Glück's originality lies. She takes a closed case, presented in a triple repetition ("brutal") and in banal conventions of neoclassical diction ("the harsh destiny inscribed for her by the Fates"), and she allows her Dido to make several small but crucial discoveries for psychic survival. The first concerns passion and time: the longest line of the poem stretches out in its discovery that a moment of intensity has the expansiveness of eternity: ". . . What difference/between that and a lifetime: in truth, in such moments,/they are the same, they are both eternity." This remarkable line ("between that and a lifetime: in truth, in such moments"), poised on the fulcrum of the colon at its center, places "a lifetime" in balance with "moments," and both in balance with that large noun "truth." The truth of lyric time is not clock time, as each poem determines in its own way; "The Queen of Carthage" works out its equation of passion as a discovered equality: a lifetime and a moment "are both eternity."

The second discovery, the acceptance of Fate, allows Glück's speaker to accept her own abandonment and to find in it a cold distinction, even an identity, instead of annihilation. In fact, she finds in it the power to grow beyond the first-person singular pronoun, and to see herself as a character: the Queen of Carthage, as she refers to herself. In that self-detachment and theatrical self-projection, the persona within the poem becomes a poet herself, and thereby masters her suffering. The third and most original—most characteristically Glückian—discovery occurs in the final couplet:

> Or should one say, to have honored hunger,
> since the Fates go by that name also.

It is the modernist diminishing move, to see in the Fates merely the lowercase appetite, hunger. Yet one doesn't have to be sensitive to the powerful role of hunger as a metaphysical state in other poems by Glück to feel that this last couplet is not reductive: it endows a classical personified abstraction, the Fates, with physiological and ethical urgency and realism. It breaks beyond the classroom decorum of pious Aeneas and suffering Dido, and the poem's own earlier, purposefully stilted diction; it sees passion as an eternal, ferocious, and ever-lively force; it insists on some nobility in that degree of openness to experience. The poem would have achieved nothing without those last two lines: merely to have claimed "distinction" would not have been worth the candle. Its final swerve of recognition ("Or should one say") presses into a dangerous realm of candor, the admission of hunger, and in so doing sees the ancient story as present, even timeless, elemental conflict and drive. Its reductive poetic method turns out to be justified as the form for disciplined lucidity in the wake of grief. The reduction intensifies. It becomes, even, a form of amplification.

A few pages later, in "Roman Study," Glück projects herself into the other partner in this misery, Aeneas. This poem's deadpan manner may almost mask the subtlety with which the pronoun "he" slides from referring to Aeneas, to suggesting Virgil himself. The dilemma of a fugitive Trojan-turning-Roman-warrior imitating a Homeric warrior (Aeneas imitating Achilles) embodies the dilemma of a Roman poet imitating Homer (and of an American poet imitating Virgil):

He felt at first
he should have been born
to Aphrodite, not Venus,
that too little was left to do,
to accomplish, after the Greeks. . . .

And both Roman warrior and Roman poet provide the occasion for Glück's own discreet *ars poetica*. As she meditates how to funnel epic into lyric, ancient into modern, myth into analysis, she turns story into examination. The prosaic, the downbeat, even deadbeat, antisublime discovers, en route, from clause to clause, the cadences of a poetry of mind:

      . . .

And the longer he thought
the more plain to him how much
still remained to be experienced,
and written down, a material world heretofore
hardly dignified.

And he recognized in exactly this reasoning
the scope and trajectory of his own
watchful nature.[29]

This may sound like an antipoem. It *is* an antipoem, of a particularly bold sort. That is to say that it is a true classic, renewing as classic art renews, a fully dignified work, cleansing in its rigor of insight and method, and in its refusal to indulge in emotional bombast or to cash in on old or new sublimities. In any period, but especially in a time like ours when the public appetite for the exposure of private horror seems insatiable, this poem's detachment is a triumph. In her own way, Louise Glück has made good the promise of Pound's conjunction, "and." Classic art always works with that conjunction between the art of past and present. Following the dictates of her own watchful nature, she has fashioned an art that is both personal and impersonal, both continuation and invention, worthy of the vernacular and classical traditions from which she springs.

Section II

FRANCE: "I" AS ANOTHER

CHAPTER 8

The "Last Madness" of Gérard de Nerval

W hen Gérard de Nerval hanged himself on the night of January 25, 1855, in rue de la Vieille Lanterne, a sordid Parisian alley, he inscribed himself into an already hackneyed Romantic mythology which mingles poetry with death in a peculiar eros. In life he had already demonstrated himself picturesquely mad, walking his pet lobster on a blue ribbon in the park of the Palais-Royal; his death by hanging from the Queen of Sheba's garter (an old apron string) was more fantastic still. His contemporaries were not slow to respond to the event. In that year Gustave Doré created his famous lithograph depicting the slightly paunchy poet dangling from a grille fence while his female soul, of Rubenesque proportions, leans lovingly over him; a trumpet-playing skeleton pulls her up out of the shadows into what appears to be a cataract of heavenly ladies in negligé whooshing from a Gothic cathedral. So Nerval entered the ranks of the romantically insane, the martyrs to art. Years later, it was this stereotypical image of the poet that the young Mallarmé exorcised in "Le Guignon," in which the Romantic poets, after a life of insult and torment, "ridiculously hang themselves from lamp posts." And it was as a charming madman that Nerval appealed to André

Breton, Paul Éluard, and other twentieth-century Surrealists enamored of the unconscious.

Nerval was a mystic, and a learned one. He dreaded rather than encouraged his fits of madness. Yet it was not only the romanticization of his insanity and death that obscured the real nature of his work for so long. For one thing, his close friends in writing of him tended to pass over the horror of his crises as well as the courage and clarity with which he made them into art. In *L'Histoire du Romantisme*, the poet Théophile Gautier, Nerval's friend from school days and a veteran with him of the theater battles in 1830 over Victor Hugo's *Hernani*, depicts only the charm of his comrade's divagations. Alexandre Dumas, the novelist and playwright, also a close friend of Nerval, is similarly delicate in treating his insanity. In these affectionate writings Nerval appears as a sort of angelic and witty will-o'-the-wisp, but not, certainly, as the enduring poet and prose writer he has turned out to be—in the words of Marcel Proust, "surely one of the three or four great writers of the nineteenth century."[1]

A later barrier to appreciation of Nerval's worth took the form, curiously enough, of misplaced appreciation. It required his kindred spirit Proust to point this out more than half a century after the poet's death. For if Nerval was noted at all by critics after Sainte-Beuve had called him the traveling salesman between Munich and Paris, it was as the prose restorer of traditional French qualities of balance and moderation, notably in the story "Sylvie." Such a characterization not only ignored the poetic achievement of his sonnets, *Les Chimères*, but distorted the nature of his fiction, which, as Proust showed, was so far from being a demonstration of rationality that it depended for its very method on an intrinsic madness. Proust called "Sylvie" "the dream of a dream," and it was precisely its intense subjectivity and its bizarre narrative transitions incited by memory and obsession that so appealed to him.[2]

The modern reader finds still another barrier in much twentieth-century criticism of Nerval. In looking up the sources of that mysterious poem "El Desdichado" (a fragment of which found its way into *The Waste Land*), one is plunged into a stew of occult erudition which includes Apuleius, alchemy, the mysteries of Eleusis, the Rosicrucians, Freemasonry, Pythagorean mysticism, eighteenth-century Illuminists, the tarot, and Swedenborg. Although most of this information is eventually useful in understanding Nerval's myth-making, it provides only the beginning, not the conclusion, of the investigation. All too often his devotees manage to present him only as a crazed pack rat of esoteric lore.

Who, then, is Gérard de Nerval? The question leads into the heart of his work. Baptized Gérard Labrunie, he used pseudonyms obsessively, writing as "Lord Pilgrim," "Ex," "Cadet Roussel," and others until settling in 1844 on "de Nerval" from a property of his uncle's. Across his own portrait by Nadar he scrawled, "Je suis l'autre" (I am the other). His attempt to define a self beyond the bounds of space and time animates the entire oeuvre, in drama, fiction, poetry, and journalism, and leads as well to a nightmare doubling of identity as the finite, "real" self opposes the infinite longings of the spirit. Nerval uses a doubled self, often personified, as in the novella *Aurélia*, as the doppelgänger, to explore the boundaries of conscious and unconscious life and to evolve poetic and fictional techniques that seem to dissolve time and space. In so doing he places himself, as heir to Rousseau, in the main line of the Romantic enterprise, but of all his contemporaries of the heyday of French Romanticism of 1830, he survives not as a period piece but as a peculiarly modern artist. Richard Sieburth beautifully describes the subversive effect of Nerval's fables of self: "Catering to a readership increasingly eager to enter into the intimacy of its favorite writers—as Coleridge grumbled, literature had now entered 'the age of personality'— Nerval discovered that there is no deeper resource of fiction, no more powerful strategy of illusion than the autobiographical 'I.'"[3]

The modernity pertains as much to the use of the unconscious as a theme as to the literary techniques devised to register it. Nerval remained lucid to an extraordinary degree during his attacks and felt it his duty to transcribe these journeys to the land of the dead, as he regarded his crises. Again and again the myth of the Descent to Hell recurs in his work, as in "El Desdichado" (The Disinherited), which concludes with the Orphic poet singing about a woman of dangerously double nature:

> Et j'ai deux fois vainqueur traversé l'Achéron:
> Modulant tour à tour sur la lyre d'Orphée
> Les soupirs de la sainte et les cris de la fée.

> (And twice, triumphant, I crossed Acheron:
> modulating in turn on the Orphean lyre
> the sighs of the saint and the fairy's wild cry.)

But the most poignant expression of the Descent to Hell appears in *Aurélia*, his last work, whose epigraph is "Eurydice! Eurydice!" Nerval's *Vita Nuova*, it is both an account of madness and a spiritual diary, begun just after his first breakdown in 1841, continued in 1853 as the attacks intensified, and finished in 1854. Part I came out in *La Revue de Paris*, January 1, 1855, just before Nerval's death; Part II was published posthumously from uncorrected proofs apparently found on his corpse. In those last years he lived wretchedly in and out of clinics, and yet it is from that feverish period that his major works date: *Voyage en Orient* coming out in its definitive version in 1851; *Lorely, Souvenirs d'Allemagne, Les Nuits d'octobre, Les Illuminés, La Bohème galante,* and *Contes et facéties*—all in 1852; and, finally, the monuments of *Les Filles du feu* (stories), *Les Chimères* (poems), and *Aurélia*. It was also in this period that Nerval met another version of his Orphic self, a poor, mad soldier in the clinic who, when asked why he would not eat, replied, "It's because I'm dead. I was buried in such and such a cemetery, at such and such a place . . ." "And where do you think you are now?" Gérard asked him. "In Purgatory. I'm working out my expiation."[4]

Aurélia unites two dominant themes of Nerval's work: the Orphic Descent and the pursuit of the Eternal Feminine—a figure he idealized in various works as Aurélia (a name taken from stories of his adored E. T. A. Hoffmann, another artist of the Double). Aurélia is a composite of his mother, dead in his infancy; the Baroness Sophie Dawes, whose image haunted his childhood and who died shortly before his first breakdown; and the actress Jenny Colon, dead in 1842. The madness described in *Aurélia* is an attempt to transcend his temporal identity in order to join the spirits of the beloved dead, but from another level of detachment the narrator observes his own visionary labor as it proceeds through memories, dreams, and hallucinations. So Nerval appears as a "doubled" figure in the very structure of his work: "If I did not feel that the mission of a writer is to analyze sincerely what he feels in the most serious circumstances of life, and if I were not setting myself a goal I consider useful, I would stop here, and wouldn't attempt to describe what I went on to experience in a series of visions, perhaps mad, or vulgarly morbid. . . ."[5]

For Nerval, as for Proust's narrator, true perception requires a dissolution of the normal logics of time and identity. Only then can the fundamental patterns within experience be revealed. It is significant that most of his protagonists are wanderers whose watches have stopped and who are propelled only by their own psychic fluctuations. Memory and dream, then, because they permit that double transcendence (of sequential time and of the ego-bound identity), function as laboratories of the spirit. In their radically disordering capacity they are paradigms of death. And a ritual death is required, in Nerval's conception, both for the reintegration of the individual soul into the world soul[6] and for the creation of a work of art. Hence, all through his work the strong attraction to death, often personified as a seductive woman (as in the story translated here, "Octavie")—particularly after the literal death of Jenny Colon in 1842.

For Nerval, the reality underlying the world of contingency and appearance is an order both spiritual and outside of time, and it is in that order that his protagonists try to move. In the preface to the third edition of his translation of Goethe's *Faust* he writes, "It would be consoling to think that nothing dies which has struck the human intelligence, and that eternity preserves in its breast a kind of universal history, visible to the eye of the soul, a divine synchronicity which would allow us someday to share in the knowledge of him who sees all future and all past in a single glance."[7] And it is in *Faust*, which he translated at eighteen and for which Goethe complimented him, that he found already dramatized the themes of transcendence of time and the pursuit of the Eternal Feminine (Helen), as well as the Descent to the Underworld, which he would make his own and live out so tragically in trying to possess Jenny as Faust tries to possess Helen.

In Nerval's work, as in Proust's, memory presides over the soul's voyages, a memory both personal and collective. In the "Letter to Dumas" introducing *Les Filles du feu*, Nerval writes, "To invent is, ultimately, to reremember. . . ."[8] His characters, delving into their own childhoods, are brought back by geographical, musical, genealogical, and etymological clues into pre-Christian antiquity, both Druidic and classical, and experience the past as a living and present force. Concurrently, the world perceived as spirit entails a constant transmigration of souls, so that the type is always visible behind the particular. Just as Orpheus and Dante, voyagers to Hell, stand in shadowy lineaments behind the crazed soldier in *Aurélia*, so the merged figures of Isis, Venus, and the Virgin Mary stand behind Aurélia; Aurélia and Adrienne of the story "Sylvie"; the queens and saints of the sonnets; and the actress, the Bohemian girl, and Octavie of "Octavie." As the Great Goddess herself says, when she appears to Gérard in a dream in *Aurélia*: "I am the same as Mary, the same as your mother, the same as you have always loved, under all forms. . . ."[9] Each story, therefore, becomes a structure of mirroring identities.

These identities migrate not only within the frame of each tale or poem, but throughout Nerval's whole oeuvre. The same types keep reappearing in different incarnations; the sonnets can be read as glosses on the stories, and vice versa. But where the flux of identities becomes terrifying is in Nerval's own conception of himself; the fanciful pseudonymic games lead eventually to *Aurélia*, in which the narrator is haunted by a mystic double who appears at times as a hostile usurper, at times a guide and brother. In the "Letter to Dumas" Nerval tries to explain another, but related, form of what is in essence radical self-doubt: the process of imaginative identification with a fictional character. Here the prose enacts the process of doubling by "doubling" a rhetorical image. In the first section, written in the author's voice, Nerval tells how a writer can "incarnate himself within his imaginative hero" so that he "burns with the factitious flames of his ambitions and his loves." The middle section is written in the voice of the fictional hero in whom Nerval-author is thus smoldering. The hero is an actor, playing the part of Nero—a role, he says, "that identified itself with me, and Nero's tunic stuck to my scorching limbs like the centaur's cloak which devoured the dying Hercules." Author and character are united in the flame of fictitious identification, in the introduction to a book which is itself defined by fire, *Les Filles du feu* (The Daughters of Fire).

Nerval's Faustian attempts to surpass a selfhood contained in space and time take form, in his fiction, as challenges to conventions and genre, plot, and sustained illusion. Travelogues shade unexpectedly into romances, journalism into novellas, novellas into confessions and letters. The confusion of modes results partly from the pressure of debts which forced Nerval to compose hastily for piecemeal publication, but in a much more significant sense it derives from his refusal to accept boundaries, in literary form as well as in life, and from his desire to break through the surface of conventionally perceived reality to the spirit world beyond. The story "Angélique," for instance, purports not to be a work of fiction at all but an account of scholarly research. The narrator—invoking Diderot, Sterne, Swift, Rabelais, and the supposedly original Homer— leads us on a scramble through historical documents and wild fantasies, involving us somewhat in the adventures of the maiden Angélique but more in the adventure of composition itself.

These dramas of illusion and disillusion, peculiarly modern in their attention to the act of fiction-making, call for a great range of style, from bald narration of facts to the most impassioned and lyrical outcries, with elegant flicks of the pen all along the way. Action follows hard upon action; time is continually disrupted by flashbacks, detours, authorial reflections, and prefigurations. Within any particular frame of time, actions erupt mysteriously into the text and disappear without explanation after a single sentence. It is a poetic and elliptical juxtaposition of images that is at work here, not the discursive linking of events the fictional form has led us to expect. Both structure and style are designed to annihilate time.

Reality and hallucination melt together terrifyingly, as in the scene in *Aurélia* in which the narrator, who has been conversing with a star, is picked up by the night watch and spends the night on an army cot hovering between two worlds as short phrases like "lying on an army cot" hover between extravagant passages of supernatural description. Nerval's visions are potent because one very observant eye never loses sight of *this* world. The Bohemian girl who appears in "Octavie" is a poor little seamstress *and* Isis; as for Aurélia, the star both of theater and sky, Nerval acknowledges, "What madness, I told myself, to love a woman platonically who doesn't love you. My reading is to blame for this: I took the poets' inventions seriously, and made myself up a Laura or a Beatrice out of an ordinary little person of our century. . . ."[10]

Proust defined Nerval's madness as essentially literary. In *Aurélia*, the narrator asserts, "However it may be, I believe the human imagination has invented nothing that isn't true, in this world or in others, and I could not doubt what I had *seen* so distinctly."[11] He had a Keatsian faith in the imagination, refusing to distinguish not only genre from genre, but his life from his creations. Of Nerval it can truly be said that his biography lies in his works. Finally his visions overtook him, and he could no longer contain himself in his mortal time and body. But through the disorder and suffering he remained faithful to his vocation, and it was only in his third month out of the sanatorium, when he was wandering from one flophouse room to another and his poverty and sense of abandonment grew so great that he could no longer write, that he succumbed to the temptation to join his mother and his various long-dead loves. For all his fantastic scrambling of identities, he essentially knew himself, as the letter to Dumas reveals, just a year before his death: "The last madness I'll persist in is believing myself a poet."[12] Not only his sonnets, but his stories as well, have proved him right.

GÉRARD DE NERVAL: "LETTER TO DUMAS"

To Alexandre Dumas

I dedicate this book [*Les Filles du feu*] to you, my dear master, as I dedicated *Lorely* to Jules Janin. You have the same claim to my gratitude.

A few years ago, I was believed dead, and he wrote my biography. A few days ago, I was believed mad, and you devoted some of your most charming lines to my spirit's epitaph. That's a good deal of glory anticipated on my due inheritance. How will I dare wear these brilliant crowns on my brow while I'm still alive? I'd better paste on a modest air and beg the public to prune back these encomia granted to my ashes, or to the vague contents of that bottle I went looking for in the moon, like Astolfe, and which I have now returned, I hope, to the normal seat of thought.

And now that I'm no longer astride the hippogriff, and in the eyes of mortals have recovered what is vulgarly known as reason—let us be reasonable.

Here is a fragment of what you wrote about me last December 10: "He is a charming and distinguished spirit, as you can judge for yourselves, to whom a certain phenomenon occurs from time to time, which, thank goodness, we hope, is not seriously disturbing either for him or for his friends; from time to time, when some task has powerfully preoccupied him, his imagination, the house madwoman, momentarily chases out his reason, who is only the mistress there; then the former remains all alone and all-powerful in this brain nourished on dreams and hallucinations no more nor less than an opium smoker of Cairo or an Algerian hashish eater; and so, tramp that she is, she launches him into impossible theories, into unwritable books. One day he's Solomon, king of the Orient; he's rediscovered the seal for calling up spirits, he waits for the Queen of Sheba; and at that point, believe me, there's no fairy tale or story from Arabian Nights that can hold a candle to the stories he spins out for his friends, who don't know whether to pity or envy him, for the nimbleness and power of these conjured spirits, and the beauty and wealth of this queen. Another day he's Sultan of Crimea, Count of Abyssinia, Duke of Egypt, or Baron of Smyrna. Still another day he thinks he's mad, and tells how it befell him, with such gaiety, passing through such amusing adventures, that everyone yearns to follow him to the country of chimeras and hallucinations, full of oases more refreshing and shaded than those on the scorched road from Alexandria to Ammon. Another day, finally, Melancholy becomes his Muse, and then just see if you can hold back your tears, for never did Werther, never did René, never did Anthony make more grievous lamentations; more poignant sobs; more tender words; more poetic cries . . . !"

I shall try to explain to you, my dear Dumas, this phenomenon you have mentioned. There are, as you know, certain tale-tellers who cannot invent without identifying themselves with their imagined characters. You know with what conviction our old friend Nodier used to tell how he'd had the misfortune to be guillotined during the Revolution; he was so persuasive that we wondered how he'd managed to glue his head back on. . . . Well, you see, the seduction of a story can produce the same result. You can incarnate yourself, so to speak, within your imagined hero so well that his life becomes your own, and you burn in the factitious flames of his ambitions and his loves! This is just what happened to me in undertaking the story of a character who figured, I believe, around the time of Louis XV under the pseudonym of Brisacier. Where did I read the fatal biography of this adventurer? I did rediscover that of the abbot de Bucquoy; but I can't come up with the slightest historical proof for the existence of this illustrious stranger. What would have been only a game for you, master—who have played so well with our chronicles and memories, that posterity will never untangle the true from the false, and will consider as your own inventions all those historic figures you used in your novels—became an obsession for me, a madness. To invent is, ultimately, to re-remember, as some moralist has said; not being able to find proofs of the material existence of my hero, I suddenly believed in the transmigration of souls as firmly as Pythagoras or Pierre Leroux. The eighteenth century itself, in which I believed I'd lived, was full of these illusions. Voisenon, Moncrir, and Crébillon the Son all wrote a thousand such adventures. Remember the courtier who recalled having been a sofa; upon which Schahabaham cried out enthusiastically: What! You were a sofa! But that's terribly elegant. . . . Tell me, were you embroidered?

Well, as for me, I was embroidered with every possible stitch. From the moment I'd seized the series of all my previous lives, it didn't matter whether I'd been prince, king, magus, genius, or even God, the chain was broken and hours passed like minutes. It would have been the Dream of Scipio, Tasso's *Vision*, or Dante's *Divine Comedy* if I'd been able to concentrate my memories into a masterpiece. Renouncing fame as genius, visionary, or prophet, I can only offer you what you so aptly call "impossible theories," and "unwritable books," of which this is the first chapter, apparently a sequel to Scarron's *Comic Novel*. . . . Judge it for yourself:

I'm still in prison, Madam; still rash, still guilty, it appears, and still trusting—alas!—in that beautiful star who was pleased to consider me, for a moment, her fate. "The Star" and "Fate"; what a charming couple in the poet Scarron's novel! But it's hard to play those two roles well these days. The heavy cart that once jolted us over the uneven paving stones of Mans has been replaced by carriages, post chaises, and other new inventions. Where is adventure, nowadays? Where is that charming poverty that made us your equals and your companions, madam actresses, we, always "poor poets," and often as not poverty-stricken? You betrayed us, denied us! And you used to complain of our arrogance! You began traipsing after rich lords, dandified, gallant, and bold, and left us in some wretched inn to foot the bill for your crazy orgies. And so I, the brilliant actor of the old days, the unknown prince, the mysterious lover, disinherited, exiled from happiness, the handsome shadowed one, adored by marchionesses and presidents' wives, I, the unworthy favorite of Madame Bouvillion, I've not been better treated than that wretched Ragotin, a provincial poetaster, a lawyer! . . .

My good complexion, disfigured by a great bandage, only helped to condemn me all the more absolutely. The innkeeper, seduced by La Rancune's arguments, was satisfied to hold me as security, the true son of the Great Khan of Crimea, sent here to study, and well known throughout Christian Europe under the name of Brisacier. If that lout, that worn-out conniver, had just left me a few old louis, some carolus, or even some poor old watch set with fake gems, I could at least have demanded some respect from my accusers, and avoided the pathetic misadventures of such an idiotic intrigue. You went one better; the only clothes you left me were a horrid puce frock coat, a black-and-blue-striped jerkin, and breeches in a highly questionable state of repair. As a result, the worried innkeeper, lifting up my valise after your departure, began to suspect a part of the sad truth and came to accuse me right out of being a prince of smugglers. At that, I was about to snatch up my sword, but La Rancune had carried it off with him under the pretext that he had to keep me from thrusting it through my breast before the eyes of the ungrateful woman who'd betrayed me. This last precaution was useless, oh La Rancune! You can't thrust a stage sword through your heart, you don't play the cook Vatel, you don't act like the hero of a novel when you're really a tragic hero: and I call all our companions to witness that that kind of death is impossible to stage effectively. I know very well you can stick the sword in the ground and throw yourself on it with your arms flung wide; but here we are in a room with a parquet floor and no rug in spite of the cold season. And anyway, the window is quite large enough and high enough over the street to permit any tragic desperation to finish its course out there. But . . . but, I've told you a thousand times, I'm an actor with religious faith.

Do you remember the way I played Achilles, when, by chance, passing through some third- or fourth-rate city, we got the whim of spreading the neglected cult of ancient French tragedy? I was noble and powerful, wasn't I, in the gilt helmet with the purple crest, under my sparkling breastplate, draped in a blue cloak? And what a shame it was then to see a father as vile as Agamemnon quarreling with the priest Calchas for the honor of shoving poor tearful Iphigenia even more quickly under the knife! I burst like lightning into the midst of this cruel and forced scene; I gave hope back to the mothers and courage to the poor young girls, always sacrificed to some duty, God, nation's revenge, honor or profit of a family! . . . Because it was well understood that such is the eternal story of human marriage. The father will always give up the daughter through ambition, and the mother will always be eager to sell her; but the lover will not always be that honest Achilles, so handsome, so well-armed, so gallant and fearsome, even though a bit too much of a rhetorician for a soldier. As for me, I was outraged sometimes at having to spout such long speeches for such a clear-cut case, and before an audience easily won over to my side. I was tempted to run them all through, the king of kings' whole imbecile court with his honor guard of sleeping extras! The public would have been delighted; but would have ended up thinking the play too short, and deciding you need time to see a princess, a lover, and a queen suffer; to watch them cry, fly into rages, and spew out a torrent of harmonious insults against the old authority of priest and king. All that is worth at least five acts and two hours, and the public wouldn't put up with anything less; it has to have its revenge on the brilliance of this unique family, pompously seated on the Greek throne, before which Achilles himself can only fly off the handle in words; it has to know all the suffering under that purple—and yet irresistible majesty! Those tears fallen from the loveliest eyes in the world onto Iphigenia's radiant breast intoxicate the crowd just as much as her beauty, grace, and the brilliance of her royal dress! That gentle voice begging for life, reminding them that she has not yet lived; those soft eyes, holding back tears to flatter a father's weakness, first coquetry, alas! her lover will never see! . . . Oh, how they concentrate, every one of them, to take it in! Kill her? Her! But who would dream of it? Great gods! Perhaps no one? . . . But no; everyone has privately decided she must die for them all, rather than live for one; everyone has found Achilles too handsome, too great, too proud. Will Iphigenia be carried off again by the Thessalian vulture, as that other, Leda's daughter, was once before by a shepherd prince from the voluptuous coast of Asia? That's the question for all the Greeks, and that's also the question for the public that judges us in these hero roles. And I, I felt myself as despised by the men as admired by the women when I played one of those proud conquering lover parts. For instead of some chilly backstage princess brought up to intone these immortal lines lugubriously, I had to defend, astonish, preserve, a true daughter of Greece, a pearl of love, grace, and purity, worthy indeed of being claimed by men from the jealous gods! Was she Iphigenia alone? No, she was Monime, Junie, she was Bérénice, she was all the heroines inspired by the beautiful blue eyes of Mademoiselle Champmesle, or by the adorable graces of the noble virgins of Saint-Cyr. Poor Aurélia! Our companion, our sister, won't you have any regrets, in these times of rapture and pride? Didn't you love me just for a moment, Cold Star! seeing me suffering, fighting, or weeping for you? Will the glory the world surrounds you with today wipe out the radiant image of our common triumphs? They all asked, every night: Who is this actress so far above everything we've applauded? Aren't we mistaken? Is she really as young, as fresh, as honest as she seems? Are those real pearls and opals streaming in her ash-blond hair, did the poor child come by that lace veil quite legally? Isn't she ashamed of that brocaded satin, of that heavily draped velvet, of those peluches and ermines? All that is so old-fashioned, it hints of fantasies beyond her years. . . . The mothers whispered like that, even as they admired the consistent choice of finery and ornaments from another century reminding them of their own happier days. The young women envied, criticized, or sadly admired. But I, I had to see her all the time not to feel dazzled by her, and to be able to meet her eyes as our roles demanded. That's why Achilles was my triumph; but how often the other roles embarrassed me! The misery of not daring to change scenes as I pleased, even sacrificing the thoughts of genius to my respect and love! The Britannicuses and Bajazets, those timid, captive lovers, were not for me. Young Caesar's purple: now that seduced me! But what a pity, then, to have nothing to say but cold treacheries. Alas! Was that Nero, so famous in Rome? this handsome fighter, this dancer, this ardent poet, whose only wish was to please everyone? Here's what history's made of him, and what the poets, following history, have dreamed. Oh! give me his rages to act out, but as for his power, I'd be afraid to accept it. Nero! I understand you, alas! not from Racine, but from my own torn heart when I dared to borrow your name! Yes, you were a god, you wanted to burn Rome, you had the right to, maybe, since Rome had insulted you! . . .

A whistle, a vile whistle, before her eyes, near her, because of her! A whistle she blames on herself—though my fault (understand this!). And you ask what one does when one is holding lightning bolts! . . . Oh! Come, my friends! For a moment I had the idea of being true, of being great, of immortalizing myself, finally, on your stage of planks and back cloths, in your trivial comedy! Instead of replying to one insult with another, which earned me the punishment I'm still suffering, instead of provoking the whole vulgar audience to hurl itself onstage and to beat me shamefully . . . I had, for a split second, the idea, the sublime idea, worthy of Caesar himself, the idea they'd all have admitted was equal to the great Racine, the august idea, finally, to burn down the theater and the audience, and all of you! and to carry her out alone through the flames, disheveled, half-naked, true to her role, or at least according to Burrhus's classic account. And you can be sure that nothing would have snatched her from me then, from that instant, until the scaffold! and from there into eternity!

Oh, remorse of my feverish nights and my days drenched in tears! What! I could have done it and didn't want to? What! You insult me again, you who owe your lives more to my pity than to my fear! I could have burned them all! Think about it: the Theater of P*** has only one exit; ours let out on a little back street, but the hall where you all sat is on the other side of the stage. I only had to detach a lamp to ignite the backdrops, and that without any fear of being surprised since the guard couldn't see me, and I was all alone listening to the tired exchange between Britannicus and Junie, waiting to reenter and make my scene. I fought with myself throughout this interval; back onstage I clenched a glove I'd picked up in my fingers; I waited to revenge myself more nobly than Caesar himself for an insult I'd felt with all the heart of a Caesar. . . . Well! Those cowards didn't dare start up again! My eye shot lightning at them fearlessly, and I was going to pardon the public, if not Junie, when she dared. . . . Immortal gods! . . . Here, let me say what I want! . . . Yes, ever since that evening, my madness is to believe myself a Roman, an emperor; my role identified itself with me, and Nero's tunic sticks to my limbs and scorches them, as the centaur's cloak devoured the dying Hercules. Let's not fool around anymore with holy matters, even from a people and an age long since extinguished, for some fire may still be left under the ashes of the Roman gods! . . . Friends! You must understand that for me it was not a matter of a cold translation of formal words; but of a scene where everything was alive, where three hearts fought with equal chances; where, just as in circus games, real blood might run! And the audience knew it perfectly well, that small-town audience so well informed of all our backstage carryings-on; those women, quite a few of whom would have loved me if I'd been willing to betray my only love! Those men, all jealous of me because of her; and the other, the well-chosen Britannicus, poor confused lover who trembled before me and before her as well, but who was to vanquish me in this terrible game, where the newcomer has all the advantages and all the glory. . . . Ah! Love's neo-phyte knew his business well . . . but he had nothing to fear, for I'm too just to commit a crime against someone who loves as I do, and it's just there that I differ from the ideal monster the poet Racine dreamed up: I'd burn Rome without a second thought, but in saving Junie, I'd save my brother Britannicus too.

Yes, my brother, yes, like me, poor child of art and imagination, you conquered her, you deserved her merely in claiming her from me. The heavens keep me from abusing my age, my strength and this noble mood health has restored to me to attack her choice, or her whim—hers, the all-powerful, the just, the goddess of my dreams as of my life! . . . Only, for a long time I feared my distress would do you no good, and that the handsome dandies of the town would steal from both of us what was lost only to me.

The letter I've just received from La Caverne clears up this point com-pletely. She advises me to give up forever "an art which is not made for me, which I don't need. . . ." Alas! It's a bitter joke, for I never needed it so much, if not the art itself, at least its brilliant products. That's what you haven't understood. You think you've done enough in recommending me to the authorities in Soissons as a noble person whose family wouldn't abandon him, but whom you were obliged to leave, in mid-journey, because of the violence of his illness. Your La Rancune introduced himself at the town hall and to my host, putting on the airs of a Spanish grandee forced by a sad accident to pause for a couple of nights in this miserable place; you others, obliged to leave P*** in a hurry the day after my dis-comfiture, you had no desire to pass yourselves off here as infamous actors, I can understand that: it's bad enough to have that mask nailed to your face on the occasions you can't avoid. But I, what am I supposed to say, and how can I disentangle myself from the infernal web of intrigue La Rancune's stories have trapped me in? Corneille's great couplet from *Le*

Menteur surely helped him make up his tale, for the cad could never have invented it for himself. . . . Imagine. . . . But what can I tell you that you don't already know, and that you haven't plotted together in order to ruin me? Hasn't that ingrate, the cause of all my trouble, spun together all the most inextricable satin threads her Arachne's fingers ever stretched around a poor victim? . . . A pretty piece of work! Well, I'm taken, I admit it; I give up, I ask for mercy. You can take me back with you without fear, and if the swift post chaises that carried you off on the Flanders road almost three months ago have already been replaced by the humble cart of our first escapades, deign to accept me at least in the capacity of monster, of phenomenon, of wide-eyed marvel to bring in the crowd, and I agree to carry out these various assignments in such a manner as to please the severest of provincial amateurs. . . . Answer me now at the post office, for I don't trust my host's curiosity: I'll send one of the servants to pick it up, a man who's devoted to me. . . .

—The Illustrious Brisacier.

What can be done now with this hero abandoned by his mistress and companions alike? Is he really only a stray actor, justly punished for impudence toward the public, for his idiotic jealousy, his mad pretensions? How will he manage to prove he's the true son of the Khan of Crimea, as La Rancune's cunning story proclaimed him? How, after such an extraordinary downfall, will he throw himself into more exalted destinies? . . . These are problems which wouldn't give you the slightest trouble, but which have plunged me into a strange spiritual distemper. Once convinced that I was writing my own story, I set myself to translating all my dreams, all my emotions, I lingered tenderly over this love for a fugitive star who left me alone in the night of my fate, I wept, I shuddered at the empty apparitions in my sleep. Then a ray of divine light gleamed in my hell; surrounded by monsters with whom I wrestled obscurely, I grasped Ariadne's thread and since then all my visions have been celestial. Someday I'll write an account of this Descent to the Underworld, and you'll see that if it was always irrational, it was not entirely lacking in reason.

And since you had the imprudence to mention one of the sonnets composed in a state of "supernaturalist reverie," as the Germans would say, you must hear them all. You'll find them at the end of the book. They are no more obscure than Hegel's *Metaphysics* or Swedenborg's *Memorabilia*, and would lose their charm in being explicated, even if that were possible.

Admit, at least, their excellence in style;—the last madness I'll persist in is believing myself a poet: it's up to the critics to cure me.

GÉRARD DE NERVAL: "OCTAVIE"

In the spring of 1835 a keen desire to see Italy took hold of me. Every day, waking up, I breathed in the bitter scent of alpine chestnut trees, in anticipation; in the evening the waterfall at Terni and the foaming fountainhead of the Tiber gushed forth for me alone between the frayed side flaps of the wings in a little theater. . . . A lovely voice, like the Sirens', whispered in my ears, as if the reeds of Lake Trasimeno had suddenly begun to speak. . . . I had to go, leaving in Paris a difficult love from which I wished to escape by distracting myself.

Marseilles was my first stop. I went to the beach every morning at Château-Vert, and as I swam I could see the bay's laughing islands in the distance. Every day, also, in the azure gulf, I met with a young English girl; her flowing body cut through the green water close to mine. This water maiden, called Octavie, came to me one day all radiant in triumph at a strange catch she had made. She held a fish in her white hands, and gave it to me.

I couldn't stop myself from smiling at such a present. Meanwhile, cholera had taken over the city, and to escape the quarantine I decided to continue my journey by land. I saw Nice, Genoa, Florence; I admired the Duomo and the Baptistry, the masterpieces of Michelangelo, the Leaning Tower, and the Campo Santo of Pisa. Then, taking the Spoleto Road, I settled down for ten days in Rome. The cupola of St. Peter's, the Vatican, the Coliseum appeared to me as in a dream. I hurried to take the coach to Civitavecchia, where I was to board the boat.—For three days, the raging sea held up the arrival of the steamship. One day, as I walked lost in thought along that desolate beach, I was almost eaten alive by dogs.

The night before my departure, the local theater put on a French vaudeville show. A blond and lively head attracted my attention. It was the young English girl, sitting in a box over the front stage. She was with her father, who seemed weak, and to whom the doctors had recommended the climate of Naples.

The next morning I bought my ticket joyfully. The English girl was on deck, pacing up and down with large steps, and, impatient at the ship's slowness, she printed her ivory teeth into the rind of a lemon.—Poor girl, I said to her, you have a chest ailment, I'm sure, and that's not what you need. She gazed at me fixedly and replied, Who told you?—The Tiburine Sibyl, I said, unruffled.—Go on! she said, I don't believe a thing you say.

With that, she looked at me tenderly and I couldn't keep myself from kissing her hand.—If I were stronger, she said, I'd teach you how to lie! . . . And, laughing, she threatened me with the gold-headed cane she held in her hand.

Our ship was approaching the port of Naples and we crossed the bay between Ischia and Nisida, washed in the fires of the Orient. She spoke again:—If you love me, wait for me tomorrow at Portici. I don't make this kind of appointment with everyone.

She stopped at the Piazza del Molo and went with her father to the Hotel Roma, newly built on the quay. As for me, I took lodgings behind the Florentine Theater. I spent the day exploring the Via Toledo, the Piazza del Molo, and visiting the Museo degli Studii; then in the evening I went to see the ballet at the Teatro San Carlo. There I met the Marquis Gargallo, whom I had known in Paris and who invited me to tea, after the show, at his sisters' house.

I'll never forget the enchanting party that followed. The marquise presided over a vast reception hall filled with foreigners. The conversation was a little like that of the Précieuses; I thought I was in the blue room at the Hotel Rambouillet. The marquise's sisters, beautiful as the Graces, reawakened my interest in ancient Greece. They argued for a long time about the shape of the stone at Eleusis, wondering whether it was triangular or square. The marquise could have settled the question, for she was as beautiful and proud as Vesta. I left the palazzo so dizzy from this philosophic discussion I couldn't find my way back to my lodgings. Wandering about the city like that, I was bound to end up as the hero of some adventure or other. The encounter I had that night is the subject of the following letter, which I later sent to her whose fatal love I had tried to escape in leaving Paris.

"I am extremely troubled. I haven't seen you for four days, or else I only see you surrounded by company; I have dire forebodings. I do believe you've been sincere with me; whether or not you've changed in the last few days, I don't know, but I fear that you have. My God! Have pity on my uncertainty, or you'll call down some grief upon us. You see, I should be accusing myself. I've been more timid and devoted than a man should show. I've surrounded my love for you with such shyness,

I've been so frightened of offending you—you, who already punished me so cruelly once before—that I have perhaps pushed my delicacy too far, and made you think I had cooled toward you. Well, I respected your important day, I suppressed emotions sufficient to have shattered the soul, and I hid myself under a smiling mask while my heart panted and burned. Others would not have had such self-control, but then perhaps no one else has given you proof of such real affection; or has known so well what you are worth.

"Let us speak frankly: I know there are ties a woman can cut only with pain, and inconvenient relationships that can only be broken off slowly. Have I asked too painful sacrifices from you? Tell me your sorrows, I will understand them. Your fears, your whims, the requirements of your position, none of all this can shake the immense affection I feel for you, or disturb the purity of my love. But we will see together what must be admitted or fought, and if there are knots which must be cut and not untied, let me take responsibility for it. It would be inhuman, at this point, not to be frank; for, as I've told you, my life hangs on your will, and you know well that my greatest desire is only to die for you!

"To die, Great God! Why does this idea continually recur to me, as if only my death could equal the happiness that you promise? Death! Yet the word does not fill my thoughts with gloom. She appears to me crowned with pale roses, as after a banquet; I have dreamed sometimes that she waited for me, smiling, at the bedside of a beloved woman; after the happiness and intoxication, saying to me:—Come, young man! You've had your share of joy in this world. Now, come sleep, come rest in my arms. I'm not beautiful, no, but I'm good-hearted and I care for you; I don't give pleasure, but eternal peace.

"But where had this image already appeared to me? Ah, I've told you, it was at Naples, three years ago. One night, near the Villa Reale, I came across a young woman who looked like you, a sweet creature who made her living doing gold embroidery on church vestments. She seemed bewildered; I brought her back to her house, though she told me of her lover in the Swiss Guards, whose arrival she feared. Even so, she didn't have to be pressed to admit that she preferred me. . . . What can I tell you? A whim seized me to lose my head for a whole night and to pretend that this woman, whose language I could barely understand, was you, come down to me by magic. Why should I hide this whole adventure from you, and the strange illusion my soul accepted painlessly, especially after the glasses of bubbling Lacrymae Christi that had been poured for me at supper? The room I entered had something mystical about it, by chance or by the odd choice of objects it contained. A black madonna covered with trinkets, whose antique costume my hostess had been hired to repair, stood on a bureau near a bed with green serge curtains; farther off, a figure of Saint Rosalie, crowned with violet roses, seemed to guard a cradle where a child slept; the whitewashed walls were decorated with old paintings of the four elements representing mythological deities. Add to all this the beautiful disorder of shining cloth, artificial flowers, Etruscan vases; mirrors in gilt frames brightly reflecting the light from the one copper lamp; and on a table, a Treatise of divination and dreams that made me think my companion must be a bit of a sorceress, or at least a gypsy.

"A good old woman with large, solemn features went back and forth, waiting on us; I think it must have been her mother! Lost in thought, without saying a word, I kept staring at the young woman who reminded me of you so exactly.

"She kept asking me: —Are you sad? And I told her: —Don't talk to me, I can hardly understand you. It tires me out to hear and to speak Italian. —Oh! she said, I can speak differently. And she broke into a language I had never heard. It was all sonorous and guttural syllables, delightful warblings, probably some primitive tongue; Hebrew, Syriac, I don't know what. She smiled at my astonishment, and going over to the bureau, she pulled out costume jewelry with fake gems, necklaces, bracelets, a crown; decked out in these, she returned to the table, and remained serious for a long time. The old woman burst out laughing when she came back in, and told me, I think, that that was how she dressed herself up for festivals. At that moment the child woke up and began to howl. The two women ran to the cradle, and soon the young one came back to me proudly holding the calmed bambino in her arms.

"She spoke to it in the secret language I had admired, and teased it gracefully; as for me, not accustomed to the burning wines of Vesuvius, I felt everything spinning in front of my eyes: this woman with her strange manners, dressed like a queen, proud and whimsical, appeared to me like one of those Thessalian witches to whom you gave your soul in exchange for a dream. Oh! Why was I not afraid to tell you this story? It's because you know perfectly well it too was only a dream, in which you alone were queen.

"I tore myself away from this ghost who both fascinated and frightened me. I wandered in the empty city until the first church bells; then, sensing the arrival of morning, I followed the little streets behind Chiaia and began to climb Posilippo above the cave. At the summit, I strolled about, gazing at the sea, now blue; at the city with its waking noises; and at the islands in the bay, where the sun began to gild the villa roofs. I wasn't a bit sad; I paced with large steps, I ran, I charged down slopes, I rolled in the damp grass; but the idea of Death was in my heart.

"Oh gods! I don't know what deep despondency possessed my soul, but it was only the cruel thought that I was unloved. I had glimpsed the ghost of happiness, I had tried all the gifts of God, I was beneath the most beautiful sky in the world, in the midst of the most perfect nature, the most spectacular view that has ever been given to man; but four hundred leagues from the only woman who existed for me, a woman who was ignorant of my very existence. Not to be loved, not even to have the hope of it! It was then that I was tempted to go settle my accounts with God for my singular life. It required only a step: at the spot where I stood, the mountain was sliced like a cliff, the sea muttered below, blue and pure; only a moment of suffering remained. Oh! This thought dizzied me frightfully. Twice I launched myself, and twice some unknown force threw me back, alive, on the earth which I clutched. No, my God! You didn't create me for everlasting grief. I don't want to outrage you with my death; but give me the strength; give me the power; above all, give me the will; that guides some to the throne, others to glory, and others to love!"

Throughout this strange night, a rather rare event had occurred. Toward dawn, all the windows of the house in which I found myself had lit up; a hot and sulfurous dust choked my breath, and, leaving my easy conquest asleep on the terrace, I started up the alleys leading to the Castle of St. Elmo. As I climbed, the pure morning air filled my lungs; I rested deliciously beneath the villa arbors, and without terror I contemplated Vesuvius still covered by a dome of smoke.

It was at that moment that I was seized by the dizziness I mentioned; the thought of the appointment with the young English girl tore me away from the fatal notions I had conceived. After refreshing my mouth with one of those enormous bunches of grapes the women sell in the market, I set out for Portici and went to visit the ruins at Herculaneum. The streets were powdered with metallic ash. At the ruins, I climbed down to the underground city and roamed for a long time from building to building, asking the monuments for the secret of their past. The temples of Venus and Mercury spoke in vain to my imagination. They had to be peopled with living figures. I climbed back up to Portici and waited in a pensive mood beneath an arbor for my mystery woman.

She appeared soon, guiding her father's painful steps, and shook my hand firmly, saying: —Good. We picked a carriage and went to visit Pompeii. I led her happily down the silent streets of the ancient Roman colony. I had already studied its most secret passageways. When we came to the Temple of Isis, I had the joy of explaining to her faithfully the details of the cult and ceremonies I had read about in Apuleius. She wanted to play the part of the goddess herself, and I was ordered to take on the role of Osiris, whose divine mysteries I unfolded.

Returning, shaken by the grandeur of the ideas we had resurrected, I didn't dare speak to her of love. . . . I was so cool that she reproached me. Then I admitted I no longer felt worthy of her. I told her the mysterious story of the apparition that had reawakened an old love in my heart, and all the sadness following that fatal night in which the ghost of happiness had been only a reproach for a perjury.

Alas! How far away it all is now! Ten years ago, I passed through Naples again, coming back from the Orient. I stopped at the Hotel Roma, and there I found the same young English girl. She had married a famous painter who had been stricken with total paralysis soon after their wedding. Bedridden, in his whole face he could move only his large black eyes, and though he was still young there was no hope for recovery, even in other climates. The poor girl had dedicated herself to living sadly between her husband and her father, and not even her gentleness and virginal candor could calm the atrocious jealousy the husband nursed in his soul. Nothing could persuade him to allow his wife to take her walks freely; he reminded me of that black giant who keeps eternal vigil in the cave of the spirits, and whose wife is forced to thrash him to keep him from falling asleep. Oh, mystery of the human soul! Is such a scene a cruel sign of divine revenge?

I could devote only one day to the spectacle of this suffering. The ship which brought me to Marseilles carried away the memory of that darling apparition like a dream, and I told myself that perhaps I had left all happiness there, behind me. Octavie has kept its secret to herself.

GÉRARD DE NERVAL: FROM "LES CHIMÈRES"[1]

EL DESDICHADO

I am the Man of Darkness—the widower—unconsoled,
the Prince of Aquitaine in the ruined tower;
my only star is dead, and my sky-charted lute
bears Melancholy's sign, the black sun, for her.

In the night of the tomb, you who comforted me,
give back Posilippo and the Italian sea,
the flower that charmed my desolate heart,
the arbor where the grapevine twined with the rose.

Am I Amor or Apollo? Lusignan or Biron?
My forehead still burns with the queen's kiss.
I have dreamed in the cave where the siren swims. . . .

And twice, triumphant, I have crossed Acheron:
modulating in turn on the Orphean lyre
the sighs of the saint and the fairy's wild cry.

MYRTHO

I think of you, Myrtho, divine sorceress; of high
Posilippo blazing in thousandfold fire;
of the Orient luster flooding your brow;
of the black grapes twined in the gold of your hair.

I was drunk on your wine, and the secret flash
of your smiling eyes, when they found me in prayer
in the feet of Iacchus. For the Muse
has made me one of the sons of Greece.

I know why the crater there gaped wide once more.
Yesterday you brushed it with a nimble foot,
and the sky was suddenly choked with ash.

Ever since a Norman duke smashed your gods of clay,
always, beneath Virgil's laurel, the pale
hydrangea has grown with the green myrtle bough.

HORUS

The god Kneph, trembling, trembled the world:
Isis, the mother, sat up on her bed,
gestured in hatred at her savage mate,
and again in green eyes her old passion flared.

"Look at him croak, the old lecher," she said.
"All the world's storms have heaved from his mouth;
bind up his bowleg, put out his squint eye,
he's the god of volcanoes, winter's king!

"The eagle's just flown, the new spirit calls,
I have put on Cybele's gown for him:
Osiris and Hermes' darling child!"

The goddess had fled in her gilded shell;
we saw her loved image gleam back from the sea
and the skies shone beneath Isis's veil.

ANTEROS

You ask why I hold such rage in my heart
and on my neck, bending, a still unconquered head:
it's because I spring from Antaeus's seed
and fling his spears back against the victor god.

Yes, I am of those the Revenger inspires,
he has marked my brow with his angry lip;
beneath Abel's pallor, stained—alas!—with blood,
I burn sometimes with Cain's implacable fires.

Jehovah! The last one subdued by your power
who cried from Hell's depths, "Oh tyranny!"
was my ancestor Baal, or Dagon my sire.

They dipped me three times in Cocytus's flood:
and protecting alone my Amalek mother
I again sow the old dragon's teeth at her feet.

DELFICA

Daphne, do you know that old sentimental song,
under the sycamore, or white laurel tree,
the olive, the myrtle, or trembling willows,
that love song, Daphne, that comes back and back again?

Remember the temple of vast colonnades,
the bitter lemons your teeth once printed,
and the sea cavern, fatal to careless guests,
where the conquered dragon's ancient seed still sleeps?

They'll return, these gods you mourn for still.
Time will restore ancient days, and their law.
The earth shudders with prophetic breath.

Meanwhile, the sybil with the Latin face
drowses beneath the Arch of Constantine
—and nothing disturbs the grave lintel above.

ARTEMIS

The Thirteenth returns . . . The first hour again.
The only one, always—or the instant alone.
Are you queen, you, the first, or the last of the hours?
Are you king, you the only or last of her loves?

In her grave, love her, who loved you in the womb.
She whom alone I adored loves me tenderly still.
It's death—or the dead girl. O torture, delight:
The rose she clasps is the *rose tremière*.

Neapolitan saint with your hands full of flames,
rose of violet heart, bloom of Saint Gudula:
have you found your cross in the desert of skies?

White roses, fall. You insult our gods.
Fall, white phantoms, from your burning sky.
The saint of the abyss is more blessed in my eyes.

CHAPTER 9

Rimbaud: Insulting Beauty

"**M**esdames, Messieurs. J'apporte, en effet, des nouvelles. Les plus surprenantes. Même cas ne si vit encore. On a touché au vers" (Ladies and Gentlemen. I bring news. Most remarkable news. The like was never seen before. Verse has been tampered with). With these words, Mallarmé, high priest of Symbolism, carried the news of radical French poetry to Oxford and Cambridge in his lectures in March 1894. Mallarmé went on in his sibylline fashion to describe the disturbance of the classical Alexandrine line in its evolution into two experimental forms, the prose poem and *vers libre*. Supremely sensitive to the displacement of a single syllable, feeling its effect as though a star had moved from its normal place in the heavens, Mallarmé, oddly, does not notice the crucial role played in this poetic revolution by his younger contemporary Arthur Rimbaud, who had died three years earlier. Other innovative poets, more clearly Mallarmé's acolytes, absorb his attention: Gustave Kahn, Jean Moréas, Francis Viélé-Griffin. Yet it was Rimbaud who had most decisively shown the way in this tampering with verse, in both the prose poem and *vers libre*, in *Une Saison en enfer*, obscurely published in 1873, and in *Illuminations*, published without the author's knowledge in 1886. I would like to examine Rimbaud's assault on the classical ideal of beauty in the Alexandrine line, and to suggest some of the costs as well as gains of that assault.

We should start with the line itself. Dominant in serious French poetry since the seventeenth century, the Alexandrine had the force of an institution, and had outlived governments and political revolutions. With its twelve syllables symmetrically balanced at the central pause, or caesura, and its hemistiches—half lines—dividing into predictable units, the line embodied a metaphysical unity and a centralizing power, resonating from Racine through Hugo and Baudelaire and on into the boyhood verse of Rimbaud—this "strict observer of the ancient game," as Mallarmé called him.[1] In Rimbaud's hands, the Alexandrine concentrated an infinity of desire into its vatic abacus of twelve syllables. "Qui ne sait se borner, ne sut jamais écrire," had propounded Boileau, legislator of La Pléiade, in 1674 in his didactic poem "Art Poétique" (he who knows no limits, never learned to write).[2] The young Rimbaud made of limitation not only a prosodic art, but also a theme and a form of precocious wisdom. His Drunken Boat's delirious vowels and enjambments create an oceanic dream of erotic and spiritual expansion, but the poem comes to rest in a dirty puddle in which a crouching child launches his paper boat. Expansion, in Rimbaud's early poems, is always tested against contraction.

Let us tune our ears, first, to the beauty in the ratios of expansion and limit Rimbaud had already mastered at the age of seventeen, and which he would, in a heartbeat, set about to destroy.

In "Le Bateau ivre" (The Drunken Boat), Rimbaud's Alexandrine launches into ecstasy in the intercourse of vowels and dipthongs, creating le Poème de la Mer—the Poem of the Sea—

. . .

> Où, teignant tout à coup les bleuités, délires
> Et rythmes lents sous les rutilements du jour,
> Plus fortes que l'alcool, plus vastes que nos lyres,
> Fermentent les rousseurs amères de l'amour![3]

(Where, dyeing suddenly the blue washes, deliriums/And rhythms slow under the shimmering of day,/Stronger than alcohol, vaster than our lyres,/Ferment the bitter rose blushes of love!)

The young poet plays a subtle game here with the caesura, imposing its classical halfway arrest softly in the first and fourth lines of the stanza, and clangorously in the third line ("Plus fortes que l'alcool/plus vastes que nos lyres"), but letting the second line extend in a single breath. For every reason of decorum of sense and syntax, one cannot retard the line after the article *les* in the sixth syllable: "Et rythmes lents sous les/rutile-ments du jour." One senses a ghost of a pause after the fourth syllable ("Et rythmes lents . . ."), but the line primarily wants to stretch out and luxuriate in its own slow rhythms without interruption. This stanza is a laboratory experiment in the figurative and expressive power of metrics, and it uses symmetry (like the equal balance, in the fourth line, of the phonemes *er* and *ou*—"*fer*ment les *rou*sseurs am*ér*es de l'am*our*") as a form of narcotic seduction. That seduction depends on the presence of clearly marked and regular sonic boundaries.

When the poem contracts to its conclusion, it tolls the speaker back to his sole self with the tragic self-awareness of the speaker of Keats's "Ode to a Nightingale" (". . . forlorn. / Forlorn, the very word is like a bell / To toll me back from thee to my sole self . . ."):

> Si je désire une eau d'Europe, c'est la flache
> Noire et froide où vers le crépuscule embaumé
> Un enfant accroupi plein de tristesse, lâche
> Un bateau frêle comme un papillon de mai.

> (If I desire a European water, it's / The black, cold puddle where, in scented twilight, / A crouching child full of sadness lets loose / A boat as fragile as a butterfly in May.)

This stanza acts out a limitation of consciousness, but its syntax, metrics, and rhythm, in the single four-line sentence with its strong enjambments and elided caesuras, insist on an emotion that swells beyond the boundary of each line or half line. One hears the twelve precise syllables in each line, and their nuanced variations as the caesura shifts from line to line, finally appearing after the eleventh syllable to launch the verb *lâche* (releases), as the child releases the boat. This is a perfectly incarnate and dramatizing poetics; it is the beauty Rimbaud would methodically insult.

To demonstrate the insult, I will concentrate on one prose poem from *Illuminations*, "Antique." But let me start by glancing at the theme of beauty in *Une Saison en enfer* (A Season in Hell). "Un soir, j'ai assis la

Beauté sur mes genoux.—Et je l'ai trouvée amère.—Et je l'ai injuriée."[4] "One evening, I sat beauty on my knees. And I found her bitter. And I insulted her," Rimbaud writes in his preface. What does he mean by this insult to Beauty? And where does it lead him?

In the controversy over the chronology of composition on Rimbaud's two masterworks, *Une Saison en enfer* and *Illuminations*, I am persuaded by Henri de Bouillane de Lacoste and Suzanne Bernard that Rimbaud wrote the *Illuminations* over an extended period, somewhat coinciding with *Une Saison en enfer*. The prose poems of *Illuminations* can have come from as early as 1872, but Rimbaud seems to have taken them up again during his stay in London in 1874. In thinking about Rimbaud's reinvention of Beauty, I shall move flexibly back and forth between these two related but distinct works.

In *Une Saison en enfer* the speaker has taken Beauty on his knees, found her bitter, and insulted her. It is no accident that he allegorizes Beauty as a woman. *Une Saison* follows a dual course: we cannot detach its reinvention of poetic form from its reinvention of love. "L'amour est à réinventer" (Love must be reinvented), the Infernal Bridegroom declares in the Verlainian section of *Une Saison*.[5] Love must be reinvented, without women: "Je n'aime pas les femmes" (I don't like women). Women, throughout Rimbaud's work, are felt as an oppressive force, and have contaminated the whole idea of love. "Et la Mère, fermant le livre du devoir, / S'en allait satisfaite et très fière, sans voir" (And the Mother, closing the book of duty, / Went off satisfied and proud, seeing nothing) ("Les Poètes de sept ans").[6] In its methodical insult to feminine and poetic conventions of beauty, *Une Saison* starts from an ancestral curse in "Mauvais sang," and its spasm of release in appetite and movement: "Faim, soif, cris, danse, danse, danse, danse" (Hunger, thirst, cries, dance, dance, dance, dance). The work then ricochets through the hallucinations of "Nuit de l'enfer" (Infernal Night). Section I of "Délires," "Vierge folle" (The Mad Virgin), spoken in the voice of Verlaine, narrates the homosexual "drôle de ménage" (hell of a household) as a form of occult research. Section II of "Délires" continues the quest in "Alchimie du verbe" (The Alchemy of the Word), the reformation of love turning to the reformation of verse as it glides between Rimbaud's rhythmical prose and his last, mysterious, irregular verses. The section concludes in two rapid-fire sentences that seem to reclaim the ideal of beauty: "Cela s'est passé. Je sais aujourd'hui saluer la beauté"[7] (That's over. Now I know how to greet beauty). But the whole of *Une Saison en enfer* ends with a rejection of old forms of beauty and the old lying forms of love; in fact, it exchanges truth for beauty as the goal: "Et il me sera loisible de *posséder la vérité dans une âme et un corps*"[8] (And I will have the right *to possess the truth in a soul and a body* [italics are Rimbaud's]). The work follows an arc from the insult to Beauty to the embrace of Truth, a trajectory followed by any innovative work in art, correcting aesthetic convention with a new realism that engenders new forms adequate to its vision.

Une Saison en enfer was composed in lyrical prose chapters with some inset verses. *Illuminations* is quite another matter. In this revolutionary work, we can see two newly amphibious creatures crawling up the beach of modernity: the prose poem and *vers libre*. Now, prose poems were not new in 1872 when Rimbaud began *Illuminations*. The form was invented in 1842 by Aloysius Bertrand with the flashing vignettes of *Gaspard de la nuit*. Baudelaire had explored allegorical, rhythmical prose poems as expansions of his verse lyrics in the early 1860s, and Mallarmé took up the experiment as early as 1864. But in *Iluminations*, Rimbaud leaves exposition and description behind, and invents new kinds of prose poems as compressed sequences of images and explosive declarations. They have little in common with the works of Baudelaire or Mallarmé.

Rimbaud's prose poems are forms of action, not description. If they are communications, it is of an intensely private nature. I use the plural advisedly. Look at the pages of *Illuminations*: not one resembles another. From page to page, Rimbaud shifts shapes: some of the poems are built in paragraphs so short they almost constitute versets; some in traditional indented paragraphs; some in one-line paragraphs that almost assume the status of verse lines; some, like our poem "Antique," in a chunk of prose as solid as a block of masonry. In yet another modulation, in two pieces from *Illuminations* the lines shake themselves loose of prose and parade as an entirely new kind of nonmetrical verse: *vers libre*. These two poems, "Marine" and "Mouvement," were written as *verse* in Rimbaud's manuscript and were rightly printed that way in *La Vogue* in the spring of 1886, the first free verse to be published in France.

Illuminations, as it reinvents love, reinvents writing, and with a kind of violence. In "Conte" (Story), the prince massacres all his concubines: "What a pillage in the garden of beauty!"[9] And that in a sense is what the young poet has done, massacred the norms and forms of poetic beauty which he had already conquered. In presenting "Antique," I must point out the extraordinary decision of Rimbaud's American translator, Paul

Schmidt, to represent the prose poem in free-verse lineation. I give Schmidt's translation for polemical reasons; I hope to show that by cracking a prose poem into verse fragments, he has done incalculable harm and lost its central resistant tension.

ANTIQUE

Gracieux fils de Pan! Autour de ton front couronné de fleurettes et de baies tes yeux, des boules précieuses, remuent. Tachées de lies brunes, tes joues se creusent. Tes crocs luisent. Ta poitrine ressemble à une cithare, des tintements circulent dans tes bras blonds. Ton cœur bat dans ce ventre où dort le double sexe. Promène-toi le nuit, en mouvant doucement cette cuisse, cette seconde cuisse et cette jambe de gauche.[10]

ANTIQUE

Graceful son of Pan!
Around your forehead, circled with berries and flowers,
    Your eyes, those glittering spheres, revolve.
Stained with the dregs of wine, your cheeks
  Become hollow.
           Your fangs gleam.
The curve of your breast is a lyre;
    Tinklings vibrate in your blond arms.
  Your heart beats in those loins
      That cradle a double sex.
Wander about through the night,
    Softly moving this thigh,
         That second thigh . . .
    And this leg,
        The left. . . .[11]

Modernity always defines itself in relation to a past it attacks and transforms. Here, the poet of modernity ("Il faut être absolument moderne"— We must be absolutely modern)[12] presents us with the figure of a faun: just the sort of neoclassical kitsch we'd expect him to despise. What does he do with it? He brings it to life; he awakens a myth.

The opening invocation—"Gracieux fils de Pan"—sets off no alarms.

This little faun, not Pan himself but a minor derivative, is *gracieux*—graceful, gracious—an apparently safe quality; it would only be by pressing hard on the word *gracieux* that we would touch on any source of lively religious energy, "grace" pagan or Christian. As the faun's anatomy assembles before our eyes, however, the creature grows less and less gracious and more and more dangerous. The poet invites us to contemplate the faun from the head down, moving from the eyes down past cheeks, fangs, chest, arms to belly, genitals, legs. We move to a visceral core of energy, and that core releases movement: Walk around. But the movement begins in the head, with the surreal action of the eyes, which roll back and forth *around* the forehead crowned with blossoms and bay leaves. If the classical faun and the classical paraphernalia of his crown represented a safe ideal of beauty, the crazy movement of the eyes disturbs that ideal and reawakens the older, Dionysian forces latent in the little goat-god. The disturbance grows: the creature's wine-stained cheeks are hollow, his fangs gleam, and as he comes more and more to life, we see him as a kind of ancient Greek stringed instrument, a cithara, whose vibrations circulate in the blond arms, uniting corporeal and musical erotic excitement. The mystery intensifies as we move down to feel the heartbeats, the life-energy pulse, in the stomach where the double sex sleeps. *Ventre*, the word for stomach, is often used as a euphemism for womb, so the faun is felt as all the more intimately hermaphroditic. Heart, stomach/womb, double sex sleeping . . . Sleep, yet the poem awakens the pagan energy with the final imperative: "Promène-toi"—Walk around—rousing the creature, and setting him into still more mysterious motion. How many legs does he have? In another insult to classical codes of beauty, the faun is commanded to move this thigh, this second thigh, *and this left leg.* To understand the scene, you should imagine Muybridge's photographs of animals in motion, or Duchamp's *Nude Descending a Staircase.* Rimbaud is turning a static block of prose and a static neoclassical myth into a form of action. And this action—erotic, pagan, numinous—unites beauty and ugliness, grace and wine dregs, seduction and danger, as well as female and male.

We have already noted, in *Une Saison en enfer*, Rimbaud's call for a reinvention of love. The prose poems of *Illuminations* resound with such appeals. "Being Beauteous" cries out, "Oh, nos os sont revêtus d'un nouveau corps amoureux"[13] (Oh, our bones are clothed in a new body of love); "Vies" declares, "Je suis un inventeur bien autrement méritant que tous ceux qui m'ont précédé; un musicien même, qui ai trouvé quelque chose comme la clef de l'amour"[14] (I am an inventor far more worthy than all those who came before me; a musician, even, who has found something like the key to love). All these elements come together in the hermaphrodite faun: a new body of love, a new music, and a new hybrid form of writing.

French poetry, unlike poetry in English, is numerical. Every syllable counts. So much so that French poets for centuries have availed themselves of tricks to contract or elongate vowel clusters and diphthongs, like playing with soft taffy, to fit the strict requirements of a line. In *dièrèse*, a diphthong normally pronounced as one syllable can be drawn out into two, as in Baudelaire's famous line from "Correspondances" which acts out its expansion of imagination in the *dièrèse*: "ayant l'expansion des choses infinies" (having the expansion of infinite things—where the word *expansion* in French is drawn out into four distinct syllables: *ex-pan-si-on*). The opposite maneuver, *synérèse*, allows a poet to mash two vowels into one syllable. In "Antique," Rimbaud acts out a poetically hermaphroditic form, both prose and verse. To test this hypothesis, just count syllables and you will find yourself hovering indecisively over vowel clusters with *i*, and diphthongs, and the mute *e* normally unvoiced at the end of words. If you stretch a little, you will have classical French verse cadences of six, eight, and ten syllables. If you don't use the *dièrèse*, you will have odd-numbered units that feel like prose. The point is, the passage is *both* verse and prose. Its heart beats truly with a double sex.

Let's count. "Gracieux fils de Pan"—six, or five. "Autour de ton front couronné"—eight. "De fleurettes et de baies"—six, or seven. "Tes yeux, des boules précieuses, remuent"—nine/ten. "Tachées de lies brunes"—five/six. "Tes joues se creusent"—four/five. "Tes crocs luisent"—three/four. "Ta poitrine ressemble"—six. "À une cithare"—five. At the crescendo, the Alexandrine strongly emerges with its six-syllable hemistich units: "Ton cœur bat dans ce ventre"—six. "Où dort le double sexe"—six. "Promène-toi la nuit"—six. "En mouvant doucement"—six. "Cette cuisse, cette seconde cuisse"—ten. The final, anatomically revolutionary phrase, with the extra leg and the disturbing crazy movement, has an extra syllable, and returns us to prose: "et cette jambe de gauche."

Rimbaud's prose poem, his hermaphroditic form, is not free verse. That is why Paul Schmidt's disintegration of Rimbaud's highly wrought piece into its constituent phrases and clauses does such violence to the poem's mode of meaning. The only justification for it I can propose is heuristic: he has printed a concentrated prose poem, compact in its hybrid formal contradictions, as a poem in flaccid *vers libre*. He did so, I imagine, as the kind of analytic exercise in which we have just engaged, by counting syllables and pointing to verse units within prose. But in that way he turned a poem into a classroom demonstration, and a flat one at that.

In the sequence of prose poems in *Illuminations*, two, as we have seen, emerge as a new genre, *vers libre*. "Marine" and "Mouvement" are both studies in movement. They were published in May and June 1886 in *La Vogue*, the same journal and the same year in which Whitman found his way into French in the translations by Jules Laforgue. This is not the place to enter into arcane discussions of priority in the invention of *vers libre*: Marie Krysinska has her partisans and made her claims for the versets she published in *Le Chat Noir* in 1882. But versets are not *vers libre*. It was the masterful Laforgue and the less masterful Gustave Kahn who pioneered these new subjective, exploratory rhythms of consciousness. In terms of priority, there is no doubt that Rimbaud, all on his own, and before anyone else, derived his two *vers libre* poems, "Marine" and "Mouvement," out of his experiments with line, sentence, and paragraph in the prose poems of *Illuminations*, between 1872 and 1874. And did he gain very much by them?

Both poems depict movement in water and landscape. Both define the line as a subjective unit shaped by a noun phrase or clause. Both make heroic claims for vision: *tourbillons de lumière* (whirlwinds of light) in "Marine," and *l'héroisme de la découverte* (the heroism of discovery) in "Mouvement." Both have given up two sources of power: the high-pressure verse chamber of the Alexandrine line, and the containment of the prose poem with its dramatic pacing of consciousness and abrupt contrasts of sentence and paragraph length. That prose instrument made possible the delivery of the short, isolated, solar-plexus punch of statement as a single-sentence paragraph standing out from the block of prose: "J'ai seul la clef de cette parade sauvage"[15] (I alone have the key to this wild parade; from "Parade"); "Arrivée de toujours, qui t'en iras partout"[16] (Arrival from always, who will leave for everywhere; from "À une raison"); "La musique savante manque à notre désir"[17] (Sophisticated music falls short of our desire; from "Conte").

"Marine," the shorter of the two poems in *vers libre*, illustrates both the resources and the squandering of power the young poet found in his new form:

MARINE

Les chars d'argent et de cuivre—
Les proues d'acier et d'argent—
Battent l'écume,—
Soulèvent les souches des ronces.
Les courants de la lande,
Et les ornières immenses du reflux,
Filent circulairement vers l'est,
Vers les piliers de la forêt,
Vers les fûts de la jetée,
Dont l'angle est heurté par des tourbillons de lumière.[18]

MARINE

Chariots of copper and silver
Prows of silver and steel—
Thresh the foam,—
Plough up the roots of the thornback.

Currents of the heath
And boundless ruts of ebb tide,
Swirl in circles toward the east,
Toward the pillars of the forest,—
Toward the trunks of the pier,
Its edge struck by whirlwinds of light.

(translated by Holly Tannen)

I chose Holly Tannen's version because she is the only translator I know of to have caught the pun on *ronces*, which means both bramble and blackberry, and the flatfish known as the "ray." In a stroke of brilliance, she found an equivalent pun in English in the word "thornback," a kind of ray. Her discovery matters, because Rimbaud is relying on concentrations of diction and imagery in this poem for its major effects; its play of syntax against rhythms is paltry, and constitutes a poetic sacrifice. (She has, however, unaccountably broken the poem in two by introducing a space, whereas the French poem maintains its single, forward-rushing momentum toward its epiphany).[19]

"Marine" proceeds by mingling scenes of land and sea in a series of parallelisms and puns: the chariots are placed symmetrically with the prows, likening the ships' prows to plow blades cutting through soil. "Thresh" is an appropriately agricultural translation for *battent* (beat, linking maritime and terrestrial action). We have already seen how *ronces*, Tannen's "thornback," mingles fish and plant. Each succeeding line marries sea and land: the heath flows in currents, the tide has ruts like a muddy field, the jetty is seen as a forest with tree trunks. But what would turn a merely clever perception of analogy into the dynamic symbolic action we know as a poem? What are the spiritual and emotional consequences of the perception as presented in this arrangement of words?

Rimbaud is a poet unreconciled to life on earth. Years before he had seen the sea in real life, he saw it in imagination as the space of freedom. "Marine's" three main verbs, "thresh," "plough up," and "swirl," lead the ocean smack into the jetty, the outpost of the land, and their collision results in the whirlwinds of light that appear as the visible form of that union. Rimbaud is toying here with his old concern for ecstatic vision reaching its limits, as he had in his boyhood masterpiece, "Le Bateau ivre." But whereas in "Le Bateau ivre" the oceanic dream contracts to a sad puddle by the end, and leaves us with the scene of the child and the paper boat and the drunken boat confessing its exhaustion while still dreaming of escape, "Marine" concludes in a triumphant extension of syllables—the longest line in the poem, with its thirteen syllables by far outpacing the earlier lines of six, seven, eight, and ten. In this regard, one might fault Tannen's translation, as she tames Rimbaud's line by reeling it in, and misrepresents the formal proportions of his poem.

"Marine's" expansive versification in the last line echoes its transcendent claim of vision and action: an obstacle overcome (the angle of the jetty struck) gives rise to an explosion of light. Duality (of sea and land) is reconciled, limitation is erased. The trouble is, this transcendence occurs only as a statement, not as realized poetic movement. Because the poem, in its lazy *vers libre*, presents itself with no structural limitations—no internal jetty, so to speak—and because its clauses and noun phrases sit so inertly upon their lines like canned goods upon a kitchen shelf, it has no rhythmical or syntactic obstacle to overcome, and it therefore exists only at the level of a proposition. Its assertion of victory sounds all the more hollow against the weakness of its means.

Rimbaud's brilliance, as a poet, was to redefine ratios of limitation and expansion. As long as he retained some structure of limit, in verse or in the prose poem, he generated the internal resistance necessary for the buildup and release of poetic energy. "Marine" and "Mouvement," lacking an objective logic of containment, are at the mercy of their own vagaries, and are—to my mind—the weakest pieces in *Illuminations*, however promising they turned out to be for free-verse poets in the century to come. In a terrible way, they confirm the bitter justice of Rimbaud's statement in "Conte": "La musique savante manque à notre désir" (Sophisticated music falls short of our desire). The sophisticated music, the truly knowing music of *Illuminations*, the music carved out of silence, is all in the prose poems and their struggles with boundaries. Even for the avant-garde, it turns out that crusty old Boileau was right: "Qui ne sait se borner, ne sut jamais écrire" (He who knows no limits, never learned to write).

CHAPTER 10

Mallarmé and Max Jacob:
A Tale of Two Dice Cups

L et us consider the avant-garde, the old avant-garde, at a time when it was new, and had not yet subsided into a reigning academicism.[1] I want to follow the arc of thought from Mallarmé's *Un Coup de dés jamais n'abolira le hasard* (A Throw of the Dice Will Never Abolish Chance) of 1897 to Max Jacob's *Le Cornet à dés* (The Dice Cup) of 1917; that is, the leap from the High Symbolism of the *fin de siècle* to the brash, Cubist poetics of the dawning twentieth century. Mallarmé and Max Jacob have in common a conception of poetry not as an utterance of sincerity and truth, but as a game, a set of rules and conventions. I propose to look at the challenge to conventions of meaning in some of their poems, and to consider some of the forms that the poetic avant-garde, in its hectic logic of self-renewal, has taken in the modern era in France. More particularly, I want to suggest a context for reading Max Jacob, the experimental French poet, novelist, and painter. Born in Quimper in Brittany in 1876, a Jew from a nonbelieving family, a homosexual, Jacob converted to Roman Catholicism in 1915, withdrew to a Benedictine monastery for two distinct periods of seven years each, and died in 1944 at the age of sixty-eight in the Nazi camp at Drancy in a suburb of Paris.

What is the avant-garde? In *The Theory of the Avant-Garde*, Renato Poggioli confesses that he cannot trace the term back to its earliest use as a metaphor for progressive art. But he points out that the military term *avant-garde*, the advance troops, first began to be used as a metaphor for radical politics in France in the first half of the nineteenth century, just in time to contribute to the rhetoric of the Revolution of 1848. It was not until France's defeat by the Prussians in 1870 that the term *avant-garde* began commonly to designate radical art as well as politics. But in a larger sense, I think we can reach back before 1870 and identify the spirit of the avant-garde—the spirit of novelty, of self-conscious rupture with the past—with the movement we know loosely as Romanticism in the arts.[2]

Bluntly stated, the poetic avant-garde is characterized by a break with the past, even outrage to the past; dismantling of inherited poetic structures and diction; and (at times) obscurity, even hermeticism. It is a staged violence to language, as in Apollinaire's call for the suppression of syntax. One *locus classicus* in English literature for the appearance of a self-consciously modern ethos occurs in Wordsworth's preface to the second edition of *The Lyrical Ballads* in 1800, revised in 1802. Wordsworth casts his argument in terms of a contract, or promise, broken between author and reader: "It will undoubtedly appear to many persons that I have not fulfilled the terms of an engagement thus voluntarily contracted," he states.[3] Why? Because he proposes to throw out conventions both contemporary and inherited, what he calls "the gaudiness and inane phraseology of many modern writers," as well as older devices of personification and periphrastic diction, in order to write instead what he calls "the very language of men"—men, he means, "of low and rustic life."[4] In seeking his elemental language and access to the truth of human nature, Wordsworth invokes not only the promise broken (but renewed) between author and public, but also the interruption of lineage and inheritance: his new practice has cut him off from "a large portion of phrases and figures of speech which from father to son have long been regarded as the common inheritance of Poets."[5]

Wordsworth helped to set the terms—of a broken contract with the reader, and revolt against tradition—that would increasingly define modern poetry in Europe. Victor Hugo is more violent, and also more egocentric, in making similar claims for his liberation of French verse. In "Réponse à un acte d'accusation" (Reply to an Act of Accusation), written in the intoxication of 1834, four years after the successful revolt of the

French middle class against the Bourbon monarchy and the enthroning of Louis-Philippe, the so-called bourgeois king, Hugo shanghais the great French Revolution of 1798 for his own purposes: "Oui, je suis ce Danton! je suis ce Robespierre!" (Yes, I am that Danton, that Robespierre!). In his rhetorical cataract, he overwhelms the neoclassical rules of French versification, letting line after line enjamb promiscuously, loosening the sacrosanct caesura from its place at the center of the twelve-syllable Alexandrine line and, most provocatively, opening the poem to plebian diction: "Je fis souffler un vent révolutionnaire, / Je mis un bonnet rouge au vieux dictionnaire" (I blew a revolutionary wind. / I dressed the old dictionary in liberty's colors). He goes on:

> J'ai dit à la narine: Eh mais! Tu n'es qu'un nez!
> J'ai dit au long fruit d'or: Mais tu n'es qu'une poire!
> J'ai dit à Vaugelas: Tu n'es qu'une machoire!
> J'ai dit aux mots: Soyez République! Soyez
> La fourmillière immense, et travaillez! Croyez,
> Aimez, vivez!—J'ai mis tout en branle, et, morose,
> J'ai jeté le vers noble aux chiens noirs de la prose.[6]

> (I said to nares: "Why, you're just a nose!"
> To the long golden fruit: "You're just a pear!"
> To Vaugelas: "You're just a pair of choppers!"
> And to the words I said: "Be a republic!
> Be one vast anthill—work! Believe, love, live!"
> Yes, I upheaved it all—relentlessly
> Threw noble verse to the black dogs of prose.)[7]

I have cited two Romantic manifestos. Such revolutions, once set in motion, tend to accelerate, and it is hardly surprising to find the young Rimbaud, just back from the Revolutionary Commune in Paris in 1871, castigating Hugo: "Hugo, trop cabochard . . ." (Hugo, too thickheaded . . . *Stella* just about takes the measure of his vision. Too many Belmontets, Lamennais, Jehovahs, old collapsed enormities).[8] Rimbaud advocated and practiced a poetry still more *en avant* than anything Hugo had dreamed.

Though later avant-garde movements—Symbolism, Cubism, Futurism, Dada, Surrealism—defined themselves polemically as breaking with Romanticism, I would argue that in essence they adhere to the revolutionary script provided by the major Romantic writers, while continually upping the ante in destructive rhetoric. The language of perpetual artistic revolution is by now, early in the twenty-first century, wearyingly familiar, however intoxicating it was in its own day. Ezra Pound, who learned his *vers libre* from the French Symbolists ("To break the pentameter—that was the first heave," he announced in a pentameter in Canto LXXXI), declared in 1918, "I believe in technique as the test of a man's sincerity; in law when it is ascertainable; in the trampling down of every convention that impedes or obscures the determination of the law, or the precise rendering of the impulse."[9]

Celebrating an art "pure" of rhetoric, he congratulated Yeats for stripping "English poetry of its perdamnable rhetoric. He has boiled away all that is not poetic—and a good deal that is."[10] Across the English Channel, five years earlier, Guillaume Apollinaire had opened his book of poems *Alcools* with "Zone": "À la fin tu es las de ce monde ancien" (In the end you're sick of this ancient world),[11] and later the same year he published his manifesto "Anti-tradition futuriste," outflanking the Italian Futurists by calling for the suppression of "poetic sorrow, of snobbish exoticism, of artistic imitation, of syntax, of adjectives, of punctuation, of tense and person of verbs, of harmonious typography, verse and stanza form . . ." etc. He covers with "shit" all "critics, pedagogues, professors, museums . . . historians . . . philologues. . . ."[12] At the same time, the doctrinaire Futurist Marinetti was calling for *l'immaginazione senza fili e le parole in libertà* (imagination untrammeled and words set free), printing, as examples, totally nonsyntactic and unpunctuated shock typography as poems in the Italian journal *Lacerba*.[13]

The revolt against tradition did not always confine itself to literary form. It turns up also as a fury against women, seen as embodying social convention and order, the primal Mother, the sexual trap. In April 1914 Marinetti's collaborator Giovanni Papini, a noted Italian intellectual, published in *Lacerba* a call (symbolic of course) for *il massacro delle donne* (the massacre of women). "It wouldn't be a massacre of the innocents," he wrote. "Because the female sexual organ is empty, and we *intrepidi coglioni* [literally, intrepid balls, but in American slang, intrepid pricks] love the abyss. A tiny abyss, to be sure! When we've built up too much internal vitality, we feel the need to piss it out somewhere. And Woman—this fleshly urinal which our desire represents to us as the chosen vessel— Woman demands our entire lives in return for this service. It's a bit much. Women should be suppressed."[14]

We have come a long way from Wordsworth's "real language of men," and Futurism and Surrealism are a far cry from the Lake Poets. I will call a halt to this survey of avant-garde provocation, and return to a quiet, masterful moment in the refashioning of French verse. When Mallarmé lectured at Oxford and Cambridge in 1894, he described for his English audience the jarring of the Alexandrine line and the emergence of the prose poem.[15] He then evoked a far more seismic disturbance, one whose magnitude very few even of his initiates quite took in. He proposed a "lustral storm," and asked, fundamentally, *s'il y a lieu d'écrire* (if there is a place, permission, reason, to write). The new poetry he championed was an act not of description, communication, or persuasion, but of suggestion and allusion; its sorcery, he said, "is to liberate, from a handful of dust or reality, without confining it to the book, even as a text, the volatile dispersal, or spirit, which has no purpose other than total musicality" ("La dispersion volatile soit l'esprit qui n'a que faire de rien outre la musicalité de tout").[16]

Any translation of Mallarmé's subtly strung clauses deforms them, because their sense inheres in their paced deferral of sense, very much an effect of his syntax. But the essential point, reiterated over and over again, is the conception of a verbal art tending to abstraction, a poetry that not only approaches the condition of music, but surpasses it.

One may object that an abstract poetry is impossible, since it is in the nature of words to be semantic, to mean. The crudely semantic aspect of words, their information-bearing, appeared to Mallarmé mere contamination. His verse is, however, neither senseless nor nonsense. Instead, it intensifies the semantic force of language by setting the plural meanings in words vibrating against one another. In his essay "Crise de vers," written the year after his Oxford and Cambridge lectures, Mallarmé urges poets to *reprendre notre bien à la musique* (to take back our rightful property from music). For, he continues, "it is not from elementary sonorities of brass, strings, and woodwinds certainly, but from the intellectual word at its zenith, that with fullness and manifest reality, as the union of the relations binding all, Music must result."[17] And this art purified of utilitarian significance, this "intellectual word at its zenith," demands the purification of the author, the disappearance of the author.

This absolutist notion of poetic purity links the anonymity of the poet to the refusal of the full referential function of words. Turning from Mallarmé's prose to his poems, we note that he crystallizes his poetic theory in several key words, of which *rien* (nothing) holds pride of place.

It launches the definitive sonnet "Salut" (which means champagne toast, greeting, and salvation) offered by Mallarmé to his followers at a poetic banquet in Paris in 1893.

SALUT

Rien, cette écume, vierge vers
À ne désigner que la coupe;
Telle loin se noie une troupe
De sirènes mainte à l'envers.

Nous naviguons, ô mes divers
Amis, moi déjà sur la poupe
Vous l'avant fastueux qui coupe
Le flot de foudres et d'hivers;

Une ivresse belle m'engage
Sans craindre même son tangage
De porter debout ce salut

Solitude, récif, étoile
À n'importe ce qui valut
Le blanc souci de notre toile.[18]

Prose translation of "Salut":

TOAST (CHEERS, SALVATION)

Nothing, this foam, virgin verse
To designate but the cut/cup;
Thus far off a flock of mermaids/Sirens
Drowns itself, many, frolicking backward.

We sail, O my various
Friends, I already on the poop,
You the proud prow that cuts
The flood of lightnings and winters;

A lovely drunkenness commits me
Without even fearing the pitch (of the boat)
To raise aloft this toast

Solitude, reef, star
To whatever was worth
The white care (anxiety, scruple) of our canvas.

"Salut" was important to Mallarmé, and he placed it at the head of his collected poems. It is his micro-*Odyssey*, complete with Sirens, but lacking Ithaca and Penelope. In Mallarmé's poem, no island kingdom, no marital embrace, call the poet home. The first word, *rien* (nothing), controls the experience, and is linked to Mallarmé's recurrent images of virginity. Here, the *vierge vers* (virgin verse) designates a virginal poetics, resistant to paraphrase; reluctant, we might say, to consummate meaning. We can trace Mallarmé's nonreferential poetics of virginity back almost thirty years to his dramatic fragment "Hérodiade," composed between 1864 and 1867. Hérodiade, the Salomé princess figure, refuses sunlight, food, human contact, and marriage, preferring her sterility reflected in gems, precious metals, and mirrors. "J'aime l'horreur d'être vierge," she asserts (I love the horror of being virgin).[19] The virgin verse of "Salut," pointing to nothing but *la coupe* (that is, the occasion, the literary toast, the champagne glass, but also the cut, the layout, of the lines and the page, and of the sail in the boat imagery), flirts with signification but partially dodges it, providing *rien*—virginal vacancy, the melodious numbers of the pure poetic act in these octosyllabic lines: solitude, reef, star. This seascape describes the elemental situation of the writer, alone, menaced by danger below (reef), guided by an ideal conception of cosmic order above (star). The key words, *salut*, *coupe*, and *toile*, are puns, and defy a single reading. *Salut* and *coupe* we have already considered. *Toile* is both the painter's canvas and the sail of the boat; in an old topos, the sea journey represents the journey of art. We are left with *rien*, nothing, a very positive and present nothing, the indefinite ("To whatever was worth"), the blank possibility of poetry as an ideal formal order: the form of the champagne glass with nothing in it but foam, which is liquid frothed to air, the perfect figure for the vacancy of content in Mallarmé's work.

Mallarmé extended this potent formalist charm in his last work, *Un Coup de dés jamais n'abolira le hasard*. The "chance" against which the poet pits himself may be seen as the fundamental disorder, the chaos of meaninglessness, of a world without God; Mallarmé is very much a man of his century in feeling the loss of faith in a transcendent deity as a crisis which threatened to annihilate any attachment to life or reason to live. Composed almost entirely in the subjunctive and conditional moods, *Un Coup de dés* is a poem/musical score/star chart that broke conventions of legibility in its own time, and still breaks them today. You have to read it along both horizontal and vertical axes, following the major sentences in capital letters and Roman typography, while holding the subordinate clauses and subordinate italics in mind. Paul Valéry, Mallarmé's young devotee, left an eerie account of his first encounter with his master's radical "Summa":

> I think I am the first man to have seen this extraordinary work. As soon as he had finished it, Mallarmé invited me to come over. . . . On his dark wooden table, square, with twisted legs, he placed the manuscript of his poem, and began to read it in a low, level voice, without the slightest emphasis, almost to himself. . . . Finally, he showed me the manuscript. I thought I saw the shape of a thought placed for the first time in our space. . . . Here, truly, Space spoke, dreamed, gave birth to forms of Time. . . . On March 30, 1897, handing me the corrected proofs of the text *Cosmopolis* would publish, he said, with an admirable smile, ornament of the purest pride a man's feeling of the universe can inspire, "Don't you think it's an act of madness?"[20]

Un Coup de dés still qualifies as avant-garde today, more than a century after its composition. It projects the mystic champagne and seascape of "Salut" into a shipwreck of human meaning. Again, its central words are puns, oscillating in sense and in gender: *la voile*, the feminine noun, means "sail"; *le voile*, the masculine noun, means "veil." *La vague*, the feminine, means "wave" (in the sea); *le vague*, the masculine, means "the indefinite." These puns point to the poet's dominant concerns: meaning is to be veiled, and deliberately "vague." The poem's central act is the articulation by the doomed captain of an utterance in the void, an utterance not inscribed in the poem, by the way, so remaining virtual: absolutely meaningless, but heroic and formally beautiful. As the poem states: NOTHING / WILL HAVE TAKEN PLACE / BUT THE PLACE.[21] Mallarmé had asked, in the Oxford and Cambridge lecture three years earlier, if there were *lieu d'ecrire*—a place, reason, permission to write. We encounter Mallarmé's *lieu*, the place of writing, again here in *Un coup de dés* as number, the constellation of words on the page, the dots on the dice. It is a purely formalist poetics: the highest roll of the dice would give six plus six, the number of syllables in the canonical Alexandrine line. The poem leaves us with a cosmic proviso, "Excepté" (EXCEPT PERHAPS A CONSTELLATION), a hypothetical constellation memorializing the arbitrary order of human thought imposed upon the void: "Toute pensée émet un coup de dés" (Every thought emits a roll of the dice).

In *Igitur*, Mallarmé's sketch of a play unpublished in his lifetime, he inscribed an early version of this throw of the dice and defiance of chance. Here, in sheer mental space and immemorial night, amid allusions to Hamlet and Poe's Raven, the poet conjures the dark room of the mind. His adverbial hero, whose name Igitur means "thus" in Latin and derives from Genesis 2:1 ("Igitur perfecti sunt coeli et terra"—Thus the heavens and the earth were finished), is about to commit suicide; he descends from his heavily draped room down dark and whispering stairs to the family vault where he will shake the dice, blow out the candle, and lie down in the ashes of his ancestors to die, "having drunk that drop of nothingness which the sea lacked."[22] Igitur's shaking of the dice (we never actually see him throw them) makes a gesture of meaning against the vast equivocation of space and time: "Igitur simply shakes the dice—a movement, before going to join the ashes, the atoms of his ancestors; the movement within him is absolved" ("Le mouvement qui est en lui est absous").[23]

The concluding passage is dominated by the word *Absolu* with an initial capital letter, an Absolute now weirdly incorporated into the hero "who feels within himself, thanks to the absurd, the existence of the Absolute" ("Qui sent en lui, grâce à l'absurde, l'existence de l'Absolu"), a state of purity, a purity cognate, Mallarmé insists, with the purity of Igitur's aristocratic blood. That biological fantasy provides a figure for the metaphysical purity the poet has imagined for a being who refuses contact with ordinary life. The tension of the scene concentrates in the wordplay between the words *absous* (absolved), and *Absolu* (the Absolute). The verb *absoudre* (to absolve) has already been ignited in section I, in the phrase "la parole qui absolut Minuit" (the word which absolved Midnight).[24] *Absolut* used as a verb this way is a wild neologism, a grammatical invention of Mallarmé's, a made-up *passé simple* (past perfect tense) stirring into life the latent etymological kinship between *Absolu* (the Absolute, a noun) and the verb *absoudre*, to absolve. Both stem from the Latin *absolvere*, to loosen, or free—from sin in the case of absolution, and from relation, division, and connection in the case of the Absolute. And Midnight might be considered an absolute time, a time out of time.

The Absolute Absolution envisaged in Mallarmé's poetry is a pure blasphemy as well as an impossible grammatical form. Poetry is that art which converts impossibility to possibility in the very structures of language, in this case presenting an apotheosis of *rien*, nothing, a void purified of the vulgarity of meaning human or divine. God's divine "thus," His agency in Genesis, has been detached from the sacred, and now attaches to sheer movement, the words in numerical dance, the ballet of prosody and syntax. As Igitur shakes the dice and prepares to lie down forever in his tomb, Mallarmé insists on the magic of the number 12: ". . . si je compte, comédien, jouer le tour—le 12—pas de hasard dans aucun sens" (if as an actor I count on playing the trick—the 12—no chance in any way).[25] The pun on "counting" intensifies the kabbalistic force of the power of number at work here as an order imposed upon reality through poetry. Igitur lies down in his tomb, for a poetry divorced from meaning is ultimately suicidal. The play concludes, "Le Néant parti, reste le château de la pureté" (With Nothingness banished, the castle of purity remains).[26] Not for nothing is the hero an adverb, movement without content. Mallarmé had transformed his own literal suicidal impulses of his period of despair in Tournon in 1866 and 1867 into a symbolic self-extinction that allowed him to go on living and writing, living and writing the death he had not accomplished. "I am perfectly dead . . ." he wrote his friend Henri Cazalis in May 1867, the same year as *Igitur*. "It's to let you know that I am now impersonal, and no longer the Stéphane whom you knew."[27] And not for nothing (or, indeed, for Nothing, we might say) did the poet's son-in-law recall the Master's delicate inflection of the word "sinister" in describing the impenetrability of *Igitur*,

> . . . a book abounding in probable delights and which he would desire not absolutely stripped of significance for everyone; so that, just as the maid entering the room during a performance of a piano piece by Schumann finds it beautiful because she is not resistant to the harmony of the chords, in the same way the man in the street should be able to draw out some meaning that satisfies him and is worth his 3 francs 50. He thinks he understands, and, in the Master's phrase, "it's thereby all the more sinister."[28]

We can turn now to Max Jacob in 1917, and see another insult to the reading public. Jacob's *Le Cornet à dés*, his Dice Cup, responds directly to Mallarmé's throw of the dice, and both respond indirectly (and in different ways) to Pascal's wager. Like Mallarmé's *Un Coup de dés*, Jacob's poems are aggressively obscure and disruptive to literary convention. But whereas Mallarmé played his godless game for the stakes of Absolute formality, the ruled structure of words reflecting some vaguely Hegelian mystique of pure intellect, Jacob's dice cup scrambles the rules of various games—semantic, logical, prosodic, narrative, fictional, social—; uses a mixed and popular vocabulary; and in breaking up human orders, eventually cracks open a space for the sacred. If Mallarmé gambled on purity and human order, Max Jacob gambled on impurity and divine order. A mystical Jewish Catholic, he took fallen language for his medium, and in its deformations saw traces of that god who was thought to have taken on flesh as the Word. And here we arrive at a crucial juncture in the development of poetic modernism: the aesthetic generally known as the avant-garde, applying to such diverse movements as Symbolism, Cubism, and Futurism, and in general associated with a defiantly secular outlook, provided one poet at least with the structures for his religious experience. Moving from Mallarmé to Max Jacob, we move from a poetry of the Absolute to a poetry seeking absolution, a poetry that finds its way through the fractures of language to confession and prayer.

When Jacob published *Le Cornet à dés* in 1917, he was forty-one, living in a miserable room in Montmartre. Breton, Jewish, homosexual, he was triply marginal to the dominant life of Paris. As a new convert to Roman Catholicism (baptized in 1915, with Picasso for godfather, after a vision of Christ in 1909), he was soon marginal to the avant-garde as well: his Cubist friends and proto-Surrealist devotees regarded his conversion as treachery, or an extravagant joke. His rejection of his Jewishness is a sad, complex, and important story that deserves its own longer account. Suffice it to say, for now, that he had grown up in a secular, atheist Jewish family in the intensely Catholic town of Quimper, and that his religious instincts seem early on to have attached him to the folkloric religion whose rites and art saturated his childhood.

Composed between 1905 and 1916, *Le Cornet à dés* was not Jacob's first book, but it was his first "hit"—a hit, that is, in the small world of literary sophisticates. Overnight, one witness has recorded, Jacob's shabby room became the "Grand Central Station" of the avant-garde.[29] Besides his old companions-in-arms from the heyday of Cubism, Picasso, Braque, Derain, and Apollinaire, young writers now swarmed there to try to glean the secret from the fey, witty, hypersensitive, malicious, and mystical poet who had refashioned the prose poem. The neophytes included those who would soon carry the banner of Surrealism: in 1917, André Breton, Aragon, and Philippe Soupault went to pay homage to Max Jacob and to learn from him how to woo the irrational.

What did the old, *fin de siècle* avant-garde, Symbolism, look like in the early years of the new century? Oddly enough, two of the second-generation, influential Symbolists in France were American. Francis Viélé-Griffin and Stuart Merrill, truly bilingual and partly educated in France, stood among the foremost poets of the era (and like many eminences, are today almost utterly forgotten). Equally eminent and equally forgotten is René Ghil, who took Mallarmé's theory of the musicality of verse almost literally and tried to enforce a strict orchestration of vowels, relating them to colors and to musical instruments. Like Mallarmé, he eschewed comprehensibility; he laced his "Pantoun," for instance, with Malay, the better to deter any unseemly lust for meaning in his French readers: "Mais on l'entend se lamenter s'âme d'amour / heurtant de gounoun'g en gounoun'g des gong'latents. . . ."[30] One hardly needs to translate these lines since their impact is mostly phonetic in French: a crude prose trot would give us, "But one hears the soul of love lamenting / striking from gounoun'g to gounoun'g hidden gongs." Ghil did go so far as to supply footnotes to Malay words—*gounoun'g* is volcano, for example—so the effect of auditory hallucination and nonsense is only provisional.

Viélé-Griffin, Merrill, and Ghil illustrate well the enervation of Symbolist poetry after the deaths of the great masters. Ghil's solemn phonetic mystification, however, would provide rich material for Max Jacob, who parodied Ghil in *Le Cornet à dés* in the prose poem "Poème du Java de M. René Ghil et s'appelant les Ksours" (Javanese Poem by Mr. René Ghil Called "The Ksours"). In Viélé-Griffin's polite *vers libre*, we find Verlaine's melancholy, vocabulary, and uneasy versification, but none of the poetry in any real sense. Verlaine's melodic undershocks, veiled intensities, and improprieties, the true sources of his power, have gone missing, and what remains is a manner and a mood. It is worth looking at a poem by Viélé-Griffin to take the full measure of the poverty of French verse in the period of Max Jacob's renovation.

Demain est au vingt ans fiers;
Leurs rires passent, et l'on reste accoudé;
On a honte, un peu, de ses joyeux hiers,
Comme d'un habit démodé.

Demain, c'est l'automne qui parle
De plus près à l'oreille qui l'écoute.
Je suis sans regret, mais j'ai mal;
Je suis sans effroi, mais je doute;

Non, certes, de ma journée:
J'ai vécu, au mieux, le poème;
Mais l'âme reste étonnée
De n'être plus elle-même.

Prose translation:

Tomorrow belongs to the proud twenty-year-olds;
Their laughs pass, and one stays leaning on one's elbows;
One is a little embarrassed by one's giddy past,
As by an old-fashioned suit.

Tomorrow, it's autumn that speaks
More and more closely to the listening ear.
I have no regrets, but I suffer;
I have no fear, but I doubt.

Not, certainly, [do I doubt] my day:
I lived, as well as I could, the poem;
But the soul remains astonished
No longer to be herself.[31]

Stuart Merrill's eight-syllable lines take their cue from Mallarmé, reproducing the master's recondite gemlike and musical vocabulary. His characteristic poem "Celle qui prie" is all mechanical expertise and recycled vocabulary, totally missing the point of Mallarmé's resistant syntax and disquietude. What started as quest has become mannerism. One stanza should suffice to make the point:

Ses doigts gemmés de rubacelle
Et lourds du geste des effrois
Ont sacré d'un signe de croix
Le samit de sa tunicelle.

Prose translation:

Her fingers begemmed in red topaz
And heavy with the gesture of fears
Have blessed with a sign of the cross
The samite of her tunicle.[32]

In all three of these late Symbolists—Ghil, Viélé-Griffin, and Merrill—
we see the after-twitch of poetry, forms and words repeated almost as if by
the autonomic nervous system. No wonder the real young writers rebelled.
Gide, who had once haunted Mallarmé's famous Tuesday evening gather-
ings, took refuge in North Africa and in writing novels; Claudel turned
to plays, to poetry in magnificently fulsome biblical versets, and to a dip-
lomatic career in Asia; Charles Péguy, always a contrarian, defined a new
terrain in his visionary *Cahiers* and in book-length poems that stretched
back to Corneille in verse form and had all the force of the great combers
of the North Atlantic.

Enter Max Jacob. Enter Max Jacob, that is, and Picasso. For after 1904,
the primary model for experimental poetry was no longer music, but
painting; no longer Wagner, but Picasso. We have moved from immaterial
to material poetics. And in painting, with the researches of Picasso and
Braque in elemental form, we move from an art of representation, trying
for the illusion of volumetric objects in space, to an art exploring the conditions and conventions of representation: an art of discontinuous visual
codes (perspective drawing, crosshatching, volumetric shading, contour)
jammed together within a single frame. An art, that is, of presentation.
Picasso enters the story not to provide some facile inter-art analogy, but
because he and Max Jacob formed the nucleus of the Cubist revolution
in painting and poetry at the ramshackle congeries of studios called "le
Bateau-Lavoir" (the washerwoman's barge) in Montmartre. From their
meeting in 1901, after Picasso's first Parisian show, Picasso and Jacob
recognized each other as comrades in art. In 1903, when the painter was
penniless, Jacob took him into his cramped lodgings and supported them

both on his janitor's salary. In 1904, Picasso moved to le Bateau-Lavoir, soon followed by Jacob, and as the circle enlarged to include Apollinaire, Braque, Derain, and others, the Cubist era emerged. "You are the only poet of the age," Picasso had declared to Max Jacob. For his part, Jacob saw Picasso as genius incarnate.[33]

Picasso's painting from 1907, *Les Demoiselles d'Avignon*, prefigures the startling turns art was about to take as Picasso and Braque invented Cubism. The painting, with its dark terra-cotta hues in the congealed curtain to the left, and the icy blue shards that separate the figures on the right, sent many of the painter's friends and patrons (like Leo Stein, Gertrude's brother) away with sick headaches. Early versions contained the figure of a sailor, modeled on Max Jacob, the painter no doubt taking a perverse pleasure in placing his homosexual friend in a brothel. In its deliberate ugliness *Les Demoiselles d'Avignon* remains shocking, and the frontal stare of the prostitutes (the *demoiselles*) still boldly challenges the viewer. Of particular importance to Jacob's poetics is the clash of codes of representation. Some of the women are flatly outlined, some are shaded volumetrically, while some (on the far right) have suddenly acquired the violent stylization of African masks. One challenge in viewing this centrifugal painting is to identify the elements of its underlying unity: the rhyming crescent shapes multiply from the slice of melon in the foreground into thighs, arms, and curtain folds; the same earth reds, blues, and white play across the whole surface; and the same vocabulary of dark lines recurs throughout. In reading Max Jacob, one engages in a similar search for continuity amid abrupt discontinuities.

Le Cornet à dés is mostly composed of small, blocklike prose poems. But to begin to take the measure of Jacob's perversity, "Le Coq et la perle" (The Cock and the Pearl), the longest piece in the book, provides a convenient entry. An assemblage of shards of statement in non sequiturs, "Le Coq et la perle" provides a little repertoire of Jacobian moves. Its title is emblematic of the whole, asserting relation between elements (a rooster and a pearl) that seem at odds in every way, not least of which is gender. To re-create the novelty of this poem in its own time, one must imagine having grown up reading not only Racine and Corneille, but with the established Symbolists Merrill, Viélé-Griffin, and Ghil, and the Gallicized Greek Jean Moréas, whose earnest volume from 1886, *Le Pèlerin passionné* (The Passionate Pilgrim), Jacob parodies in "Le Coq et la perle" as "le Pèlerin carapassionné" (a wild pun, impossible to translate: something like "the Shellfish Pilgrim").

Opening "Le Coq et la perle," we see, first, that these writings appear to be flashes of prose, not poetry. They refuse all the seduction, the lulling psychic transport, that the recurrences of verse provide. Secondly, we observe that what we're reading makes no sense, but skips from one subject, tone, and genre to another, all apparently unrelated. We notice, further, that whatever internal sense any particular statement may begin to make is vitiated by rampant phonetic play, so that syllables seem more important than words (and then what happens to meaning?). We romp among phonemes: Algérie/Egérie, coin de doublure/fourrure, bleu pâle/ pan de ciel/coin du pôle. Translation falters because semantic meaning is not the primary point, but literally these words indicate: Algeria/Egeria, corner of [cloth] lining/fur, pale blue/patch of sky/corner of the pole. I shall quote from the first few pages in the translation by Christopher Pilling and David Kennedy, indicating where I have skipped sections, and inserting the French where the puns demand attention.

THE COCK AND THE PEARL

I thought he was bankrupt, but he still has slaves and a house with several rooms. On the rocks, the divas were half-naked in their swimming-costumes. In the evening, everyone climbed into the railway carriages and the little trains glided beneath the pines. I thought he was bankrupt! . . . he's even found me a publisher! The publisher's given me a tortoise, one with a pink and shiny shell: the least ducat would do me much more good.

Are you off? People will see how ill you are: the lanterns on castors are watching you and the zebra on rockers is doing its level best to make you go dizzy.

I hereby declare that I am world-wide, oviparous, a giraffe, parched, sinophobic and hemispherical. I quench my thirst at the well-springs of the atmosphere which laughs concentrically and farts at my uncertainty.

And when all that remained of the Polish lancer, with his limbs cut off and his bottle broken, was a single eye, the eye sang *The Two Grenadiers*.

O skull, what do you need to look like a parson's nose? a stretched bladder? and to look like an ostrich? goose pimples?

[The game here is all in the play of vowels: "Que te manque-t-il, ô crane, pour avoir l'air d'un cul de poulet? la baudruche? et pour avoir l'air d'une autruche? la chair de poule." The near rhyme between *baudruche* (bladder) and *autruche* (ostrich) sets the basic structure. *Cul de poulet*—parson's nose—is considerably more vulgar in French than in English: chicken's ass.]

Wearing a cap and bells, the scissor-grinder (it's death himself) opens his short cape lined with cherry-red silk to sharpen a huge sabre. A butterfly on the wheel stops him.

His white arms became my whole horizon.

A blazing fire is a rose on the fan-tail of a peacock.

. . .

If you put your ear to the tick-tock of your ear, you can be sure to hear something inside which is not yourself but a demon or the Devil himself.

When you're painting a picture, with every brush-stroke it changes completely, it turns like a cylinder and it's almost interminable. When it stops turning, the picture's finished. My last one portrayed a Tower of Babel in lighted candles.

. . .

It so happens that, when you snore, the world of matter wakes the other world.

Walking down the Rue de Rennes, I bit into my bread with such emotion that it felt as if I was biting into my heart.

A pale blue thorn-bush is a steeple in the moonlight.

In the Andean *cordillera*, grapes grow on the hops, but no one sees them.

. . .

On a trip through Algeria with his Egeria, the Empress, the Emperor Napoleon III was obliged to save his skin by going in full regalia through a mangrove swamp. What increased their sluggishness was the fact that the Emperor wore Wellingtons that pinched his feet.

The infant, the effant, the elephant, the frog and the sauté potato.

. . .

A screw, ridged as it spirals; expressed at the tip: a screw!
A vice, it squeezes tight; when we squeeze tight; it's vice!
[A valiant attempt to squeeze the sense from the French pun on *la vis*, the screw, and *le vice,* vice.]

. . .

The artillery of the Sacré-Coeur or the cannonisation of Paris.

. . .

The sun is in filigree lace.

A fraction of pale blue lining, a strip of fur like a patch of sky over a stretch of the polar region.

. . .

When my brother returned from his travels, he embraced me. "What are you reading?" he asked me, "or rather, how old are you? for you can tell someone's age by their book." It was *The Carapacious Tartar* or was it *The Passionate Pilgrim* by the author of *The Tartan Cape* or *The Pilgrim Lassie.*[34]

The sequence concludes:

I am bringing you my two sons, said the old acrobat to the Virgin of the Rocks, who was playing the mandolin. The younger knelt in his pretty little suit; the other was holding out, on the end of a stick, a fish.

At this point, a reader new to Max Jacob might be tempted to throw the book across the room. But supposing that we keep the book in hand with a little patience, and supposing that we are readers who relish words even when they are turning somersaults, we may find that "Le Coq et la perle" rewards our attention. If we let it teach us how to read, we find that we are in a world of rapid transitions and logical leaps; a world where propositions are made and then negated; where the ordinary sense we are used to making finds itself in danger. If style enacts consciousness, Jacob's style here initiates us into a state of mind that can survive the rapid assault of shifting data: that can survive modernity. Like Picasso in *Les Demoiselles d'Avignon*, Jacob invites us to see representation as a convention. "Le Coq et la perle" plunges us into a structure of shifting and competing conventions so that we are compelled to see writing itself as a set of provisional illusions. But the exercise of alienation allows, finally, a new language of oblique truth-telling no longer possible in the older dialect.

In the opening fragments of "Le Coq," we move from a bit of nineteenth-century realist narration ("I thought he was bankrupt"), to a joke on the conditions of writing ("he's even found me a publisher!"), to a dizzyingly unstable world of the second-person singular with lanterns on castors and a zebra on rockers, to a multifarious self-portrait: "I hereby declare that I am world-wide, oviparous, a giraffe. . . ." This self-portrait undoes the conventions of Romantic singular identity, the heroic "I" of Victor Hugo, and carries the ascetic absence of Mallarmé and the objectivity of Rimbaud ("Je est un autre"—I is another) into the direction of the carnivalesque and the absurd. In a few rapid gestures, Jacob has undone the dominant conventions of nineteenth-century fiction and poetry and its postures of both objectivity and subjectivity. The task of the new art will be to create new grounds for both.

Several preoccupations begin to emerge which will prove to be keys to Jacob's later art as well as to this book. One is the love story. Too painful to be told "straight," love in Jacob's landscape appears in flashes and sidewise glances, its intense vulnerability protected by the surrounding ironies. So the line "His white arms became my whole horizon" compresses Romantic diction into a modernist metaphoric fragment, as the grandeur of the experience ("my whole horizon") is compressed into a single embrace ("his white arms"). As modernist narration, the scene presents only a snapshot from which a story must be inferred; as modernist poetry, the line stops a syllable shy of the canonical Alexandrine, and focuses on an image, not an explanation or elaboration of emotion. It would be possible to read the elliptical presentation of love in Jacob as an aspect of the life of the closet in his generation, but to limit it to a queer reading, I think, would be to neglect the philosophical as well as emotional range of his radical privacy.

Another concern surfacing again and again here is a method of image-making. Sometimes it takes the form of an outright metaphorical assertion: "A pale blue thorn-bush is a steeple in the moonlight." At other times, it comes as a meditation about visual art: "When you're painting a picture . . ." In either mode, it forces us to see reality anew as a set of unlikely resemblances. The painting evoked here turns out to be an exercise in synesthesia as the picture turns like a cylinder, evoking the multiple perspectives of Cubist art, and concludes as sound, not vision, in the Tower of Babel, and as multiplicity, not unity of sense. A reader of such work must be an active partner, collaborating in the play of sense-making, and recognizing it as play. Allied to the visual inventions of the poem is its project of revelation, its hyperreality, each little epiphany leading to an altered state of awareness: "It so happens that, when you snore, the world of matter wakes the other world." The poet behind such a statement has trained himself in Kabbalah, in astrology, in mystic numerology, in the rich, more or less cranky world of the *fin de siècle* occult.

One of the shortest sections of "Le Coq et la perle" will serve as a molecule which recapitulates in miniature the structure of the whole:

L'enfant, l'éfant, l'éléphant, la grenouille et la pomme sautée.

(The infant, the effant, the elephant, the frog and the sauté potato.)

The part reflects the whole in presenting a sequence that both does and does not exhibit a logical order. It is an unsatisfactory statement syntactically, since it is not a grammatical sentence: its incompletion demonstrates the method of the whole book. Lacking a verb, it forces the reader to supply a verb mentally, and thereby to make a private sense of the sequence. The first three words appear to follow a phonetic pattern ("L'enfant, l'éfant, l'éléphant . . ."); only similarity in sound holds them together, and one of them, *l'éfant*, is a nonsense word engendered by the other two. Then the line—if we can call it that, for it lives uneasily between verse and prose—switches from phonetics to image-making in its mode of communication with "frog," a creature whose leaps seem the figurative equivalent of the whole poem. From the frog, the conjunction "and" comfortingly and fallaciously asserts linkage, and joins the preceding nouns to the further leap in the pun on *pomme sautée*, a culinary joke on the idea of leaping already suggested by the frog. The *pomme sautée* is literally a jumping apple, but in French culinary argot *pomme* is short for *pomme de terre*, or potato, and "sautéing" is not jumping but rapid frying in a skillet. So nothing is what it seems, and meaning leaps from unit to unit; meaning is the leaping itself, the motion. And of paramount importance in measuring Jacob's leap from Mallarmé is his rejection of Symbolist hieratic diction and imagery: with Jacob, we are in a world of high jinks and low art, all the hierarchies scrambled and aesthetic categories turned inside out.

Just as Jacob hides his erotic experience between the lines, so does he fold his religious faith into serious pranks. The old acrobat who presents his sons to the Virgin of the Rocks seems to have stepped out of one of Picasso's Blue Period paintings of circus performers into Leonardo's canonical painting in the Louvre, and the virgin herself has picked up a mandolin, a recognizable prop from Cubist painting. The boys, who may or may not be John the Baptist and the Christ child, embody that sacred possibility that Jacob saw everywhere around him, as he said, in the gutter, the streets, the commonest of everyday life. The fish dangling at the end of the child's stick concludes this whole phantasmagorical poem with a perfectly commonplace noun that also contains the Christian mystery of sacrifice and its most ancient symbol.

Some might call Jacob's work "metapoetry." I prefer to say simply that Jacob, as fed up with Parnassian neoclassical formalities as with the equally mechanical and airless leftover Symbolism, has chosen to do a little demolition work, clear some space, and begin sorting out, afresh, the elements of poetry. When we turn to the "dice," the block-shaped prose poems that form the bulk of *Le Cornet à dés*, we find an expansion of similar techniques and frames of mind. The prose poem is a hybrid form, begging every question about the nature and limits of genre. Furthermore, Jacob's prose poems sidestep the anecdotal coherence of the earlier prose poems of Aloysius Bertrand, Baudelaire, and Mallarmé. Rimbaud is a more serious competitor to Jacob's lucid art of the irrational, and it is therefore Rimbaud he takes pains to attack in the preface to *Le Cornet à dés*:

> Rimbaud widened the field of sensibility and all writers owe him a debt of gratitude, but authors of prose poems cannot take him as a model, because the prose poem, in order to exist, has to submit to the laws of all art, which are style or intention, and the situation or feeling, and Rimbaud leads only to disorder and exasperation. . . . The prose poem is a constructed object and not a jewelry shop window. Rimbaud is the jewelry shop window, not the jewel: the prose poem is a jewel.[35]

(Jacob had, earlier in the preface, insisted on a distinction between "style" and "situation" that to many readers will feel arbitrary: "The style or the intention creates, that is to say, separates. The situation distances, that is to say excites artistic emotion; we recognize that a work has style when it gives the sense of having closure; we recognize that it's situated from the little shock it gives or from the margin that surrounds it, the special atmosphere in which it moves.")[36] Both style and situation, by which Jacob seems to mean characteristic choice of diction and syntax, and characteristic imagery and action, serve to distinguish the literary work, to set it apart from other works and from reality, and to insist on its internal coherence.

Let us examine one of Jacob's jewels. "Roman d'aventures" (Adventure Story) tells us by its title that it's a pastiche of a popular genre of fiction. It works through a collision of styles and tones, and through its comic polarities: ancient versus modern, French versus English, chastity versus sexual innuendo, homosexual versus heterosexual, nature versus city, logic versus illogic. And we may as well say, verse versus prose, the polarity underlying any prose poem.

ROMAN D'AVENTURES

C'est donc vrai! me voilà comme Philoctète! abandonné par le bateau sur un rocher inconnu, parce que j'ai mal au pied. Le malheur est que mon pantalon me fut arraché par la mer! Renseignements pris, je ne suis pas ailleurs que sur le rivage de la pudique Angleterre. "Je ne tarderai pas à trouver un policeman!" C'est ce qui arriva: un policeman et qui parlait français: "Vous ne me reconnaissez pas, dit-il en cette langue, je suis le mari de votre bonne anglaise!" Il y avait une raison que je ne le reconnusse pas, c'est que je n'ai jamais eu de bonne anglaise: il me conduisit dans une ville voisine en cachant ma nudité avec des feuillages tant bien que mal et, là, chez un tailleur. Et, comme je voulais payer: "Inutile, me dit-il, fonds secrets de la police" ou "de politesse," je n'ai pas très bien compris le mot.[37]

ADVENTURE STORY

So it's true! Here I am, like Philoctetes! Cast away on an unknown reef by the ship, because my foot hurts. The awkward thing is that my trousers were ripped off by the sea! Upon inquiry, I am, of all places, on the shores of chaste England. "It won't be long before I find a policeman!" That's what happened: a policeman, one who spoke French: "You don't recognize me," he said in that language, "I'm the husband of your English maid!" There was a reason why I hadn't recognized him; it's that I never had an English maid: hiding my nudity as well as could be expected with a leafy branch, he led me to a nearby city, and there, to a tailor's shop. And as I tried to pay, "Don't bother," he told me, "Secret police funds," or "politeness funds," I couldn't quite catch the word.[38]

This poem cannot be translated effectively because its action springs from its being written in French and placed in England, and using the English word "policeman" within the French text. The English policeman speaks French. Setting aside the question of its linguistic tensions, we see how it uses the conventions of rationality and logic of a detective story and then turns them inside out. Just as the narration seems to promise a logical order ("There was a reason why I hadn't recognized him"), the next assertion contradicts the story's coherence: "I never had an English maid." The punctuation intensifies the delirious character of the episode: reasons and actions spill forward, directed and connected by commas and a colon: ". . . I never had an English maid: he led me to a nearby city. . . ." Even granted the tolerance for run-on sentences in French prose, this sentence accelerates the sequence of events across normal boundaries of plot and place. The most serious polarity, and auditory confusion, is the last, between *police* and *politesse*. The near rhyme raises the question of the nature of social order, and the question of whether it is enforced, linguistically and otherwise, by habits of courtesy and convention (politeness) or by the threat of force (police). One remembers that homosexuality was a crime punishable by fines and imprisonment in France at this time, and that even in the relatively tolerant city of Paris, gay bars were routinely raided and their clients arrested or harassed. It is also in the police force that Jacob found some of his lovers; the flipping valences in his prose poems to some extent reflect the paradoxes and hypocrisies of his actual social world.[39] In all of Jacob's work, fractures in language tend to fracture, as well, illusions of stability in social order and categories of experience.

In 1921, Max Jacob, tired of his worldly life in Paris and the bickering among the avant-gardes, withdrew to the Benedictine monastery of Saint-Benoît-sur-Loire, where he remained until 1928 with rare jaunts to Paris and to his native Brittany. He could not live in the monastery as monastic life in France had been dismantled by the anticlerical edicts of the French government between 1902 and 1905, and in any case he had not been accepted into a monastic order. But he lived first in the priest's house attached to the basilica, and then in lodgings in the village, following a monastic routine of prayer and meditation which still left him time to write and paint. From 1928 to 1937 he had another swing of life in Paris, and then from 1937 to his death in 1944 he lived again in retreat at Saint-Benoît. During all those years, he continued to evolve as a poet, writing eight more books of poems, a number of highly unusual novels, plays, and story collections, and two treatises on poetry.

The gambits of *Le Cornet à dés* were really only the beginning. The later poems represent something we might call the mystic avant-garde. Part of the story of twentieth-century philosophy in France is the quest by atheists for a vocabulary and even a practice to give them access to mystical experience and contact with a sublime Other that is not divine. The work of Georges Bataille, starting in the twenties, can be seen in this light, as can that of Maurice Blanchot. Jacob, by contrast, believed ardently in the Catholic god he had annexed partly from the colorful folkloric rituals of his childhood in Brittany, and partly from his need for a philosophy of consoling love. His poems, from the twenties on, unfold within the context of his highly personal adopted faith and his Jewish background and lifelong interest in Kabbalah. Starting from the vantage point of the secular avant-garde, he devised a set of radical linguistic maneuvers in his poems which form exercises for the change of consciousness and preparation for visionary experience. "Colloque III" from *Fond de l'eau* in 1927 provides a characteristic example:

COLLOQUE III

—Regardez-moi. Vous fais-je peur?

—Quelles petites flammes autour de Votre Visage? Seigneur, que ne pouvez-vous être aussi fier de moi que je le suis de Vous.

—Vous avez trop de vie. L'améthyste a la couleur de la nuit, soyez comme l'améthyste. Vous ne vous trompez pas.

—J'ai rechauffé dans mes mains qui sont l'esprit l'oiseau qui est le Saint Esprit.

—Posez l'oiseau sur le marbre de la Vérité.

—Je m'aime en Vous.

—Vous m'aimez en vous.[40]

DIALOGUE III

—Look at me. Do I frighten you?

—What are those tiny flames around Your Face? My Lord, would that you could be as proud of me as I am of You.

—You're too lively. The amethyst is the color of night, be like the amethyst. You won't be mistaken.

—In my hands which are ghostly I've warmed the bird which is the Holy Ghost.

—Place the bird on the altar of Truth.

—I love me in You.

—You love me in you.

The dialogue form maintains the distinction between the two speakers, one divine, one human, but the separation is, if not canceled, at least radically exchanged in the play of pronouns at the end: "I love me in You. / —You love me in you." In that exchange, the word "you" serves as a vessel that can carry divine and human substances, and love reveals both transformation and affirmation of Being in simple and almost algebraic terms.

Almost all of Jacob's later poetic works are love poems in some fashion, derived from traditions of mystical eroticism he found in *The Song of Songs*, the works of the Catalan mystic Raymond Lulle, whom he had translated, and Saint John of the Cross. But Jacob's poems are far more troubled than the earlier works, and human, sexual love looms tormentingly in them. "Vision infernale en forme de madrigal" (Infernal Vision in the Form of a Madrigal) appeared in the collection *Les Pénitents en maillots roses* (The Penitents in Pink Drawers) in 1925. It pours its fluid Alexandrine lines with irregularly placed half lines for emphasis against eight-syllable insets: Jacob has taken over two of the traditional lines of French verse, the Alexandrine and the octosyllabic, and molded them to his own dreamlike transitions. The poem plays between inherited orders—of metrics, rhyme, and spiritual experience—and the eruption of irregularity: the balance of strophes is thrown off after the sixth, and sacred love is blasphemously replaced by human, erotic, and personal love. The absurd, in this poem, is no longer a gesture to *épater le bourgeois*; it's the presence, in this world, of mystery, the mystery of love, with all its impersonal and personal force.

VISION INFERNALE EN FORME DE MADRIGAL

"Beaux chevaliers d'Alcantara
Vénus de Marnes la Coquette
Le nabab de Calatrara
Vous fait offrir sa goélette
pour partir au Guatemala."

Quand j'avais renoncé à votre amour, ô femmes
quand j'avais du plaisir chanté le requiem
et conquis Bethléem

Quand du monde j'avais repoussé la jusquiame
Du voyage éternel d'Isaac Laquedem
quand j'avais pris la rame

Quand sous l'étroit balcon la patrouille des vices
et ses rires sonnants comme un de profundis
frappant comme jadis
ma porte afin de me pousser dans ses milices
j'avais fait de ma chambre une secrète oasis
ou plutôt un hospice

je n'avais pas connu le ciel clair de tes yeux
le neigeux univers de ton corps estival
ni l'enfer embaumé de tes épais cheveux
ni ta beauté qui me sera le Saint Graal
ni ton âme dont je serai le Parsifal.

"Beaux chevaliers d'Alcantara
Beaux chevaliers d'Alcantara
le bateau part! on n'attend pas!
—Qu'ils s'en aillent vers les tropiques,
je n'ai qu'une exode mystique
qu'un reliquaire et sa relique
je n'ai plus qu'une tendre oasis
ce sont tes yeux de myosotis."[41]

INFERNAL VISION IN THE FORM OF A MADRIGAL

"Handsome knights of Alcantara
Venus of Marnes-la-Coquette
The nabob of Calatrara
Offers you his private yacht
to sail away to Guatemala."

When I had renounced your love, O women,
when I had of pleasure intoned the requiem
    and conquered Bethlehem

When I had cast off the henbane of this world
And of the Wandering Jew's eternal
    voyage the sail unfurled

When, beneath the cramped balcony, the vice
squad and its laughter ringing de profundis
    knocking as in the old days
at my door to enroll me in its militias
I had made my room a secret oasis
    or almshouse

I did not yet know the clear sky of your eyes
the snowy kingdom of your limbs in summer
nor the perfumed hell in your thick hair
nor your beauty which will be my Holy Grail
nor your soul for which I shall be Parsifal.

"Handsome knights of Alcantara
Handsome knights of Alcantara
all aboard! anchors aweigh!
—Let them rush off toward the tropics,
I have only one mystic exodus
one reliquary and its relic
I have one tender oasis only: you,
your eyes, their forget-me-not blue."[42]

In "Angoisses et autres" (Agonies and More), Jacob uses a Verlainian *vers impair*, the odd-numbered syllable line. In English the fact of writing a line of seven, nine, or eleven syllables hardly registers; in France, where since the seventeenth century both art and politics have been so dominated by ideas of symmetry and centrality, the *vers impair* hit the nineteenth century as a major upheaval, and it is still felt as an irregularity in the twentieth century. In "Angoisses et autres," which appeared in *Fond de l'eau* in 1927, the pronouns slide metamorphically. By this time, Jacob's earlier multiplication of identities ("I hereby declare that I am worldwide, oviparous, a giraffe, parched . . .") has a definite theological and erotic purpose. The first stanza plays the "I" of the poet-speaker against the capitalized "You" of God ("I'm afraid You'll take offense"). Stanza 2 moves in to the intimate, lowercase "you" which now designates the poet-speaker ("God whom you nag day in day out"). Stanza 3 flows out into the impersonal psychic realm of poetry and sorrow, with no "I," and with "you" now addressing Poetry itself: "this evening Poetry your horse / wears a black veil." These poems have dropped the obscurities of *Le Cornet à dés*, but maintain the psychic liberties gained in those first experiments.

ANGOISSES ET AUTRES

J'ai peur que Tu ne t'offenses
lorsque je mets en balance

dans mon cœur et dans mes œuvres
ton amour dont je me prive
et l'autre amour dont je meurs

Qu'écriras-tu en ces vers
ou bien Dieu que tu déranges
Dieu les prêtres et les anges
ou bien tes amours d'enfer
et leurs agonies gourmandes
Justes rochers vieux molochs
je pars je reviens j'approche
de mon accessible mal
mes amours sont dans ma poche
je vais pleurer dans une barque

Sur les remparts d'Edimbourg
tant de douleur se marie
ce soir
avec tant d'amour
que ton cheval Poésie
en porte une voile noire[43]

AGONIES AND MORE

I'm afraid You'll take offense
as I weigh and weigh again
in my works and in my heart
your love from which I live apart
that other love I'm dying in

What will these lines be about
God whom you nag day in day out
God his angels and his priests
or your love's infernal feasts
and their gobbling agonies
Righteous rocks old blood-soaked gods
I leave return veer close again
to my all-too-easy sin
my loves are in my pocket here
I'll sail weeping out to sea

On Edinburgh's city wall
so much sorrow marries so
much love
this evening Poetry your horse
wears a black veil[44]

Mallarmé was a poet of a pure and Absolute atheism, and Max Jacob a poet of impurity and the quest for absolution. Both placed poetic language under a pressure so great they threatened intelligibility. "Vision infernale en forme de madrigal" and "Angoisses et autres" show Jacob more concerned with earthly than with divine love. But the two were never separate for him, though they existed always in a kind of Petrarchan tension. If one is drawn into his work, one finds him working out, at length and in many variations, his lifelong confession, his sexual remorse, his fear of Hell, his hope of salvation through a fixation—quasi-erotic—on the figure of Christ, a sublimed version of the beautiful male body it was permissible to love. One can grieve that he never met the work of Gerschom Scholem, and never found a way to accept his own Jewishness: his studies in Kabbalah nourished him, but not sufficiently to provide him with a full religious practice. Judaism, as Jacob experienced it in his extended family and their social world both in Quimper and in Paris, was a religion of secular rationalism and the assimilated middle class; how delusional that assimilation was to prove became clear only in the family's near extinction under the Nazi Occupation. He lived in a profoundly anti-Semitic country, and internalized some of its poison. Similarly, one can grieve that he lived in a culture in which his kind of love—the love of men for men—was viewed as criminal and shameful, a shame he also took into his psyche and lived as hell. It was a hell that engendered some of his most powerful poems.

Max Jacob used (and invented) disorienting avant-garde techniques to dissolve the social and psychological "ego" and to open the spirit to revelations beyond conventions of selfhood his rational and materialistic culture provided. I conclude with an excerpt from a long poem from *La Défense de Tartufe* (The Defense of Tartufe), Jacob's book from 1919, an account partly in prose, partly in verse, of his vision and his conversion. "Le Christ au cinématographe" (Christ at the Movies) is written in Alexandrine rhyming couplets slapped down with nonchalant expertise. In my translation, I've tried to give the clash of tones—the faux naïf, the savvy cliché, the jargon, the wit, the eruption of prayer. For Jacob, God *was* everywhere, especially in slips of the tongue, in the gutter, in the human welter, in fractured language. This poem rises out of that welter, in its cheap shots, its awkwardness, its gimcrack phrasing. It defies sophistication. But then, so does the love of God, in any faith.

. . .

On me traite de fou! oui! j'entend le lecteur,
Ou bien de sacrilège et l'on fait le docteur:
Fous vous-mêmes, si la vérité vous fait rire.
Le Seigneur est partout et dans les endroits pires:
Sentir en soi son Dieu, l'écouter, lui parler,
Qu'on soit dans un théâtre, dans la rue, au café,
Ce miracle commun n'a rien qui scandalise;
On parle à Dieu partout en dehors de l'église.
Ma folie est ailleurs puisque fou l'on me croit.
Sachez que je L'ai vu! que je L'ai vu deux fois:
C'était rue Ravignan, chez moi, le sept octobre;
—Non! je n'étais pas gris, je suis un homme sobre—
Le sept octobre de l'année dix-neuf cent neuf;
Je te prends à témoin, Seigneur, qui mis à neuf
Mon âme de pécheur empli de turpitudes;
Tu sais de quelles péchés j'avais pris l'habitude,
Dans quel gâchis je vivais, tu sais dans quel enfer,
Quelles résolutions ta visite a fait naître
Dans le chrétien que, grâce à toi et aux bons prêtres,
Me voici devenu, plein de sens et de raison.
Donc, la première fois, Tu vins dans ma maison.
Et la seconde fois, au Cinématographe . . .
"Vous allez donc au Cinématographe,
Me dit mon confesseur, la mine confondue.
—Eh! mon père! le Seigneur n'y est-il pas venu?"

Bande des habits noirs, drame de Paul Féval;
Le drame est dans mon cœur et non pas sur le film.
Les agents de la gendarmerie en cheval
Encerclent un voleur dans un mortel dilemme,
Une taie sur la foule et les pleurs dans mes yeux!
La tache était un nimbe, le nimbe entourait Dieu.
A moi, cette faveur. pourquoi cette venue?
Sur l'écran! dans ce film au coin de cette rue,

C'est pour moi les plis du manteau blanc comme un cierge,
Abritant les quatres bambins de ma concierge
Dont tu voulus un jour que je prisse soin.
Ah! notre âme à tes yeux ne peut cacher de mystère?
Tu pénètres dans tous les êtres de la terre?
Alors! pourquoi? Pourquoi cette faveur
Si tu connais ma vie et toute sa noiceur?
Si tu connais mes fautes et toutes mes faiblesses?
Qu'y a-t-il donc en moi, mon Dieu, qui t'intéresse?[45]

FROM "CHRIST AT THE MOVIES"

. . .

They call me crazy! Yes! I hear the reader now—
Or blasphemous, you scold with furrowed brow.
Madmen yourselves, if truth can make you laugh.
The Lord is everywhere, and with the worst riffraff.
To feel God in oneself, to hear him, to reply,
Whether at the movies, in the street, at a café,
This common miracle shouldn't start a fuss:
Outside of church, God's everywhere, and speaks with us.
My madness, if I'm mad, is of a different brand.
Listen: I've seen him! Twice, close at hand:
It was October seven, rue Ravignan, in my room—
No! I wasn't drunk, nor in delirium—
In the year nineteen-oh-nine, October seven;
I take you as witness, Lord, who put new leaven
Into me, sinning lump of filthiness;
You know what sins had seized me in their fists,
What hell I lived in, what a squalid mess,
What resolutions you raised up like yeast
In this Christian whom, thanks to you and the good priests,
I've become, endowed with sense and reason.
So, the first time, you appeared in my room.
And the second time, it was at a film.
"You go to the movies, then?" with dumbfounded air
Demanded my confessor. —Yes, Father,
What if I did? Didn't Our Lord come there?"
The Gang in the Black Suits, thriller by Paul Féval;

The plot's in my heart and not on the screen.
The cops and Mounties close round and corral
A thief in dire straits: a sudden sheen
Spreads over the crowd, my eyes fill with tears!
The sheen is a halo, in its light God appears.
To me, this gift! Why did you choose to meet
Me here? In this movie on a little side street
The drapes of a taper-white mantle enfold
My concierge's four urchins you once told
Me to care for. Can the human soul
Hide no scrap from your eyes, must it be seen whole?
Is there for your vision no mystery in our heart?
Do you penetrate all beings in every part?
Then why? Why this grace
If you know my life in all its ugliness?
If you know my faults and my weaknesses too?
What in me, Oh Lord, could interest you?[46]

CHAPTER 11

Orpheus the Painter:
Apollinaire and Robert Delaunay

In its typography, Mallarmé's *Un Coup de dés* (1897)[1] raised once again the perennial problem of the relation, in poetry, between the senses of hearing and vision, and between their corresponding arts, music and painting. If Symbolist poetics had seemed to aspire to the condition of music,[2] *Un Coup de dés* shifted its allegiance toward the pictorial, and may be said to be a pivotal text, a turn toward a new poetry which would take its cue from Cubist painting.

Already, in the essays preceding *Un Coup de dés*, "La Musique et les lettres" (1894) and "Crise de vers" (1896), Mallarmé had affirmed the dual and intermediary nature of poetry, which draws lifeblood from both seeing and hearing. In his letter to Gide about *Un Coup de dés*, Mallarmé insisted on the bodiliness of his poem: "The constellation will assume there, in accordance with precise laws and insofar as the printed text permits, fatally the bearing [*l'allure*] of a constellation . . . for, and this is the whole point of view . . . the *rhythm of a sentence* concerning an act, or even an object, makes no sense unless it *imitates* them, and *figured upon the paper*, taken back by the letter from the original printed impression [*l'estampe*], contrives to *render*, in spite of everything, something of them [*n'en sait rendre, malgré tout, quelque chose*]"[3] (italics mine).

Roger Shattuck has aptly described this attitude as Mallarmé's Cratylism.[4] He quotes from the letter to Gide, and puts his finger precisely on the pictorial allegiance of Mallarmé's text: "Mallarmé is very precise: words can usually mimic their meaning. But this is heresy! Here is the patron saint of Symbolism attaching poetry not to music but to painting!"[5] Shattuck adds this footnote: "Mallarmé's Cratylism was also auditory. He complained almost petulantly about the inappropriate nocturnal hollowness of the French word jour, and of the complementary brightness and airiness of nuit." In both cases, the visual and the auditory, what Mallarmé insists on, and what Shattuck so rightly observes, is the doctrine of literal embodiment of sense, and as so often with Mallarmé, a Platonic dialogue supplies the correlative.

On the other hand, Un Coup de dés, that hymn to the conditional and subjunctive moods and to multiple vibrations of meaning, denies its own textual materiality, and the materiality of the world. In that hallucinatory seascape, all reality dissolves "in these latitudes / of the vague."[6] Mallarmé's puns and his hovering syntax point to the white spaces, the blanks of meaning beyond the surface of the text. Such wordplay, emphasizing language as a Gnostic veil, undermines the notion of the literal as the primary level of representation, and returns us to a notion of the literal as that which pertains simply to printed letters. The letters, however, for Mallarmé serve in their turn to define the blank spaces, which in their turn evoke l'immortelle parole,[7] the silent, paradisal language preceding Babel. In an ascension reminiscent of stages of eros in The Symposium, Mallarmé's poetics pass from the textual and pictorial to the musical, and then take a vast step further into the realm of pure essence, the Idea.

We can observe the first transformation, from image to music, in a paragraph from "La Musique et les lettres" which Mallarmé inserted into "Crise de vers." The passage starts with visual evocations: "Monuments, the sea, the human face, in their fullness, native. . . ." The power of such images cannot be described, but must be evoked, alluded to, suggested. The passage concludes with a paean to literary art: "Its own sorcery is to liberate, from a handful of dust or reality, without confining it to the book, even as a text, the volative dispersion, or spirit, which has no purpose other than total musicality."[8] And just as the poem transcends its textuality, this music has nothing to do with instruments. Later in this essay comes Mallarmé's famous exhortation to writers to reprendre notre bien (take back our property) from music.[9] He aims at a spirituality transcending music as well as the pictorial. The "elocutory disappearance of the poet" leads, by the end of the essay, to an implicit disappearance of the text itself into the pure contemplation of the Book of the Universe, "the magic concept of the Great Work. In a similar way, that symmetry linking the placement of verses within the poem to the authenticity of the poem within the volume flies, beyond the volume, to any number of poets who inscribe, on spiritual space, the larger signature of genius, anonymous, and perfect as an existence of art."[10] Such space is spiritual, not textual; and one notes the force of Mallarmé's simile, "perfect as an existence of art," which leaves the work of art hypothetical, a state of mystic virtuality.

Apollinaire cultivated the poetic place, the textual, musical, and pictorial *lieu*, bequeathed by Mallarmé. With the advent of Cubism, painting—which was beginning to examine more consciously its own semiotic nature—became the dominant model for poetic practice. Even before Braque included the letters *BAL* in his painting *Le Portugais* in 1911, Cubist art had been implicitly asserting the conventionality of pictorial signs by incorporating contradictory codes of representation within a single canvas.[11] The transaction between poets and painters, between verbal and visual signs, was mutual, if not equal: the outstanding poems of the period, by Jacob, Reverdy, Cendrars, Huidobro, and Apollinaire himself, spring largely from procedures and attitudes learned from the painters at le Bateau-Lavoir.

The poets reflect the painters' practices in multiple and mischievous ways. One thinks of the "Cubist" fracturing of narrative, semantic, and syntactic conventions in the works of these loosely connected poets as well as in the prose of Gertrude Stein. The multiplication of pictorial perspectives in Cubism found a literary analogue in multiple and shifting pronoun patterns. An underlying vision of discontinuity heralded by Picasso's *Les Demoiselles d'Avignon* (1907), a challenge to mimesis as the goal of art, and a self-conscious testing of the medium and conditions of representation seem to motivate the work of all the writers associated with le Bateau-Lavoir. Specifically pictorial notions of ideogrammatic typography operate in such pieces as *La Prose du Transsibérien*, the two-meter poem-painting scroll produced in 1913 by Blaise Cendrars and Sonia Delaunay; in Huidobro's *Tour Eiffel* (1918) dedicated to Robert Delaunay,[12] and in many of the poems in his volumes *Horizon Carré* (1917), *Ecuatorial* (1918), and *Poemas articos* (1918); and in the rather willful experiments of the poet Pierre Albert-Birot, editor of *SIC*. Reciprocally, Cubism's triumph owed much to the enthusiastic promotion it received at the hands of writers, especially Gertrude Stein, Apollinaire, and, later, Pierre Reverdy.

The latter's journal *Nord-Sud* reproduced Cubist art and published the poetry associated with Cubism (Jacob, Apollinaire, Huidobro, Salmon, Reverdy); Reverdy himself was recognized by the painters as a lucid interpreter of their work.[13] Reverdy's essay "Sur le cubisme," published in *Nord-Sud* in 1917, is a rare document in Cubist criticism, emphasizing each art's responsibility to its own medium, and defining Cubism, in its celebration of the pictorial medium, as an art, not of realism, but of "reality": the reality of paint on canvas, line, shape, value, and hue.[14]

Apollinaire published articles about Picasso from 1905 on,[15] and in 1913 assembled his various writings about art in the ambiguously titled *Méditations esthétiques: LES PEINTRES CUBISTES*, whose publisher, Eugène Figuière, capitalized the wrong phrase, thus skewing Apollinaire's emphasis.[16] In some ways, Apollinaire understood little about painting. At least, he rarely seems to have looked at it with much precision. Picasso, Braque, Jacques Villon, and the art dealer and publisher Kahnweiler have all spoken critically of Apollinaire's lack of visual comprehension[17]; his classification of "cubisms" into the "scientific," the "physical," the "orphic," and the "instinctive" was regarded as absurd, and his mystagogic reflections on the fourth dimension ("It figures the immensity of space eternalizing itself in all directions at a given moment. It is space itself, the dimension of the infinite . . .") seemed, to most painters, pure nonsense. Picasso has spoken of Apollinaire's art criticism as "shallow," "containing little good sense"; Daniel-Henry Kahnweiler is still less tolerant: "What unleashed his enthusiasm was novelty, true or false. His work on the Cubist painters is a conglomeration of passages written under the dictation of the painters themselves (sometimes altered at the last moment as the result of quarrels), magnificent lyrics flights, and a number of purely pataphysical elucubrations, for instance the classification of the painters into 'physical,' 'scientific,' 'instinctive,' and 'Orphic' Cubists."[18] Worse still, for Picasso and Braque, was Apollinaire's blithe skipping off into the camp of Sonia and Robert Delaunay.

Robert Delaunay's "Orphism" owed to analytic Cubism its freedom in breaking down hierarchies of perspective and volume, and its elevation of abstract geometric elements—triangular wedges, discs, arcs, straight lines—to the roles of major actors. Delaunay's treachery was his luscious celebration of hue but relative neglect of value, tone, and volumetric tension: a glorying in primary chromatic play that seemed, to Picasso and Braque, a betrayal of their rites of purification. But Delaunay's misreading of Cubism, a deviance which was to prove so fruitful for Paul Klee, also released a new poetry in Guillaume Apollinaire.

Apollinaire's earliest reference to Robert Delaunay, in 1910 in an article in *L'Intransigeant*, is hardly complimentary: ". . . solidly painted canvasses which have the unfortunate air of commemorating an earthquake."[19] But over the next two years, the tone grows much more sympathetic, not to say adulatory. Delaunay is partly credited with inventing "pure painting,"[20] a judgment which must have raised hackles at le Bateau-Lavoir, stronghold of analytic Cubism. Apollinaire's major essay on Robert Delaunay comes in 1912 and was printed in slightly varying versions both in France, in *Les Soirées de Paris*, and in Germany in *Der Sturm*. In this essay, Apollinaire, quoting Delaunay, celebrates color as "the problem of modern painting" (as opposed to the concern with two-dimensional rendering of volume that had motivated the researches of Picasso and Braque, and had in fact severely limited the Cubist palette). In line with this reversal of priorities, color over structure, space, and volume, Seurat is elevated over Cézanne as the father figure for modern painting, for it is in Seurat that Delaunay found inspiration for his theory of the simultaneous contrasts of colors: "The simultaneity of colors by the simultaneous contrasts and by all the unequal measures resulting from the colors according to their expression in their representative movement: this is the only reality for structuring a painting."[21] (The translation is faithfully turgid.) Delaunay, quoted by Apollinaire, goes on to associate pictorial simultaneity, the contrasts of complementary hues, with eternity: "The subject is the harmonic proportion, and this proportion is composed of various simultaneous members in one action. The subject is eternal in the work of art, and must appear to the initiate in all its order, all its science."[22] The crucial concept here is the interpenetration of spatial and temporal categories, which corresponded, for Apollinaire, to the visual and auditory elements of poetry. Delaunay's language of musical and mystical initiation so appealed to Apollinaire that it led him to conclude his essay with the announcement that "simultaneity is life itself,"[23] relegating all previous art, including, presumably, Cubism, to the realm of mere "succession" or death.

By 1913, Apollinaire was equating light with poetry when writing of the art Delaunay was now calling Orphism.[24] The poet had, indeed, received a new vision of the universe. He had long associated himself with the mythic lord of music and poetry, Orpheus, also important, in his role as mediator between life and death, as the founder of Greek and later Roman mystery cults.[25] In 1911, Apollinaire had published a charming collection of poems illustrated by Raoul Dufy's woodcuts, *Le Bestiaire, ou Cortège d'Orphée*, in which the first poem, "Orphée," celebrates the union of vision, music, and mystical knowledge. The reader is asked to admire "the line"—Dufy's line: "Elle est la voix que la lumière fit entendre" (It is the voice that the light made audible).[26] Delaunay's pictorial Orphism, which presumed to transcend the physicality of the canvas and the bounds of sequential time by making a mystery religion of colored light, suited Apollinaire's occult imagination perfectly. It remains to be seen with what precision Apollinaire would translate Delaunay's pictorial elements into poetic ones. As for Apollinaire's art criticism, it is not criticism at all: it is notes for a new translation of painting into poetry, the visualization of a new poetic space, a zone beyond "Zone."

Apollinaire's poem "Les Fenêtres" (1912) and the *Calligrammes* (1917) which closely followed it are inscribed in a long Western tradition of ekphrasis whose genealogy has been admirably traced by Jean Hagstrum, John Hollander, Wendy Steiner, and Albert Cook, among others.[27] I will not rehearse it here. But before turning to Delaunay's paintings, *Les Fenêtres*, and to Apollinaire's poem to and for them, I want to recall Lessing's sober separation of the media, visual art into the spatial mode and writing into the temporal, lest Apollinaire's pictorialism seem too facile an enterprise. When he declared, "Poésie cubiste? Idée ridicule!"[28] Pierre Reverdy was reformulating Lessing and helps remind us that Apollinaire's attempt to render painting into poetry was something of an unnatural act. But then, so is all art.

Delaunay exhibited a series of the window paintings in Berlin in December 1912 with Apollinaire's poem, produced on commission, as a catalogue copy. Briefly, we should note the shattering of the represented cityscape, Paris, into a self-reflective act of vision, a look through a hypothetical window whose frame is invisible (see Figure 1).

The window asserted by the title serves to focus the act of looking, and, indeed, makes "looking" a major theme by partitioning off the segment of cityscape we are to contemplate. In addition, Delaunay was studying the prismatic effect of the passage of light through panes of glass, studies he would carry on soon in paintings such as *Formes circulaires: le soleil et la lune* (1912–13).[29] The totemic figure of the Eiffel Tower, symbol of "pure" structure and, as we learn from Roger Shattuck, an emission station for a signal for the synchronization of world time,[30] has become the constitutive element, its triangle wedge shape organizing the rhythm of the color across the surface. Delaunay's catchword for his painting was "simultaneity," by which he meant the orchestrated contrasts of complementary hues; it is a term to which Apollinaire would give full temporal and metaphorical force.

Figure 1. Robert Delaunay, *Première Fenêtre simultanée*

One of the conversation poems (exercises in eavesdropping, and pre-Surrealist collaborative ventures, controlled in this case by Apollinaire), "Les Fenêtres" first took shape in a café with intervention by André Dupuy and André Billy; Apollinaire finished it in the Delaunay studio.[31] *Ut pictura poesis*: how does he translate the paintings? The secret, I believe, is his refusal to describe. Instead, the poem discovers the principle of action in the paintings, and invents an analogous linguistic enactment.

LES FENÊTRES

Du rouge au vert tout le jaune se meurt
Quand chantent les aras dans les forêts natales
Abatis de pihis
Il y a un poème à faire sur l'oiseau qui n'a qu'une aile
Nous l'enverrons en message téléphonique
Traumatisme géant
Il fait couler les yeux
Voilà une jolie jeune fille parmi les jeunes Turinaises

Le pauvre jeune homme se mouchait dans sa cravate blanche
Tu soulèveras le rideau
Et maintenant voilà que s'ouvre la fenêtre
Araignées quand les mains tissaient la lumière
Beauté pâleur insondables violets
Nous tenterons en vain de prendre du repos
On commencera à minuit
Quand on a le temps on a la liberté
Bigorneaux Lotte multiples Soleils et l'Oursin du couchant
Une vieille paire de chaussures jaunes devant la fenêtre
Tours
Les Tours ce sont les rues
Puits
Puits ce sont les places
Puits
Arbres creux qui abritent les Câpresses vagabondes
Les Chabins chantent des airs à mourir
Aux Chabines marronnes
Ét l'oie oua-oua trompette au nord
Où les chasseurs de ratons
Raclent les pelleteries
Étincelant diamant
Vancouver
Où le train blanc de neige et de feux nocturnes fuit l'hiver
Ô Paris
Du rouge au vert tout le jaune se meurt
Paris Vancouver Hyères Maintenon New York et les Antilles
La fenêtre s'ouvre comme une orange
Le beau fruit de la lumière

WINDOWS

The yellow fades from red to green
When aras sing in their native forest
Pihis giblets
There is a poem to be done on the bird with only one wing
We will send it by telephone
Giant traumatism
It makes one's eyes run

There is one pretty one among all the young girls from Turin
The unfortunate young man blows his nose in his white
    necktie
You will lift the curtain
And now look at the window opening
Spiders when hands were weaving light
Beauty paleness unfathomable violet tints
We shall try in vain to take our ease
They start at midnight
When one has time one has liberty
Periwinkles Burbot multiple Suns and the Sea-urchin of the
    setting sun
An old pair of yellow shoes in front of the window
Towers
Towers are streets
Wells
Wells are market places
Wells
Hollow trees which shelter vagabond Capresses
The Octoroons sing songs of dying
To their chestnut-colored wives
And the goose honk honk trumpets in the north
When the racoon hunters
Scrape their pelts
Gleaming diamond
Vancouver
Where the train white with snow and fires of the night flees
    the winter
O Paris
The yellow fades from red to green
Paris Vancouver Hyères Maintenon NewYork and the Antilles
The window opens like an orange
Lovely fruit of light

               (translated by Roger Shattuck)[32]

Delaunay's principle, as we have seen, is to break the represented hierarchies of volume and space into abstract elements, the wedge shape and
the color contrasts. The paintings also rely on the play between *passage*,
the passing of one plane into another or into contiguous space, and its

opposite maneuver, the abrupt meeting of planes along the line Leo Steinberg has called the "arris." *Passage*, as practiced by Cézanne and elaborated by Picasso, involved strenuous discontinuity in the representation of solid volumes, and since the Delaunay window paintings do not seriously articulate volume, the smoky blurring of planes into one another is a rather weak brand of *passage*.[33] Similarly, the hard edges separating planes hardly make three-dimensional suggestions in Delaunay's windows, and have, consequently, a much lazier time of it than in a Picasso. Still, Delaunay organized his surface by contrasts in complementary hues and in planar arrangement, and the effect of such contrasts is to disintegrate Renaissance perspectival assumptions about volume, space, and distance.

Apollinaire, for his part, must break the hierarchy of time, that is, sequence. He tries to do this by interrupting the story, by a new simplified syntax which makes each line an independent unit, and by mixing up verb tenses:

> Voilà une jolie jeune fille parmi les jeunes Turinaises
> Le pauvre jeune homme se mouchait dans sa cravate blanche
> Tu soulèveras le rideau

> (Here is a pretty young girl among the young girls of Turin
> The unfortunate young man was blowing his nose in his
> white necktie
> You will lift the curtain)

> [In discussing the poem line by line, I will not always follow
> Roger Shattuck's translation, as I need to make points about
> the literal sense of the French, such as the verb tenses, that he
> does not always represent.]

Such narrative and temporal discontinuity is an easy game, however, which never succeeds in simulating real "simultaneity" since even the non sequiturs are condemned to sequential presentation. The real discovery of the poem is not to have imitated pictorial simultaneity, but to have disrupted and reconstituted syntactic and semantic order through the exploitation of an abstract linguistic element analogous to the colored wedge, the syllable.

Like the wedge in Delaunay's paintings, the syllable defines both *passage* and disjuncture. The very first line announces the theme of *passage*: "Du rouge au vert tout le jaune se meurt" ("From red to green all the yellow dies out"). The [o] in "jaune" mediates between the [u:] in "rouge" and the [ɛ:] in "vert"; but Delaunay prefers contrast to mediation, and the color yellow dies out, in the paintings, in favor of more vibrant complementarities, just as the rainbow of vowels disappears into the insistent [a], [ã], and [i] of the following lines: "Quand chantent les aras dans les forêts natales / Abatis de pihis . . ." (When the macaws sing in their native forests / Giblets of pihis). The poem will continue to advance like this, not by a logic of description or narration, but in the phonetic engendering of one syllable by another, all the while maintaining a strong semantic vibration, an appeal to reference, just as the paintings keep appealing to representation and never entirely lose sight of Paris.

The poem, then, is a *lieu* for generating new relations between phonetic and semantic sense, a kind of paradisal laboratory. The next lines present the theoretical intention: "Il y a un poème à faire sur l'oiseau qui n'a qu'une aile / Nous l'enverrons en message téléphonique" (There is a poem to be made on the bird which has only one wing / We will send it as a *message téléphonique*). Here, technology becomes mythology: the new, winged poem (the ambiguous pronoun in *l'enverrons*, "we will send it," confuses bird and poem) to be sent through the new urban telegraph system is a revolutionary communication designed to crack the hierarchies of space and time: therefore, *traumatisme géant* (giant traumatism).

With the anonymous young man and young girl we are on the familiar terrain of Cubist narrative discontinuity; but line 10, "Tu soulèveras le rideau" (You will lift the curtain), introduces a new, heroic pronoun, "you," herald of the theatrical vision which opens as if of its own accord into the mystical present-tense eternity of the poem: "Et maintenant voilà que s'ouvre la fenêtre" (And now the window is opening). The next lines veer close to description as they evoke, in their sonorities, Delaunay's colors: "Araignées quand les mains tissaient la lumière / Beauté pâleur insondables violets."

The metaphor of weaving carries the material into the immaterial, and hints at the transcendental nature this poem's *lieu* will assume.

> Nous tenterons en vain de prendre du repos
> On commencera à minuit
> Quand on a le temps on a la liberté

(We'll try in vain to rest
We'll begin at midnight
When one has time one has liberty)

Here Apollinaire redoubles the assault on time. As Albert Cook has observed, *commencera* (will begin) is doubly future[34]; and the poem transfigures the cliché about having free time, and the clichéd names of newspapers, *Le Temps* and *La Liberté*, into a literal and revolutionary declaration. In Apollinaire's sparkling and aerial poetics, such a platitude ("When one has time one has liberty") has a special rhetorical function, *qua* platitude, dramatically placed to focus attention on the worn-out and commercial words. Just as Delaunay's Orphic vision redeems the ordinary visual world by rearranging it, Apollinaire aims at shocking into life all metaphors latent in common parlance. To have time and liberty, as pure essences, would be revolutionary indeed.

Its overt narration fractured, the poem lets its new freedom blossom into a cosmic allegorical vision which evolves, in a sustained *passage*, from the sea to the heavens, from green to red, from the material to the immaterial, with a Cubistically multiplied solar system in the center: "Bigorneaux Lotte multiples Soleils et l'Oursin du couchant" (Winkles Burbot multiple Suns and the Sea-urchin of sunset). Albert Cook has registered the reverberations of this line: "The opening aphorism has been spelled out and also emblazoned. Added to all this play of 'light' across the line is another grammatical alignment: The singulars and the plurals alternate—*Bigorneaux*, *Lotte*, *Soleils*, *Oursin*; and this alternation cuts across that between possibly literal (the first three) and certainly metaphorical (the last), as well as across that between sea creatures (the first, second, and fourth) and suns (the third and, in its figure, the fourth)."[35] I would like to point, additionally, to its astonishing juxtaposition with the line which follows: "Une vieille paire de chaussures jaunes devant la fenêtre" (An old pair of yellow shoes in front of the window). The point of view precipitates us from exterior to interior, from cosmic to domestic space, from red and green to yellow, and produces that "simultaneist" vertigo that Apollinaire admired in his friend's paintings. This effect of juxtaposition is analogous not to pictorial *passage*, but to its opposite, the articulation of the hard edge, or arris, between planes; it shows that Apollinaire, for all his palaver, was acutely sensitive to the multiple constructive procedures of the painting. When he wrote to his fiancée Madeleine Pagès that he liked this poem "*beaucoup, beaucoup*," it was to this new articulation, this flexible, line-by-line, mobile syntax that he referred.

The visionary pilgrimage continues with a series of semantic eviscerations: like Delaunay's overworked wedges, Apollinaire's phonemes have multiple duties to perform, and in performance they collapse height into depth, vertical into horizontal, space into time:

> Tours
> Les tours ce sont les rues
> Puits
> Puits ce sont les place
> Puits
>
> (Towers
> Towers are streets
> Wells
> Wells are market places
> Wells)

Tours: the word means towers, circular movements, turns, magic tricks. The poem exploits all senses. Towers melt into streets, wells turn into town squares; but *puits* is also an unstable syllable, since the same combination of sounds, [pui], means "then" as well as "wells," and launches us back into the sequential narration the poem has denied.

In the newly cleared poetic space an Edenic vision rises, time and space delivered up to the play of vowels, and especially to the familiar caresses of [a], [ã], and [i]:

> Arbres creux qui abritent les Câpresses vagabondes
> Les Chabins chantent des aires à mourir
> Aux Chabines marronnes
>
> (Hollow trees sheltering vagabond Capresses
> The Octoroons sing songs of dying
> To their chestnut-colored wives)

In its final phase, the poem enters a phonetic and onomatopoetic delirium in which the goose identifies "utterly" with its cry, and in which the word seems truly incarnate, hence untranslatable: "Et l'oie oua-oua trompette au nord" (And the goose honk honk trumpets in the north). The aural identity of *oie* (goose) with *oua* (honk) imitates the visual rhyming of Delaunay's wedges, which "signify" everything from the Eiffel Tower itself to the negative space defined by its base to rooftops to the patterned refraction of light. The poem concludes in a crescendo of phonetic identities. We must listen now to the flight of syllables, their metamorphoses, their undermining of syntactic and semantic order. The ear attends especially to the syllable [vɛr] which is a color, *vert*, green, and a line of verse, *vers*, but also the preposition *vers* (toward), essential but always suppressed in this poem of transition, of *passage*; *ver* shares also in the name of a city and a season: Vancou*ver*, hi*ver*. Ear and eye collaborate intimately to seize the identity of space and time in the rhyming couples Hyères/*hier*, Maintenon/*maintenant*. And the impossible geographical flight between cities ("Paris Vancouver Hyères Maintenon New York et les Antilles") simulates pictorial *passage*, while the sound [ã] frolics between color in *blanc*, space in *Van*couver, and time in the suggested but not quite present "mainte*nant*."

The poem concludes almost at the place of its beginning, thus in a near-cyclical eternity and denial of progression, with the repetition of its first line, "Du rouge au vert tout le jaune se meurt." Like the window, the poem opens "like an orange," offering slices of fruit, the wedges displayed, and splayed, in Delaunay's paintings: "La fenêtre s'ouvre comme une orange" (The window opens like an orange). The simile seems to leave us with a figurative incarnation, the fruit. But just as the sea urchin turned into a sunset, the last line takes yet another turn, and turns the comparison inside out, transforming matter, the orange, into spirit and light: "Le beau fruit de la lumière." The incarnation proposed was unstable and temporary, and leaves us merely with the echo of a familiar sound in "Le beau fruit de la lumi*ère*."

If *Un coup de dés* set out to be a musical score,[36] but remained, in part, typography and painting—if it wanted to be spirit but could not deny its flesh—"Les Fenêtres" aspires to the condition of painting but remains, in part, music, and spirit. It is Apollinaire's triumph to have endowed poetic music with a new phonetic fleshliness, a new way of irritating sound into sense.

Since a major source of Apollinaire's inspiration lay in painting, most vitally in the work of Picasso and Delaunay, it is not surprising that soon after his pictorial experiment in "Les Fenêtres" he should have pressed his medium still further in the direction of the visual. Huidobro, the Italian Futurists, and the Russian "Rayonists" Larionov and Goncharova were already experimenting, in poems and on posters, with wildly various and wildly placed typography.[37] In *Calligrammes* Apollinaire formalized those impulses, and seemed driven to transform Mallarmé's transcendent *lieu*, the text which is, finally, a sign to be erased, into an entirely earthly and incarnate space, a text-picture which literally embodies itself, a *lieu* not so much significant as self-signified. The poem-as-emblem, a familiar creature in the lineage extending from Simmias of Rhodes (ca. 300 B.C.E.) through George Herbert, gains new life in the post-Symbolist linguistic context.

The first version of *Calligrammes* was a small collection of *idéogrammes lyriques* scheduled to appear in August 1914. It was entitled *Et moi aussi je suis peintre* (And I also am a painter). The outbreak of war interrupted the publication of the book, which did not come out until April 1918, much expanded, with the title *Calligrammes*. If Apollinaire's pictorial ambition declared itself more modestly in the new title—*gramma* in Greek means the line of a drawing as well as an alphabetical letter—that ambition was hardly diluted in the pictorial typography of the poems. The *calligrammes*, poems shaped like watches, neckties, crowns, fountains, the Eiffel Tower, and so forth, seem to break the tenuous equilibrium between image and sound established in *Un coup de dés* and "Les Fenêtres," and seem to affirm the pictorial materiality, the physical presence, of the text.

Perhaps not surprisingly, in subjecting language to such strains, the *calligrammes* end up meditating not about the pictorial, but about the poetic: in courting the literal, they explore the resources of the symbolic, which refuses to be suppressed. Looking into an alien medium, Apollinaire sees himself reflected; looking into painting, he *hears* poetry. In the *calligramme* "Cœur couronne et miroir," which juxtaposes three objects on one page, each is an emblem of the poet: the heart is his own, a flame reversed; the crown (disentangled from its image) tells us that "Les Rois qui meurent tour à tour renaissent au cœur des poètes" (Kings dying one by one are reborn in the hearts of poets); and the circular mirror, which is a circular sentence, encloses the inscription GUILLAUME APOLLINAIRE. It would appear, then, that, for this poet at least, painting is a place in which to encounter poetry, that is to say, himself.

Apollinaire formalizes, as well, what might be considered a dual phenomenology of reading. Pondering themes of loss and evanescence, eternal lyric motifs given special poignance by the wartime context of this book, the *calligrammes* seem to oppose the passage of time in reading by presenting each poem as a "simultaneous" shape which can be grasped with the illusion of immediacy. In "La colombe poignardée et le jet d'eau" (see

Figure 2), the poet arrests a bird in flight over a spurting fountain, and immortalizes in each fugitive emblem the names of the lost: women in the bird, his dispersed male companions in the ejaculating water.

Such is the perennial ambition of poets, Horace's "exegi monumentum aere perennius," Shakespeare's "That in black ink my love may still shine bright." Apollinaire's shaped poem, the text-as-*lieu*, rescues not only loves and friends and the erotic moment itself lost to time, but strains to remove the very act of reading from time by encoding it in a visual image. Reading itself, then, could be construed as an erotic act, perishable but solicitous of immortality. On the other hand, the poem can only be deciphered in time; it is only in time that its haunting rhymes and eight-syllable units reveal themselves. All reading of poetry depends on such a dual awareness of a poem's iconic unity and of its musical passage; in the *calligrammes*, Apollinaire dramatizes and makes explicit what every reader of poetry must perform.

In conclusion, I would like to look briefly at one of the *calligrammes*. "Il pleut" (see Figure 3) appeared in 1916 in Pierre Albert-Birot's journal *SIC*.

Even before reading the poem, we are confronted, visually, by its offense against our habit of reading horizontally. At first glance, "Il pleut" may appear a fairly juvenile exercise: words become rain, sound becomes image. But its power rises from an opposite impulse: the metamorphosis of image into music.

Most of the lines have a rather conventional prosody. Given the liberties that Apollinaire habitually takes with the final *e* and with the pronunciation of verbs in the third-person plural, the lines fall (literally) into fairly regular eight- and ten-syllable units, and into Alexandrines. The poem presents an equally traditional lyric subject matter: the ephemeral nature of love. It is a complaint against time. And with the pressure of this subject, the poem-painting shades into the poem-score, into music. It also remembers Verlaine's hypnotic poem of raining and weeping, an exercise in oneiric repetition from the rain song, "Il pleure dans mon coeur" (It rains in my heart).

We can trace Apollinaire's transformation of the poem-painting into the poem-score. In the first half line, "Il pleut des voix de femmes comme si" (It rains voices of women as if), a material reality, the rain, dissolves into sound, the women's voices. In the half line's complement, "elles étaient mortes même dans le souvenir" (they were dead even in memory), the ambiguous pronoun *elles* could refer either to the voices or to the

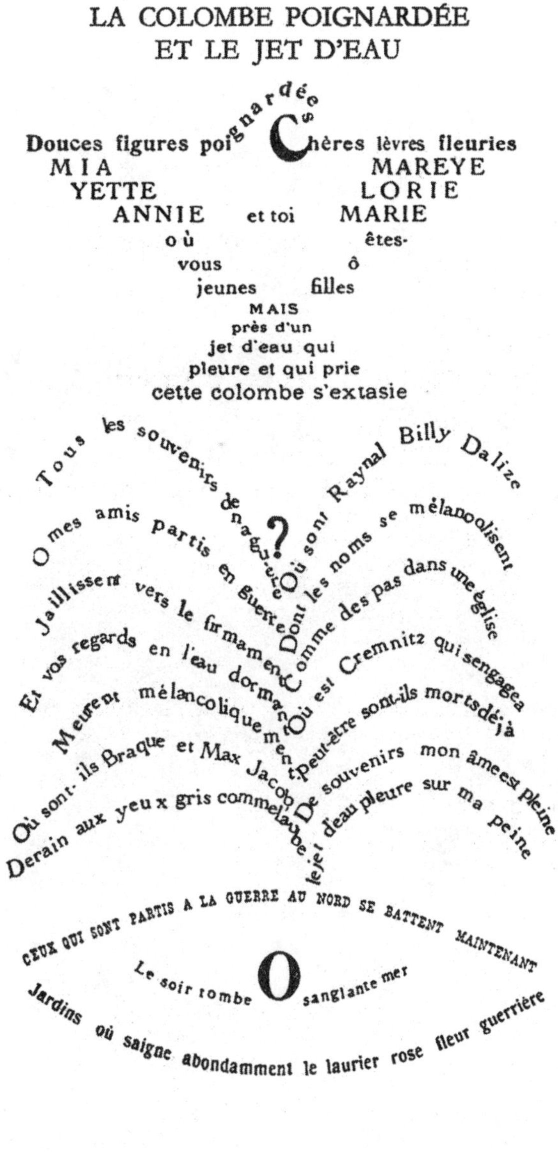

LA COLOMBE POIGNARDÉE
ET LE JET D'EAU

Douces figures poignardées Chères lèvres fleuries
MIA MAREYE
YETTE LORIE
ANNIE et toi MARIE
où êtes-
vous ô
jeunes filles
MAIS
près d'un
jet d'eau qui
pleure et qui prie
cette colombe s'extasie

Tous les souvenirs de naguère
O mes amis partis en guerre
Jaillissent vers le firmament
Et vos regards en l'eau dormant
Meurent mélancoliquement
Où sont-ils Braque et Max Jacob
Derain aux yeux gris comme l'aube
Où sont Raynal Billy Dalize
Dont les noms se mélancolisent
Comme des pas dans une église
Où est Cremnitz qui s'engagea
Peut-être sont-ils morts déjà
De souvenirs mon âme est pleine
Le jet d'eau pleure sur ma peine

CEUX QUI SONT PARTIS A LA GUERRE AU NORD SE BATTENT MAINTENANT
Le soir tombe O sanglante mer
Jardins où saigne abondamment le laurier rose fleur guerrière

Figure 2. Guillaume Apollinaire, "La Colombe poignardée et le jet d'eau"

IL PLEUT

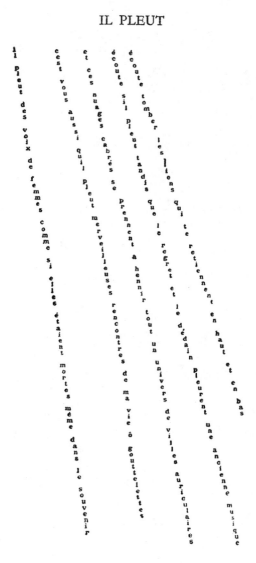

Figure 3. Guillaume Apollinaire, "Il pleut"

women: we are witnessing still another dissolution, that of the women themselves into sound, and of sound into uncertain memory.

The second line, or line of rain, precipitates memory back into its liquid state, but with such metaphoric intervention that we can no longer trust the materiality of these raindrops: "C'est vous aussi qu'il pleut merveilleuses rencontres de ma vie ô gouttelettes" (It's you also that it rains marvelous encounters of my life O droplets). In the third line, each hemistich evolves from the visual to the auditory: "et ces *nuages* cabrés se prennent à *hennir* tout un *univers* de villes *auriculaires*" (and these clouds start whinnying a whole universe of auricular cities).

The penultimate line contains a chiasm of auditory/emotional/emotional/auditory: "*écoute* s'il pleut tandis que le *regret* et le *dédain* pleurent une ancienne *musique*" (listen if it's raining while regret and contempt weep an ancient music). We should note as well a near pun in French between the verbs for raining and weeping, *pleuvoir* and *pleurer*, reinforcing the line's inner symmetry. If the poem concluded here, it would leave us with a simple resolution in favor of the last word, *musique*. But that would be too simple a reversal of the apparent pictorial pretensions. It concludes, instead, with a new and precarious balance between the claims of the ear and those of the eye: "écoute tomber les liens qui te retiennent en haut et en bas" (listen to the fall of the ties which hold you high and low). I hope it is not too willful of me to understand *liens* (ties, bonds, ligatures, lines) as an allusion to the lines of verse; this poem which holds and doesn't hold in its lines, in defiance of typographical gravity, seems an emblem of loss as well as of paradoxical restitution. Love falls from memory, the poem falls out of its prosody, image dissolves into music and music into memory. But the emblem itself, the image, the idea of form, remain, and hold us "high and low." It is the profession of an ancient and subtle faith in the resources of poetic form. And this poem, so aggressively situated in the *lieu*, the space, of vision, discovers that it is a space haunted, even consecrated, by music.

Section III

POETRY AND CONSCIENCE: "I" AT WORK

CHAPTER 12

Words and Blood in Dante

Although the Logos is common to all, most men live as if
each of them had a private intelligence of his own.
—Heraclitus

R eaders of the *Divine Comedy* find there a vastly complex medieval theology penetrating all order—moral, aesthetic, political,
and scientific—along with a lifetime's reading list of sources and
corollary texts. This is not the hunger I bring to the poem. What struck
me, when I blundered into its precinct as a teenager, was its dramatic
spiritual psychology in a poetry embodied in sounds, objects, and action.
I can still hardly write about it, because I absorbed the poem first in the
almost prearticulate fervor of late adolescence. This was poetry to be
tasted, gnawed, turned on the tongue.

I was eighteen, living alone in Rome, wandering through a canto or
two a day in my grandmother's shabbily elegant calfskin edition before
wandering later each day through the hallucinatory city. These grandeurs
seemed mystifying, urgent. Like the city, the poem appealed to the sensory
intellect, drawing its sense from the senses. I felt then, I still feel, that we
can recognize our own desires and deformations in Dante's cast of char-

acters, as we recognize our physical world in his, boiling pitch, fireflies, mirrors, candles, shadows, and all. Such a poetry is incarnational in a lowercase, secular sense. But its majesty, strain, and challenge arise from its profane communions being set always in the light of a specific religious communion, its human words in the light of a sacred Word. Into that gulf between word and Word, the poem radiates its illusion and its promise.

As Virgil describes the journey to be taken through Hell, he promises the wayward pilgrim an experience as powerfully auditory as it will be visual:

> ove udirai le disperate strida,
> vedrai li antichi spiriti dolenti,
> ch'a la seconda morte ciascun grida . . .

> (*Inferno* I.115–17)

(. . . where thou shalt hear the desperate lamentations / shalt see the ancient spirits disconsolate, / who cry out each one for the second death. [All translations are by Henry Wadsworth Longfellow.])[1]

Before the character Dante even enters the gates of Hell, it is the infernal cacophony that strikes his imagination. Light is mute here, but sighs, groans, cries, keening, and curses resound in every language of the earth. The deeper he descends, the greater the range of utterances of grief and fury he will hear. There is political rhetoric, obscenity, slang, nonsense (the quasi-significant gibberish of Pluto and Nimrod) and, almost at the bottom, the heartbreaking echo of the sacred in Ugolino's tale of his dying son Gaddo: "Padre mio, ché non m'aiuti?" (*Inferno* XXXIII.69: My father, why dost thou not help me?), the "Eli, eli, lamma sabacthani" still misunderstood, misheard, by Ugolino, who seems impervious to the model of sacramental sacrifice his son has offered him. Hell is the grimly familiar landscape of most human desire and action, and its sounds, too, are familiar. This is our language. This is what we have made of the Word that was in the beginning, and was with God, and was God. Dante the pilgrim has traveled as if with a tape recorder, preserving our distortions; Dante the poet plays them across the potentially redemptive grid of *terza rima*, so that they may take on meaning beyond our meanness.

If the poet can do this, it is because the Bible has already schooled him in the drama of the Word's falling and rising, its corruption and regeneration. Language falls throughout the Hebrew Bible, even before

Babel, in the seductions of Eden, in Cain's insolent question, and in the whole sordid unwinding of vice and stupidity we call history. It is saved in the declaration and redeclaration of the Covenant, and in each self-positioning by those who have heard the Lord's voice ("Here I am"); it is saved and codified in the Law, in prophecy, and most intimately in the Psalms. Throughout the Hebrew Bible, human language, in a world created initially by God's speech, struggles back toward sacred sense. In the Gospels that sense is understood, quite physically and even primitively, as the Word made flesh. If Christ's injured flesh can redeem the lost likeness of the Divine Image in our ruined faces, so his flesh as Word can be felt—is felt, I think, by Dante—to heal our mangled speech. But the poetic word is not a sacred word, as the poem warns us over and over in its images of literary pride and delusion: Arachne, the magpies, the Siren, Marsyas. The poem not only depicts the language of its characters as deformed and reforming, but works, itself, within the medium of deformation. No telepathies or instant fixes here. The poet slogs through the mire of fallen language, and it is a long haul through narration, dialogue, meditation, exposition, and prayer, all organized by *terza rima*. Even the visions and voices of Paradise, increasingly transmitted as brain waves though they seem to be, have to be represented, if at all, as traces in human language moving through the ordered time of verse.

It is the *morta poesia* of *Inferno* that I most recognize. Facing again in memory the frozen lake of traitors in *Inferno* XXXII, the poet laments not having rhymes sufficiently harsh and grating to "press out the juice of his conception." But the Muses, whose help he implores, have already given him a transfusion of bubbling, gurgling, hissing syllables, doubled glottals, grating vowels; in vocabulary, the poet has felt free not merely to use the vernacular, but to ransack it, serving up tar, shit, farts, and assholes along with Francesca's romantic and courtly self-justifications and Farinata's eloquence.

In *Purgatorio*, the cantica of redemptive imagination, Hell's physical and literal imagery gives way to a dazzling series of moving pictures and speaking bas-reliefs, a compendium of ways in which an art of hyperrealism instructs the mind. In kindred spirit, poetry in *Purgatorio* meditates on the conditions of its own making and higher purposes, as individual poets, ancient and modern, find their verses trained upon the larger trellis of collective and sacred words: psalms, scriptural quotation, prayer. Before we experience poetry's reintegration, however—before Dante, Virgil, and the questing souls are scolded for dallying, listening to Casella sing one of Dante's own earlier love poems; before Arnaut speaks in Provençal out of the refining fire; before Virgil's own verses for Marcellus and Dido are recycled in a context of new loss and new love—in Hell we chew and gag on the raw material of language. Our language. For we are made by language, as Genesis 1 teaches: God creates by speaking. If Dante the pilgrim has any hope, it is a grace that comes to him not *from* language—his love for Beatrice must have been, originally, a shock beyond speech—but *through* language: through his experiences of reading Virgil's Latin and hearing Beatrice's Italian, through his whole emotional and intellectual landscape embodied in words. The Word will come to him, if it comes, translated through words. If we as readers find ourselves touched by this poem, it will be because we, too, have tasted the language of delusion, and recognize it to be soiled, rotten, or toughened as beef jerky.

Inferno has a full menu of such anticommunions. Francesca's hash of Guido Guinizelli's *canzone* of courtly love is one: "Amor, ch'al cor gentil ratto s'apprende . . ." (*Inferno* V.100: Love, which is quickly kindled in a gentle heart . . .). The wrathful sinners burbling in the slime are another: "Quest' inno si gorgoglian ne la strozza, / ché dir nol posson con parola integra" (*Inferno* VII.125–26: This hymn do they keep gurgling in their throats, / for with unbroken words they cannot say it). So is Brunetto Latini's perversion of the rhetoric of learning. So are the desperate mechanics by which Ulysses and Guido da Montefeltro force human speech from the tongues of flames they inhabit. Language betrayed is the very medium of Hell: there's no dearth of examples. But one scene in particular has haunted me for years, perhaps since it so incarnates the conditions of struggling speech: Pier della Vigna, the suicide, imperial minister, ambassador, and poet trapped in a tree.

In the seventh circle where the violent are punished, the suicides suffer for violence against the self. At every level, the canto reminds us of the claustrophobia and self-entrapment that define suicide. Pier della Vigna seems trapped by the figurative force of his own name: Pier of the Grapevine, his soul now enclosed in a twisted thorn tree on which he will hang the rags of his body at the Last Judgment in a meaningless parody of the Crucifixion. He is entrapped, too, in the model of *Aeneid* III, doomed to repeat the suffering of Polydorus from Virgil's poem; but whereas Polydorus is imprisoned in a mound beneath his bleeding thornbush in Thrace as a victim of murder, Pier has murdered himself, further tightening the circle in around the self. In yet another intensification of the Virgilian scene, Pier is embodied *within* his tree, not just under it. The violence with which Aeneas yanked at the bleeding bush in Thrace is repeated here as a consciously cruel experiment inflicted by the poet Dante through the agency of Virgil, as a way of educating the pilgrim. Virgil's apology to Pier for the violation seems oddly ambivalent in the script provided by Dante, sympathetic but at the same time competitive, demonstrating Dante's superior realism: "'Had he been able sooner to believe,' / My Sage made answer, 'O thou wounded soul, / What only in my verses he had seen, / Not upon thee had he stretched forth his hand; / Whereas the thing incredible has caused me / To put him to an act which grieveth me'" (*Inferno* XIII.46–51).

And then there is the self-enclosure of Pier's own speech. Ornate as befits a court poet, minister, and counselor to the Emperor Frederick II, Pier's speech rounds in on itself in elaborate repetitions, variations, and antitheses. The harlot envy, Pier says,

> infiammò contra me li animi tutti;
> e li infiammati infiammar sì Augusto. . . .
>
> (Inferno XIII.67–68)

(. . . inflamed against me all the other minds, / And they, inflamed, did so inflame Augustus. . . .)

Pier's chiastic description of his own suicidal impulse acts like an architectural figure for self-destruction. His mind, he says, "ingiusto fece me contra me giusto" (*Inferno* XIII.72: made me unjust against my just self). The Italian word order builds an arch: paradoxically opposed and symmetrical, *ingiusto* and *giusto* sustain the foundations. The repeated first-person singular pronoun "me," in the sadly objective case, flanks the keystone: the self as object, multiplied and detached. In the center, holding together the whole sorry structure, is poised the adversarial preposition *contra*, which in its own way embodies the spirit of suicide.

A master of rhetoric in life, Pier della Vigna in Hell must struggle to enunciate. Only in Italian does this passage spit and whistle as it must:

> Come d'un stizzo verde ch'arso sia
> da l'un de' capi, che da l'altro geme
> e cigola per vento che va via,

sì de la scheggia rotta usciva insieme
  parole e sangue; ond' io lasciai la cima
  cadere, e stetti come l'uom che teme.

(Inferno XIII.40–45)

(As out of a green brand, that is on fire / At one of the ends, and
from the other drips / And hisses with the wind that is escaping; /
So from that splinter issued forth together / Both words and blood;
whereat I let the tip / Fall, and stood like a man who is afraid.)

Here, the fallen word is made flesh in the onomatopoeia of the doubled
z of *stizzo*, in the hissing *s*'s, *sc*'s, and *c*'s. It is made drama in the enjambments: the broken bough spits words and blood, *parole e sangue*, out from
the broken end of its line: "sì de la scheggia rotta usciva insieme / parole
e sangue. . . ." The astounded pilgrim lets the twig fall from one line to
the next: ". . . ond' io lasciai la cima / cadere. . . ." The language of suffering issues, physically, as blood sizzling off the page.

Poetry is, by itself, a secular art. Dante has achieved in this passage
a piece of bravura mimesis, a phonetic, syntactic, and metrical rendi-
tion of the action he describes. Like the astonishingly lifelike paintings
and sculptures in *Purgatorio* (and their forebears in *The Aeneid*), Dante's
own figuration can take the breath away. Logically, however, nothing
requires a relation to be established between the injured, lowercase words
of human pain, and the uppercase incarnate Word of Christian promise.
We can recognize the truth of the symptoms described in *Inferno* without
buying the prescriptions that follow: acceptance of Christ's sacrifice,
belief in the efficacy of penitence, redirection of desire from earthly
objects to the Christian God. Theology, though, presses to connect
word and Word, arguing through analogy. Dante's narrative will try to
shape such a relation imaginatively, bringing into hierarchical association
the fallen word and the divine Word, Adam and Christ. The trinitarian
verse form and the triple rhymes of *Cristo* with itself urge that association, and *Paradiso* takes us far toward its fulfillment before Dante's *alta
fantasia* fails him.

Failure is, of course, written into the literary, if not the religious,
endeavor, as human and divine can never be commensurate, however
analogous. Christ as human, as Word made flesh, uneasily connects the
two realms, but the poet's account at the end of *Paradiso* of gazing into
the heart of Light, absolute love, can only be made in the negative and
imagistic terms suited to mortal cognition:

Così la neve al sol si disigilla;
    così al vento ne le foglie levi
    si perdea la sentenza di Sibilla.

(*Paradiso* XXXIII.64–66)

(Even thus the snow is in the sun unsealed, / Even thus upon the wind in the light leaves / Were the soothsayings of the Sibyl lost.)

There is a far earlier scene, however, in the lower reaches of *Purgatorio*, that seems to me to dramatize convincingly the redemption of lowercase language in Christian terms, and to bring word into experiential relation to the Word. Like the episode of Pier della Vigna, it has to do with gargled and agonized speech. In the case of Buonconte di Montefeltro, however, the last strangled utterance in life is enough to save him. We find him near the base of the mountain of Purgatory, not even in Purgatory proper, among those who sinned up until the last moment and died violently. Buonconte compresses his life story into the few moments that matter to him:

"Oh!" rispuos' elli, "a piè del Casentino
    traversa un'acqua c'ha nome l'Archiano,
    che sovra l'Ermo nasce in Apennino.
Là've 'l vocabol suo diventa vano,
    arriva'io forato ne la gola,
    fuggendo a piede e sanguinando il piano.
Quivi perdei la vista e la parola;
    nel nome di Maria fini', e quivi
    caddi, e rimase la mia carne sola."

(*Purgatorio* V.92–102)

("Oh!" he replied, "at Casentino's foot / A river crosses named the Archiano, born / Above the Hermitage in Apennines. / There where the name thereof becometh void / Did I arrive, pierced through and through the throat, / Fleeing on foot, and bloodying the plain; / There my sight lost I, and my utterance / Ceased in the name of Mary, and thereat / I fell, and tenantless my flesh remained.")

Buonconte's last-minute salvation balances his father's damnation: we had met Guido da Montefeltro with Ulysses among the false counselors in the speaking flames of *Inferno* XXVII. Whereas Guido had converted late in life, in outward form at least, thinking to assure his salvation, only to be brutally surprised at the outcome, his son dying at the Battle of Campaldino concludes with a prayer of a single name which saves him. Buonconte's story, the story of a name choked out by a man wounded in the throat, occurs in a canto running with appalling liquids: blood, swamp water, torrents, an infernal rainstorm, the marshes of Maremma. Between Jacopo del Cassero dying in the mire in the pool of his own blood, and the sibylline Pia whose life is concentrated in a one-line chiasmus of place ("Siena mi fe, disfecemi Maremma" [*Purgatorio* V.134]: Siena made me, unmade me Maremma), Buonconte participates, through his wound, in his entire watery landscape. The place incarnates his story. There where the river Archiano loses its name in a densely alliterative line ("Là've 'l vocabol suo diventa vano"), Buonconte also loses his *vocabol*, wounded in the throat, making of his blood another tributary to the river. Though he loses speech, he saves the essential word, *Maria*, and the enjambment of his dying is not a prelude to damnation: "nel nome di Maria fini', e quivi / caddi . . ." (I ended on the name of Mary, and there / I fell . . .). In a touch of brilliant irony, the devil who feels cheated of the soul sneers that this salvation occurred "per una lagrimetta"—one tiny teardrop to be weighed against the rivers of blood, sin, and diabolical revenge, and, most astonishingly, against a lifetime of violence.

We may also weigh that teardrop, and that gurgled prayer, against the self-involuting language of Pier della Vigna. In both cases, Dante has made the language physically present. Ink, in both scenes, has become transubstantiated as blood. The question is whether, in each case within the fiction, the blood will have sacrificial efficacy. A doctrine concerning damnation and grace takes on substance as drama. More than doctrine, it is Dante's dramatic psychology and embodied phonetics that allow us to sense in Pier della Vigna what a soul feels like, trapped in self-destruction, spitting out its painful account of itself like sap from a green bough in flame. It is the dramatized, imagistically embodied landscape of *Purgatorio* V that allows us to absorb the saving force of Buonconte's last gasped word.

The doctrine itself is shocking: a split-second repentance outweighs years of destruction. But does that intellectual and moral shock become an obstacle to apprehension of the poem by nondoctrinal readers? Modern readers have dashed themselves over and over at this question, and so forceful and provocative is Dante's theology that each new reader, I suspect, is drawn back to grapple with it personally in spite of Eliot's useful suspension of "both belief and disbelief," and Auerbach's bold assertion that in the *Divine Comedy* "the image of man eclipses the image of God."[2] Eliot and Auerbach, each in his way, might have been thought to have settled certain matters of literature and belief. In fact, they settled very little. The *Comedy* continues to be a monumentally unsettling poem. For myself, I have found it indispensable to recognize that a vast, systematic theology undergirds the poem, while at the same time reminding myself not to read sclerotically: not to allow attention to congeal, in approval or indignation, around any particular theological point. This is, after all, a poem: a course of action, not a *summa*. In an important sense, the poem's reality overflows its doctrine. That reality is made present, substantial, and dynamic in many ways, but especially in language's corporeality: onomatopoeia, lineation, and imagery. It appeals to the mind through the nervous system, and leaves us room to apprehend Pier della Vigna's and Buonconte's tortured syllables as universal examples of human speech.

When we try to tell the truth, whoever we are, of whatever faith or nonfaith, the best we can do, often, is to sputter. We will be fortunate if the truth we spit out is not entirely self-concerned. Poetry heals nothing. But by placing its lowercase communion upon our tongues, it can draw us into imaginative relation with truths beyond our own, and can place the personal pronoun—subjective or objective—in the neighborhood of far greater words.

CHAPTER 13

Dark Knowledge:
Melville's Poems of the Civil War

M y subject is knowledge. In particular, the way in which several poems of Herman Melville dramatize the dawning of knowledge through struggle: in theme, the fratricidal national struggle of the American Civil War; in form, the in-wrought, crabbed, ponderous, grimed verse through which Melville fought his way to private perception. *Battle-Pieces and Aspects of the War*, published in August 1866, involves us as modern readers in a more general struggle: the ever-renewed attempt by the present to envision or to evade the past. The Civil War represents, for citizens of the United States, a parental past which it is convenient to forget but which continues to work upon us and through us. As a nation we still suffer variously the aftershocks of slavery; and we are still, 140 years after Lee's surrender at Appomattox, half bewildered by the strains of being no longer an agricultural and maritime Jeffersonian democracy. We are, instead, an industrialized, militarized imperial nation whose "dream" has taken expansionist forms, as Melville foresaw, in the poem "The Conflict of Convictions," observing the new iron dome on the Capitol:

Power unanointed may come—
Dominion (unsought by the free)
    And the Iron Dome,
Stronger for stress and strain,
Fling her huge shadow athwart the main;
But the Founders' dream shall flee.[1]

This project of looking at Melville's poems commits me to a particularly filial encounter. The Civil War, while largely forgotten in the North (though slavery is not), is still *the* war in the South, and I am the child of a Northern mother and a Southern father. Furthermore, my Southern father loved and edited the poems of Melville. For years I sought, with half my mind, to forget "my father's war" and the literature of that war: hadn't the elders sufficiently raked over those ashes? But the knowledge that counts most, I think, is tragic knowledge; so I find myself returning to those ancestral battlefields to try to understand where we have come from. All Americans are children of the Civil War whether we know it or not.

Melville, too, had an instinct for evasion. After the successes of his early books of travel adventures, *Moby-Dick* had met with incomprehension in 1851, and his successive works—the sprawling, haunted novel *Pierre; or The Ambiguities, Israel Potter, The Piazza Tales*, and the bitter, self-canceling *The Confidence Man* in 1857—had flopped, leaving Melville with only family and friends for a reading public. Attempts at lecturing had failed as well. When in April 1860 the Democratic National Convention split into Northern and Southern factions at the meeting in Charleston, South Carolina, and a few weeks later the Republican Convention nominated Lincoln for president, Melville took flight, shipping out on May 30 on the clipper ship the *Meteor* of which his younger brother Tom was the captain. Stanton Garner has told this story well in *The Civil War World of Herman Melville*, documenting how closely connected to the war Melville would be through his large network of friends and family, including two cousins who took part in the fighting. The *Meteor* was bound around Cape Horn to San Francisco, a voyage of many months. Leaving behind his wife and four children, a literary career in ruins, and a country on the verge of Civil War, Melville was scudding south toward Cape Horn through ferocious storms. The Horn itself, when they rounded it, struck him as "horrible snowy mountains—black, thundercloud woods—gorges—hell-landscape."[2] A sailor fell from the main topsail yard, crashing to his death on the deck. In this oblique approach of his to the Civil War, Melville read

Milton, Chapman's Homer, Schiller, the New Testament, and the Psalms. When the *Meteor* docked in San Francisco in October, Melville headed home, taking a steamer south to Panama City, a train across the isthmus, and another steamer north to arrive in New York City on November 13. Lincoln had just been elected, and South Carolina had seceded.

Melville wrote *Battle-Pieces and Aspects of the War* in the last months of the conflict and after its conclusion. The book appeared in August 1866. Reviews ranged from polite to indignant; the *American Literary Gazette and Publishers' Circular* declared, "He has written too rapidly to avoid great crudities. His poetry runs into the epileptic. His rhymes are fearful."[3] It is these crudities I want to examine. "The real war," wrote Whitman, who had nursed his brother and countless other wounded soldiers for three years in the war hospital in Washington, D.C., "will never get in the books."[4] It certainly did not get in the books in the patriotic, self-righteous, and popular regularities of John Greenleaf Whittier, whose ease of prosody carried the correspondingly easy freight of his abstractions and undisturbed convictions:

> The storm-bell rings, the trumpet blows;
> I know the sign and countersign;
> Wherever Freedom's vanguard goes,
> I know the place that should be mine.[5]

Nor does the "real war" make much of an appearance in James Russell Lowell's elegy for the young white colonel Robert Gould Shaw who died leading the heroic black Fifty-fourth Massachusetts Volunteer Infantry in their assault on Battery Wagner in Charleston, South Carolina, or in Lowell's "Ode Recited at the Harvard Commemoration, July 21, 1865," one of the most famous poems of the war. "Brave, good, and true, / I see him stand before me now," wrote Lowell of the young Shaw, but the reader sees neither the young man nor more than a glimpse of the action which killed and glorified him. The Harvard Commemoration Ode begins, "Weak-winged is song," quite true in this case; Lowell's praise of Lincoln is high-minded and well-meant, but doesn't bring the assassinated hero to life in the mind's eye: "The kindly-earnest, brave, foreseeing man, / Sagacious, patient, dreading praise, not blame, / New birth of our new soul, the first American."[6]

While Whittier confidently and easily declared, "I know," Melville's *Battle-Pieces* labor for their knowledge, and engage the reader in that struggle. Poem after poem pursues its quarry of truth, casting off illusory knowledge along with conventional poetic solutions. The hunt after the white whale had prepared for this probe into his country's nature and into human nature; Chapman's Homer had shown him a radiantly factual, unsentimental view of men at war, passion recorded with both supreme detachment and supreme detail of spear crunching through ligament and bone. The greatest art wars *against* illusion, as Simone Weil, one of *The Iliad*'s best readers, would write: "To love truth means to tolerate the void, and consequently to accept death. Truth is on the side of death."[7] Melville's poems constitute such an art: it tolerates the void and accepts death.

It also accepts mystery. The introductory poem about the execution of John Brown, "The Portent," simultaneously reveals and veils. It gives no easy clue for the deciphering of its sign: "Hidden in the cap / Is the anguish none can draw; / So your future veils its face, / Shenandoah! / But the streaming beard is shown / (Weird John Brown), / The meteor of the war."[8] God, in "The Conflict of Convictions," says neither "Yea" nor "Nay": "None was by / When He spread the sky; / Wisdom is vain, and prophesy."[9] And how do civilians know a war? The long poem "Donelson" unfolds the progress of the three-day battle by Union forces to capture Fort Donelson on the Cumberland River in Tennessee, in February 1862, from the perspective of Northerners milling about the bulletin board in sleet to read the latest telegraphed news. "Washed by the storm, till the paper grew / Every shade of a streaky blue," the news changes shape through three days of rain until finally, after Grant's costly victory, "The death-list like a river flows / Down the pale sheet, / And there the whelming waters meet."[10] "The House-Top" ambiguously presents the New York City draft riots of July 1863, evoking both the vicious violence of the rioters, who lynched blacks and burned a black orphanage, and the viciousness of the force brought in to repress them. In "The Armies of the Wilderness," a long, ambitious poem drawing on the three battles fought, between 1863 and 1864, in that infernal wooded section of Virginia where the forest caught fire and hundreds of the wounded burned to death, the horror emerges through the splicing of lyric and narrative passages, but finally cannot be described:

> None can narrate that strife in the pines,
>   A seal is on it—Sabaean lore!
> Obscure as the wood, the entangled rhyme
>   But hints at the maze of war—

Vivid glimpses or livid through peopled gloom,
　　And fires which creep and char—
A riddle of death, of which the slain
　　Sole solvers are.[11]

Because Melville's poems look to the outer void, they brave the inner depth as well. Whereas Emerson, in "Grace," thanks his "preventing God" for the defenses (against his own inner darkness) of "example, custom, fear, occasion slow," and confesses, "I dare not peep over this parapet / To gauge the roaring gulf below,"[12] Melville—who had savaged Emerson as Mark Winsome, "more a metaphysical merman than a feeling man," in *The Confidence Man*—could never resist a parapet. One such poem, "The Coming Storm," meditates upon a lowering landscape painting of that title by S. R. Gifford, exhibited in Washington in April 1865. The fulfilling impulse to the poem rises not from the landscape itself, but from the fact of its ownership by Edwin Booth, the famous Shakespearean actor whose brother, John Wilkes Booth, had just shot Lincoln: "No utter surprise can come to him / Who reaches Shakespeare's core; / That which we seek and shun is there— / Man's final lore."[13] For a fratricidal war, a poem of dread fraternal acknowledgment.

I want now to look in detail at several of the poems, considering them as modes of action precipitating a provisional but tragic knowledge. The whole book, *Battle-Pieces and Aspects of the War*, can in a sense be regarded as one sustained action, a chronological sequence responding to significant points in the war; but the poems were, for the most part, written after the events they describe. They were not versified reports from the front like Henry Howard Brownell's popular *Lyrics of a Day: Newspaper Poems by a Volunteer in the U.S. Service*, published in 1864. The dates affixed to each of Melville's poems refer, not to composition, but to the place of narrated events within the unfolding drama of the war. The introductory poem, "The Portent," isolated in italics at the outset and not included in the table of contents, throws down the initial challenge of vision and interpretation.

THE PORTENT
(1859)

Hanging from the beam
　　Slowly swaying (such the law)
Gaunt the shadow on your green,

Shenandoah!
The cut is on the crown
(Lo, John Brown),
And the stabs shall heal no more.

Hidden in the cap
　　Is the anguish none can draw;
So your future veils its face,
　　Shenandoah!
But the streaming beard is shown
(Weird John Brown),
The meteor of the war.

Where to start? With the action the poem contemplates, or the action the poem *is*? In the poem itself, they fuse: historical event becomes event in the mind of the reader through the event in language. The brute data: On October 16, 1859, the abolitionist John Brown—already guilty of the murder of five pro-slavery settlers in Kansas—attacked the federal arsenal at Harper's Ferry, Virginia, with a band of followers. As is well known, he hoped his act would stir up a slave revolt. As is also well known, Colonel Robert E. Lee led the company of Marines who recaptured the arsenal and wounded and arrested Brown. Brown's hanging in Charleston, Virginia, on December 2, 1859, contributed to the passions, in both North and South, that would erupt into war: Union soldiers would march into battle singing, "John Brown's body lies amouldering in the grave. . . ."

But there all certainty stops. For a figure who assumed mythic proportions, Brown provoked wildly varying reactions, even among Northerners. Emerson was quoted as saying his execution would "make the gallows glorious like the Cross"; Hawthorne responded, in his essay "Chiefly about War Matters, by a Peaceable Man," "Nobody was more justly hanged. He won his martyrdom fairly, and took it firmly."[14] Melville's poem takes shape and life in the gap between these two statements. Anyone seeking clear-cut approbation or condemnation of Brown will leave "The Portent" baffled.

How does the poem behave? Look, first, at the obvious: its shape. Two symmetrical chunks. A central division. Presentation, and complication? And the meter: it's not revolutionary; it's far more irregular than Longfellow or James Russell Lowell, but this kind of varying line length within the stanza was standard within the lyric tradition in English. Its most startling move, metrically, is the elimination of all unstressed syllables in the penultimate line of each stanza: "(Lo, John Brown)"; "(Weird John Brown)." I'll have more to say about those parentheses and those three-beat, all-stress lines: it's not often that a poem names its main subject only in parenthesis. On the other hand, the parentheses and the stress focus the reader's attention on the deferred subject—"(Lo, John Brown)"—and so, like the poem as a whole, simultaneously conceal and reveal the heart of the matter.

Consider for a moment the meter and prosody. The poem observes a rigorous symmetry. First line of each stanza: trochaic trimeter catalectic. That is to say, three trochees, the last not having a fit but simply missing its last, unstressed syllable: "*Hanging from* the *beam*"; "*Hidden in* the *cap*." Both ear and eye are working intensely here. First word and first stress: *Hanging*. Something—we don't yet know it is a corpse—is hanging. Last word of the first line, stressed: *beam*. There we have the elemental scene: action and noun. Second line in each stanza: trochaic tetrameter catalectic. Our poet is sticking with trochees, but he's lengthening his breath to four beats. He still ends on a strong stress, however. What is he showing us now? "*Slowly swaying, such* the *law*." It's the action of hanging these trochees are suffering: one feels the sway. But physical action observed and participated in gives rise to a parenthetical abstraction, a declaration that brooks no disagreement and concludes in one powerful, stressed monosyllable: *law*. Alliteration, in the repeated *s*'s, seems to bind the physical motion of what we do not yet know is a corpse to the legal enforcement: "Slowly *s*waying, *s*uch the law." What law? It is the law of gravity that suspended bodies, under stimulus, swing in pendulum-fashion; it was the law of the United States—and certainly of the state of Virginia—in 1859 that murder and insurrection be punished by death. Meter, too, is a law, and enforces its argument.

The first sentence has not yet concluded, and we still don't know *what* is hanging. Third line: "Gaunt the shadow on your green": more trochees, another tetrameter, also catalectic; this hanging meter is becoming insistent. So is the alliteration, with *g* this time: *g*aunt/*g*reen. Often in poetry when sound enforces a likeness—*g/g*—the deeper sense vibrates with significant difference, and that is the case here: the suggestions of starvation and death in "gaunt" collide with the fertility implicit in "green." In the "shadow"—squarely placed in the center of the line—we seem to have discovered the subject of the sentence, though not of the poem. But what kind of subject is this: not the thing itself, but its projection, its dark two-dimensional image? Phonetically, "shadow" generates the whole fourth line, echoed symmetrically in the next stanza: "Shenandoah." The subliminal suggestion of "valley" in relation to "Shenandoah," combined with "shadow" and the ominous implications of the poem thus far, may call to mind "the valley of the shadow of death" from Psalm 23. The echo provokes ironic dissonance, not consolation. Still trochees, but contracted from four feet to two, from tetrameter to dimeter. And since the poet addresses the valley directly—"your green"—and concludes his first sentence here with an exclamation, we feel a corresponding quickening of dramatic interest. Still, the major point is that the poem continues to conceal its ostensible subject.

Line 5 comes as a jolt: a rapid shift from trochees to iambs—"The *cut* is *on* the *crown*"—with the harshness of alliterated *c*'s in the powerful nouns: *cut/crown*. Still mysterious. What cut? Whose crown? Is there a king here? Line 6, as noted before, appears to resolve the mystery: "(Lo, John Brown)." It has eliminated all unstressed syllables, and in keeping with the visual logic of the poem seems to point a finger at its subject: "Lo." The rhyme of "Brown" with "crown" appears to confer the crown of martyrdom upon the insurrectionary: Edmund Wilson in *Patriotic Gore* reminds us that Emerson was not alone in regarding Brown as a Christ figure. The sentence, however, has still not concluded. The last line of the stanza, an anapestic/iambic trimeter, rhymes with nothing in this stanza; it must await its sinister partner in the last line of the poem, and match "shall heal no more" with "war": "And the stabs shall heal no more."

The last three lines of stanza one provide a superficial and misleading clarity. The trimeter, basically iambic, seems consolingly familiar. But the images delivered in elemental monosyllables—cut/crown/John/ Brown/stabs—are more troublesome the more one ponders them. In some loose symbolic manner the poem invites us to see in John Brown the conventional figure of abolitionist martyr; though hanged, he was also during his capture slashed by a sword on the head as on the symbolic kingly headgear betokening his martyr's station. Melville leaves the crown, however, unspecified, and since the poem is addressed to the green and fertile Shenandoah Valley, the reader's imagination is free to wander. The cut, perhaps, is on the crown of peace? Of the Union? And what about those "stabs"? Melville has introduced a grisly historical literalism which immensely complicates the reading of martyrdom. For the stabs associated with John Brown are not only the gashes he suffered from Lieutenant Green's sword at Harper's Ferry; the gashes are also those he and his two sons and henchmen inflicted in May 1856 in Pottawattomie Creek, Kansas, when they dragged out of bed, shot, stabbed in the face, and hacked off the fingers and arms of five illiterate poor whites from Tennessee—three men and two boys—who owned no slaves. Brown executed his massacre as retaliation for the murder of five Free-Soilers, two days before, by a pro-slavery gang in the melee of Bleeding Kansas. Behind that violence, implicit in the poem, looms the still greater violence of slavery itself. The hanging in "The Portent" has been preceded by many stabs, none of them innocent.

The second stanza reproduces the metrical pattern of the first, with minor substitutions. How does it contribute, however, to the slowly emerging image of John Brown? Stanza 1 had at least come around to naming the figure who cast the shadow over the green Shenandoah, soon to become a battlefield. Stanza 2, which like the first seems to contemplate a picture of the hanging, rebels against the visual medium and begins by insisting that the truth cannot be represented: "Hidden in the cap / Is the anguish none can draw." Metrical symmetry, syntactical parallelism, and alliteration insist on the kinship of "Hanging" and "Hidden." But more than the hanged man's individual face is hidden behind the cap. Once again the poem addresses the valley, which seems to expand so as to include the whole land in its illusion of prewar innocence: "So your future veils its face, / Shenandoah!" The poem exploits its privilege of tragic hindsight: to the eyes of 1859, the future did veil its face. The last three lines break from concealment to revelation. Unwilling to make a simple moralizing pronouncement, the poem instead enacts a startling metamorphosis. Prompted by the visual detail of the beard, the relatively small object which we saw as passive in stanza 1—the hanging corpse—becomes a heavenly body of terrifying scale, motion, and power: a meteor. This meteor may in turn call upon demonic energies if we remember, as Melville surely did, Satan's great banner streaming in *Paradise Lost*: "The imperial ensign, which, full high advanced / Shone like a meteor streaming to the wind . . ." (*Paradise Lost* I.537). "Weird" brings to the transformation its etymological force, meaning not merely "strange," but, as Melville knew from the Weird Sisters of *Macbeth*, "having the power to control the fate or destiny of men, etc.; later, claiming the supernatural power of dealing with fate or destiny" (*OED*). While the poem does not presume to explicate Brown's moral nature, his role as portent is clear in the last, fatal monosyllable: war.

We are dealing, on the evidence of "The Portent," with a concentrated, elliptical art, which instead of delivering a ready-made judgment, forces readers to participate in the chiaroscuro process of arriving at judgment. In "The Portent," the reader may be induced to share, as a sensation of sound, in the rhythm of hanging. This is also an art of isolated visual details and shadows—Brown's shadow across the Shenandoah Valley, the shadow of the iron dome across the Potomac—rather than direct description. But Melville was creating himself as a poet in the course of writing these poems, experimenting with still other ways to dramatize the act of knowing.

The Civil War was for the United States a bloody ceremony of coming of age. It provided that experience for thousands of young soldiers from North and South, and Melville—who like Stephen Crane did not fight in the war—was fascinated by their transition from innocence to experience. A number of his poems focus on this testing of youth: "The March into Virginia, Ending in the First Manassas," "Ball's Bluff," "The College Colonel," "On the Slain Collegians." "All wars are boyish and are fought by boys," is his compact, aphoristic pentameter in "The March into Virginia," and these poems—composed by a forty-six-year-old noncombatant, a man of physical strength who suffered from rheumatism and neuralgia—are haunted by the figure of the sacrificed Boy. Melville does not take either side in his grief; these lines from "On the Slain Collegians" have a bitterness one might expect from Blake:

> What could they else—North or South?
> Each went forth with blessings given
> By priests and mothers in the name of Heaven;
>   And Honor in both was chief.
> Warred one for Right, and one for Wrong?
> So be it; but they both were young—
> Each grape to his cluster clung,
> All their elegies are sung.[15]

Reading these poems as dramas of initiation, I reach out to clasp my father by his spectral hand. For that is how he read them, especially "The March into Virginia," which he loved. To read them in the light of his love is something of an initiation in itself: I come to them, no longer young, with the line ringing in my ear, "Youth must its ignorant impulse lend." I will not try to improve on, or rehearse, my father's description of the rhythmical shifts in the poem's three sections—from gnomic abstraction, to the frolicking tetrameters of ignorance, to the lengthened, "experienced" pentameters of the conclusion; I will mention but not dwell on his remarking the pun on "berrying party" ("burying party") in line 18. But here is the poem:

THE MARCH INTO VIRGINIA
ENDING IN THE FIRST MANASSAS
(July 1861)

Did all the lets and bars appear
    To every just or larger end
Whence should come the trust and cheer?
    Youth must its ignorant impulse lend—
Age finds place in the rear.
    All wars are boyish, and are fought by boys,
The champions and enthusiasts of the state:
    Turbid ardors and vain joys
        Not barrenly abate—
    Stimulants to the power mature,
        Preparatives of fate.

Who here forecasteth the event?
What heart but spurns at precedent
And warnings of the wise,
Contemned foreclosures of surprise?
The banners play, the bugles call,
The air is blue and prodigal.
    No berrying party, pleasure-wooed,
No picnic party in the May,
Ever went less loth than they
    Into that leafy neighborhood.
In Bacchic glee they file toward fate,
Moloch's uninitiate;
Expectancy, and glad surmise
Of battle's unknown mysteries.
All they feel is this: 'tis glory,
A rapture sharp, though transitory,
yet lasting in belaureled story.
So they gayly go to fight,
Chatting left and laughing right.

But some who this blithe mood present
    As on in lightsome files they fare,
Shall die experienced ere three days are spent—
    Perish, enlightened by the vollied glare;
Or shame survive, and, like to adamant,
    The throe of Second Manassas share.[16]

The Battle of Bull Run, which this poem commemorates, delivered the first shock to Union confidence. On July 21, 1861, the federal army, 35,000 strong under General McDowell, marched from Washington, D.C., to attack the Confederates, who had 31,000 men under the generals Beauregard and Johnston at Manassas Junction, Virginia. So convinced were the Union troops and their officers of their superiority that spectators from Washington accompanied them with picnic baskets to delight in the victory. The advantage swayed back and forth sickeningly on the murderous field, but General Thomas J. Jackson, standing like a "stonewall" to earn his nickname, broke the Union army's resolve and sent it scrambling back to the Capitol. Six months later, Hawthorne visited Washington and recounted: ". . . all of us were looking toward the terrible and mysterious Manassas, with the idea that somewhere in its neighborhood lay a ghastly battlefield, yet to be fought, but foredoomed of old to be bloodier than the one where we had reaped such shame. Of all haunted places, methinks such a destined field should be thickest thronged with ugly phantoms, ominous of mischief through ages beforehand."[17] Whitman, who was not present at the battle, described the retreat with a journalist's vigor in *Specimen Days*:

The defeated troops commenced pouring into Washington over the Long Bridge at daylight on Monday, 22nd—day drizzling all through with rain. The Saturday and Sunday of the battle (20th, 21st) had been parched and hot to an extreme—the dust, the grime and smoke, in layers, sweated in, follow'd by other layers again sweated in, absorb'd by those excited souls—their clothes all saturated with the clay-powder filling the air—stirr'd up everywhere on the dry roads and trodden fields by the regiments, swarming wagons, artillery, &c.—all the men with this coating of murk and sweat and rain, now recoiling back, pouring over the Long Bridge—a horrible march of twenty miles, returning to Washington baffled, humiliated, panic-struck. Where are the vaunts, and the proud boasts with which you went forth? Where are your banners, and your bands of music, and your ropes to bring back your prisoners? Well, there isn't a band playing—and there isn't a flag but clings ashamed and lank to its staff.[18]

Like "The Portent," Melville's "The March into Virginia" is a poem of grim retrospective knowledge. It proceeds through the interplay of questions ("Whence should come the trust and cheer?" "Who here fore-casteth the event?"), glimpses of description, and declaration; it moves also from a reflective present tense, to the past tense of narrative, to the suspended narrative present of innocence ("So they gayly go to fight"), to give birth to a future tense of futile enlightenment: "Shall die experienced. . . ." We should notice certain currents of sound and the burden of imagery and thought they bear, to see (and hear) how the poem acts out its enlightenment.

Take the letter *b*. Along with the obvious pattern of rhyme at line ends, modulating from interlaced rhymes to couplets and back again, an alliterative pattern of *b*'s guides us through the poem like a nerve: *b*ars (as in hindrances to youth's impulsiveness); *b*oyish; *b*oys; tur*b*id; not *b*arrenly a*b*ate; *b*anners; *b*ugles; *b*lue; *b*errying; neigh*b*orhood; *B*acchic; *b*attle; *b*elaureled; *b*ut; *b*lithe. That tells just part of the story, but an important part: the boyish, exuberant part. "Turbid ardors," a phrase that can scarcely be imagined in James Russell Lowell, swells with a sexual suggestiveness in the vicinity of "not barrenly abate"; the confused erotic energy of youth turns out, surprisingly, not to be "barren," but to have a sinister fertility: it fuels the war, "Stimulants to the power mature, / Preparatives of fate." Melville liked this word "abate"; it adhered in his mind to boyishness, as in the description of the slain collegians: "Each bloomed and died an unabated Boy." In both cases, a mortal irony attends the negative formula of "abate"; the boys have died; it is their boyish energy, translated into myth and memory, that does not "abate." The fertility they sow is a prodigality of death: "Not barrenly. . . ."

"Bacchic" concentrates and elevates this erotic energy. But "prodigal" prompts a pause and a detour. From *prodigus* in Latin, meaning "extravagant," the word awakens in English hearers immediately the image of another boy, the wastrel, the biblical son returned and redeemed. Two lines earlier the poem has hinted, in legal parlance, that redemption will be "foreclosed" for these young soldiers who have spurned "at precedent / And warnings of the wise, / Contemned foreclosures of surprise. . . ."

For the moment, it's the air, not the boys, that's blue and prodigal, but the word has subliminally raised the question: Will these sons return home?

Returning to the trail of *b*'s, we should consider "leafy neighborhood." This is the Edenic wood, unillumined by experience; the very word "neighborhood" carries connotations of fraternal play, vicinity, and intimacy. For a brotherly war—Bull Run was just twenty miles from Washington—"neighborhood" has a fatal appropriateness. The boyhood woods of "The March into Virginia" give way later in the sequence to ghastly metaphysical versions of wilderness in which men discover their bestial selves and brothers, signally in the poems "The Armies of the Wilderness" and "The Scout toward Aldie." "The March into Virginia," however, concerns itself only with the revelation of the first Battle of Bull Run, the knowledge that springs on the poem in a traplike rhyme: "In Bacchic glee they file toward Fate, / Moloch's uninitiate."

"Fate," in lowercase, had already slipped into the poem at the end of stanza 1, rhyming with "not barrenly abate." Now the rhyme with "Fate" acts out the destiny of the boys; unwittingly, they rhyme with their own deaths as they pass from the sphere of a celebratory god to a god worshipped in the immolation of children: Moloch's uninitiate. The negative, as always in Melville, acts stressfully. Moloch breaks into the poem, inducing a horrible prescience in the reader, and perhaps, too, a retrospective Miltonic shudder at the thought of Satan's fierce companion-in-arms from *Paradise Lost*; but the boys, still *un*initiate, retard the discovery, so this blocklike, multisyllabic line—just two words holding the whole tetrameter fort— quivers with the contradiction of knowledge proposed and resisted.

The adversative "But," starting the third stanza, swings the poem from Bacchus to Moloch, from innocence to experience, from life to death. The blue air and "lightsome files" give way to the enlightenment of "the vollied glare"; the *b*'s surrender to a new but insistent pattern of sound, the *sh* of "*sh*all," "peri*sh*," "*sh*ame," and "*sh*are." Even in Melville's crossed-out manuscript versions of the last line, the *sh* dominates: "Thy after-*sh*ock, Manassas, *sh*are"; "Thy second *sh*ock, Manassas, *sh*are." But the elemental story had already been told by the key words; "shock," as Melville decided, was both too obvious thematically to be stated, and an overblowing of the alliteration. The deep instruction of defeat—one Melville knew well—was, for the survivors, to outlive shame, and define tempered forms of shared experience.

Only poetry of the highest order weaves its strands of sound so complexly into its semantic and syntactic orders, converting the arbitrary into the provisonally significant. What, then, about Melville's "crudities"? Why were his rhymes considered "epileptic"? He was not the only nineteenth-century American poet to fall afoul of a reading public accustomed to the confirmations of regularity. It is not insignificant that in 1855 Whittier threw his copy of *Leaves of Grass* into the fire; that the book sold poorly; that one reviewer called it "a gathering of muck . . . entirely destitute of wit," and another described Whitman as "this arrogant young man . . . who roots like a pig among the rotten garbage of licentious thoughts."[19] Whitman rebelled: in the poem "1861," he declared, "No dainty rhymes or sentimental love verses for you terrible year, / Not you as some pale poetling seated at a desk lisping cadenzas piano. . . ."[20] In the mid-century in the United States the genteel and expert mellifluousness of Longfellow and Lowell held sway. In the work of Jones Very, a devotional poet of urgent simplicity and intensity, or in the intimate, slightly irregular sonnets of Frederick Goddard Tuckerman, the inherited versification could find its own peculiar and forceful realization and reach a modest audience; but the expressive irregularities in rhythm, diction, and syntax with which Whitman, Melville, and Dickinson responded to the strongest promptings in English had almost no purchase on the minds of contemporary readers.

But new truths, inwardly felt, demand new forms. The American Civil War, with its massive industrialization in the manufacture and distribution of weapons, its development of repeating rifles and ironclad warships, and with Sherman its total assault on the means of sustaining life, was immediately recognized as a novel kind of conflict by military specialists abroad and at home. Melville, Hawthorne, and Mark Twain, among others in the broader public at home, saw that the Romantic era had passed in literature as in warfare. Like the poets of a later modern war, Wilfred Owen, Isaac Rosenberg, Ivor Gurney, and David Jones, Melville found himself writing poems of undeception ("What like a bullet can undeceive!"), not so much jettisoning poetic decorum as insisting on a new standard of fitting language to fact. In such terms Melville salutes the retiring *Temeraire*, the wooden warship in the British fleet famous from the Battle of Trafalgar:

> A pigmy steam-tug tows you,
>   Gigantic, to the shore—
> Dismantled of your guns and spars,
>   And sweeping wings of war.
> The rivets clinch the iron-clads,
>   Men learn a deadlier lore. . . .
>
> ("The *Temeraire*")[21]

In another poem responding to the fight between the ironclad ships in March 1862, "A Utilitarian View of the *Monitor*'s Fight," Melville faces head-on the challenge of readjusting poetic convention: it may have been his rhyming "heroic" with "caloric" that so distressed the reviewer at the *American Literary Gazette and Publishers' Circular*. The poem runs:

A UTILITARIAN VIEW OF THE *MONITOR*'S FIGHT

Plain be the phrase, yet apt the verse,
   More ponderous than nimble;
For since grimed War here laid aside
His Orient pomp, 'twould ill befit
     Overmuch to ply
   The rhyme's barbaric cymbal.

Hail to victory without the gaud
   Of glory; zeal that needs no fans
Of banners; plain mechanic power
Plied cogently in War now placed—
     Where War belongs—
   Among the trades and artisans.

Yet this was battle, and intense—
   Beyond the strife of fleets heroic;
Deadlier, closer, calm 'mid storm;
No passion; all went on by crank,
     Pivot, and screw,
   And calculations of caloric.

Needless to dwell; the story's known.
   The ringing of those plates on plates
Still ringeth round the world—
The clangor of that blacksmiths' fray.
     The anvil-din
   Resounds this message from the Fates:

War shall yet be, and to the end;
   But war-paint shows the streaks of weather;
War yet shall be, but warriors

> Are now but operatives; War's made
> > Less grand than Peace,
> And a singe runs through lace and feather.[22]

"Plain be the phrase," indeed. The poem achieves itself not merely by intruding an industrial vocabulary upon a diction inherited from Scott ("plain mechanic power"; "crank, / pivot and screw"; "plates on plates") but, more dynamically, by using its few rhymes to rivet the argument. Contrast the rhymes of Lowell's "Commemoration Ode" with those of Melville's "A Utilitarian View." In Lowell's first stanza, what Pope had called "the sure returns of still-expected rhymes" ferry the song along its untroubled current of feeling: song/height/light/wrong/hearse/verse/come/drum/desire/fire/strong/save/grave/throng. Melville, not wanting "Overmuch to ply / The rhyme's barbaric cymbal," reduces his rhymes to the second and sixth lines of each stanza, relying on meter to discipline his lines. With the exception of nimble/cymbal in the first stanza (which associates the action of verse with the action of the ship), each rhyme registers the collision between romance and realism: fans/artisans, heroic/caloric, plates/Fates, weather/feather. This new, deadlier mechanical warfare continued to develop through our own century's wars and has culminated, most recently, in the smart bombs and video-game warfare that so charmed the American public during the Gulf War and the invasion of Iraq. More than the shot for liberty heard round the world in Emerson's "Concord Hymn," Melville ironically predicts, "The ringing of those plates on plates / Still ringeth round the world."

I have been speaking of the Civil War, and of different kinds of knowledge born of that war in Melville's poems. One crucial truth was born for the nation as a whole only imperfectly and through the agony of the conflict itself, and that was the real purpose of the war. Even now, people disagree about that purpose. Lincoln in his First Inaugural Address stated, "I have no purpose, directly or indirectly, to interfere with the institution of slavery in the states where it exists. I believe I have no lawful right to do so, and I have no inclination to do so."[23] Some white Southerners seceded, less to protect slavery than to insist on the principle of states' rights; the majority of white Northerners supported the war for the preservation of the Union, not for the abolition of slavery; when Lincoln signed the Emancipation Proclamation on January 1, 1863, many white Northern soldiers simply quit. But by the Second Inaugural Address, Lincoln admitted that slavery "constituted a peculiar and powerful interest. All knew that this interest was, somehow, the cause of the war."[24] For many Northern whites, including abolitionists, it was difficult to keep black people in their human reality, as opposed to abstractions, in focus, and this difficulty—by no means entirely outgrown in our time—is evident in the treatment of black and other nonwhite figures in the works of Melville, Whitman, and Hawthorne.

For these writers—even for Melville, who felt much less racial animosity toward nonwhites than Whitman did, as his portrayal of Queequeg suggests—the black stands as a haunting enigma, at times seen hopefully as "benign," at times as murderous and vengeful. After his trip to the war zone around the Capitol in January 1862, Hawthorne described a party of escaped slaves:

> So rudely were they attired,—as if their garb had grown upon them spontaneously,—so picturesquely natural in manner, and wearing such a crust of primeval simplicity (which is quite polished away from the Northern black man), that they seemed a kind of creature by themselves, not altogether human, but perhaps quite as good, and akin to the fauns and rustic deities of olden times. . . . At all events, I felt most kindly toward these poor fugitives, but knew not precisely what to wish in their behalf, nor in the least how to help them. For the sake of the manhood which is latent in them, I would not have them turned back; but I should have felt almost as reluctant, on their own account, to hasten them forward to the stranger's land; and I think my prevalent idea was, that, whoever may be benefited by the results of this war, it will not be the present generation of negroes, the childhood of whose race is now gone forever, and who must henceforth fight a hard battle with the world, on very unequal terms.[25]

Whitman and Melville both interrogate the sibylline figure of an old black woman, and leave us with a portrait not of her, but of their own estrangement and bewilderment: "Who are you dusky woman, so ancient hardly human, / With your woolly-white and turbann'd head, and bare bony feet?" asks Whitman in "Ethiopia Saluting the Colors."[26] Melville, reflecting on the portrait *Formerly a Slave* by Elihu Vedder, tries to see hope in the suffering face of Jane Jackson: "Her dusky face is lit with sober light, / Sibylline, yet benign."[27] John Hollander, in *The Gazer's Spirit*, has acutely observed the various senses of "light" and the play of retrospection and prophecy in Melville's poem, which seems to have influenced later work by the painter. But in other works Melville allows for a far more troubled apprehension. In "The Swamp Angel," the great cannon of that name used to bombard the city of Charleston, South Carolina, in August 1863, is associated explicitly with the justified vengeance of former slaves:

> There is a coal-black Angel
> With a thick Afric lip,
> And he dwells (like the hunted and harried)
> In a swamp where the green frogs dip,
> But his face is against a City
> Which is over a bay of the sea,
> And he breathes with a breath that is blastment,
> And dooms by a far decree.[28]

As he had a few years earlier in the tale "Benito Cereno," the story of a ferocious revolt on board a slave ship and of an amiable white visiting captain who cannot for the whole length of the tale read the signs, Melville apprehends in "The Swamp Angel" the violence of revenge, the complex layerings of guilt, and the motion of the soul toward the kind of forgiveness that can emerge only from an encounter with truth:

> Who weeps for the woeful City
> Let him weep for our guilty kind;
> Who joys at her wild despairing—
> Christ, the Forgiver, convert his mind.

I want to conclude on this note of chastened forgiveness. It is the note on which Lincoln closed his Second Inaugural Address just weeks before his death: "with malice toward none; with charity for all." It is the deepest knowledge born of Melville's *Battle-Pieces*, when the delusions of partisanship fall away in the face of shared suffering and death:

SHILOH

> Skimming lightly, wheeling still,
> The swallows fly low
> Over the field in clouded days,
> The forest-field of Shiloh—

Over the field where April rain
Solaced the parched ones stretched in pain
Through the pause of night
That followed the Sunday fight
    Around the church of Shiloh—
The church so lone, the log-built one,
That echoed to many a parting groan
      And natural prayer
    Of dying foemen mingled there—
Foemen at morn, but friends at eve—
    Fame or country least their care:
(What like a bullet can undeceive!)
    But now they lie low,
While over them the swallows skim,
    And all is hushed at Shiloh.[29]

The hush with which Melville concludes his poem, in the mysterious, prolonged syllables of Shiloh (where dwelt the house of the Lord for the kingless and divided Israelites in Judges 18), grants tragic silence and recognition, but not absolution. In his refusal of facile comfort, Melville shows how art points the way to the life of conscience, however fitfully illuminated. In establishing his silence, he educates our speech. Perhaps in that hush we can hear the dead speak.

CHAPTER 14

Hardy's Undoings

Hardy is famously a haunted poet, attuned to otherworldly voices, glimpsing spectral flickers from the corner of his eye. And he is a haunting poet. His voice rises, for me, out of the otherworld of childhood, with "Neutral Tones," "Channel Firing," and "The Oxen" so shaped by the harmonics of the paternal voice that I can hardly distinguish whose voice is whose in such a chord: Hardy, Ransom, my father.[1] A chord I loved and, naturally, resisted, fleeing to other countries and other languages to find words I could imagine my own. It was Hardy, reencountered in a volume of *Selected Poems* in a dim, dank country house in the Veneto, when I was twenty-two and footloose in Italy, who lured me back to English. That return has been the work of years, a widening of the inner ear to receive frequencies from beyond the grave. And it gives me a figure for literature itself: the written evidence of such listening.

Hardy himself listened hard. What he heard—not only the voices of his imagined dead, but the hymns of Tate and Brady, the English ballads, Virgil's Latin, Shelley and Swinburne—he wove into his own poems. I want to describe briefly some of what I have heard in Hardy: what strains and dissonances in his poems enliven them, and prompt the disorientation that prepares for revelation. In *The Life of Thomas Hardy* (purporting to have been composed by his second wife, Florence Hardy), Hardy wrote, "There is no new poetry; but the new poet—if he carry the flame on further (and if not he is no new poet)—comes with a new note. And that note it is that troubles the critical waters."[2] In Hardy's own day as well as later in our century, critics have condemned and patronized the roughnesses in his meters and diction. Even a reader as percipient as Blackmur fell into the trap, declaring that "what Hardy really lacked was the craft of his profession—technique in the widest sense. . . ."[3] The poet, however, knew just what he was after in the exercise of his art, an art, as he described it by analogy to Gothic architecture, of "cunning irregularity." Of himself, he wrote that "he carried on into his verse, perhaps in part unconsciously, the Gothic art-principle in which he had been trained—the principle of spontaneity, found in mouldings, tracery, and such like—resulting in the 'unforeseen' (as it has been called) character of his metres and stanzas, that of stress rather than of syllable, poetic texture rather than poetic veneer. . . ."[4]

Poets in our century, with the exception of Eliot, have harkened gratefully to Hardy's expressive irregularities and roughing up of veneer: Ransom, Davie, Larkin, Gunn, and Mezey, among others, have recorded their debts. Among critic-scholars, Leavis stood out, early, in admiring the realistic logic motivating apparent oddnesses in Hardy's poems, arguing for their artistic superiority on representational grounds in his essay "Reality and Sincerity."[5] More recently Dennis Taylor, revealing Hardy's responses to the quickened and complex world of Victorian philology and prosodic studies, has demonstrated in a manner both broad and detailed how consciously the poet constructed his verse; and Eric Griffiths has explored with sensitive ingenuity the ethical dimensions of what he calls Hardy's "drama of formality."[6] Yet it appears that scholars, on the whole, are still adjusting their sights to the kind of sophisticated purposefulness in Hardy observed by Taylor and Griffiths.

I think of a poem as a structure of weights and balances, and of a fine poem as one whose resources—syntax, meter, rhythm, etymology, soundplay—work as carefully placed fulcrums to hoist statement to figurative height. I want to look now at a few such fulcrums in Hardy's verse—negative prefixes, to be specific—and argue that in their resistance to "veneer," to smooth reading, we can intuit not only something of the strenuous structural logic of the poems, but also something about their spiritual energy: something about the power of negation employed as leverage to the sense, and about the "sense" of a poem dynamically conceived. Right in Hardy's awkwardness, I suggest, we find his greatest strength, and his greatest testing of his medium.

Hardy was responding to negations already active in English poetry: Hamlet the King's "unhouseled, disappointed, unaneled"; and, to snatch a few from that majestic compilation of warring negations, *Paradise Lost*, grace which to all "Comes unprevented, unimplored, unsought"; Satan leaving God's throne "unworshipped, unobeyed," while Abdiel the faithful seraph remains "unmoved, / unshaken, unseduced, unterrified . . ."; or Adam lamenting Eve "defaced, deflowered, and now to death devote." Hardly a new matter, this poetry of internal contradiction, the prying up of words by the wedges of prefixes. But Hardy practices it so consistently and recurrently it begins to be a defining feature of his art.

As soon as one begins to collect instances, one notices the range and variety in the kind of force the negative prefixes exert. Taking *Paradise Lost* as an example, we find that just as Hell reproduces but parodies and deforms divine structures, presenting an infernal Genesis and an infernal Trinity, so the negative prefixes, though superficially similar, act in radically different ways depending on the spiritual context. Satan embodies the principle of negation, and his negative prefixes act destructively, undoing God's work and the responsive virtues of worship and obedience (God's throne "unworshipped, unobeyed . . ."). Abdiel's faithfulness, however, also takes a powerful negative form, the prefixes in his case dramatizing the struggle in which the solitary noble spirit stands against a crowd and against an eloquent argument for self-enfranchisement (Abdiel remains "unmoved, / unshaken, unseduced, unterrified"; the last three epithets amplify and gloss the possible senses of the first, "unmoved"). In Hardy, syntax and etymology collaborate so vigorously that a consideration of his prefixes often leads right into the central action of a poem, and opens a wide spectrum of interpretive possibilities.

Not only the negative prefixes exert their force in his poems. Sometimes a single poem, like "A Commonplace Day" from his second book, *Poems of the Past and Present* (1902), presents an anthology of compacted and self-correcting prefixes. In this case, they are concentrated in the last two stanzas where they enact the drama of cognition, possibility, and quenching which the poem as a whole considers in its ghostly and sterile day. The last stanzas each open with another of Hardy's characteristic gestures, one related in spirit to the negatings by so many of his prefixes: the adversative conjunctions "yet" and "but" which signal swerves in thought, countermovements surging into the poem's structured refusals, the enactment of the regret that was only named at the end of stanza 4. In tracing the prefixes as a sequence—*un*discerned, *en*kindling, *be*numbed, *em*bodied, *under*voicings—we track thought in motion, and watch it produce a word we might use to describe in a general sense Hardy's technique: undervoicings. The last stanzas read:

> —Yet, maybe, in some soul,
> In some spot undiscerned on sea or land, some impulse rose,
>   Or some intent upstole
> Of that enkindling ardency from whose maturer glows
>   The world's amendment flows:
>
> But which, benumbed at birth,
> By momentary chance or wile, has missed its hope to be
>   Embodied on the earth;
> And undervoicings of this loss to man's futurity
>   May wake regret in me.[7]

Hardy used a great range of prefixes, but the specifically negative ones are the most telling, especially those that wrench normal diction. Early and late, they obtrude in his lines and titles; from "Hap" ("And why unblooms the best hope ever sown?"); "miscompose" and "unknows" in "At a Bridal"; "unheed" in "A Sign-Seeker"; or the poem entitled "Unknowing," all in his first book, *Wessex Poems* (1898); through "The Self Unseeing" in *Poems of Past and Present* (1902); to late instances like "unknown, unrecked, unproved" (giving way to "enearthed") in "I Worked No Wile to Meet You" in *Late Lyrics and Earlier* (1922); and "unwitting" and "disfigured" in "Unkept Good Fridays" from the last book, *Winter Words in Various Moods and Metres*, published posthumously in 1928. Some of these instances—"unwitting," "disfigured"—in no way disturb conventional usage, and it is only in the larger context of Hardy's poems with their ostentatious negations that such common prefixes gain any noticeable force. Others, however, like "unknows" and "unblooms," wreak violence upon convention, and in their insistent oddity demand a reckoning.

One notes at once how intimately Hardy connects these negations with the ideas of knowledge and vision. It is as if perspective can be established only through the positing of an illusion which the poems must strain to lift away, in an effort often linked with the struggle of absence with presence. These pangs of negation give rise, not to vision, but to the mere possibility of envisioning the dead and once beloved cousin in "Thoughts of Phena," where through the reiterated negations ("Not a line of her writing have I, / Not a thread of her hair, / No mark of her late time . . ."[8]) the poet urges his "unsight" to conceive the lost figure. Hardy did not coin the unusual noun "unsight," but it is so rare that the 1971 compact edition of the *Oxford English Dictionary* gives only two instances, one from Hoccleve in 1412, and the other from "Thoughts of Phena." Since the poem's task is to "picture" the dead woman, "unsight" in its rarity calls attention to that struggle. Like so many of Hardy's poems, this one works against itself and against its own posited conditions and circumstances: the speaker wrests not a vision of Phena, but a possibility of such vision, from years deprived of sight and sign of her. That wresting, embodied in the contradictory noun "unsight" (which distinctly does not mean "blindness"), is at work also in the repetition of the clause "whereby / I may picture her there," which in the last lines of the poem reverses its earlier sense. In stanza 1, it confesses the speaker's powerlessness to envision, but by the end "whereby" could be taken as referring not to the lack of mnemonic signs but to the envisioning power released by that lack: ". . . yet haply the best of her—fined in my brain / It may be the more / That no line of her writing have I /. . . /. . . whereby / I may picture her there."[9]

Given the ambiguities embedded in "unsight" and "whereby," all the speaker can manage here is the confrontation of radiant hypotheses (enray; enarch) with the dire (mischances; unease; forebodings; disennoble). One notable effect of this poem, emphasized by the prevalence of prefixes, occurs in the removal of a prefix: ". . . yet haply the best of her—fined in my brain," where the contraction of "refined" to "fined" suggests the process of purification and simplification which the poem seeks in the act of memory.

Two well-known poems can serve as exemplary dramas of negation. "In Tenebris I" comes from Hardy's second collection, published in 1902, well before the death of his first wife, Emma. I can offer here only hints toward a fuller discussion. One remarks, first, the poem's symmetries: its dimeter, trimeter, trimeter, dimeter pattern with the dimeters behaving like jammed trimeters with syllables lacking; its quatrains designed with narrow base, squat column, pinched capital; the initial noun in all but the last stanza; the opposing "but" in all but the third stanza.

IN TENEBRIS I

"Percussus sum sicut foenum, et aruit cor meum." —*Ps. ci.*

Wintertime nighs;
But my bereavement-pain
It cannot bring again:
    Twice no one dies.

Flower-petals flee;
But, since it once hath been,
No more that severing scene
   Can harrow me.

Birds faint in dread:
I shall not lose old strength
In the lone frost's black length:
    Strength long since fled!

Leaves freeze to dun;
But friends can not turn cold
This season as of old
    For him with none.

Tempests may scath;
But love can not make smart
Again this year his heart
    Who no heart hath.

Black is night's cope;
But death will not appal
One who, past doubtings all,
    Waits in unhope.[10]

Next to this poem of living death, the "nothing" of Stevens' "The Snow-man" seems a plenitude. With Hardy the neo-Gothic architect in mind, one notes how expression bucks against the formal order: the adjective "black" replaces the sequence of nouns (wintertime; flower-petals; birds; leaves; tempests). The last lines of the third and fifth stanzas refuse the trimeter and square off as double spondees: "strength long since fled," "who no heart hath." Which brings us to the negative prefix in the last, monumental noun, "unhope." Toward that word the whole poem has urged itself over the self-erected obstructions of its "but," "but," "but," even as it rehearsed its bereavement pain through progressive losses: severing scene; strength fled; friends and love gone. Every stanza doubles its initial negation, and in Hardy's spiritual math, two negatives do not make a positive. The final stanza diminishes even death next to the certainty of depair: "one who, past doubtings all, / Waits in unhope." We have been prompted by the previous stanza to stress every syllable of that dread conclusion ("Waits in unhope") where movement comes to stasis. What is the philosophical status of this noun "unhope"? Is it hope once entertained and now foreclosed? Or is it the exclusion of any possibility of hope, ever? Like the negation that concludes "The Darkling Thrush" ("Some blessed Hope, whereof he knew / And I was unaware"), simultaneously proposing and denying awareness, "unhope" plays both possibilities off against one another: hope *had been*, and is annihilated by the prefix; the condition of unhope, more actively anguishing than despair, erases even past hope, but reminds us constantly of its severed possibility.

Like "unsight," "unhope" is not an invention of Hardy's but a word dragged out of the deep, old chest of English. The *Oxford English Dictionary* lists two citations from the thirteenth century and one from the fifteenth. One must turn to Gerard Manley Hopkins, Hardy's obscure contemporary, for prefixes as essential to the poem's dynamism and as true, even in their strangeness, to the nature of English: the "widow-making, unchilding, unfathering deeps" of "The Wreck of the Deutschland," "wanwood" from "Spring and Fall," "no-man-fathomed" of "No worst, there is none"; but Hopkins so activates every syllable that prefixes and suffixes surge up as full-fledged compounds. Both poets treat a poem as a complex action that unbuilds and rebuilds received language as it flexes and finds its singular sense, but Hopkins goes much further than Hardy in jarring conventional word-sense.

Hardy's contradictory enactments, jarring enough, reach a crescendo in "The Going," the first of the great elegies for Emma Hardy from 1912–13. I would point to the way the warp of negatives (no hint; not follow; not speak; not think) pulls against the woof of the three "why's" in the symmetrically alternating stanzas. I would point also to the play of past against present tenses, for instance in the shift from the past participle "gone" ("you would close your term here, up and be gone") to the dreadfully present and continuous recognition of "going" as a noun with verbal force: "Unmoved, unknowing / That your great going / Had place that moment, and altered all." We might trace the plot from the depriving prefixes which describe the speaker's ignorance of his wife's death (and, by contagion, of her life)—*un*moved, *un*knowing—back to the innocent negative prefix of happy courtship in the past ("While Life *un*rolled us its very best"). This plot intensifies in the course of rhymes, moving from the participial pair unknowing/going in stanza 2 to the more highly charged verbal forms of the conclusion, go/know. In the last stanza, the prefix "un-" has migrated to the unhappy past, now seen as "*un*changeable" in that paradoxical line: "Unchangeable. It must go." Stasis and the fugitive collaborate in this act of grief, the indefiniteness of the pronoun (*what* must go?) expanding the eerie power of "going" from the dead wife to the whole world of recollected and injured happiness and aborted hope that died with her. In the last line, the prefix "un-" wheels upon the speaker himself with a ferocity unforeseen in the poem: ". . . O you could not know / That such swift fleeing / No soul foreseeing— / Not even I—would undo me so!" If what tortures the speaker about his past is lack of feeling, lack of knowledge, the eruption into present consciousness of both feeling and knowledge have almost unstrung the sentence and left him near annihilation. He is the one in the end, "on end," to "go." And the deepest and characteristic story is told, not by the end rhyme, but by internal rhyme: the homophony of *know* and *no* defines knowledge as Hardy austerely understood it and played it out in the structure of verse.

Inspired by Bergson, Kenneth Burke would later take the concept of the negative as the second clause in his definition of the human: "Man is / the symbol-using (symbol-making, symbol-misusing) animal / inventor of the negative (or moralized by the negative). . . ."[11] Burke immediately qualified his clause: ". . . it might be more accurate to say that language and the negative 'invented' man."[12] However truly this definition and its qualification may describe humanity in general, they seem particularly apt for Hardy. His fictions in verse and prose explore the consequences of the hortatory negative (the "Thou shalt nots" of the Decalogue); but even more deeply they probe what Burke calls the "propositional negative"— for Hardy, the sense that human reality is essentially structured around cancellation: of hope, of illusion, of life itself. He built this cancellation into the very shapes of his words. Underwriting the multitude of Hardy's negatives—the unseeings, unknowings, undoings—stands death, the ultimate negation. No wonder so many of Hardy's poems are populated by ghosts; his is an art undertaken not so much *sub specie aeternitatis* as in the perspective of death, and the negative prefixes are the scars inflicted by that art upon language, which gains thereby its most intense life.

These negations of Hardy's are not idiosyncrasies of temperament. They partake in one, at least, of the labors of twentieth-century poetry in English, that clearing of space for the disillusioned imagination one finds in Frost's desert places and "diminished thing," and in Stevens' "the the." Hardy dramatized a vision of what Stevens called "Modern Poetry": "The poem of the mind in the act of finding / What will suffice." Only through the embodied agony of interrogation and negation do Hardy's poems earn their way; and only by participating in that agony do we earn our way as readers. To return to the personal: in partaking of Hardy's poems, I find myself at once mourning, and severely consoled: taught over and over the lesson of relinquishment which can be learned only "by heart," and by the heart in action.

CHAPTER 15

Meeting H.D.

Hilda Doolittle was an American poet who left the United States. H.D.—as Ezra Pound, her poetic initiator and onetime sweetheart, nominated her in 1912, and as she remained all her literary life—takes her place in that American tradition of retreat from the New World and its bustling future. These expatriate Americans, Henry James, Edith Wharton, Ezra Pound, T. S. Eliot, and Gertrude Stein, among others, reveal by their *via negativa*, by their nostalgia for the European parent cultures, by their citizenship in a *patria* of the imagination, much about their homeland and ours. H.D. is of that family. She was born in Bethlehem, Pennsylvania, to Moravian stock in 1886, and she left the United States (what her friend Pound, in "Hugh Selwyn Mauberley," called "a half-savage country") in 1911 to settle first in London, then Switzerland. She hardly ever returned to the country of her birth. A trip to California in 1920; another short trip in 1937; another in 1957, when she was old and fragile, to be honored at Yale University, where the Beinecke Library was amassing a collection of her papers; in 1960, a brief final trip to New York City to receive the Gold Medal in Literature from the American Academy of Arts and Letters. She died the following year in Switzerland. She is buried in the family plot in Bethlehem.

She was born and is buried in Bethlehem. But which Bethlehem? The name opens up the double exposure of colonial place names, the traces of the Old World inscribed upon the New: Troy, New York; Athens, Georgia; New England. H.D. paid a considerable poetic price for identifying with the biblical, original Bethlehem rather than with her prosaic Pennsylvania town. The prophetic temptation to which she succumbed was, I believe, very nearly a poetic catastrophe—though to say "catastrophe" melodramatizes the fate of a precise but slender talent. But art arises most vigorously out of the jaws of its own defeats, or near defeats. In considering H.D., I want to look at a particular case of the prophetic and visionary claims sometimes made by poetry.

H.D. comes aptly to hand because she has not—or has not yet—been installed in a mausoleum of greatness. Her reputation is an unstable element whose electrons keep bouncing about their outer rings. Though her admirers—and she has many these days—would establish her work "in its rightful place in the canon of great modernist writers,"[1] it is by no means clear that she belongs in that canon, and this lack of clarity forces us to acts of evaluation that test our own resources as readers. What is greatness in poetry? What is goodness, even?—perhaps a harder question to answer.

Let me put the case most provocatively. On the one hand, she is a writer, dead forty-five years ago, whose hefty *Collected Poems, 1912–1944*, introduced by a discriminating and learned scholar, Louis Martz, is still in print, along with numerous novels, memoirs, and later book-length poems; the not inconsiderable poet Robert Duncan devoted twenty-three years of essays to her, creating, piecemeal, what he called "the H.D. Book"; she is claimed by many as a major modernist figure; the annotated bibliography of work about her runs to 112 pages. But this is also the poet of whom Laura Riding and Robert Graves wrote, in 1927, in *A Survey of Modernist Poetry*, "Her work is so thin, so poor, that its emptiness seemed 'perfection,' its insipidity to be concealing a 'secret,' its superficiality so 'glacial' that it created a false 'classical' atmosphere."[2] T. S. Eliot, a friend of hers, wrote to her estranged husband Richard Aldington, in 1921, "I did not conceal from you that I think you over-rate H.D.'s poetry. I do find it fatiguingly monotonous and lacking in the element of surprise. I mean that this last book [*Hymen*] is inferior to her earlier work; that many words should be expunged and many phrases amended; that the Hellenism lacks vitality; and also morally, I find a neurotic carnality which I dislike."[3] Even Pound, who had nurtured her work, corrected it, gotten it published, and established her in the Anglo-American literary scene in 1912, by 1917 was writing to a common acquaintance, "I don't think any of these people have gone on; have invented much since the first *Des Imagistes* anthology. H.D. has done work as good. She has also (under I suppose the flow-contamination of Amy [Lowell] and [John Gould] Fletcher) let loose dilutions and repetitions, so that she has spoiled the 'few but perfect' position she might have held on to."[4]

Let us turn to that Imagist anthology, and to those early poems of H.D.'s, and let us consider how—to use Pound's phrase—she "went on."

Imagism was a minor literary movement in London in an era of avant-garde movements all hectically proclaiming themselves and succeeding one another like Shakespeare's waves, each changing place with that which goes before. Such as it was, Imagism began as a small group that cohered around T. E. Hulme at the Poets' Club in 1908, publishing a little plaquette of hard-edged, objective poems called *For Christmas MDCCCCVIII* containing, among others, Hulme's poem "Autumn" which has become a standard illustration for the Imagist aesthetic. The movement gathered definition in a famous scene in the tea shop of the British Museum in September 1912, where Pound, who had been establishing himself in London for four years, looked over the drafts of a few poems Doolittle—recently arrived—had given him. "But Dryad, this is poetry," he exclaimed (he called her "Dryad" because in the days of their early romance they used to kiss and discuss poetry in the tree house of her Philadelphia yard). Out came the red pencil; he corrected a few words, and signed them with a new name for her, in a flourish, "H.D. Imagiste."[5] Thus was Hilda Doolittle, daughter of an American astronomer, and a dropout from Bryn Mawr College, transformed into an author, an author backed by a movement (though the "movement" hardly existed). She kept those initials all her life, weaving them into her work: her last, book-length poem is entitled *Hermetic Definition*.

Recalling the Imagism of 1912—one sees how quickly the movement, *qua* movement, had flared and guttered out, replaced, for Pound, by Wyndham Lewis's Vortex—Pound said, "The whole affair started not very seriously, chiefly to get H.D.'s five poems a hearing without its being necessary for her to publish a whole book. It began certainly in Church Walk with H.D., Richard Aldington, and myself."[6] Ever the impresario, Pound had immediately sent H.D.'s poems to Harriet Monroe at *Poetry* magazine in Chicago: "It is in the laconic speech of the Imagistes," he wrote Monroe. "Objective—no slither—direct—no excess use of adjectives etc. No metaphor that won't permit examination.—It's straight talk—straight as the Greek!"[7] Monroe accepted three poems, "Hermes of the Ways," "Priapus," and "Epigram," and they appeared in the January 1913 issue of *Poetry*.

This critical vocabulary directly reflects the Imagist manifesto Pound would publish in the March 1913 issue of *Poetry*, over the signature of his companion-in-arms F. S. Flint:

1. Direct treatment of the "thing" whether subjective or objective.
2. To use absolutely no word that does not contribute to the presentation.
3. As regarding rhythm: to compose in the sequence of the musical phrase, not in the sequence of the metronome.[8]

Pound backed up this declaration with a more extended prescription under his own name in "A Few Don'ts": "'An Image' is that which presents an intellectual and emotional complex in an instant of time . . ."; "It is better to present one Image in a lifetime than to produce voluminous works"; "Use no superfluous word, no adjective which does not reveal something. Don't use such an expression as 'dim lands of peace.' It dulls the image. It mixes an abstraction with the concrete. It comes from the writer's not realizing that the natural object is always the adequate symbol.—Go in fear of abstractions . . ." ("dim lands of peace" is Pound's swipe at a poem by his friend Ford Madox Ford).[9]

All of this polemic was an attack on Pound's immediate literary inheritance, Romantic and Victorian poetry at its most decorative, and the sub-Wordsworthian, sub-Tennysonian, sub-Arnoldian imitations that continued to constitute much of the verse published in Britain and the United States in those prewar years. "As for the 19th century," Pound wrote, "with all respect to its achievements, I think we shall look back upon it as a rather blurry, messy sort of a period, a rather sentimentalistic, mannerish sort of a period."[10] Let us ignore for the moment the blur in Pound's own rhetoric here, all those "sort of's," and even the injustice of his characterization of the art of Tennyson, Browning, Hopkins, Meredith, Swinburne, and others. In trying to focus on Imagism, we may allow—provisionally—certain of its enabling prejudices.

Pound had launched Imagism, and with it, H.D. He had already used the name of the movement to introduce poems by Hulme in his book *Ripostes* in the fall of 1912; now Flint and Pound agitated for Imagism in the pages of *Poetry* in 1913, and by the summer of that year had sent off to New York the manuscript of an anthology of Imagist poems by various hands to be published as *Des Imagistes* in a new journal called *The Glebe*. Publication was held up until the spring of the following year, by which time Pound was absorbed in the more dynamic Vortex, leaving Imagism—or Amygism as he came to call it—in the busy hands of Amy Lowell.

It is instructive to look at H.D.'s defining poem, "Hermes of the Ways." Defining not only because it helped to initiate her life as a writer, but because Hermes—god of theft, of roads, of passage between realms, of alchemical transformation—was to remain one of her patron deities.

"Hermes of the Ways" was inspired by Anyte, the Greek woman poet of around 300 B.C.E. Aldington would later translate all of Anyte's surviving work. The following epigram by Anyte (translated here by Diane Rayor) gives an idea of the compressed material H.D. was expanding:

> I, Hermes, stand here by the windy tree-lined
> crossroads near the white coastal water,
> sheltering men weary from the road—
> my fountain murmurs cold water.[11]

The landscape is recognizable. From Anyte, H.D. has taken the terrain of her whole first book, *Sea Garden*, which would appear in 1916, a landscape of contradiction, sea and land, wind and water, the roads themselves at cross-purposes. But in adopting Anyte's latent contradictions, H.D. has urged them to outright conflict in her vision of breaking, fronting, rushing, whipping, gnashing, and a desperate sun. In H.D.'s poem, it is an exalted, perhaps exasperated lyric human self that speaks, not the ancient god-voice; and in spite of Pound's Imagist ethos of objectivity, it is an irritated subjectivity I most hear throughout H.D.'s early poems in *Sea Garden* (1916), *The God* (1913–17), and in *Hymen* (1921). "Heu, / it whips around my ankles!" exclaims the speaker in "Hermes of the Ways." "Shall I hurl myself from here, / shall I leap and be nearer you?" she asks in "The Cliff Temple"; "O wind, rend open the heat, / cut apart the heat, / rend it to tatters," she commands in "Garden."

HERMES OF THE WAYS

I

The hard sand breaks
and the grains of it
are clear as wine.

Far off over the leagues of it,
the wind,
playing on the wide shore,
piles little ridges,
and the great waves
break over it.

But more than the many-foamed ways
of the sea,
I know him
of the triple path-ways,
Hermes,
who awaits.

Dubious,
facing three ways,
welcoming wayfarers,
he whom the sea-orchard
shelters from the west,
from the east
weathers a sea-wind;
fronts the great dunes.

Wind rushes
over the dunes,
and the coarse, salt-crusted grass
answers.

Heu,
it whips around my ankles.

II

Small is
this white stream,
flowing below ground,
from the poplar-shaded hill,
but the water is sweet.

Apples on the small trees
are hard,
too small,
too late ripened
by a desperate sun
that struggles through sea-mist.

The boughs of the trees
are twisted
by many bafflings;
twisted are
the small-leafed boughs.

But the shadow of them
is not the shadow of the mast head
nor of torn sails.

Hermes, Hermes,
the great sea foamed,
gnashed its teeth about me;
but you have waited,
where sea-grass tangles with shore-grass.[12]

Certainly, H.D. is not composing in the sequence of the metronome. Almost every line is a syntactic unit corresponding to an essence or an act perceived, and placed like a mosaic chip. "Direct treatment of the thing," yes, and economy of presentation. Within this economy, however, one notices how much repetition piles its little ridges of words to shape the scene: the hard sand breaks, the great waves break; "the grains of it" abut "the leagues of it"; dunes pile upon dunes; stream, apples, and trees are all small. In a chiasm, boughs are twisted, twisted are boughs. What is this psychic landscape? It has hardness, clarity, particularity. Appropriately, the vision initiates with sand, and even that breaks. Almost every line, a contained phrase or clause, has its own crystal structure, and seems as irreducible as a grain of sand. Within this landscape/seascape of distance and intimacy, of great and small, the "I" grows from knowledge of the god ("I know him") to exclamation ("Heu, / it whips around my ankles!") to invocation ("Hermes, Hermes"). In a further contradiction, the poem plays action (breakage, rushing, frontage) against essences. Notice the staging of the copulative verbs in section II, some placed at line ends ("small is"; "twisted are"), some at line heads ("are hard"; "are twisted"; "is not"), some in mid-line ("but the water is sweet"); but all tend to immobilize some essence. Against that incipient stasis, the poem twists and baffles, discovers its nervous life as much in the sequence of adversatives ("But the water is sweet"; "but the shadow"; "but you have waited") as in its gnashing verbs. Like most of the poems in *Sea Garden*, like the notion of a sea garden itself, "Hermes of the Ways" celebrates adversity and the richness of fertility balked, with apples ". . . hard, / too small, / too late ripened." The whole book sounds this note, like the roses in the opening poem: "Rose, harsh rose, / marred and with stint of petals."[13]

This is a deliberately limited art, and it gains both its strength and its weakness from that limitation. In this first book, the poem that achieves the most is "Sea Violet."

SEA VIOLET

The white violet
is scented on its stalk,
the sea-violet
fragile as agate,
lies fronting all the wind
among torn shells
on the sand-bank.

The greater blue violets
flutter on the hill,
but who would change for these

who would change for these
one root of the white sort?

Violet
your grasp is frail
on the edge of the sand-hill,
but you catch the light—
frost, a star edges with its fire.[14]

The phonetic power of the name "violet" conspires, in its hard dental consonant, with the poet's will to hardness, a psyche that is both fragile and rocklike, tiny and strong. The ligature of off-rhymes binds the violet to its fate as a creature of edges, boundaries, fronting "all the wind," fronting sea and land, star and earth, frost and fire. The teeth-clicking sound pattern tells the story: white violet/agate/root/white/sort/light. Another is told in the intensifying repetition, "but who would change for these / who would change for these," as the poem builds to a crisis of recognition. The end, propelled by another adversative ("but you catch the light"), rises to a line of mysterious, concentrated richness: "frost, a star edges with its fire."

I have spoken of limitation, and it seems only honest to reckon some of its costs. All art works within chosen limits, but H.D. chose with particular severity, in her free-verse architecture, to align lines with phrases and clauses, and in doing so she sacrificed the power gained by playing syntax against line ends. The danger in her mosaic technique is inertness, relieved only rarely by enjambment. We should remember that in 1916, when *Sea Garden* came out, Yeats had published *Responsibilities* two years earlier, with its majestic and various rhythmic propulsions, including "The Cold Heaven": "Suddenly I saw the cold and rook-delighting heaven / That seemed as though ice burned and was but the more ice . . ."[15] In the very year in which *Sea Garden* appeared, Frost published *Mountain Interval*, ringing its changes on the vernacular within the pentameter frame; Edward Thomas, soon to fall in the Great War, was composing his own tough and subtle lines: "The last light has gone out of this world, except / This moonlight lying on the grass like frost / Beyond the brink of the tall elm's shadow" ("Liberty").[16] It is not only a matter of enjambment, which can be a crude invigoration of syntax against line; it is a matter of the dynamism of phrasing; the distribution of weights, measures, and breath within the line; and the greater resonances available when syntactic units are not boxed into line units and when the line allows more internal variation. As one more contrast, perhaps unfair, to H.D., listen to these lines from Ivor Gurney, fighting in France in 1916. His slightly later poem "Smudgy Dawn," written around 1921, sets a standard of force and subtlety to which English poems should be answerable: "Smudgy dawn scarfed with military colours / Northward, and flowing wider like slow sea water, / Woke in lilac and elm and almost among garden flowers."[17]

H.D. could hardly have been reading Gurney between 1912 and 1916. But she read Pound. Nearer to her purpose, and hugely instructive for any consideration of the renewal of verse in English, is the evolution of his "In a Station of the Metro." The first version, printed in *Poetry* in 1913, experimented with isolated noun phrases, and dislocated the larger line:

IN A STATION OF THE METRO

The apparition   of these   faces in the crowd :
Petals on a wet, black   bough .[18]

The revision, printed in his volume *Lustra* in 1916, subordinated the noun phrases to the larger flow of the line, and so threw more emphasis on the pivotal action of the colon (or semicolon); the revision emphasizes, too, the change in rhythm from the pentameter of the faces to the freer metric of the line with the petals:

IN A STATION OF THE METRO

The apparition of these faces in the crowd;
Petals on a wet, black bough.[19]

Such rhythmical intelligence, such subtlety of play in surge against pause and of meter against *vers libre*, is rarely audible in H.D.'s lines.

And how did H.D. "go on" after her Imagist successes in *Sea Garden, The God,* and *Hymen*? Her sequences of novels, ambitious later collections of poems, her memoirs (including the powerful account of her friendship with Pound, *End to Torment,* and *Tribute to Freud,* a free-associative record of her psychoanalysis), her involvement in avant-garde film, form too large a body of work to consider within the confines of one essay. I want to focus on two dramas particular to this poet. One is her poetry of escape, often imagined in the context of eluding the magnetizing men from whom she learned so much: Pound, D. H. Lawrence, and Freud. The second involves her growing sense of herself as a prophetic poet as, increasingly, she broke from her Imagist self-confinements.

While the escape poems reveal a great deal about her struggles to conceive of herself independently of men, and throw a strong light on a persistent psychic mechanism in her work, they do not necessarily make for poetic strength. The address to Pound, "Toward the Piraeus" from 1924, has only documentary interest; its Greek mannerisms do not convert autobiographical pain into symbolic form. The words remain merely a record of pain, a clinical notation. "You would have broken my wings," the speaker declares, "I loved you." "It was not chastity that made me wild, but fear . . ." that your hand " . . . might break // with the slightest turn—no ill will meant—my own lesser, yet still somewhat fine-wrought, / fiery-tempered, delicate, over-passionate steel."[20]

Of greater interest are the several poems to Freud and Lawrence, though all have their botched passages. "The Master," addressed to Freud, contains this austere and surprising section, where H.D.'s gift for compression works at full horsepower to link the cosmic and the human, and even to discover a kind of wit:

> I had two loves separate;
> God who loves all mountains,
> alone knew why
> and understood
> and told the old man
> to explain
>
> the impossible,
>
> which he did.[21]

In the midst of her praise of this master, H.D., devotee of Hermes the patron of thieves, steals herself away from too great a subservience:

> only I,
> I will escape.

The repetition of the pronoun, concluding one line, starting the next, pivots the affirmation. Paradoxically, it is an affirmation made possible by the master's clarification of herself to herself: "And it was he himself, he who set me free / to prophesy."

That setting free was in some ways dangerous. For H.D., born in Bethlehem and already given to thinking of herself as a Pythian priestess of the oracle, had a strong urge to prophesy. She had experienced some trancelike visions, one in 1919, in the Scilly Isles, and several more the following year as she traveled to Greece with Bryher, the novelist, her female partner of many years. On shipboard, H.D. seemed to see an island and dolphins take shape, visible to no one but herself; on Corfu, what she thought of as elements of a Delphic vision—a head, a chalice, a lamp like the Pythia's tripod, the Winged Victory—seemed to "write themselves" on her hotel wall, and later during that visit to Corfu she danced for Bryher some scenes of hallucinated possession, taking on the identities of a tree, an Indian medicine man, a Japanese girl, a Tibetan priest, and the lady goddess Rhea.

In the long poems collected in *Trilogy*, composed during the Second World War in London under the Blitz, H.D.'s prophetic strain declared itself more emphatically. The poems are *The Walls Do Not Fall*, published in 1944 by Oxford; *Tribute to the Angels*, published by Oxford in 1945; and *The Flowering of the Rod*, published—again by Oxford—in 1946. Great claims have been made for them. Albert Gelpi asserts, "*Trilogy* marks the opening of the late, great phase of H.D.'s poetry and must be ranked with *Four Quartets* and the *Pisan Cantos* as the major poems in English to come out of the war."[22] Within the context of a thoroughly syncretic vision, H.D. splices in scenes of prophetic possession, Judaic, Hellenic, and Christian: "unaware, Spirit announces the Presence; / . . . we know not nor are known; / the Pythian pronounces—."[23] In *Tribute to the Angels* she usurps the voice of the Book of Revelation, with just enough tact to leave the quotation in italics: "*I John, saw. I testify.*"[24]

The Walls Do Not Fall starts with a street scene from London in the bombing, and migrates rapidly:

I.

for Karnak 1923
from London 1942

An incident here and there,
and rails gone (for guns)
from your (and my) old town square:

mist and mist-grey, no colour,
still the Luxor bee, chick and hare
pursue unalterable purpose

in green, rose-red, lapis;
they continue to prophesy
from the stone papyrus:

there, as here, ruin opens
the tomb, the temple; enter,
there as here, there are no doors:

the shrine lies open to the sky,
the rain falls, here, there,
sand drifts; eternity endures;

ruin everywhere, yet as the fallen roof
leaves the sealed room
open to the air,

so, through our desolation,
thoughts stir, inspiration stalks us
through gloom:

unware, Spirit announces the Presence;
shivering overtakes us,
as of old, Samuel:

trembling at a known street-corner,
we know not nor are known;
the Pythian pronounces—we pass on

to another cellar, to another sliced wall
where poor utensils show
like rare objects in a museum;

Pompeii has nothing to teach us,
we know crack of volcanic fissure,
slow flow of terrible lava,

pressure on heart, lungs, the brain
about to burst its brittle case
(what the skull can endure!):

over us, Apocryphal fire,
under us, the earth sway, dip of a floor,
slope of a pavement

where men roll, drunk
with a new bewilderment,
sorcery, bedevilment:

the bone-frame was made for
no such shock knit within terror,
yet the skeleton stood up to it:

the flesh? it was melted away,
the heart burnt out, dead ember,
tendons, muscles shattered, outer husk dismembered,

yet the frame held:
we passed the flame: we wonder
what saved us? what for?[25]

The early stanzas show H.D. at her best. The parentheses in the first
stanza—"(for guns)," "(and my)"—open the potentially static lines to
breathing room and a self-interrupting scruple. The quotidian diction
("an incident here and there") establishes the world in a scene of shared
modern experience, the *koine*, the common language for matters too grave
to be pumped up immediately with rhetorical adrenaline. The simple
adverbs of place, "here" and "there," worked and reworked in different
configurations, carry out the spiritual engineering suggested by the epigraph: "for Karnak 1923, from London 1942"; they place in vital relation
ancient Egypt with its ruin and its eternity ("there") with contemporary
London in ruins ("here"). In stanzas 4 and 5 the adverbs continue to do
fulcrum work: "there as here, there are no doors"; "the rain falls here,

there." Most effective is the seeing of "another sliced wall / where poor utensils show / like rare objects in a museum": here one senses that one can trust the speaker to report on something observed and translated imaginatively without distortion.

In this scene of communal suffering, the prophetic voice, whether as Samuel or the Pythian priestess, remains plural. Equally plural is the bewilderment of the survivors: "what saved us? what for?" The statement that "Pompeii has nothing to teach us" retains an objective and colloquial probity. But the poet loses her balance in that tercet with the adjectival inflation of "slow flow of terrible lava." And the poem as a whole is leaden in its lineation, obvious in its self-interpreting ("through our desolation . . .").

Section II of *The Walls Do Not Fall* begins the struggle for prophetic power, as the vatic "we" confront the reproving "they": "they snatched off our amulets, / charms are not, they said, grace."[26] Here begins a poetry, not of observation, but of assertion; not of conflict faced, but of wish fulfillment. The speaker exhorts, "so let us search the old highways / for the true runes, the right-spell, / recover old values. . . ." "Let us, however, recover the Sceptre, / the rod of power."[27] That rod of power cannot just be claimed. It must be won, in poetry, through a language that overcomes itself, and though "they" accuse the speaker, "your stylus is dipped in corrosive sublimate," that image pays this poem too great a compliment. I smell and taste no corrosive sublimate, either in the facile vowel spell of true runes/right-spell, or, still worse, in the sermonizing literalness of the prescription "recover old values."

The Walls Do Not Fall discovers a first-person singular pronoun, an "I" seen as nugget of selfhood, shellfish within its shell, and worm waiting to be made butterfly. This "I" promises itself a birth endowed with biblical power from the Gospel of Matthew 13:46: "so that, living within, / you beget, self-out-of-self, // selfless / that pearl-of-great-price."[28] In a weave of singular and plural, the consciousness of this poem, surviving war, imagines a meeting with the sacred—Sirius, Osiris, O-Sire—at a tomb transformed to a temple gate.

Tribute to the Angels, the second poem in *Trilogy*, unfolds under the protection of Hermes, H.D.'s tutelary deity. But it claims prophetic authority from the Book of Revelation, and proceeds by a sequence of invocations to Hebrew angels, the most important of whom for this work is Azrael, angel of death, and angel of *writing*, who writes and then erases mortal names. H.D. envisions art here as a theft ("steal then, o orator / plunder, o poet").[29] It is a theft of vision from a host of orthodoxies to "reinvoke, recreate" a private vision. Such a project is Blakean and Promethean in its ambition. Its success depends on the tensile strength of its language. It comes closest to earning its keep in odd moments of dynamic lineation: "is fresh-fallen snow (or snow / in the act of falling) dim?"[30] It also does honest work when it struggles toward essences through wordplay:

> Now polish the crucible,
> and in the bowl distill
>
> a word most bitter, *marah*,
> a word bitterer still, *mar*,
>
> sea, brine, breaker, seducer,
> giver of life, giver of tears;
>
> now polish the crucible
> and set the jet of flame
>
> under till *marah-mar*
> are melted, fuse and join
>
> and change and alter
> mer, mere, mère, mater, Maia, Mary,
>
> Star of the Sea,
> Mother.[31]

For this bisexual poet—"the perfect bi," Freud called her—the discovery of the mother goddess at the heart of male religious structures constitutes at least part of the heart of the matter (or the *mater*).[32] The matter is regeneration within scenes of ruin, regeneration seen as "a half burnt-out apple tree / blossoming," a tree as emblematic as Wordsworth's "but there's a tree, of many, one," from "Intimations of Immortality from Recollections of Early Childhood."

How does this regeneration, for which the speaker gives thanks, occur? Partly through the perception of life's continuance through ruin; partly through the perception of the sacred permeating the ordinary. And yet, and yet. I find myself resisting. At one level, because some of the writing is simply bad. That Zeus's lightning "shattered earth / and splintered sky" comes as no revelation.[33] Nor are we much illuminated on the subject of lightning by the phrasing of "people / daring the blinding rage / of the lightning."[34] Lightning seems to bring out some of H.D.'s most flaccid effects. A more serious, though not unrelated, problem involves the narrative. Who *are* these people, in section 1 of *The Walls Do Not Fall*, who do not survive? Whose flesh melts away? Whose hearts burn out and muscles shatter? Who are the children crying for food while flaming stones fall on them in section 29 of *The Walls Do Not Fall*? The question, rightly put, is not: Who are they? We know generally who they are. The question is: What becomes of them in this poem? And does the poem lead us to care? H.D. evokes these victims of war as backdrop to her own drama of spiritual renewal. My doubt about H.D.'s claimed regeneration in *Trilogy* resembles the resistance some readers feel to T. S. Eliot's "Little Gidding," where rhyme and meter so willfully enforce a transcendence of the terror of the bombing:

> The dove descending breaks the air
> With flame of incandescent terror
> Of which the tongues declare
> The one discharge from sin and error. . . .

A situation to be resolved in:

> All manner of thing shall be well
> When the tongues of flame are in-folded
> Into the crowned knot of fire
> And the fire and the rose are one.[35]

Section I of *The Flowering of the Rod* moves from the beautiful garment of a deity and the snow on Hermon (a mountain in Syria visible from the northern border of the Hebrews' promised land, associated, in the Psalms, with the Lord's blessing), to the bombing ("the terrible banner / darkens the bridgehead"), to a blithe impulse to "leave the smouldering cities below / (we have done all we could)"; to leave pity and "mount higher / to love—resurrection." Those civilians with burned hearts and shattered muscles have simply been left behind, not spiritually absorbed. Section II begins in a most ill-judged maneuver, "I go where I love and where I am loved, / into the snow." Like (and yet in fundamental ways unlike) Eliot with his fire and rose, *The Flowering of the Rod* pursues its argument by imagistic assertion:

> Yet resurrection is a sense of direction,
> resurrection is a bee-line,
>
> straight to the horde and plunder,
> the treasure, the store-room,
>
> the honey-comb;
> resurrection is remuneration,
>
> food, shelter, fragrance
> of myrrh and balm.[37]

The writing here is clean and clear. But in the larger spiritual architecture of the poem, it could be seen as dangerously decorative, self-pleasing, and offensive in its celebration of the singular "resurrected" self: "I go . . . where I am loved. . . ." *The Flowering of the Rod*, a complex poem, works its way, like the rest of *Trilogy*, through wordplay (rod, to rood— the crucifix—to reed, the female bending plant, the writing instrument) and through a multiple exposure of divinities: Attis, Adonis, Tamnuz, have their sacrificial roles to play, as Isis-Astarte-Cyprus (Venus) do their part. All tends toward the sacrifice and implied resurrection of Christ, seen undoctrinally as the precious bundle of myrrh, the precious herb for burial. In this prolonged tale, Mary Magdalen obtains myrrh from Kaspar, one of the Magi. With this dissident Mary, this interplay of youth and sorrow, life and death, the poem gracefully concludes:

> But she spoke so he looked at her,
> she was shy and simple and young;
>
> she said, Sir, it is a most beautiful fragrance,
> as of all flowering things together;
>
> but Kaspar knew the seal of the jar was unbroken.
> He did not know whether she knew

the fragrance came from the bundle of myrrh
she held in her arms.

Too gracefully. H.D.'s old Imagist elegance, beautifully executed here, should have been dipped in corrosive sublimate. Nor can sacred power be so easily annexed into the narcissism of a private religion. The writer of these delicate final lines also wrote, with flabbergasting blindness and self-absorption in her memoir of Ezra Pound in 1958, "The prison actually of the Self was dramatized or materialized for our generation by Ezra's incarceration."[38] By *Ezra's* incarceration, in the century of Hitler and Stalin, the death camps and the gulag?

If H.D. was in a certain prison of the Self as she wrote those lines, she is also the author of such moments of true vision as "I have lost pace with the wind"[39] and "O heart, small urn."[40] She is a stronger poet when she is not claiming a scepter, but recognizing her vulnerability; she sees better not when she is announcing herself as a Seer, but when she actually looks and can show us ". . . another sliced wall / where poor utensils show." It is by such sightings, and such reverberations, that she earns a lasting place in the art.

CHAPTER 16

Adventures of the "I": The Poetry of Pronouns in Geoffrey Hill

Almost at the end of his book-length poem *The Triumph of Love*, Geoffrey Hill refers once again to the poem by the nineteenth-century Italian poet Leopardi, "A se stesso," "To oneself":

> *A se stesso:* of Self, the lost cause to end all
> lost causes; and which you are not (are you?)
> so hopeless as to hope to defend. You've
> *what?*

Hill's poem invites us to examine some structures of poetic selfhood. Listen again to these lines from section CXL of *The Triumph of Love*:

> *A se stesso:* of Self, the lost cause to end all
> lost causes; and which you are not (are you?)
> so hopeless as to hope to defend. You've
> *what?* Leopardi for the New Age? Mirageous
> laterite highway—every few miles
> a clump of vultures, the vile spread.

> *Fama/Fame* [It.—ED]: celebrity and hunger
> gorging on road–kill. *A se stesso.*[1]

Many of the radical maneuvers of Hill's recent poetry are on display here: a notation both dense and rapid; self-interruption; interruption by a fictive busybody of an editor; an aggressive challenge to an imagined interlocutor, "you" (You've / *what?*); physically repulsive imagery; shifts in register from the colloquial to the complexly rhetorical. Just in these eight lines, if we wanted to be fancy about it, we could identify two figures of speech with solemn names: polyptoton, the repetition of a word in different cases or inflections in the same sentence (lost cause/lost causes; you are not (are you?); hopeless/to hope). And epanalepsis, a figure to which the poet has alerted us back in section X, the use of the same words to open and close a passage: *A se stesso, a se stesso*. These figures are neither ornamental nor ostentatious here. In their claustrophobic structure, they embody a fundamental feature of the argument: that the lost cause of the Self *is* a lost cause because of its self–enclosure. To confirm the deliberateness of this gesture, we have only to turn back to the earlier invocation of Leopardi in section LXI to find another enclosing epanalepsis and another polyptoton:

LXI

> *A se stesso.*
> Not unworded. Enworded.
> But in the extremity
> of coherence. You will be taken up.
> *A se stesso.*[2]

If we raise our heads to a wider-angled view of the whole poem, we find that it is one large epanalepsis, or *almost*, with one crucial alteration. It opens in a one-line section that is a descriptive sentence fragment: "Sun-blazed, over Romsley, a livid rain-scarp." It concludes in section CL in almost the same line: "Sun-blazed, over Romsley, the livid rain-scarp." The intervening 148 sections will have taken us on a wild ride of confession and anticonfession, and will have confronted us with the paradox of a poem which on the one hand accuses the Self of being a lost cause, and on the other seems to make the Self and its guilts the center of the enterprise. Section II reads:

Guilts were incurred in that place, now I am convinced:
self-molestation of the child-soul, would that be it?[3]

The penultimate section, bracketing the poem and echoing section V, stretches the arc of the whole from original guilt to the difficulty of forgiveness:

Obstinate old man—*senex*
sapiens, it is not. Is he still
writing? What is he writing now? He
has just written: I find it hard
to forgive myself. We are immortal. Where
was I?—[4]

Before plunging into this morass of guilt, confession, and paradox, I want to suggest some context for my question about poetic selfhood, both as it takes shape in Hill's last three books, and in broader terms as a preoccupation of twentieth-century poetry. First, the modernist doctrine of impersonality. Geoffrey Hill's first two books, *For the Unfallen* (1959) and *King Log* (1968) hew fairly strictly to a code of non-self-revelation. If the first-person singular pronoun is used at all, it appears as a distanced, prophetic "I" ("Against the burly air I strode," in "Genesis"), or as an obvious mask ("I love my work and my children. God / is distant, difficult," in "Ovid in the Third Reich"). More often than not these early poems act through an impersonal "we" ("We grasp, roughly, the song," from "Two Formal Elegies") or a fictive "you," but most often these poems operate in the third person. Some have no specified grammatical subject at all, as in "Solomon's Mines": "Anything to have done!"[5] This severity, we may imagine, is in part temperamental hauteur and stoic detachment, and stems in part from the modernist ethos of impersonality articulated by T. S. Eliot in his essay "Tradition and the Individual Talent" in 1919: "What happens to the artist," Eliot famously claims, "is a continuous surrender of himself as he is at the moment to something which is more valuable. The progress of an artist is a continual self-sacrifice, a continual extinction of personality."[6] Behind Eliot looms the magus-like figure of Mallarmé with his declaration that the pure work implies the elocutory disappearance of the poet.

At the opposite end of the spectrum from this disappearance flail the paroxysms of self-revelation of what we have come to call "confessional poetry." The publication in 1959 of Robert Lowell's *Life Studies*—itself a masterfully composed and imaginative work—opened the floodgates to a spate of anecdotal poems of suffering selfhood in which the claim to the reader's attention seemed increasingly to rest, not with formal properties of language, but with the sensational personal subject matter presented and the demands of a self seen as imperially interesting in and of itself. Anne Sexton was one of the early practitioners of this new literalism ("I hold a five-year diary that my mother kept / for three years, telling all she does not say/of your alcoholic tendency . . .").[7] She is by no means the worst of the lot, nor has the charm of this irregularly lineated gossip worn off for the public at large. In this context, Hill's project in the later books can be seen as counterconfession. As he savagely asks through the clashing voices of *Mercian Hymns* (1971), "What should a man make of remorse, that it might profit his soul? Tell me. Tell everything to Mother, darling, and God bless."[8]

The question is the serious one, the central one. What *should* a man—or a woman, for that matter—make of remorse? And how do poems make it? One way Hill's poems approach the matter is through a *via negativa*, a negative way, to use the term of the mystics. "I may be gone some time. Hallelujah! / Confession and recantation in fridge," announces section LXXIII of *The Triumph of Love*; section CXLV bursts out, "Incantation or incontinence—the lyric cry? / Believe me, he's not / told you the half of it. (*All who are able may stand*)."[9]

For Hill, a Christian poet, confession does *not* mean self-advertisement. Whether in the fridge or not, confession as he conceives it implies a formal relation of the penitent to God. *The Confessions* of Saint Augustine, written in the fourth century C.E., set the model: the self of the confessing speaker is composed of an intricate tissue of quotations from the Bible and direct addresses to the Lord. The self takes shape, rhetorically, through quotation and prayer, and assumes self-consciousness in relation to the radical otherness of the divine. This model of confession contrasts sharply with the Romantic, self-centering confessions of the eighteenth-century philosopher Jean-Jacques Rousseau, who quotes only his own earlier works in a way that verges on the autoerotic, and who addresses the reader for a confirmation of his own reality, uniqueness, and ultimate innocence. With this latter, secular form of confession—the one that, in debased form, dominates our own era of *Self* magazine—Geoffrey Hill's poems are violently at odds.

As for that lyric cry, it is a match Hill has struck several times. The joke on incantation and incontinence in *The Triumph of Love* in 1998 lit the fuse for the phonetic explosion verging on nonsense in *The Orchards of Syon* in 2002: "lyric cry lyric cry lyric cry, I'll / give them lyric cry! / Whose is the voice, faint, injured and ghostly, / trapped in this cell phone, if it is not mine?" (XXX).[10] Note the pun on "cell phone" and "self-phone": a "self-phone" could be seen as a comic model of the personal lyric. Whose is the voice: that is the matter I am trying to tease out. The lyric poem in the West is generally dated to the Greek poets of the seventh century B.C.E.: Archilochos, Sappho, Alcaeus among them. In their monodies— songs for a single voice accompanied by flute or lyre, as opposed to choral odes of praise or mourning—these ancient poets seem to have invented a new language for subjectivity, quite different from anything in Homer. We can hear the origin of Hill's lyric cry in Archilochos lamenting, "And I, alone in the dark, / I was promised the light"[11]; and in Sappho, wrung by erotic desire, describing her own near extinction: "sweat pours from me, a trembling seizes me all over, I am greener than grass, and it seems to me that I am little short of dying."[12]

"I seem"—the Greek verb *phainomai*—gives the key to this new poetry of the inner life. It is important for us, still the heirs of European Romanticism, to recognize that the "I" enunciated by Archilochos and Sappho has some profoundly conventional features—just how many, scholars are still arguing about. We should be wary of projecting back on these poets our modern notions of autonomous individuality and of sincerity. We are speaking about a language for the inner life, about the intensity of this new fictive interiority. To say "fictive" is not to say "false": but it is to insist on the difference between the composed voice and the biographical individual mired in her circumstances and contradictions.

After these early Greeks, the lyric cry rolls down the centuries, inflected differently in different eras and languages, but usually saying or pleading or insisting "I want" and "I hurt." In its great forms, it preserves that startling freshness that makes us believe that Catullus, and Villon, and Baudelaire are our contemporaries and soul mates. "I" resonates with "I." This is not the place for a Cook's Tour of Western inwardness. Let me notice a few emblematic instances, however, to show what Hill is rejecting. Five centuries after Sappho, the Roman poet Catullus addresses himself in poem after poem: "Miser Catulle, desinas ineptire" (Wretched Catullus, stop driveling), he snorts in one poem, making an art of this exhibition of himself.[13] One thousand three hundred years after Catullus, his fellow Italian Petrarch, inventing the sonnet sequence in the *Rime sparse*, balances an intensely personal voice against an elaborate set of Neoplatonic poetic conventions to celebrate his lady Laura. The very grammar of his first sonnet insists on a hyperbolic inwardness which is at the same time public:

> Ma ben veggio or si come al popol tutto
> Favola fui gran tempo, onde sovente
> Di me medesmo meco mi vergogno.[14]

(But now I see well how to everyone I was for a long time a public story [*favola*, fable], for which often of me myself within myself I am ashamed of myself.)

Hill's recent poems, and his question "Whose is the voice?" assault the kind of single self performed in these lyrics by Sappho, Catullus, and Petrarch. In chronology of composition, the books I am considering are *The Triumph of Love* (1998), *Speech! Speech!* (2000), and *The Orchards of Syon* (2002). I propose a specific approach for tracking his adventures of the "I." If we inject a radioactive dye into the pronouns and observe their activity— rather as doctors inject dye into patients to observe specific functions of the brain under a CAT scan or an MRI—we will not obtain a comprehensive account of his poems, but we will have an insight about one of their central concerns: How does the self grow capable of redemptive love? Poetry is neither philosophy, nor psychology, nor theology; it arrives at its truths through a musical-verbal process, cadence leading to cadence, clause to clause, in the compromised, slipshod medium of language. Hill's process is more exacting than most, more purgatorial, dragging through pain, obscenity, curse, question, argument, solecism, and deliberate misprision to prayer and guarded blessing. In this labor, his pronouns do much of the heavy lifting, and it is the pronouns we will try to watch in action. "Excuse me," blurts the shifting speaker in *The Triumph of Love*:

> Excuse me—excuse me—I did not
> say the pain is lifting. I said the pain is in
> the lifting. No—please—forget it.
> $\qquad\qquad\qquad$ (XLII)[15]

In considering personal pronouns as the actors in the drama, we may turn for a moment to the linguist Emil Benveniste. He sets the first and second grammatical persons—"I" and "you"—in a totally different category from the third-person "he," "she," and "it." "I" and "you," according to Benveniste, are not referential nouns. They refer to no "fixed or objective notion." He goes on: "Each I has its own referent and corresponds each time to a unique being who is set up as such. . . . I cannot be defined except in terms of 'locution,' not in terms of objects as a nominal sign is. I signifies 'the person who is uttering the present instance of the discourse containing "I."' . . . It has no value except in the instance in which it is produced."[16] The same goes, of course, for "you." Benveniste says of "I" and "you" that their job is to solve the problem of "intersubjective communication": "Language has solved the problem," he argues, "by creating an ensemble of 'empty' signs that are nonreferentia with respect to 'reality.' These signs are always available and become 'full' as soon as a speaker introduces them into each instance of his discourse."[17]

Language may have "solved the problem of intersubjective communication" (rebarbative phrase!) in some abstract and general way, but we mortals need to solve it again and again, in action, and that is what the pronouns strain to do in Hill's late poetry. The strain emerges partly from the fact that Hill's pronouns are, if not "empty" signs, signs that shift their reference with almost every enunciation. No "I," no "you," no "we" can be trusted to remain the same even in the course of a short passage in these poems, and in the struggle to track them, the reader is jarred into an uncomfortable, radicalized vision of selfhood and its relations.

To complement Benveniste, let us draw into the orbit of our reading the name of the French philosopher Emmanuel Levinas. Benveniste's analysis would leave us with the exhilarating, mobile notion of "I" as an empty sign, but Levinas's religious perspective, from his Jewish tradition, builds off Martin Buber's classic work *I and Thou* of 1923 and Gabriel Marcel's *Metaphysical Journal* of 1927 to emphasize, more dynamically, the relations *between* "I" and "you." We need such an emphasis in reading Hill, whose long poems are both erotic and theological. "To say 'you,'" writes Levinas, "is the primary fact of Saying."[18] Levinas meditates upon the mystery of distance and intimacy between "I" and "you," what he calls "the marvel of the social relation"; behind that marvel stands for him, as for Buber, the greater marvel of a God who sums up the possibility of all human connectedness.

We now have a context in which to approach Hill's adventures of the "I." Already years ago he was composing occult autobiographies in "The

Songbook of Sebastian Arrurruz" in *King Log*, and in *Mercian Hymns*. The persona of Arrurruz, an imaginary Spanish poet whose dates are 1868–1922, freed Hill to write an erotic sequence in which "I" and "you" emerge in a numinous directness he had not otherwise allowed himself: "'One cannot lose what one has not possessed.' / So much for that abrasive gem. / I can lose what I want. I want you."[19] In the multiple exposure of personae in *Mercian Hymns*, the eighth-century Anglo-Saxon king Offa is crossed with the twentieth-century boy: "Dreamy, smug-faced, sick on outings—I who was taken to be a king of some kind, a prodigy, a maimed one" (V).[20] It was from *Mercian Hymns* that I lifted the challenge "What should a man make of remorse?" And in the dance of "I" and "he" in the hymns we find a dry run for the phantasmagorical pronouns of the late work.

We face a paradox. In these long poems, as Hill leaves behind the subjective genre of lyric, he lets in a far more unruly autobiography. The voices fracture and multiply, and the lines, already disarticulated in many of the poems in *Canaan* (1996), devolve further from metrical order to a subtle, frequently enjambed free verse. Two more general observations: in these long poems, Hill uses polyphony, multiple voices, as a discipline, and a method of inquiry and transformation. Part of the discipline is the task of integrating a poetry of private confession and quest for absolution within a poetry of public, ethical discourse.

The Triumph of Love, whose 150 sections pay homage to the 150 Psalms, starts teasingly with five sections coordinating the number of lines in each section to the section number: one line for section I, two for section II, and so forth. After the fifth section the symmetry peters out and we are already over our heads, in the deep end. The first line abstains in several ways. "Sun-blazed, over Romsley, a livid rain-scarp." It is not a full sentence, and it has no pronouns, no human actors. Dense with two noun compounds, which are metrically two emphatic spondees (Sun-blazed; rain-scarp), it sets us in a highly visual landscape. Even without a verb, the line acts. It plays opposites against one another: sun against rain, a blaze against the blue-black of livid, celebration (in sun) against harm (livid, bruise color). "Scarp" itself is an aggressive word, meaning the pitch of a hill, but also a fortified bank. Along with the destructive possibilities in "blaze," "scarp" charges the line with contained force. And what of the keystone, the name "Romsley"? Readers unfamiliar with Hill's native Worcestershire won't have to look far to discover that Romsley is a town close to Bromsgrove, where Hill was born. So we find ourselves in an obscurely autobiographical landscape, both personal and impersonal: no "I," but the land itself, eloquent with mute personal history, brilliant and bruised.

Section II thickens the plot. The passive verb of the first clause leaves the question of culpability open: "Guilts were incurred"—by whom? That is one mystery the whole rest of the poem will try to solve. Guilt for the death of the Kenelm, the boy martyr murdered there in the ninth century, we learn in section VII; diffuse guilt for the dead of World War II; personal guilts never directly confessed, but requiring the whole poem's purgatorial labor. Then the first-person singular enters, "now I am convinced." This "I" purports to be a center of consciousness and judgment in the poem: we shall see how soon he is dislodged from that position. "Now" suggests a present vantage point for surveying the past, a bifocal vision confirmed in the next line, "self-molestation of the child-soul," which brings the child and the adult "I" into alignment. Almost at its conclusion, in section CXXI, the poem will pick up this motif of doubled vision as it imagines a source of redemption in childhood innocence:

> Light is this instant, far-seeing
> into itself, its own
> signature on things that recognize
> salvation. I
> am an old man, a child, the horizon
> is Traherne's country.[21]

The line "am an old man, a child, the horizon" holds in its single horizon the old man and the child; the abrupt enjambment, isolating "I" on the line above, dramatizes the mystery of the self composite in time that both is and isn't the child and the old man, the arc of its own biography. Thomas Traherne, we remember, is the seventeenth-century English poet of landscapes of visionary innocence. But in the early stages of *The Triumph of Love*, childhood is felt as a source of guilt, not innocence, and is obscurely linked to the martyrdom of Kenelm. The poem will have far to go before it redeems that child.

Section III responds to the challenge of diffuse guilt, what in Christian terms we could feel as original sin. Two guardians are invoked: Petronius Arbiter, the Roman author of the wildly decadent novel *The Satyricon*, from the reign of Nero; and Angelus Silesius, a seventeenth-century Polish Lutheran poet and doctor who converted to Roman Catholicism. The

name of Petronius warns that the poem will engage violent public corruption; the appeal to Angelus Silesius suggests the opposite extreme of
luminous *caritas*. The arc of Hill's *Triumph*—triumph in the sense, not of
victory, but of ceremonial procession, as in the *Trionfi* of Petrarch—will
extend, we may imagine, from perversion to sacred love, from public satire
to private blessing. Observing our radioactive dye, note the expanding
scope of the poem: from no pronouns in section I, to the first-person
singular in section II, and now to the first-person plural, "Take us in
charge." This move to "we" and "us" is crucial: it signals an intention to
integrate the solitary self into some larger communal experience of suffering and purgation.

Section IV withdraws to the impersonal with an oblique description
of the poem's process—"ever more protracted foreplay"—and a glimpse
of a heart attack: eternity and a sudden ending are set in violent contrast
to one another. But it is to section V I want to draw our attention. It
contains, *in nuce*, the purgatorial method of the whole work to come, and
the alternative model to the lost cause of the self:

> Obstinate old man—*senex*
> *sapiens*, it is not. What is he saying;
> why is he still so angry? He says, I cannot
> forgive myself. We are immortal.
> Where was I? Prick him.[22]

No quotation marks cordon off these statements or help us distinguish the
voices. What the poem calls for much later, a "formal / self-distancing"
(CXXXIII), is already at work in this third-person portrait of the "obstinate old man." A hostile public voice seems to launch this attack and
registers the incomprehension of so many of Hill's critics: Why is he still
so angry? But the kaleidoscope turns quickly, and the pronouns tumble
into and over one another: it, he, I, myself, we, I, him. Who is this "we"
of "we are immortal"? Is the statement contained in what "he" says? Or
is it some general claim by an authorial voice from an Archimedian point
outside the dialogue? Who asks "Where was I"? We cannot definitively
answer such questions. The poem has thrown us into a quest for self-
definition that involves guilt ("I cannot / forgive myself"), a religious
promise of immortality, a first-person singular who appears mobile and
changeable ("Where was I?"), and an inimical relation to a public world
("Prick him"). Several stylistic registers seem to be at work simultane-

ously: "Where was I?" can be read—must be read—both as the colloquial self-interruption of a speaker who has lost his train of thought, and as an existential question about the self and its origins: Where was my true being? Where did I truly exist? By the end of the poem, the wheel of the 145 sections will have brought us around again to a version of this passage, significantly changed. But we are not there yet.

The Triumph of Love is a long poem. Throughout it, we will find juxtaposed the kaleidoscope shards we saw in section V. For instance, we could make a list of the third-person portraits of the author: "Scab-picking old scab: why should we be salted / with the scurf of his sores?" (XXXI); "obnoxious chthonic old fart" (XXXIV); "shameless old man" (XXXVII); "rancorous, narcissistic old sod" (XXXIX). This is the poet seen by his public. At another extreme are the intimate enunciations of the "I" musing in solitude: "whatever may be meant by *moral landscape*, / it is for me increasingly a terrain / seen in cross-section . . ." (LI); "why do I / take as my gift a wounded and wounding / introspection?" (LXVII); and of Romsley, "Let it now take for good a bad part of my / childhood. I gather I was a real swine" (LXXXII).

The problem is one of integration. How can we as readers—how can the poem—relate the intimate confessing self to the self contemptuously seen from the outside? This is where Benveniste, in spite of his clinical vocabulary, comes usefully to hand. If we think of "I" and "you" not as referring to stable entities, but as signs waiting to be filled with the meaning of each encounter, then we will begin to have a sense of the cumulative, plural way in which The Triumph of Love works. Bearing in mind as well Levinas's sense of "I" and "you" filling each other with reciprocal meaning, we might look to the "I"/"you" constructions in the poem for the forms in which a self capable of love takes shape. The work's title is, after all, for all its invective, The Triumph of Love. A scan of the "I"/"you" passages reveals three main types: the intimate ("my dear and awkward love, we may not need / to burn the furniture" [LVII]); the embattled ("bugger you, MacSikker et al" [CXIX]); and the prayers to Petrarch's *Vergine bella* (lovely virgin) interspersed throughout. Part of the poem's labor is to find its way through the travail of intimacy and public conflict to a state in which prayer, compassion, and humility might be possible. As the poem's own lengthy procession suggests, there is no shortcut. The Triumph of Love is remarkable, among contemporary poems, in accepting its own ill nature—rage, envy, bitterness—as part of the raw material through which it must work.

The "I" that asks, in the penultimate section, "Where / was I?" has taken shape through all these encounters, and more. It is largely constituted, for instance, by its capacity for memory and mourning, processes not so easily picked up by scanning pronouns, but central to the poem. "Whose lives are hidden in God? Whose?" asks the unnamed speaker urgently about the dead of World War II in section XIII, and images of the war—the burning ghetto in film and stills, Coventry in "huge silent whumphs / of flame-shadow"—have in some sense set the terms of the need for purgation that drives the whole work. That it is a process and driven, we are never in doubt, though it proceeds by editorial interruption, doublings-back, and ironic non sequiturs, and though halfway through, the author—"I"—appears lost "in this maze of my own / devising" (LXXV).

The procession, enjoying its own form of epanalepsis, fetches up almost where it began. The obstinate old man is now writing, not saying. The act is now in the perfect tense: "He / has just written." What he has just written is, in effect, the entire poem we have just read, and here is its synopsis: instead of "I cannot / forgive myself," we have arrived at "I find it hard / to forgive myself." The forgiveness is difficult, but to the eye of faith, it is as improbably possible as that Gerard Manley Hopkins' "Jack, joke, poor potsherd, / patch, matchwood" should be simultaneously, in Christ's love, "immortal diamond."[23]

"We are immortal" claims, not so much the poet, as the poem. It is a collective, not a private, statement. The jolt back to the personal question "Where / was I?," given new point by the altered line break, has the quality of waking from a dream, not just from a lost train of thought, and delivers us back almost to our point of origin:

Sun-blazed, over Romsley, the livid rain-scarp.

Not, now, *a* rain-scarp, but *the* rain-scarp—the one known, recognized, made particular, an origin now not only for the poet, but for the reader who has shared in the purgatorial trek. One answer to the question "Where / was I?" is, not in the solitary self, for there is no such thing for true being, but in place, in time, in a set of relations the poem has now established.

We can do no more than glance at *Speech! Speech!* and *The Orchards of Syon*, but a similar attention to the adventures of "I" with "you" and "he" would show us a good deal about the processes of confession in these works. *Speech! Speech!*, the infernal canticle, welters in a stew of jargon and abused language, ferocious humor, and a harsh sexuality of checkmate condoms, exchange of love bites, the urine ceremony. In this cacophony of crossed signals ("I AM LOSING YOU," 5) the poetic self pursues its pilgrimage, though "AUTHENTIC SELF a stinker" is the message to pass on (99).[24] This burlesque show, gruesomely public and interrupted by laughter and applause, drops even the consolatory support of the shared plural: "On self-advisement I erased / WE, though I / is a shade too painful . . ." (6).

A telescopic view of this wild poem shows that, once again, the mathematical center provides a clue to its progress and goals. Midway through the 120 sections ("as many as the days that were / of Sodom," 35), section 60 takes stock of its own pilgrim's progress. We can treat this passage as a microcosm of the work. The apparently authorial, confessional "I" ("I think now I / shall get through") is no sooner proposed than he is boxed on the ears into the second person ("On thy way, Friend")—and then estranged into an allegorical landscape in the pun, "Up the Hill / Difficulty." The impudent pun, of course, thumbs its nose at the by now ritualized criticism of Hill's work as difficult, "inaccessible." The question "How do I find thee?" explodes any unitary pretensions of the initial "I." This "I" feels plural; it echoes Bunyan, it incorporates but surpasses the authorial voice, it seeks a "thee." The proper noun "Hill" has fractured into two pronouns, "I" and "thee," Hill in search of himself. But what he finds is a demonic joke, a parody of poetry's investiture. Where we had a right to expect Apollo, god of harmony, we receive Apollyon, the angel of the abyss in the Book of Revelation; and that persona degenerates, phonetically and symbolically, into a nonentity. "ANON on his knees, / sinuses choked with shit." The section doesn't leave us in Dantesque scatology, however. It is a measure of Hill's great distance from the postmodern free play of pronouns in John Ashbery, for instance, that from the wreckage of "I," this section rescues the figure of PILGRIM, and concludes in a parodied theological news bulletin: "Flash: / Bucer signs for England—*De Regno Christi*." The decomposed, isolate self in Hill opens up to a vision—borrowed from the sixteenth-century German Protestant theologian Martin Bucer, who took refuge in Cambridge—of selfhood formed in relation to national and divine orders. Not so subtly, section 60 answers accusations and questions just raised in section 59: "everyone a self-trafficker," and "And nów whose England áre you' but then whích / England wére you? Were you ever? NOW THEN!"

Speech! Speech! concludes its slapstick with phonetic nonsense which scrambles yet suggests the deep sense in all the poem's themes: love, consciousness, identity, prayer. "AMOR. MAN IN A COMA, MA'AM. NEMO. AMEN." This is Hill's hell; we are hardly to expect a redemptive promise. At best, its paronomasia and freakish juxtapositions serve the purpose of voiding bad sense. The progress in the line from AMOR through nonbeing (NEMO) to ritual prayer indicates at least a blueprint for an escape from the hell of self. It is left to Paradiso—*The Orchards of Syon*—to cash the checks written by the words AMOR (love) and AMEN.

Taking one of its many cues from Calderón's seventeenth-century play *Life Is a Dream*, *The Orchards of Syon* integrates confession with profession of faith, nature's cycles with God's time, *eros* with *caritas*, and the "I" with vastly larger orders of spirit and sense. Its method is relational, through the medium of its gently loping cadences, swift elisions, and multiple exposures. Its modes are pastoral and theatrical, both announced in the opening poem which celebrates illusionistic play: "Watch my hands / confabulate their shadowed rhetoric." As we have come to expect, "I" and "you" engage in an elaborate dance which translates them to the impersonal form of patterned action: "Tell me, is this the way / to the Orchards of Syon / where I left you thinking I would return?"

The "I" still has tricks up its sleeve, some of them confessional. "I wish I understood myself / more clearly or less well" (II); "I know breakthrough as I tell / the dream surpassed" (VI). Seen alone, "I" is a lost cause. It will be the poem's task, as it was Dante's in the *Vita Nuova* and Petrarch's in the *Rime sparse*, to absorb the private "I" through erotic experience into nuptials of the spirit; its analogous task is to assimilate Bromsgrove, the town of personal origin, to Goldengrove, Hopkins' mythically mortal wood, and to absorb Goldengrove in its turn into the higher, biblical pastoral of the Orchards of Syon, a sacred and timeless order. Autobiography is to be sublimed into collective, sacred myth. The poem moves through a panoply of intimacies between shifting "I's" and "you's"—some are remembered lovers, some are fellow writers invoked as guardian spirits. Behind poem LV stands Shakespeare's *Twelfth Night* with its plots of disguises and crossed loves. The "I" and the "you" are both seen as actors, Malvolio the abused clown, Viola the disguised heroine. Identity is understood as emerging through the play of illusion, the "self-surmounting roles," and is composed in the structure of relationship: "To you I stand / answerable." In its graceful, flexible pentameters, the poem moves through confession to various senses of "profession"—the compromised senses of "job" and even of a dubious claim, toward something close to a profession of faith. Love leads, but the "I" drops out by the last lines, to make room for "withdrawn theology": God, the ultimate source of being and relationship, is understood as hidden, even absent, but remains the primary motive force in his creatures, in whom he leaves desire. With lovely tact, this poem ends with the sun dropping below the hill (Ankerdine), as God himself has dropped from view, but not from power.

> I desire so not to deny desire's
> intransigence. To you I stand
> answerable. Correction: must once have stood.
> What's this thing, like a clown's eyebrow-brush?
> O my lady, it is the fool's confession,
> weeping greasepaint, all paint and rhetoric.
> Empower the music; I'm tired. Shakespeare, who scarcely
> brooded on perfection, perfect so many times.
> Memory! memory! *The eye*
> *elaborates its tears*, but misremembered,
> misremembering no less key-clustered
> mistletoe, the orchard's châtelaine.
> I may well carry my three engraved thoughts
> out beyond Shrawley whose broad verges once
> throve like spare garden plots with pear and apple
> or with wild damson, thinner on the ground.
> O my lady, this is a fool's profession
> and you may be dead, or with Alzheimer's,
> or happily still adoring a different
> Duke of Illyria. I have set you up,
> I confess thát, so as not to stint
> your voice of justice. Love grows in some
> way closer to withdrawn theology.
> The Deists' orb drops below Ankerdine.[25]

Section LV does not conclude *The Orchards of Syon*, but it is here that I wish to wind up my account. The self alone, in Hill's view, *is* a lost cause, but that is the beginning, not the end, of the story. His Dantesque trilogy provides a structure in which the self can be imagined as rescued. Despite the hallucinatory method, a deep and orderly logic is asserted in the architecture of each of the canticles. The lost self gathers substance in the struggle to consciousness in a series of relationships that emerge rhythmically to include the dead, an ideal of nation, and God. The poems are, in the fullest sense, comic. "Gnothi / seauton sounds like adult fun," section XXXVII had wisecracked about the Socratic injunction to know thyself, and the poems are, among other things, fiendishly funny. But they are divine comedies as well, in Dante's mode: *commedia* because they end happily.

Coda

August: Vermont. From his study: A single dry beech leaf hangs from a branch of balsam by a spiderweb strand. I saw the same leaf last August, is it possible it has survived a winter of blizzards when a man has died?

Pond water glints through pine boughs. The mind of the forest: years and years of layered decaying leaves.

You brought me a small gray stone. I showed you an empty palm. To write the icon, slide cloudlight over the surface of the pond. It will adhere. We will read it together, years from now.

> Tightening noose of a November afternoon. Sex on my
> fingers,
> honey from Mount Hymettos on our thighs. I love this hour
> of erasure,
> this season stripping down in chill rain and gray. The trees
> are di-
> vested, the suburban

lawns are numb, the twigs
and vestiges are cast down,
and whatever small knowledge remains
is to be cherished in the spine, the wrist pulse, the primitive
    mons
which guards its secret against and into the circling down of
    night,
the wheeze and shush of distant, hurrying tires.

From Marcel Schwob, *Le Livre de Monelle* (1895):

"Don't wait for death: she is with you. Be her companion and hold
her close: she resembles you."
"Die your own death; don't envy the deaths of ages past. . . ."
"Burn the dead carefully, and scatter their ashes to the four winds
of heaven. . . ."
"Bequeath yourself nothing, neither pleasure nor sorrow."
"And she said, from afar: Forget me and I will be returned to
you."

Dragging my innocence over the surface of the earth like a chain.

My spine a braid of pain.

Buber: "All real living is meeting."

Chiara, aged four, on Pierre from her day care: "Is he French, or a
human being?"

To me, the other day, objecting to my reading aloud: "I hate it when
you rhyme! Your mouth goes all wibble-wobble and you look like a
cow."
Later: "Drawing-writing is stronger than word-writing."

The father, in whom disease is chewing at lungs, brain, liver, and lymph glands, arrives to collect his young daughter from an afternoon of play at our house. He is thin, he wears a baseball cap and sunglasses. "How are you?" he asks cheerfully. "Fine, thanks," I reply, and in order not to ask him how he is, declare, with obtuse heartiness, "They played well this afternoon, they had a wonderful time." "Good, good," he says. His daughter, who does not know what is in store for them, gallops up: "Daddy!" He leans to embrace her, her arm is soft around his neck. Her light hair falls over his shoulder.

Biography: a low mimetic mode. Precisely. By any means. So let it lead me. "We are saved by what we cannot imagine" (Ashbery). (Are we saved?) Give me your hand.

1992

June 27. Matthew 3:10. "And now also the axe is laid unto the root of the trees: therefore every tree which bringeth not forth good fruit is hewn down, and cast into the fire."

3:12. "[Jesus] whose fan is in his hand, and he will thoroughly purge his floor, and gather his wheat unto the garner; but he will burn up the chaff with unquenchable fire."

VIOLENCE (Transformations require destruction: like that Tibetan deity in the Museum of Fine Arts trampling on a necklace of skulls in his marriage with Wisdom. He has the slavering, fanged mouth of a monstrous bull as he leans over her, waving his forty-odd arms; she, in his lap, twists upward, her legs twining around his waist, melon breasts pressed to his chest. The museum label helpfully notes that the figures are "anatomically correct" and that they can be separated and fitted back together in their copulation. A crowd of schoolchildren tromps by the statue; two ten-year-olds linger to peer at it while their myopic and harassed teacher tries to shoo them into a farther room. "What's the bull doing to that lady?" asks one girl. "That's Asia," says the teacher, with a vague wave of the hand. "Come on." "Look," says the other girl, "that bull is *eating* that lady.")

July 2. Ezra 6–10. Sad, terrible, and glorious rhythm. Return to Jerusalem. Ezra discovering the intermarriage of the Jews, 9:3— "And when I heard this thing, I rent my garment and my mantle, and plucked off the hair of my head and of my beard, and sat down astonied."

Matthew 5:17. "Think not that I am come to destroy the law, or the prophets: I am not come to destroy, but to fulfil." And the impossible command, "Love your enemies" (5:44).

July 6. Esther 1–3. A fairy tale: powerful stupid king; cast-off queen; beautiful virgin; persecution. . . . Also, archetypal anti-Semitism: Mordecai the Jew in the king's gate is proud, does not bow down to the favorite, Haman. Therefore: genocide. "The posts went out, being hastened by the king's commandment [of slaughter], and the decree as given in Shushan the palace. And the king and Haman sat down to drink; but the city of Shushan was perplexed" (3:15). Horrifying banal detail.

July 15. Job 14. The chapter of mortality: "Man that is born of a woman is of few days, and full of trouble." 14:2. He cometh forth like a flower, and is cut down; he fleeth also as a shadow, and continueth not." (1 Peter 1:24. "All flesh is as grass." Isaiah 40:6. "The voice said, Cry. And he said, What shall I cry? All flesh is grass, and all the goodliness thereof is as the flower of the field." 40:7. "The grass withereth, the flower fadeth: because the spirit of the Lord bloweth upon it: surely the people is grass.")

From *Zen Mind, Beginner's Mind*, Shunru Suzuki, p. 106, "Dogen-zenji became interested in Buddhism as a boy as he watched the smoke from an incense stick by his dead mother. . . ."

July 21. Yale Review, vol. 80, no. 3. Richard Poirier on William James. Literature as "performing presence," enactment (but no ??!!! social normality rubbish as in J. L. Austin!). James: "Each word appears less as a solution than as a program for more work" (p. 77). James' attention to neglected transitives rather than nominatives. From James' *The Stream of Thought*: "All dumb or anonymous psychic states have, owing to this error [substantives taken as concepts], been coolly suppressed; or, if recognized at all, have been named after the substantive perception they led to, as thoughts 'about' this object or 'about' that, the stolid word 'about' engulfing all their delicate idiosyncrasies in its monotonous sound. . . ."

July 28. End of Job. 41:18. "By his neesings a light doth shine, and his eyes are like the eyelids of the morning." (Great word.) 41:19. "Out of his mouth go burning lamps, and sparks of fire leap out." 41:20. "Out of his nostrils goeth smoke, as out of a seething pot or caldron."

July 30. Tillich, *Dynamic of Faith*, p. 100, "There is no faith without separation." (Max Jacob's love poems.)

August 4. Proverbs. Themes keep recycling: punish children, fear the Lord, be thrifty and provident, care for the poor: combination of peasant wisdom and grim faith in righteousness rewarded. Concern with language: strictures against false witness. 15:4—"A wholesome tongue is a tree of life: but perverseness therein is a breach in the spirit." Women get it hard, especially in advice to wayward sons: 23:27—"For a whore is a deep ditch; and a strange woman is a narrow pit." (Ecclesiastes 7:26. "And I find more bitter than death the woman, whose heart is snares and nets, and her hands as bands. . . .")

August 12. Proverbs rises in crescendo. 30:15. ". . . There are three things that are never satisfied, yea, four things say not, It is enough:" 30:16. "The grave; and the barren womb; the earth that is not filled with water; and the fire that saith not, It is enough. . . ." 30:18. "There be three things which are too wonderful for me, yea, four which I know not:" 30:19. "The way of an eagle in the air; the way of a serpent upon a rock; the way of a ship in the midst of the sea; and the way of a man with a maid." (Practical advice gives way to poetry, to awe.)

October 15. John Butler Yeats' letters to Willy. August 6, 1906: "Poetry is written not by Intellect but by the clairvoyant faculty."

April 6, 1913: "Personality is born out of pain. It is the fire shut up in the flint" (p. 161).

November 16. Return from D.C., conference on American Poetry at Library of Congress. Predominant thesis, that American poetry is a poetry of solitude, the new self in a new land. But my notion was different: and here I realized I'd hit on my own bent, tragic Virgilian eclogue as opposed to the intoxicant of "pure" lyric (Mallarmé, "Rien, cette écume, vierge vers"—Nothing, this foam, virgin verse). That in the U.S. we cannot be exempt from the blood guilt of our destiny, from Cortés to Puritans to Civil War to L.A. 1992. That ours is a contaminated lyric, no virgin, and that that is its force. The "self," yes, but the self in relation to God, to nature, to history. Good old WCW had it right in 1925 in *In the American Grain*: we must record these initiatory sacrifices. Remus cries out from the bloody ground (he is the great, lost figure in *The Aeneid*). The real eclogue is not safe from Caesar's soldiers: "Tityre, tu patulae recubans sub tegmine fagi . . ." (the first Eclogue: You, Tityrus, lying under the cover of a spreading beech . . .). And what is the Hebrew Bible but one ghastly long account of the fall of language into time? A thoroughly bloodied word, that covenant, with a berserk parent insisting on complete obedience, and the children forever lusting after the groves. The terrible repetitiousness of history, sacred history. A recurring dream.

December 7. Isaiah 29:4. "And thou shalt be brought down, and shalt speak out of the ground, and thy speech shall be low out of the dust, and thy voice shall be, as of one that hath a familiar spirit, out of the ground, and thy speech shall whisper out of the dust." This describes true poetry. Language suffering the condition of its utterance. Like Pier delle Vigna in Dante, "sì della scheggia rotta usciva insieme / parole e sangue; ond' io lasciai la cima / cadere, e stetti come l'uom che teme" (So from the broken twig spewed out words and blood, so that I let the branch fall, and stood like a man in fear). All spitting and hissing, primal language of pain, original language. Language is a physical medium, needs blood or dust to come true. Poetry must whisper or gurgle.

From Hofmannsthal, *The Book of Friends*:

"We are so eager to possess and are made so happy by any sign of fidelity that we can feel something like pleasure even in a regularly recurring fever."

"Reality is the fable convenue of the Philistines."

"Singing is near miraculous because it is the mastering of what is otherwise a pure instrument of egotism: the human voice."

"What is culture? To know what concerns one, and to know what it concerns one to know."

1993

January 15. Basho 1644–1694. The most "famous" Japanese haiku:
  The old pond:
  A frog jumps in—
  The sound of water[1]

(more literally—"water of sound"). Robert Aitken (*A Zen Wave*): "'Samadhi' means 'absorption,' but fundamentally it is unity with the entire universe. When you devote yourself to what you are doing, moment by moment—to your koan when on your cushion in zazen, to your work, study, conversation, or whatever in daily life—that is samadhi."

Snow today. Nino and I ran down Robinwood Avenue, almost silent over the white, in the white: it was a soft feathering snow, light as breath. The woods drew us in, we passed under a curtain of snow-embroidered boughs and were in the "other" world: silence, white, no human forms, the path beckoned us on. Nino running—a black arrow, nose slicing the wind, head low, tail ruddering straight behind, plumes in the air. His small legs flew fore and aft. He's eleven years old and sick with a tumor, but running in the snow, he's immortal.

January 18. Basho:
  In plum-bower scent
  Pop! the sun appears—
  The mountain path.[2]

Aitken: "In the *eihei koruku*, Dogen Kigen asks, 'Without bitterest cold that penetrates to the very bone, how can plum blossoms send forth their fragrance all over the universe?'" (p. 31).

> Kobayashi Issa (1763–1827). When his little daughter died:
> While the dewdrop world
> Is the dewdrop world,
> Yet—yet—[3]

Aitken: "We come and go, being seen off and seeing off. 'Yet—yet' is also the point. . . . Please stop at that point. Enter that point. Someone asked me how long it would take to attain *kensho*, realization experience. I answered, 'No time at all.'"

> *February 9.* Basho:
> Let my name
> Be traveler;
> First rains.[4]

(At the Zen temple in Cambridge, an angry cold young man resident there, filled with pride of self-mastery. The Holocaust was "a cosmic readjustment of karma." Now there is someone with a petrified heart. What hell did he crawl out of?)

February 17. From Missal: "Memento, homo, quia pulvis es, et in pulverem reverteris" (Remember, man, that you are dust, and to dust you must return). All this turning/returning/con-version— Jonah, prodigal son, Hebrews.

June 3. From *The Crown of Thorns*, Austin Farrar, lent by A.G. For Easter: "We do not come to God for a little help, a little support to our own good intentions. We come to him for resurrection."

Easter III: "Unless we agonise at some time over the birth of faith, faith is not ours, it is not a personal possession, it is not the child of our own soul . . ." (p. 31).

August 26. Jeremiah 25:11. "And this whole land shall be a desolation and an astonishment. . . ." 25:15. "For thus saith the Lord

God of Israel unto me; Take the wine cup of this fury at my hand, and cause all the nations, to whom I send thee, to drink it." 25:16. "And they shall drink, and be moved, and be mad, because of the sword that I will send among them. . . ." (Bosnia, Somalia.) 25:33. "And the slain of the Lord shall be at that day from one end of the earth even unto the other end of the earth; they shall not be lamented, neither gathered nor buried; they shall be dung upon the ground. . . ."

This desolation is MAN-MADE. God has no need to wreak vengeance: we author our own destructions.

November 27. In the detox clinic to visit X. More destructions. Thanksgiving. Glimpsed other inmates: anorexic, tall young woman—narrow foxy face; heavily made-up eyes; wore skin-tight leggings, high-heeled sandals, bodysuit. She looked like a ruined Barbie doll. Husband (?) and brother (?)—dumpy, helpless-looking young men—brought in two-year-old boy, who ran to her. "Sweetie! Did you miss me?"

In the waiting room near me, a middle-aged man with a bleary, bruised look sits with his visitor. Both men heavy. The inmate says he feels lousy, his mind's a "sieve," he can't hear what anyone's saying to him, his stomach's upset. "At least you're sober," says his friend. "You gotta give yourself that. One day atta time." "Yeah, one day atta time," replies the inmate gloomily. "What kinda life is that? No drinking, no smoking, no gambling, no going out with the guys—WHAT KINDA LIFE? WHAT'S TO LIVE FOR? It all seems so . . . mundane." "No one ever promised you a rose garden," says the friend, "That's life. Gotta accept it." "Yeah, no roses, sure ain't no bedda roses." Pause. Then the inmate: "What's worst is, now I'm sober, I don't know what's going to happen. When I'm drunk, I always know what's going to happen. But sober, I don't know."

1994

February 18. V's death. He was ninety-six, still composing.

My last conversation with him, three weeks ago: he asked whether I believed in the afterlife. "I don't know," I replied. "Do you?" He said he was skeptical, but still waiting to see: "I won't say no, I won't say yes, I'll see. . . ." He added, "But I think God is an oversimplification."

March 7. Home with rain patter, high snowbanks melt into gurgle, wash into storm drains; mist hovers over all, a palpable cloud.

Numbers 25:1. "And Israel abode in Shittim, and the people began to commit whoredom with the daughters of Moab." 25:2. "And they called the people unto the sacrifices unto their gods: and the people did eat, and bowed down to their gods."

Ends with Phinehas pursuing man of Israel and Midianitish woman into tent, "and thrust both of them through, the man of Israel and the woman through her belly. So the plague was stayed from the children of Israel."

Violence. This raging exclusive god. The need to slay all other possibilities. Psychically, depicts a mind in defensive spasm, almost a sexual spasm, "the woman through her belly."

March 9. Glaucoma, *glaukommatos*: gray-eyed. *Glaukos*, gleaming, silvery, bluish green, gray. A poem of anguish: her arm, a twig wrapped in cloth.

Afternoon falls out of itself. Hypnotic snow. The arborvitae hunches in the cold, clumps over. Rhododendron leaves curl inward, like cigars.

May 25. B.U. Student Union. Upstairs, those mortuary photographs of the Metcalf teaching award winners: most of them look miserable in the camera's eye. Trapped souls: in the bulb's glare, the skin is caught in mortal fatigue, hairdos are helmets, the eyes look out pleadingly.

June 30. Mount Larissa, behind Argos. A fort: Mycenaean, Dark Age. Byzantine, Frankish, Turkish, Venetian, Turkish, Greek. Differing wall constructions tell of the various builders, from the gigantic, ingeniously fitted Cyclopean masonry of the Mycenaeans to the small mortared Venetian and later stones. The towers and battlements—what's left of them—clutch the cliff, far over the Argive plain with its orange groves and olives. Nauplion lies down there, and the whole gulf spreads softly out in the noon sun. This was the plain sacred to Hera; she renewed her virginity every year in the fountain at what's now the monastery of Agia Moni (whose fountain is now dedicated to the Eternal Life of Christ). Up on this military crag where for millennia men have bled and shouted and cursed and rallied and vomited and died, barely a cicada grates the stillness; drought and stone preside; heat clamps over us like a white cope. Out of the drought and silence, in a corner of the high inner court, a fig tree thrusts up, outrageously green. In its shadow I imagine I hear the whisper not only of leaves, but of water. And there must be water up here. A few feet away, water is visible down an ancient cistern. From a bough of the fig, at my approach, three little dark blue birds with narrow yellowish beaks startle up noisily and flit to the near wall, where they perch, whistling, on the stones.

Notes

1. Kevin Hart brings this sort of inquiry, and his formidable philosophical and theological training, to his study of Charles Wright's poems, "*La Poesia è scala a Dio*: On Reading Charles Wright" (*Religion and the Arts* 8, no. 2 (2004): 174–99). In prying apart a notion of the solid, unified ego, Hart writes, "We have already heard Jean-Luc Nancy telling us that finitude means being 'infinitely exposed to the otherness of our own "being."' Understanding this concretely would involve establishing how I mark my plurality in a singular manner and how I form a singular contract with these pluralities. It is one of the critic's tasks to discern how Wright himself negotiates plurality and singularity, and it is a task that is best performed with a nuanced understanding of the distinction between life and work" (Hart, 189).

2. I am indebted to Ronald Schuchard for documentation on Mallarmé's influence on Eliot. Eliot first read of Mallarmé in Arthur Symons' *The Symbolist Movement in Literature* in 1908, and found there Symons' translation of the key sentence: "'The pure work,' then, 'implies the elocutionary disappearance of the poet, who yields place to the words, immobilised by the shock of their inequality; they take light from mutual reflection, like an actual train of fire over precious stones, replacing the old lyric afflatus or the enthusiastic personal direction of the phrase'" (Arthur Symons, *The Symbolist Movement in Literature* [New York: E. P. Dutton, 1958], 73). I prefer to translate *élocutoire* as "elocutory," to place the emphasis more clearly on the linguistic function of the making of any statement than on the decorative art of elocution. Mallarmé's theory of poetic impersonality contributed to Eliot's, presented not only in the famous essay "Tradition and the Individual Talent" in 1919, but also, in relation to Mallarmé, in "Modern Tendencies in Poetry" published in the journal *Shama'a* in India in 1920. There Eliot develops the analogy of the poet and scientist, each

engaged in "a complete surrender of himself to the work in which he was absorbed." Eliot goes on to say, "There is the same inevitability and impersonality about the work of a great poet," and uses the example of Villon to describe the coldness with which the poet observes his own intense feelings. He proceeds to name the French poets who pointed the way to modernity for the English: Laforgue, Corbière, Rimbaud, and, importantly, Mallarmé, whom he praises for calling attention to the fact that "the actual writing of poetry, the accidence and syntax, is a very difficult part of the problem." In 1926 Eliot published an essay in French in *La Nouvelle Revue Française* entitled "Note sur Mallarmé et Poe" in which he remarked on "the primitive power of the Word" and the obstructive syntax in both poets, and cited the line from Mallarmé's elegy for Poe ("donner un sens plus pur aux mots de la tribu") which Eliot would later incorporate into "Little Gidding": "to purify the dialect of the tribe." See *La Nouvelle Revue Française* 27 (November 1, 1926): 524–26.

3. Marcel Proust, *Contre Sainte-Beuve* (Paris: Gallimard, 1954), 157. Later in the book, Proust distinguishes inner from outer truth in the opposition of silence and speech: "Books are the work of solitude and *children of silence*. The children of silence should have nothing to do with the children of speech, with thoughts born from the desire to say something, to blame, to have an opinion, that is to say an unclear idea" (Proust, 368). My translation.

4. Roland Barthes, *Image Music Text,* trans. Stephen Heath (New York: Hill and Wang, 1978), 143.

5. Ibid., 146.

6. Kevin Hart's inquiry into the moral and spiritual dimensions of Blanchot's atheism and erasure of selfhood has guided my thinking in these matters. See Kevin Hart, *The Dark Gaze: Maurice Blanchot and the Sacred* (Chicago: University of Chicago Press, 2004).

7. Maurice Blanchot, *L'Espace littéraire* (Paris: Gallimard, 1955), 109.

8. James Merrill, *Collected Poems,* ed. J. D. McClatchy and Stephen Yenser (New York: Knopf, 2002), 184–85.

9. Louise Glück, *Proofs and Theories* (New York: Ecco Press, 1994), 45.

10. Stéphane Mallarmé, *Oeuvres complètes*, ed. Henri Mondor and G. Jean-Aubry (Paris: Bibliothèque de la Pléiade, Gallimard, 1965), 647.

CHAPTER 1   *Midi*

1. Theodore Roethke, *The Collected Poems of Theodore Roethke* (Garden City: Anchor Press, 1975; 1966), 35.

2. Thomas Hardy, *Thomas Hardy: The Complete Poems,* ed. James Gibson (New York: Macmillan, 1976), 12.

CHAPTER 2   *Sappho: Translation as Elegy*

1. Peter Sacks, *The English Elegy: Studies in the Genre from Spenser to Yeats* (Baltimore: Johns Hopkins University Press, 1985).

2. W. H. Auden, "In Memory of W. B. Yeats," in *Collected Poems,* ed. Edward

Mendelson (New York: Random House, 1976; 1991), 247; Ezra Pound, *The Cantos of Ezra Pound* (New York: New Directions, 1979), 3.

3. D. A. Campbell, *Greek Lyric Poetry: A Selection of Greek Lyic, Elegiac and Iambic Poetry* (London: Macmillan; New York: St. Martin's Press, 1967), xxv.

4. Georg Luck, *The Latin Love Elegy* (London: Methuen, 1969), 26.

5. Ovid, *The Heroides and the Amores*, ed. and trans. Grant Showerman (Cambridge: Harvard University Press, 1958), 180. Translation mine.

6. Sacks, 3.

7. Ibid., 2.

8. Ibid., 26ff.

9. In the fourth Georgic, Virgil sets the defeat of Orpheus against the life-giving success of the peasant Aristaeus. Thanks to the narration of Proteus, Aristaeus is able to appease the vexed spirit of Orpheus and bring life out of death, reviving his beehive:

> Everywhere in the bellies of the victims
> Bees buzzing in the fermenting viscera
> And bursting forth from the ruptured sides in swarms
> That drift along like enormous clouds in the sky
> And come together high in the top of a tree
> And hang in clusters from the swaying branches.

David Ferry, *The Georgics of Virgil* (New York: Farrar, Straus and Giroux, 2005), 185.

10. For an elegant and clear-sighted reading of the passage, with particular attention to the anaphora "And now" and the ambiguous "he," see Sacks, 116. I am using the text of "Lycidas" prepared by H. C. Beeching: *The Poetical Works of John Milton* (Oxford: Oxford University Press, 1904; 1938; 1941), 37–42.

11. Gregory Nagy, "Phaethon, Sappho's Phaon," *Harvard Studies in Classical Philology* 77 (1973): 173–75.

12. H. T. Wharton, *Sappho* (London: John Lane, 1898, 4th ed.; reprint, Amsterdam: Libera, 1974), 168.

13. Charles Segal, "Eros and Incantation," *Arethusa* 7 (1974): 139–60.

14. Wharton, 34–35.

15. Ibid., 36–37.

16. C. J. Fordyce, *Catullus: A Commentary* (Oxford: Oxford University Press, 1961), 218ff.

17. T. P. Wiseman, *Catullus and His World: A Reappraisal* (Cambridge: Cambridge University Press, 1985), 152–54. I am not convinced that we need accept Wilamowitz's theory of a marriage ceremony as the occasion for Sappho's poem in order to sense that poem bitterly invoked by Catullus. The elemental drama of "Phainetai moi," a happy couple excluding the former lover, suffices to charge Catullus's address to Lesbia with retrospective anguish. Yes, the symptoms he enumerates appear to be those of passion, not jealousy, since *ille* (lines 1, 2)—that man, any man—is not as definite and particular as Sappho's *keinos . . . aner* (that man). In both poems, I think, attention

focuses more on the painful mystery of love itself rather than on an interloper; and Catullus could be seen as recalling his own innocent, early passion only to underscore his disillusionment by reference to Sappho's distress as well as to the destruction of whole kingdoms in the *otium* stanza. For further discussion, see Denys Page, *Sappho and Alcaeus* (Oxford: Oxford University Press, 1955), 20–21, and Anne Pippin Burnett, *Three Archaic Poets* (Cambridge: Harvard University Press, 1983), 229–43.

18. Wiseman, 146.

19. Rosanna Warren, *Each Leaf Shines Separate* (New York: W. W. Norton, 1984), 53.

20. For a learned and lucid account of such efforts, see John Hollander's *Vision and Resonance* (New Haven: Yale University Press, 1975; 1985), 59–70. It is an indispensable book.

21. John Hall, "Phainetai moi," in E. M. Cox, *The Poems of Sappho* (New York: Charles Scribner's Sons, 1925), 34.

22. Ibid., 70.

23. Ibid., 72.

24. Mary Barnard, *Sappho* (Berkeley: University of California Press, 1958), 39.

25. Robert Lowell, *Imitations* (New York: Farrar, Straus and Giroux, 1958; 8th ed., 1969), 3.

26. Basil Bunting, *Collected Poems* (Oxford: Oxford University Press, 1978), 119.

27. Charles Baudelaire, *Œuvres complètes*, ed. Y.-G. Le Dantec (Paris: Bibliothèque de la Pléiade, Gallimard, 1958), 183.

28. Ibid., 212.

29. Charles Baudelaire, "Lesbos," in *Les Fleurs du mal*, trans. Richard Howard (Boston: David R. Godine, 1982), 123.

30. Guy Davenport, *Archilochus, Sappho, Alkman* (Berkeley: University of California Press, 1980), 93, a translation of fragment 42. Guy Davenport brought the Poundian imperative of clarity to bear in his long and honorable engagement with archaic Greek poetry.

31. A notable exception is Jerome McGann, whose *Swinburne: An Experiment in Criticism* (Chicago: University of Chicago Press, 1972) began to repair the wrong. Further, elegant reparation continues with Kenneth Haynes' edition, *Poems and Ballads, & Atalanta in Calydon* (London and New York: Penguin, 2000).

32. Haynes, 163.

33. Ibid., 49.

34. Davenport, 79; Barnard, 38.

35. Haynes, 69.

36. Algernon Charles Swinburne, *Major Poems and Selected Prose*, ed. Jerome McGann and Charles Sligh (New Haven: Yale University Press, 2004), 165.

37. J. M. Edmonds, *The Greek Bucolic Poets* (Cambridge: Harvard University Press, 1938; 1950; 1960), 445.

CHAPTER 3   *Alcaics in Exile: W. H. Auden's "In Memory of Sigmund Freud"*

1. Katherine Bucknell and Nicholas Jenkins, *W. H. Auden: "The Map of All My Youth"* (Oxford: Clarendon Press, 1990), 106; hereafter abbreviated as *WHA*.

2. John Fuller, *A Reader's Guide to W. H. Auden* (London: Thames & Hudson, 1970), 176.

3. See Monroe Spears, *The Poetry of W. H. Auden: The Disenchanted Island* (New York: Oxford University Press, 1963), 222, 248; Richard Johnson, *Man's Place: An Essay on Auden* (Ithaca: Cornell University Press, 1973), 29.

4. W. H. Auden, *The Dyer's Hand* (New York: Random House, 1962), 47; hereafter abbreviated as *DH*.

5. *DH* 296–97.

6. Lucid accounts of Alcaeus's poetry and his social role can be found in Anne Pippin Burnett's *Three Archaic Poets: Archilochus, Alcaeus, Sappho* (Cambridge: Harvard University Press, 1983), and in Bruno Gentili's *Poetry and Its Public in Ancient Greece*, trans. A. Thomas Cole (Baltimore: Johns Hopkins University Press, 1988).

7. David A. Campbell, *Greek Lyric: Sappho and Alcaeus* (Cambridge: Harvard University Press, 1982), 301–3.

8. Ibid., 296–99.

9. *DH* 17.

10. W. H. Auden and Chester Kallman, eds., Noah Greenberg music ed., *An Elizabethan Song Book: Lute Songs, Madrigals and Rounds* (New York: Doubleday Anchor, 1956), xv.

11. W. H. Auden, *Collected Poems*, ed. Edward Mendelson (New York: Random House, 1976; 1991), 253; hereafter abbreviated as *CP*. Auden later retitled the poem "They."

12. *CP*, 273.

13. *DH* 27.

14. *CP* 238.

15. *WHA* 111.

16. *WHA* 113.

17. *WHA* 115.

18. Edward Mendelson, *Early Auden* (New York: Viking Press, 1981), 332–66.

19. "New Year Letter," line 50, in *CP* 200.

CHAPTER 4 *The End of* The Aeneid

1. Robert Fitzgerald, trans., *The Aeneid* (New York: Random House, 1983; 1990), 395.

2. Alexander Pope, trans., *The Iliad of Homer* (New York: Heritage Press, 1943), 415.

3. Fitzgerald, *Aeneid*, 213–14.

4. Ibid., 313.

5. Ibid.

6. Ibid., 141.

7. Ibid., 141–42.

8. Ibid., 13.

9. Ibid., 187.

10. W. H. Auden, *Collected Poems*, ed. Edward Mendelson (New York: Random House, 1976; 1991), 346.

11. Ibid., 598–600.

12. Ibid., 637–39.

CHAPTER 5 *Negative Idylls: Mark Strand and Contemporary Pastoral*

1. Alexander Pope, *The Prose Works of Alexander Pope*, ed. Norman Ault (Oxford: Blackwell, 1936), 298–99.

2. Samuel Johnson, "John Milton," in *Samuel Johnson: Selected Poetry and Prose*, ed. F. Brady and W. K. Wimsatt (Berkeley: University of California Press, 1977), 426.

3. Robert Wells, *The Idylls of Theocritus* (Manchester: Carcanet, 1988), 55.

4. Andrew Marvell, *Complete Poetry*, ed. George deF. Lord (New York: Modern Library, 1968), 49.

5. Paul Alpers, *What Is Pastoral?* (Chicago: University of Chicago Press, 1996), 22.

6. David Ferry, *The Eclogues of Virgil* (New York: Farrar, Straus and Giroux, 1999), 3.

7. Michael Putnam, *Virgil's Pastoral Art: Studies in the Eclogues* (Princeton, N.J.: Princeton University Press, 1970), 78. Annabel Patterson has extended such questions to the whole history of the genre in her *Pastoral and Ideology: Virgil to Valéry* (Berkeley: University of California Press, 1987).

8. Wells, 56.

9. Charles Segal, *Poetry and Myth in Ancient Pastoral: Essays on Theocritus and Virgil* (Princeton: Princeton University Press, 1981), 118–21.

10. Mark Strand, *The Monument* (New York: Ecco Press, 1978), 17.

11. Segal, 42.

12. Wells, 55–56.

13. Ibid., 56.

14. Ibid., 84.

15. Segal gives a thorough account of the bibliography on Daphnis and the mystery associated with him in "Since Daphnis Dies: The Meaning of Theocritus' First Idyll," in *Poetry and Myth in Ancient Pastoral*, 25–46.

16. Wells, 58.

17. Ferry, 39.

18. Putnam shows how the Orpheus story in Georgic IV imagines the destructiveness of human desire both as a farewell to pastoral and as a prefiguration of the eruption of desire at the end of *The Aeneid*: "If the actual death of the poet is adumbrated in *Eclogue* 9 and his disavowal of bucolic poetry stressed at the conclusion of 10, the myth of Orpheus, which virtually ends *Georgic* 4, treats the same topic in a new guise. Human emotion again destroys the ideal. It kills love and the poet, and ruins the possibility of poetry, though the farmer's existence itself is renewed" (Putnam, 17).

19. Stéphane Mallarmé, *Oeuvres complètes,* ed. Henri Mondor and G. Jean-Aubry (Paris: Bibliothèque de la Pléiade, Gallimard, 1965), 366.

20. Mark Strand, *Selected Poems* (New York: Atheneum, 1980), 79; hereafter abbreviated as *SP*.

21. *SP* 9.

22. Wallace Stevens, *The Collected Poems* (New York: Random House, 1954; 1982), 383.

23. *SP* 63.

24. *SP* 65.

25. *SP* 10.

26. *SP* 49.

27. *SP* 50.

28. *SP* 51.

29. *SP* 52.

30. *SP* 59.

31. *SP* 67.

32. *SP* 73.

33. *SP* 75.

34. Mark Strand, "Views of the Mysterious Hill: The Appearance of Parnassus in American Poetry," *Gettysburg Review*, vol. 4 (1991): 669–80.

35. *SP* 63.

36. *SP* 67.

37. *SP* 70.

38. *SP* 71.

39. Linda Gregerson, "Negative Capability," *Parnassus: Poetry in Review* 9, no. 2 (1981): 90–114. Reprinted in Linda Gregerson, *Negative Capability* (Ann Arbor: University of Michigan Press, 2001), 5–29.

40. Mark Strand, *The Continuous Life* (New York: Knopf, 1990), 42–43; hereafter abbreviated as *CL*.

41. *CL* 6.

42. *CL* 7.

43. David Ferry, *The Georgics of Virgil* (New York: Farrar, Straus and Giroux, 2005), 181.

44. *CL* 8.

45. *CL* 8.

46. *CL* 9.

47. *CL* 9.

48. Mark Strand, *Dark Harbor* (New York: Knopf, 1993), vii; hereafter abbreviated as *DH*.

49. *DH* 3.

50. *DH* 5.

51. *DH* 11.

52. *DH* 30.

53. *DH* 31.

54. *DH* 38.

55. *DH* 39.

56. *DH* 48.

57. *DH* 42.

CHAPTER 6   *In Classic Guise: John Hollander's Shadow Selves*

1. John Hollander, *Types of Shape* (New Haven: Yale University Press, 1991), 3.

2. John Hollander, *The Figure of Echo* (Berkeley: University of California Press, 1981), 122.

3. John Hollander, *Selected Poetry* (New York: Knopf, 1993), 305; hereafter abbreviated as *SP*.

4. David A. Campbell, *Greek Lyric I: Sappho and Alcaeus* (Cambridge: Harvard University Press, 1982), 321–23.

5. James Michie, *The Odes of Horace* (Harmondsworth: Penguin, 1964), 117.

6. W. H. Auden, *Collected Poems*, ed. Edward Mendelson (New York: Vintage, Random House, 1976; 1991), 276.

7. John Hollander, *Selected Poetry* (New York: Knopf, 1993), 319–20.

8. Derek Walcott, *Sea Grapes* (New York: Farrar, Straus and Giroux, 1976), 3.

9. John Hollander, *Spectral Emanations: New and Selected Poems* (New York: Atheneum, 1978), 54; hereafter abbreviated as *SE*.

10. *SE* 57.

11. J. M. Edmonds, trans. and ed., *Lyra Graeca*, vol. I (Cambridge: Harvard University Press, 1922), 215.

12. Campbell, 75.

13. Dante Alighieri, *The Divine Comedy*, trans. Charles Singleton, Bollingen Series LXXX (Princeton: Princeton University Press, 1970–75). *Purgatorio* V.134, 52–53.

14. T. S. Eliot, *Collected Poems, 1909–1962* (New York: Harcourt Brace Jovanovich, 1934; 1936, 1970), 64.

15. Paul Verlaine, *Œuvres poétiques complètes*, ed. Y.-G. Le Dantec (Paris: Éditions de la Pléiade, Gallimard, 1962), 326.

16. John Hollander, *Figurehead* (New York: Knopf, 1999), 5; hereafter abbreviated as *F*.

17. *SP* 309.

18. *SP* 320.

19. *F* 31.

20. Ibid.

21. *F* 3–4.

22. *SE* 199–216.

23. *F* 86.

24. *SP* 313.

25. *F* 9–11.

26. *F* 22.

27. *F* 31.

28. *F* 45.

29. *F* 53.

30. *F* 57.

31. *F* 61.

32. *F* 76.

33. *F* 79–86.

34. Robert Lowell, "The Nihilist as Hero," in *History* (New York: Farrar, Straus and Giroux, 1973), 193.

35. *F* 9.

36. Ibid.

37. *F* 12.

38. John Hollander, *Harp Lake* (New York: Knopf, 1988), 37–40.

39. *F* 61.

40. *F* 55.

41. *F* 53.

42. *F* 58.

43. *F* 61.

44. James Merrill, *The Inner Room* (New York: Knopf, 1988), 95.

45. *F* 20.

46. *F* 22–24.

47. John Hollander, *Blue Wine* (Baltimore: Johns Hopkins University Press, 1979), 7.

48. *F* 45–48.

CHAPTER 7　*Contradictory Classicists: Frank Bidart and Louise Glück*

1. Frank Bidart, *Desire* (New York: Farrar, Straus and Giroux, 1997), 9; hereafter abbreviated as *D*.

2. Ezra Pound, *Poems and Translations*, ed. Richard Sieburth (New York: Library of America, 2003), 45.

3. Ibid., 236.

4. Ibid., 527.

5. Ezra Pound, *The Cantos of Ezra Pound* (New York: New Directions, 1948), 3.

6. Frank Bidart, *In the Western Night: Collected Poems 1965–90* (New York: Farrar, Straus and Giroux, 1990), 223–43; hereafter abbreviated as *IWN*.

7. "Elegy," *IWN* 96. "The Book of the Body," *IWN* 106. "Golden State," *IWN* 150. "Confessional," *IWN* 74.

8. *IWN* 132.

9. *IWN* 135.

10. *IWN* 167.

11. *IWN* 135.

12. *IWN* 52.

13. *D* 8.

14. By permission of the author. I am grateful to Frank Bidart for showing me the new version in manuscript.

15. *IWN* 7–11.

16. Louise Glück, *The Wild Iris* (New York: Ecco Press, 1992), 29; hereafter abbreviated as *WI*.

17. Louise Glück, *Proofs and Theories* (New York: Ecco Press, 1994), 56; hereafter abbreviated as *PT*.

18. Louise Glück, "American Narcissism," *Threepenny Review*, Winter 1998, 5–7; "Against Sincerity," in *Proofs & Theories*, 33–45.

19. *PT* 33.

20. Louise Glück, *The House on Marshland* (New York: Ecco Press, 1975), 28.

21. Louise Glück, *Averno* (New York: Farrar, Straus and Giroux, 2006), 16–19; hereafter abbreviated as *A*.

22. "Matins," *WI* 26.

23. "September Twilight," *WI* 60.

24. "Field Flowers," *WI* 28.

25. "October," *A* 13.

26. Louise Glück, *Ararat* (New York: Ecco Press, 1990), 23.

27. Louise Glück, *Meadowlands* (New York: Ecco Press, 1996), 19.

28. Louise Glück, *Vita Nova* (New York: Ecco Press, 1999), 5.

29. Ibid., 10–11.

CHAPTER 8   *The "Last Madness" of Gérard de Nerval*

1. Marcel Proust, "À propos du style de Flaubert," in *Contre Sainte-Beuve* (Paris: Gallimard, 1971), 596. Translation mine.

2. Such close affinities link Proust to Nerval that the first paragraph of Nerval's story *Aurélia* could almost have opened *Combray*: "Dreaming is a second life . . . the first moments of sleep are the very image of death: a nebulous torpor seizes our thought, and we can't determine the exact moment in which 'I,' transformed, continues the work of existence . . ." (Gérard de Nerval, *Œuvres complètes*, vol. III, ed. Jean Guillaume and Claude Pichois [Paris: Bibliothèque de la Pléiade, Gallimard, 1993], 695; translation mine). Both Marcel and Gérard suffer a strange metempsychosis as they hover between sleep and waking. It is not hard to see why Proust felt compelled to come to terms with Nerval's "excessive subjectivity" in *Contre Sainte-Beuve*, that embryonic version of *À la recherche du temps perdu*. He sees Nerval's as an essentially literary madness, an intensification of the writer's explorations in dream, memory, and personal sensation. Proust, so disposed to that same research, was driven to define Nerval's case and to distance him so that he could place his own fictional character Marcel within the corrective context of the social and dramatic world of the novel. The essay is a fascinating exorcism.

3. Gérard de Nerval, *Selected Writings*, trans. and ed. Richard Sieburth (London: Penguin, 1999), ix.

4. Gérard de Nerval, *Aurélia*, in *Œuvres complètes*, vol. III, ed. Jean Guillaume and Claude Pichois (Paris: Éditions de la Pléiade, Gallimard, 1993), 750; translation mine.

5. Ibid., 700.

6. Nerval studied occult initiation rites for years: Freemason, Rosicrucian, the rites of Isis, the Mysteries of Eleusis. One of his principal sources was the *Traité de la réintegration des êtres* by the Illuminist Martines de Pasqually (1721–1774), a Christian kabbalist who had founded the order of the Élues Coëns. The *Traité* was circulating in manuscript during Nerval's lifetime and was introduced to him by a friend, but it was not published until 1899.

7. Quoted by Jean Richer in *Gérard de Nerval et les doctrines ésotériques* (Paris: Éditions Griffon d'Or, 1947), 163.

8. Gérard de Nerval, *Les Filles du feu*, in *Œuvres complètes*, vol. III, ed. Jean Guillaume and Claude Pichois (Paris: Éditions de la Pléiade, Gallimard, 1993), 451.

9. Ibid., 736.

10. Ibid., 696.

11. Ibid., 717.

12. Ibid., 458. I am responsible for all the translations in this essay. As far as I know, English versions of the "Letter to Dumas" and "Octavie" have not been available to contemporary readers until now, although Geoffrey Wagner's excellent *Gérard de Nerval: Selected Writings* (Ann Arbor: University of Michigan Press, 1970) contains many of the other works mentioned here: "Sylvie" and "Émilie" from *Les Filles du feu*, as well as *Aurélia* and selected poems.

Gérard de Nerval, from *Les Chimères*

1. The authoritative text for *Les Chimères* is Gérard de Nerval, *Œuvres complètes*, vol. III, ed. Jean Guillaume and Claude Pichois (Paris: Éditions de la Pléiade, Gallimard, 1993), 645ff.

Chapter 9   *Rimbaud: Insulting Beauty*

1. Stéphane Mallarmé, *Œuvres complètes*, ed. Henri Mondor and G. Jean-Aubry (Paris: Bibliothèque de la Pléiade, Gallimard, 1965), 512. Translation mine.

2. Nicolas Boileau, *Œuvres complètes*, ed. Françoise Escal (Paris: Bibliothèque de la Pléiade, Gallimard, 1966), 158.

3. Arthur Rimbaud, *Œuvres complètes*, ed. Rolland de Renéville and Jules de Mouquet (Paris: Bibliothèque de la Pléiade, Gallimard, 1965), 100; hereafter abbreviated as *OC*.

4. *OC* 219.

5. *OC* 229.

6. *OC* 77.

7. *OC* 238.

8. *OC* 244.

9. *OC* 178.

10. *OC* 180.

11. Arthur Rimbaud, *Poems*, trans. Paul Schmidt, selected by Peter Washington (New York: Everyman's Pocket Library, Knopf, 1994 [Washington]; 1975 [Schmidt]), 139.

12. *OC* 243.

13. *OC* 181.

14. Ibid.

15. *OC* 179.

16. *OC* 183.

17. *OC* 178. "La musique savante manque à notre désir" is a key sentence for Rimbaud, and very difficult to translate. The otherwise masterful Wallace Fowlie did not capture its full import in his version, "Our desires are deprived of cunning music," in Jean Nicholas Arthur Rimbaud, *Complete Works, Selected Letters: A Bilingual Edition*, trans. Wallace Fowlie, revised by Seth Whidden (Chicago: University of Chicago Press, 2005), 315. Nor did I, in my own first version: "Our desire lacks a knowing music." *La musique savante* means classical music, sophisticated music, as opposed to popular music, and Rimbaud, in search of the primitive and tired of the forms of European civilization, both feels the inadequacy of those forms to express his vision, and perhaps his own inadequacy as a poet. The verb *manque*, to lack, goes both ways: the existing music fails his desires, and his desires fail to generate the adequate music. But Rimbaud is also playing on the root sense of *savante*, related to *sagesse*, wisdom, suggesting the range of hermetic and visionary wisdom he sought as a poet-seer. This further reach of *savante* is not audible, unfortunately, in the English phrase "sophisticated music." The difficulty of translation points to an essential feature of Rimbaud's poetry: its hermetic density of expression. I am indebted to Avigdor Arikha and Marie-Odile Masek for helping me sort out this conundrum.
18. *OC* 196.
19. Holly Tannen, "Marine," at hollytannen.com/play/Marine.htm.

CHAPTER 10 *Mallarmé and Max Jacob: A Tale of Two Dice Cups*

1. Peter Bürger, among others, has remarked on the institutionalization of the "historical avant-garde" in contemporary official culture. Of Duchamp's Ready-Mades, he writes, "It is obvious that this kind of provocation cannot be repeated indefinitely. The provocation depends on what it turns against; here, it is the idea that the individual is the subject of artistic creation. . . . Since now the protest of the historical avant-garde against art as institution is accepted as *art*, the gesture of protest of the neo-avant-garde becomes inauthentic" (Peter Bürger, *The Theory of the Avant-Garde* [Minneapolis: University of Minnesota Press, 1984], 52–53). Similarly, Henri Meschonnic quotes Aragon already in 1929 describing the taming of Cubism: "'We were at the period when Cubism, accepted and commercialized, contained no new idea, challenged nothing.' It concluded in 'a sort of official favor.' One couldn't put it more succinctly" (Henri Meschonnic, *Modernité Modernité* [Paris: Gallimard, 1988], 22).
2. I owe a great deal to Peter Bürger and to Henri Meschonnic, in their different ways, for my thinking about the avant-garde, but I want to be clear in distinguishing my methods and goals from theirs. Bürger's dialectical criticism, emerging from a philosophical and sociological tradition in debate with Hegel, Marx, Lukács, Adorno, and Benjamin, is essentially concerned with the structure of society and with ideologies that express that structure. For him, "one question moves to the center of literary interpretation, the question concerning the social function of literary works" (Bürger, lii). The most frequently recurrent phrase in his book on the avant-garde is "bourgeois society," and that fact shows where his real interest lies: with society, not with art. His angle of vision allows him some keen obser-

vations: "In bourgeois society, it is only with aestheticism that the full unfolding of the phenomenon of art became a fact, and it is to aestheticism that the historical avant-garde movements respond" (Bürger, 17). Furthermore, in the course of the nineteenth century, with the dominance of the bourgeoisie "the form-content dialectic of artistic structure has increasingly shifted in favor of form" (Bürger, 19). And, "with the historical avant-garde movements, the social subsystem that is art enters the stage of self-criticism" (Bürger, 22). There is truth in all these statements, but an inadequate truth for anyone who does not believe that art is a "social subsystem." My own vision differs fundamentally from Bürger's. I believe that art is not (only) a symptom of social systems, nor (only) a language of protest—failed or not—in relation to a social system, but a mode of inquiry with its own authority and vocabularies of forms developed over the ages. To relegate art to the merely "aesthetic" is to refuse to recognize its powers of radical analysis and representation. As I do not accept class structure as the key determinant of reality, I object to seeing art subordinated to philosophy and sociology and their claims of "science" (another word Bürger uses frequently). Let us turn the tables and see philosophy and sociology subordinated to art's quest for reality. Bürger himself quotes from Schiller's "On the Aesthetic Education of Man," a far more comprehensive statement of the role of art: "We must be at liberty to restore by means of a higher Art this wholeness in our nature which Art has destroyed" (Bürger, 45).

Henri Meschonnic writes much more intimately of art than Bürger does, from within the practices of poetry and poetics. Linguistics and philosophy, instead of sociology, give him his tools of analysis. His *Modernité Modernité* is dedicated to rescuing an enduringly innovative impulse in the arts from historicism and academicism: "Modernity is an effect of language—of discourse. It is history as discourse. It is irreducible to historicism, which would imprison it in the means of production of an epoch. An epoch of meaning." (Meschonnic, 35; my translation). It will be clear by now that my own approach is empirical, combining practical criticism, literary history, formal analysis, and translation to try to bring to light the forces at work in works of art, acknowledging them both as forces and as modes of work.

3. William Wordsworth, *Lyrical Ballads*, ed. Michael Mason (London and New York: Longman, 1992), 59.

4. Ibid., 65.

5. Ibid., 66.

6. Claude Favre de Vaugelas (1585–1650) was a powerful grammarian, one of the original members of the Académie Française. His treatise *Remarques sur la langue françoise, utiles à ceux qui veulent bien parler et bien écrire* helped to set standards for courtly French.

7. The translations of Hugo's poem "Réponse à un acte d'accusation" come from E. H. and A. M. Blackmore, *Selected Poems of Victor Hugo* (Chicago: University of Chicago Press, 2001), 163–77.

8. Arthur Rimbaud, letter to Paul Demeny, May 15, 1871, in *Œuvres complètes*, ed. Rolland de Renéville and Jules Moquet (Paris: Bibliothèque de la Pléiade, Gallimard, 1954), 272. Victor Hugo composed his poem "Stella" in 1853 while in exile from the Second Empire in Jersey, England. In its exalted crescendo, a star speaks

and calls men to action: "... Car celui qui me suit / Car celui qui m'envoie en avant la première / C'est l'ange Liberté, c'est le géant Lumière" (... For he who follows me, for he who sends me in front / Is the angel Liberty, is the giant Light). Louis Belmontet had been close to Victor Hugo and Sainte-Beuve, but betrayed his liberal friends by supporting Napoleon III and becoming the official poet of the Second Empire. Félicité de Lamennais was a liberal Catholic philosopher whose pamphlet *Paroles d'un croyant* provoked Pope Gregory XVI to attack him in an encyclical in 1834.

9. Ezra Pound, "A Retrospect," in *Literary Essays of Ezra Pound*, ed. T. S. Eliot (London: Faber & Faber, 1960), 9.

10. Ibid., 11.

11. Guillaume Apollinaire, *Œuvres poétiques*, ed. Marcel Adéma and Michael Décaudin (Paris: Bibliothèque de la Pléiade, Gallimard, 1965), 39. Translation mine.

12. Guillaume Apollinaire, *Œuvres en prose complètes*, vol. II, ed. Pierre Caizergues and Michael Décaudin (Paris: Bibliothèque de la Pléiade, Gallimard, 1991), 937–39. Translation mine.

13. Filippo Marinetti, "L'immaginazione senza fili e le parole in libertà," *Lacerba* 1, no. 12 (June 15, 1913): 121–24.

14. Giovanni Papini, "Il massacro delle donne," *Lacerba* 2, no. 7 (April 1, 1914): 97.

15. Stéphane Mallarmé, *Œuvres complètes*, ed. Henri Mondor and G. Jean-Aubry (Paris: Bibliothèque de la Pléiade, Gallimard, 1965), 643.

16. Ibid., 645. Translation mine.

17. Ibid., 368.

18. Ibid., 27.

19. Ibid., 47.

20. Ibid., 1581. Translation mine.

21. Ibid., 474–75.

22. Ibid., 443. Translation mine.

23. Ibid., 442. Translation mine.

24. Ibid., 436.

25. Ibid., 442.

26. Ibid., 443.

27. Stéphane Mallarmé, *Correspondance complète, 1862–1871; Lettres sur la poésie, 1872–1898*, ed. Bertrand Marchal, preface by Yves Bonnefoy (Paris: Gallimard, 1995), 342–43. Maurice Blanchot quotes this letter in *L'Espace littéraire* (Paris: Nouvelle Revue Française, 1955), 109.

28. Mallarmé, *Oeuvres complètes*, 427–28.

29. Pierre Andreu, *Vie et mort de Max Jacob* (Paris: La Table Ronde, 1982), 114.

30. René Ghil, *Choix de poèmes de René Ghil* (Paris: Albert Messein, 1928), 65.

31. Fernand Gregh, *Portrait de la poésie moderne* (Paris: Delagrave, 1939), 125. Translation mine.

32. Ibid., 126. Even the English translation needs a translation: samite is a medieval silk cloth woven in silver and gold thread; a tunicle is a priestly robe. This poem is heavily indebted to Mallarmé's "Sainte."

33. Andreu, 47.

34. Max Jacob, *The Dice Cup*, trans. Christopher Pilling and David Kennedy (London: Atlas Press, 2000), 27–38.

35. Max Jacob, *Le Cornet à dés*, preface by Michel Leiris (Paris: Gallimard, 1945), 22–23.

36. Ibid., 16. For the history of the prose poem, Suzanne Bernard's erudite compendium is still indispensable: *Le Poème en prose jusqu'à nos jours* (Paris: Librairie Nizet, 1959). *The Prose Poem in France: Theory and Practice*, edited by Mary Ann Caws and Hermine Riffaterre (New York: Columbia University Press, 1983), brings the story up to date impeccably. For Max Jacob's quarrel with Pierre Reverdy about priority in the invention of the Modernist prose poem, see Michel Décaudin, "Reverdy et le poème en prose," *Sud*, Colloques poésie-Cerisy, 1981: 279–88; and the excellent appendix by Maurice Saillet to Pierre Reverdy, *Le Voleur de Talan* (Paris: Flammarion, 1967), 174–77.

37. *Le Cornet à dés*, 131.

38. My translation.

39. Jacob's poems and novels abound in scenes with policemen. He found many of his transient lovers among the gendarmes and the Republican Guard, and he delighted in his own physical resemblance to Jean Chiappe, the famous prefect of police of Paris in the 1930s (who was also bald, and known to frequent gay bars). On the lovers, see Hélène Seckel, *Max Jacob et Picasso* (Paris: Réunion des Musées Nationaux, 1994), 35. For a fascinating account of police raids of gay bars from the point of view of the authorities, see Lucien Zimmer, *Un Septennat policier* (Paris: Fayard, 1967).

40. Max Jacob, *Fond de l'eau* (Paris: Gallimard, 1927), 124.

41. Max Jacob, *Ballades* (Paris: Gallimard, 1970), 260.

42. Rosanna Warren, *Stained Glass* (New York: W. W. Norton, 1993), 42–43.

43. Jacob, *Ballades*, 125.

44. Warren, 41.

45. Max Jacob, *La Défense de Tartufe* (Paris: Gallimard, 1964), 127.

46. Warren, 45–46.

CHAPTER 11   *Orpheus the Painter: Apollinaire and Robert Delaunay*

1. *Un Coup de dés* appeared first in the journal *Cosmopolis* in May 1897. For an extended discussion, see Robert Greer Cohn, *Mallarmé's Un Coup de dés: An exegesis* (New Haven: Yale French Studies, 1949).

2. For an erudite and levelheaded analysis of the role assigned to music in Symbolism, see Henri Peyre's chapter "Symbolism, Peinture et Musique," in *Qu'est-ce que le symbolisme?* (Paris: Presses Universitaires de France, 1974), 178ff.

3. Mallarmé, *Œuvres complètes*, ed. Henri Mondor and G. Jean-Aubry (Paris: Bibliothèque de la Pléiade, Gallimard, 1945), 1582.

4. In his essay "Apollinaire's Great Wheel," in *The Innocent Eye* (New York: Washington Square Press, 1986), 291–317, Roger Shattuck describes in loving detail the artistic and literary context from which Apollinaire's *Calligrammes* emerged, and

pays particular attention to the connection with Mallarmé. In the dialogue *Cratylus*, Plato explores a mimetic theory of language (embraced by the character Cratylus) in which words are seen as "natural" and as embodying meaning, instead of as conventional. Socrates of course complicates that theory with a fantastical satire on etymologies.

5. Shattuck, 301.

6. Mallarmé, 475. Translation mine.

7. Mallarmé, 364.

8. Mallarmé, 366.

9. Mallarmé, 367.

10. Mallarmé, 367.

11. Wendy Steiner points to the inspiration the linguist Roman Jakobson derived from Cubist art's manipulation of signs, particularly in the work of Braque. Steiner, *The Colors of Rhetoric* (Chicago: University of Chicago Press, 1982), 195.

12. Vicente Huidobro, *The Selected Poetry of Vicente Huidobro*, ed. David M. Guss (New York: New Directions, 1981), 19.

13. Francis Steegmuller, *Apollinaire: Poet among the Painters* (New York: Farrar, Straus and Giroux, 1963), 141.

14. Pierre Reverdy, *Nord-Sud, Self Defence et autres écrits sur l'art et la poésie (1917–1926)* (Paris: Flammarion, 1975), 14–21.

15. Guillaume Apollinaire, "Picasso, Peintre et Dessinateur," in *La Revue Immoraliste* (April 1905), and "Les Jeunes: Picasso, Peintre" in *La Plume* (May 1905), reprinted in *Apollinaire: chroniques d'art*, ed. L.-C. Breunig (Paris: Gallimard, 1960), 34–39. Hereafter abbreviated as Breunig *Chroniques*.

16. Guillaume Apollinaire, *Les Peintres cubistes*, ed. L.-C. Breunig and J.-Cl. Chevalier (Paris: Hermann, 1965). See introduction, pages 9–11, for an account of the mishap.

17. Francis Steegmuller, Apollinaire's magisterial biographer, has collected a formidable array of such complaints. See his *Apollinaire: Poet among the Painters*, 139–44.

18. Steegmuller, 143.

19. Breunig *Chroniques*, 96.

20. Ibid., 343.

21. Ibid., 347.

22. Ibid., 348.

23. Ibid.

24. Ibid., 352.

25. W. K. C. Guthrie, *Orpheus and Greek Religion* (New York: W. W. Norton, 1966).

26. Guillaume Apollinaire, *Alcools* (Paris: Gallimard, 1920), 145.

27. John Hollander has meditated for years on the subject of ekphrasis. His *Vision and Resonance*, 2nd ed. (New Haven: Yale University Press, 1975), is an indispensable text, for that and many other matters. His own ekphrastic poems are collected in *Types of Shape* (New York: Atheneum, 1979). *The Gazer's Spirit: Poems Speaking to Silent Works of Art* (Chicago: University of Chicago Press, 1995) represents a kind of *summa* of his thought on the subject. Jean Hagstrum's *The Sister Arts* (Chicago: University of Chicago Press, 1958) is a classic in the ekphrastic bibliography, to which

Wendy Steiner's *The Colors of Rhetoric* (Chicago: University of Chicago Press, 1982), Albert Cook's *Figural Choice in Poetry and Art* (Hanover: University Press of New England, 1985), and W. J. T. Mitchell's *Iconology* (Chicago: University of Chicago Press, 1986) are important additions.

28. Steegmuller, 151.

29. F. Gilles de la Tourette, *Robert Delaunay* (Paris: Charles Massin, 1950), 52.

30. Shattuck, 306. "The tower also stood for the synchronization of time in the world; ever since an International Congress on Time in Paris in 1912, the Eiffel Tower had been transmitting an official hourly signal by which all clocks worldwide were to be set in reference to Greenwich mean time."

31. Steegmuller, 234–39.

32. Guillaume Apollinaire, *Œuvres poétiques*, ed. Marcel Adéma and Michel Décaudin (Paris: Bibliothèque de la Pléiade, Gallimard, 1965), 168. The translation appears in Roger Shattuck, *Guillaume Apollinaire: Selected Writings* (New York: New Directions, 1971), 141.

33. For a brilliant, extended discussion of *passage* and its relevance to Cubist historiography, see Leo Steinberg's reply to William Rubin: "The Polemical Part" (*Art in America* 67 [March–April 1979]: 114–47). In an earlier essay in the same controversy, Steinberg initiates the use of the term "arris" for the line defining the meeting of planes. These terms are of particular importance in the discussion of Picasso, whose work is so insistently volumetric: "An irregular lattice of arises emerges as the condition of three-dimensionality in symbolic form" (Leo Steinberg, "Resisting Cézanne: Picasso's *Three Women*," *Art in America* 66 [November–December 1978]: 127–28).

34. Cook, 78.

35. Ibid.

36. Mallarmé, 367, in "Crise de vers": "Un art d'achever la transposition, au Livre, de la symphonie. . . ."

37. Shattuck, 297–300.

CHAPTER 12   *Words and Blood in Dante*

1. Dante Alighieri, *The Divine Comedy*, trans. Henry Wadsworth Longfellow (Boston: Ticknor and Fields, 1867).

2. Erich Auerbach, *Mimesis: The Representation of Reality in Western Literature*, trans. Willard Trask (Princeton: Princeton University Press, 1953), 202.

CHAPTER 13   *Dark Knowledge: Melville's Poems of the Civil War*

1. Herman Melville, *Selected Poems of Herman Melville*, ed. Robert Penn Warren (New York: Random House, 1967; 1970), 95. Out of filial feeling, I will use this edition, hereafter referred to as *SP*, for all the poems I quote here. Lee Rust Brown has edited a more recent, excellent edition of *Battle-Pieces and Aspects of the War* (New York: Da Capo Press, 1995).

2. Stanton Garner, *The Civil War World of Herman Melville* (Lawrence: University of Kansas Press, 1993), 54.

3. Ibid., 441.

4. Edmund Wilson, *Patriotic Gore* (New York: Oxford University Press, 1966), 481.

5. John Greenleaf Whittier, *Anti-Slavery Poems: Songs of Labor and Reform* (Cambridge: Riverside Press, 1888), 214.

6. *American Poetry: The Nineteenth Century*, vol. I, ed. John Hollander (New York: Library of America, 1993), 699.

7. Simone Weil, *La Pesanteur et la grâce* (Paris: Plon, 1988), 19. Translation mine.

8. *SP* 91.

9. *SP* 93.

10. *SP* 102.

11. *SP* 128.

12. Ralph Waldo Emerson, *Collected Poems and Translations*, ed. Harold Bloom and Paul Kane (New York: Library of America, 1994), 243.

13. *SP* 141.

14. Robert Penn Warren, *John Brown: The Making of a Martyr* (New York: Payson and Clarke, 1929), 432. Nathaniel Hawthorne, *Works: Miscellaneous*, vol. 23 (Columbus: Ohio State University Press, 1994), 397.

15. *SP* 143.

16. *SP* 96.

17. Hawthorne, 364.

18. Walt Whitman, *Poetry and Prose*, ed. Justin Kaplan (New York: Library of America, 1982), 708.

19. Paul Zweig, *Walt Whitman* (New York: Basic Books, 1984), 266.

20. Whitman, 418.

21. *SP* 117.

22. *SP* 120.

23. Abraham Lincoln, *Speeches, Letters, Miscellaneous Writings, Presidential Messages and Proclamations*, ed. Don E. Fehrenbacher (New York: Library of America, 1989), 215.

24. Ibid., 686.

25. Hawthorne, 386.

26. Walt Whitman, *Poetry and Prose*, ed. Justin Kaplan (New York: Library of America, 1982), 451.

27. *SP* 142.

28. *SP* 137.

29. *SP* 122.

Chapter 14   *Hardy's Undoings*

1. John Crowe Ransom edited *Selected Poems of Thomas Hardy* (New York: Macmillan, 1960), with an introduction no less insightful and gracefully useful today than it was forty-odd years ago.

2. Florence Emily Hardy, *The Life of Thomas Hardy, 1840–1928* (New York: St. Martin's Press, 1962), 300.

3. R. P. Blackmur, *Language as Gesture* (New York: Columbia University Press, 1952), 52.

4. Hardy, 301.

5. F. R. Leavis, "Reality and Sincerity," *Scrutiny*, 1952–53; reprinted in *The Living Principle* (New York: Oxford University Press, 1975).

6. Dennis Taylor, *Hardy's Metres and Victorian Prosody* (Oxford: Clarendon Press, 1988), and *Hardy's Literary Language and Victorian Philology* (Oxford: Clarendon Press, 1993); Eric Griffiths, *The Printed Voice of Victorian Poetry* (Oxford: Clarendon Press; New York: Oxford University Press, 1989), 200.

7. Thomas Hardy, *The Complete Poems*, ed. James Gibson (New York: Macmillan, 1976),115; hereafter abbreviated as *CP*.

8. *CP* 62.

9. *CP* 62.

10. *CP* 167. 11. Kenneth Burke, *Language as Symbolic Action* (Berkeley: University of California Press, 1966), 16.

12. Ibid., 9.

NOTE: I wish to thank John Hollander, Robert Mezey, and Christopher Ricks for their generous and helpful readings of this essay.

CHAPTER 15   *Meeting H.D.*

1. Michael King, *H.D., Woman and Poet* (Orono: National Poetry Foundation, University of Maine, 1986), 16.

2. Laura Riding and Robert Graves, *A Survey of Modernist Poetry* (Edinburgh: R. & R. Clark Limited, Folcroft Library Edition, 1979), 122. Eileen Gregory, *H.D. and Hellenism: Classic Lines* (Cambridge: Cambridge University Press, 1997), 14.

3. Eliot, *The Letters of T. S. Eliot*, vol. I, 1898–1922, ed. Valerie Eliot (New York: Harcourt Brace Jovanovich, 1988), 488.

4. Ezra Pound, *Selected Letters of Ezra Pound, 1907–1941*, ed. D. D. Paige (New York: New Directions, 1950), 114.

5. H.D., *End to Torment: A Memoir of Ezra Pound*, ed. Michael King (New York: New Directions, 1979), 18.

6. Hugh Kenner, *The Pound Era* (Berkeley: University of California Press, 1971), 177; hereafter abbreviated as *PE*. The scene is also described in Barbara Guest, *Herself Defined: The Poet H.D. and Her World* (Garden City: Doubleday, 1984), 40, and in King, 209.

7. *PE* 174.

8. *PE* 178. Pound inserted the manifesto in his own "A Retrospect" in *Pavannes and Divisions* in 1918. Reprinted in *Literary Essays of Ezra Pound*, ed. T. S. Eliot (New York: New Directions, 1968), 3; hereafter abbreviated as *LE*.

9. *PE* 181; *LE* 4.

10. *LE* 11.

11. Diane Rayor, *Sappho's Lyre: Archaic Lyric and Women Poets of Ancient Greece* (Berkeley: University of California Press, 1991), 126.

12. H.D., *Collected Poems, 1912–1944*, ed. Louis L. Martz (New York: New Directions, 1983), 37; hereafter abbreviated as *CP*.

13. *CP* 5.

14. *CP* 25.

15. W. B. Yeats, *William Butler Yeats: The Poems*, ed. Richard Finneran (New York: Macmillan, 1983), 125.

16. Edward Thomas, *Collected Poems* (New York: W. W. Norton, 1974), 78.

17. Ivor Gurney, *Selected Poems*, ed. P. J. Kavanagh (Oxford: Oxford University Press, 1990), 86.

18. Ezra Pound, *Personae: The Shorter Poems*, ed. Lea Baechler and A. Walton Litz (New York: New Directions, 1990), 251.

19. Ibid., 111.

20. *CP* 179.

21. *CP* 453.

22. King, 174.

23. *CP* 510.

24. *CP* 548.

25. *CP* 509.

26. *CP* 511.

27. *CP* 512.

28. *CP* 514.

29. *CP* 547.

30. *CP* 572.

31. *CP* 552.

32. Guest, 209.

33. *CP* 550.

34. *CP* 556.

35. T. S. Eliot, *Collected Poems, 1909–1962* (New York: Harcourt Brace Jovanovich, 1970), 207, 209.

36. *CP* 578.

37. *CP* 583.

38. *End to Torment*, 56.

39. *CP* 57.

40. *CP* 531.

CHAPTER 16   *Adventures of the "I": The Poetry of Pronouns in Geoffrey Hill*

1. Geoffrey Hill, *The Triumph of Love* (Boston: Houghton Mifflin, 1998), 76; hereafter abbreviated as *TL*.

2. *TL* 32.

3. *TL* 1.

4. *TL* 82.

5. Geoffrey Hill, *New and Collected Poems, 1952–1992* (Boston: Houghton Mifflin, 1994), "Genesis," 3; "Ovid in the Third Reich," 49; "Two Formal Elegies," 19; "Solomon's Mines," 14; hereafter abbreviated as *NCP*.

6. T. S. Eliot, *Selected Prose of T. S. Eliot*, ed. Frank Kermode (New York: Harcourt Brace Jovanovich; Farrar, Straus and Giroux, 1975), 40.

7. Anne Sexton, *All My Pretty Ones* (Boston: Houghton Mifflin, 1962), 4.

8. *NCP* 102.

9. *TL* 38; *TL* 79.

10. Geoffrey Hill, *The Orchards of Syon* (Washington, D.C.: Counterpoint, 2002), 30.

11. Guy Davenport, *7 Greeks* (New York: New Directions, 1995), 33.

12. David A. Campbell, *Greek Lyric: Sappho and Alcaeus* (Cambridge: Harvard University Press, 1982), 81.

13. Catullus, *Poems*, ed. Elmer Truesdell Merrill (Cambridge: Harvard University Press, 1893), 17.

14. Petrarch, *Petrarch's Lyric Poems*, trans. and ed. Robert M. Durling (Cambridge: Harvard University Press, 1976), 37.

15. *TL* 21.

16. Emile Benveniste, *Problems in General Linguistics*, trans. Mary Elizabeth Meek (Coral Gables: University of Miami Press, 1971; Paris: Gallimard, 1966), 218.

17. Ibid., 219.

18. Emmanuel Levinas, "The Word I, the Word You, the Word God," *Alterity and Transcendence*, trans. Michael B. Smith (New York: Columbia University Press, 1999), 93.

19. *NCP* 81.

20. *NCP* 97.

21. *TL* 64.

22. *TL* 2.

23. Gerard Manley Hopkins, *Poems of Gerard Manley Hopkins*, ed. Robert Bridges (London: Oxford University Press, 1950), 67.

24. Geoffrey Hill, *Speech! Speech!* (Washington, D.C.: Counterpoint, 2000), 3, 50.

25. *The Orchards of Syon*, 55.

CODA

1. Robert Aitken, *A Zen Wave: Basho's Haiku and Zen* (New York and Tokyo: Weatherhill, 1978), 25.

2. Ibid., 30.

3. Ibid., 40.

4. Ibid., 106.

Permissions Acknowledgments

The author is grateful for permission to reprint the following copyright material:

Robert Aitken: "In plum-bower scent . . . ," "Let my name . . . ," "The old pond . . ." by Basho, and "While the dewdrop world . . ." by Issa, translated by Robert Aitken, from *A Zen Wave: Basho's Haiku and Zen*, copyright © 2003 by Robert Aitken. Reprinted by permission of the publisher.

W. H. Auden: "In Memory of Sigmund Freud," copyright © 1940 and renewed 1968 by W. H. Auden; "Secondary Epic," copyright © 1960 by W. H. Auden; "They," copyright © 1945 and renewed 1973 by W. H. Auden; "Vespers," copyright © 1955 by W. H. Auden; "A Walk after Dark," copyright © 1966 by W. H. Auden, from *Collected Poems* by W. H. Auden. Used by permission of Random House, Inc., and Faber and Faber Ltd.

Mary Barnard: "Phainetai moi," by Sappho, translated by Mary Barnard, from *Sappho*, copyright © 1986 by Mary Barnard. Reprinted by permission of University of California Press.

Frank Bidart: "The Book of the Body," "California Plush," "Catullus: Odi et Amo" (translation of Catullus), "Confessional," "Elegy," "Golden State," "In the Western Night," "Self-Portrait, 1969," and "Vergil *Aeneid* 1.1–3.3," from *In the Western Night: Collected Poems, 1965–1990* by Frank Bidart, copyright © 1990 by Frank Bidart. Reprinted by permission of Farrar, Straus and Giroux, LLC and Carcanet Press Limited. "Odi et Amo" (translation of Catullus), from *Desire* by Frank Bidart, copyright © 1997 by Frank Bidart. Reprinted by permission of Farrar, Straus and Giroux, LLC.

E. M. and A. H. Blackmore: "Reply to a Bill of Indictment," by Victor Hugo,

frey Hill, pages 2, 6, 30, 55, copyright © 2002 by Geoffrey Hill. Reprinted by permission of the publisher. "5," "6," "59," "60," "99," and "120," from *Speech! Speech!* by Geoffrey Hill, pages 3, 30, 50, 60, copyright © 2000 by Geoffrey Hill. Reprinted by permission of the publisher. "II," "V," "XLII," "LXI," "LXXIII," "CXXI," "CXL," "CXLV," and "CXLIX," from *The Triumph of Love* by Geoffrey Hill, copyright © 1998 by Geoffrey Hill. Reprinted by permission of Houghton Mifflin Company and Penguin Books Ltd. All rights reserved.

John Hollander: "Upon Apthorp House," from *Movie-Going* by John Hollander, copyright © 1962 by John Hollander. Reprinted by permission of the author. "A Possible Fake," from *Types of Shape*, copyright © 1991 by John Hollander. Used by permission of Yale University Press. "After an Old Text," "August Carving," "Hobbes, 1651," "Lady of the Castle," "Movie-Going," and "Off Marblehead," from *Selected Poetry* by John Hollander, copyright © 1993 by John Hollander. "Across the Board," "Arachne's Story," "Beach Whispers," "A Fragment Twice Repaired," "Las Hilanderas," "Owl," "So Red," "Sun in an Empty Room," and "Variations on a Table-Top," from *Figurehead* by John Hollander, copyright © 1999 by John Hollander. "Effet de Neige," from *Harp Lake* by John Hollander, copyright © 1988 by John Hollander. Used by permission of Alfred A. Knopf, a division of Random House, Inc.

Richard Howard: "Lesbos," from *Les Fleurs du mal* by Charles Baudelaire, copyright © 1982 by Charles Baudelaire, translated from the French by Richard Howard, illustrations by Michael Mazur. Reprinted by permission of David R. Godine, Publisher, Inc.

Max Jacob: "Angoisses et autres," "Vision infernale en forme de madrigal," and "Colloque III," from *Ballades. Suivi de Visions infernales, Fond de l'eau, Sacrifice imperial, Rivage, et de les Pénitents en maillots roses* by Max Jacob, copyright © 1970 Editions Gallimard, Paris. "Le Christ au cinématographe," from *La Défense de Tartufe. Extases, remords, visions, prières, poèmes et meditations d'un Juif converti* by Max Jacob, copyright © 1964 Editions Gallimard, Paris. "Le coq et la perle" and "Roman d'aventures," from *Le Cornet à dés* by Max Jacob, copyright © 1945 Editions Gallimard, Paris. Used by permission of Gallimard, Paris.

David Kennedy and Christopher Pilling: "The Cock and the Pearl," by Max Jacob, translated by David Kennedy and Christopher Pilling, from *The Dice Cup*, copyright © 2000 by David Kennedy and Christopher Pilling. Reprinted by permission of Atlas Press: atlaspress.co.uk.

James Merrill: "The Thousand and Second Night," from *Collected Poems* by James Merrill and J. D. McClatchy and Stephen Yenser, editors, copyright © 2001 by the Literary Estate of James Merrill at Washingt on University. Used by permission of Alfred A. Knopf, a division of Random House, Inc.

James Michie: "Ode II, 13," from *The Odes of Horace* by Horace, translated by James Michie, copyright © 1965 by James Michie. Used by permission of Viking Penguin, a division of Penguin Group (USA) Inc.

Ezra Pound: "Canto I," from *The Cantos of Ezra Pound* by Ezra Pound, copyright © 1934, 1937, 1940, 1948, 1956, 1959, 1962, 1963, 1966, and 1968 by Ezra Pound. "In a Station of the Metro," from *Personae* by Ezra Pound, copyright ©

Index